The Fam

A t<

In memory of Carl Broad; 1969-2018.

Printed by CreateSpace

ISBN-13: 978-1511890335
ISBN-10: 1511890339

Original cover photograph of the Gledrid Roundabout by Arriva436.

The Family Law
A to Z

A reference book for litigants & students

Nick Langford, MA Oxon.

&

Ruth Langford, F.Inst.Pa.

Introduction

The law is an ancient vocation which has accumulated a large and distinct vocabulary over the centuries.

The legal system in England and Wales is a common-law system, which means the law applies equally to all people and regions. This is a peculiarly English structure in which there is no complete codification of the law, unlike many other European countries with systems derived from Roman law. Common law is based rather on binding legal precedents established by monarchs and justices; this is a legacy of the Norman Conquest which imposed French institutions upon the existing English ones. Unlike Roman Law, which transfers power and authority to the state, common law aspires to confine that power. As Parliament became established, there was a shift from common to statutory law, implemented through legislation. This continues to be very much the case in family law which relies on large bodies both of statutory law and precedent.

Norman law also introduced a generous stock of Latin terms, many of which derive from maxims whose ultimate origin is in Roman law. The legacy of this is short, often two-word, phrases – *ab initio, in camera*. Many common English words are used in unfamiliar and contradictory ways; as in other industries, this is designed to exclude the layman and oblige him to employ a professional guide through this linguistic labyrinth, and because *Quidquid latine dictum sit, altum viditur.*[1]

In June 2011, 20% of family cases involved at least one litigant-in-person (LiP), but the advent of LASPO – the Legal Aid, Sentencing and Punishment of Offenders Act – in April 2013 further reduced the number of litigants able to afford representation by a lawyer, forcing many to represent themselves and others to shun the courts altogether; by 2015 the proportion of cases had risen to 76%.

Changes to terminology introduced under Labour in 2007/08 were less to do with making the law accessible to litigants-in-person (LiPs) and more a part of the New Labour project to sweep aside centuries-old institutions and create cultural change. The Lord Chancellor's Department became the Ministry of Justice and the post of Lord Chancellor was effectively abolished; he lost his role chairing debates in the Lords, his position as head of the judiciary and his power to appoint judges. "Decrees" became "orders"; the decrees *"nisi"* and *"absolute"* became "conditional" and "final". "Petitions" became "applications"; "ancillary relief" became "financial remedy"; the "co-respondent" became the "second respondent"; "leave" became "permission".

Justice minister Bridget Prentice said, "The new proposals will make it easier for people to follow what is being said in court. Outdated language will

---

[1] Anything said in Latin will sound profound.

be replaced by everyday terms that reflect the way people think in the 21ˢᵗ century". In *The Guardian*, Marcel Berlins punned that the Government was taking all the romance out of divorce.

Changing the language is always easier than changing laws or improving delivery of services which remained as they had always been. The new terminology failed to catch on, and the old terms continue to be used.

Further attempts were made to simplify the language with the introduction of the Child Arrangements Programme in 2014, and a short glossary was provided. In an effort to neutralise the language of winners and losers, orders for contact and residence became Child Arrangements Orders, and "contact" was downgraded to "involvement".

The reality is that the majority of litigants are expected to know what the jargon means without having it explained to them; lawyers are unwilling to "dumb-down" the law just to make it accessible to LiPs. Trying to get to grips with this unfamiliar language can be daunting and only adds to the stress of an already traumatic situation.

Our aim in this *A to Z*, therefore, is to provide a go-to reference guide which not only offers a concise explanation of each term, but also contains interesting and practical notes or points of reference. We hope it will appeal equally to the litigant, the lay advisor and the law student.

With grateful thanks to Vincent McGovern and Paul Taylor for their continued support.

Nick and Ruth Langford, August 2018

Acronyms & Abbreviations

Text in **bold** signifies an entry in the alphabetical listing.

ACA2002 – the Adoption and Children Act 2002

AER or All ER – All England Reports

BIOC – **Best Interests of the Child**

BMLR – Butterworth's Medico-Legal Reports

CAFCASS – **Children And Family Court Advisory and Support Service**

CA1989 – the **Children Act 1989**

CAO – **Child Arrangements Order**

CAP – **Child Arrangements Programme**

CB – **Child Benefit**

CCI – **Child Contact Intervention**

CETV – **Cash Equivalent Transfer Value**

CFR – **Children and Family Reporter**

CJ – Lord Chief Justice

CMS – **Child Maintenance Service**

CNI – **Certificate of No Impediment**

COP – Court of Protection

CSA – Child Support Agency

DFJ – Designated Family Judge

DVPN – **Domestic Violence Protection Order**

ECHR – (or ECtHR) the **European Court of Human Rights** or **European Convention on Human Rights**

EWCA or CA – the **Court of Appeal** of England and Wales

EWHC – the **High Court** of England and Wales

FAO – **Family Assistance Order**

FCA – **Family Court Advisor**

FCR – Family Court Reports

FDA – **First Directions Appointment**

FDR – **Financial Dispute Resolution**

FH – **Final Hearing**

FHDRA –**First Hearing Dispute Resolution Appointment**

FLR – Family Law Reports

FMH – Former **Matrimonial Home**

FNF – **Families Need Fathers**

FPC – Family Proceedings Court

FPR 2010 – **Family Procedure Rules 2010**

HL or UKHL – the House of Lords

HRA1998 – the **Human Rights Act 1998**

J – Mr or Mrs Justice
LA – Local Authority
LAA – Legal Aid Agency
LJ – Lord or Lady Justice
LLJ – Lords or Ladies Justice
LTR – **Leave-to-Remove**
MCA1973 – **Matrimonial Causes Act 1973**
MF – **McKenzie Friend**
MIAM – **Mediation Information and Assessment Meeting**
MPS – Maintenance Pending Suit
MR – Master of the Rolls
NACSA – **National Campaign for Child Support Action**
NRP – **Non-Resident Parent**
NYAS – **National Youth Advocacy Service**
P – **President** (of the Family Division)
PIP – Parents Information Programme
PR – **Parental Responsibility**
PRO – **Parental Responsibility Order**
PRR – **Parental Responsibility & Rights**
PSO – **Prohibited Steps Order** or **Pension Sharing Order**
PSU – **Personal Support Unit**
PWC – **Person with Care**
QB – the Queen's Bench Division
QC – **Queen's Counsel**
RCJ – the Royal Courts of Justice
REMO – **Reciprocal Enforcement of Maintenance Orders**
SIO – **Specific Issues Order**
SPIP – **Separated Parents Information Programme**
SRO – Shared Residence Order (Obsolete)
UB – **Unreasonable Behaviour**
UKSC – the United Kingdom **Supreme Court**
WLR – Weekly Law Reports

Useful Contacts

Bristol Grandparents Support Group – a charity which provides support and information to grandparents denied contact with their grandchildren. Website: http://www.bristolgrandparentssupportgroup.co.uk/.

Citizens' Advice Bureaux – local branches are only as good as their volunteers who seldom specialise in family law. Specialist offices exist at the Royal Courts of Justice (Telephone: 020 7947 7701) and at the Central London Family Court in High Holborn which runs a *pro bono* Family Advice Service staffed by family law solicitors from local firms. Advice sessions in all areas of family law are run on a first-come-first-served basis from 10:00 to 13:00 and from 14:00 to 17:00 on Mondays, Wednesdays and Thursdays. They can also help with filling out forms and documents.
Website: http://www.rcjadvice.org.uk/family-law/.

Falsely Accused Carers and Teachers (FACT) – support and campaigning for those falsely accused of abusing children and vulnerable adults. Website: www.factuk.org; Telephone helpline: 0843 289 20 16.

False Allegation Support Organisation (FASO) – support for those falsely accused of abuse. Website: www.false-allegations.org.uk; Telephone helpline: 0870 242 66 50.

Families Need Fathers (FNF) – the oldest of the fathers' groups, established in 1974, FNF runs local meetings and member forums and a network of McKenzie Friends. Website: www.fnf.org.uk; Telephone helpline, 07:00 to midnight, seven days a week, 0300 0300 363.

Grandparents Apart – formerly the Grandparents' Federation; support for grandparents separated from their grandchildren. Website: http://grandparentsapart.co.uk/; Telephone: 0141 882 5658 or 01560 322937.

Grandparents' Association – support for grandparents whose grandchildren have been taken into care, or who are being denied contact. Website: http://www.grandparents-association.org.uk/; Telephone: 0845 4349585.

Grandparents Plus – national charity supporting the role of grandparents and wider family in childcare, particularly where parents are no longer able to care for their children themselves. Website: http://www.grandparentsplus.org.uk/; Telephone: 0300 123 7015.

Legal Ombudsman – for complaints about solicitors; PO Box 15870, Birmingham, B30 9EB; email: enquiries@legalombudsman.org.uk; telephone: 0300 555 0333.

Mankind – a national charity which provides support for male victims of abuse and domestic violence. Website: http://www.mankind.org.uk/; Telephone: 01823 334244.

Marriage Foundation – the "national champion for marriage" promoting healthy, stable relationships and a reduction in family breakdown and its fallout. Website: http://www.marriagefoundation.org.uk/Web/; Telephone: 0203 291 0912.

Men's Advice Line – a Home Office-run support service for male victims of domestic violence. Website: http://www.mensadviceline.org.uk/; Telephone: 0800 801 0327.

Mothers Apart from Their Children (MATCH) – support for mothers separated from their children because of ill-health, fostering, adoption, abduction, alienation following high-conflict family breakdown or family rows. Website: http://www.matchmothers.org/.

National Campaign for Child Support Action (NACSA) – the best resource for help with child support, whether for liable or receiving parents. Website: http://www.nacsa.co.uk/; Telephone: 01384 572525.

National Missing People Helpline (formerly Missing Persons) – Website: www.missingpeople.org.uk; Freephone helpline: 0500 700 700; Helpline from outside the UK: +44 (0)20 8392 4545; Message Home helpline: 0800 700 740.

Oratto – an excellent resource for connecting litigants with the most appropriate lawyer. Website: https://oratto.co.uk/wiki/family-law-solicitor; Telephone: 01243 850 603.

Relate – charity giving advice on divorcing sensibly and amicably. Website: http://www.relate.org.uk/; Telephone: 0300 100 1234.

Reunite – charity specialising in international parental child abduction. A parent's first port of call in all international cases. Website: http://www.reunite.org/; Telephone: +44 (0) 116 2555 345; Advice Line: +44 (0) 116 2556 234.

Salvation Army Family Tracing Service – a tracing service for missing persons, reporting an 85% success rate.
Website: www.salvationarmy.org.uk/familytracing; Telephone: 0845 634 4747

Society of Professional McKenzie Friends – a self-regulatory body which aims to protect consumers by offering a code of conduct for "professional" McKenzie Friends and a complaints procedure. Website: www.mckenziefriends.directory.

List of Flowcharts

À La Carte

See **Unbundling**.

A Mensa et Thoro

(Latin: "from table and bed") a form of divorce replaced in 1857 by **Judicial Separation**.

Ab Initio

(Latin: "from the beginning") used of marriages which were **Void** from the outset.

Abduction

The removal by a parent or putative father of a child under the age of sixteen across an international border without the consent of those with **Parental Responsibility** (PR) or **Leave** of the Court. It is a criminal offence under the Child Abduction Act 1984.

Removal of a child within the jurisdiction is not abduction; although Scotland operates under a different jurisdiction from England and Wales, removal of a child to Scotland does *not* constitute abduction because the

European authors of the **Hague Convention** on Child Abduction didn't understand Scotland was a separate jurisdiction.

In England and Wales, no **Child Arrangements Order** needs to be in place regulating with whom a child is to live, but if the child is resident in or was abducted from Scotland, there must be a **Residence Order**.

Abduction often follows the separation of a couple of different nationalities or faiths. It is quite common, for example, for Islamic fathers to remove their children to their country of origin and mothers will find it almost impossible to recover children taken to countries in which **Sharia** law prioritises the rights of fathers over those of mothers or children. The most common country to which children are taken is Pakistan, followed by the USA, Ireland and Spain. Around 40% of abductions are to non-Hague Convention countries, from which recovery is more difficult. There are some countries from which no child has ever been returned.

A parent who fears their child is at risk of abduction should first visit the website of the charity *Reunite* and download a *Child Abduction Prevention Guide*. He should apply to the Court immediately and *Ex Parte* for a **Summons**. He will also need a **Seek and Locate Order** and a **Passport** Delivery Order; they will be drawn up by the **Tipstaff** office and executed by them on the defendant abductor with informal notice or **Without Notice**. There is no time to waste form-filling; the parent should phone the Tipstaff in advance and wait to see the duty judge.

On no account should the potential abductor be alerted. The order will include a prohibition upon disclosing the fact of the proceedings to the defendant. The Tipstaff will take as many details as possible and liaise with the police to track the child down. The Tipstaff order can only be as useful as the information made available.

The judge will not grant the order unless the parent has everything prepared: he must give an undertaking to commence proper proceedings on the next working day and prepare a **Position Statement**, clearly setting out the facts, to convince the judge that the case is so urgent it cannot wait. Once he has the **Without-Notice** order and summons, the parent must arrange for a **Process Server** to serve them on the defendant as soon as possible. If the Court refuses to issue a search order, the decision should be appealed.

Returning home to find a child has been taken and no note left as to his whereabouts is a terrifying situation, but it is important to remain focused. There are several options open depending on the circumstances; we will assume the obvious has been tried, such as calling the other parent's mobile. It is vital to act swiftly: if the Court concludes that a new *Status Quo* has been established, and the child has become **Settled** in the new country, the chances that he will be ordered to be returned are greatly diminished.

Practice Direction 12F tells a parent what to do if his child has been taken out of the country without his consent. It should be read in full.

The best chance of return is if the child has been taken to a **Brussels II** country: jurisdiction remains with the country from which the child was taken, and it can issue an order for mandatory return.

If the country to which the child has been taken is a part of the **Hague Convention** and/or the European Convention, the abduction must be registered with the International Child Abduction and Contact Unit (ICACU), 81 Chancery Lane, London, WC2A 1DD; telephone: + 44 (0)20 7911 7045 / 7047; fax: + 44 (0)20 7911 7248; email: enquiries@offsol.gsi.gov.uk. Outside of normal working hours contact the Royal Courts of Justice, + 44 (0)20 7947 6000, or + 44 (0)20 7947 6260. ICACU will forward the application to an experienced solicitor who will take the case on and arrange **Legal Aid**.

In Hague Convention cases, public funding is not means-tested, and litigants are advised to hire a solicitor with experience of abduction cases and a proven track record. This special status does not apply to defendants. The applicant must seek legal advice immediately, both here and in the country to which the child has been abducted.

The relevant court procedure is set out in Chapter 6 of the **Family Procedure Rules 2010** which should be read in conjunction with Practice Direction 12F and the Child Abduction Act 1984. It should be borne in mind that in Hague Convention proceedings there may be several defendants pursuant to Rule 6.5. The application is made using Form C67.

It is better that the proceedings take place in London because this is where the greatest expertise is to be found. Deputy High Court judges and **Section 9 judges** should not deal with Hague and Brussels II cases.

For non-Hague countries, the Foreign and Commonwealth Office, Protection Section, Consular Division should be contacted, telephone: + 44 (0)20 7270 1500. Applications for return are made on Form C66 and are heard in the High Court.

Abortion

The intentional termination of a pregnancy.

Section 58 of the Offences Against the Person Act 1861 criminalises the *unlawful* procuring of a miscarriage and Section 59 the *unlawful* supply of poisons or instruments intended to cause a miscarriage, regardless of whether the woman is actually with child.

The Infant Life (Preservation) Act 1929 criminalised the killing of a child capable of being born alive, closing a lacuna which permitted a child to be killed during the moment of birth, although the first prosecution was not until 2007. In 1938, precedent extended the defence to abortion to include "mental and physical wreck" to allow, for example, abortion following rape (R v Bourne [1938] 3 All ER 615).

Liberal MP David Steel's Private Member's Bill was intended to clarify, not change, existing law and was partly inspired by the 1957-61 thalidomide catastrophe. The 1967 Abortion Act permitted abortion up to twenty-eight weeks to avoid injury to the physical or mental health of the woman or of her children, and up to full term to save the mother's life, to prevent grave permanent injury to her physical or mental health, or if the child was likely to be severely physically or mentally handicapped.

Such a termination became lawful if conducted by a medical practitioner and if two practitioners were of the opinion it was justified. It is nearly always considered safer for a mother to terminate a pregnancy than to allow it to continue. The 1929 Act, however, continued to prevent the abortion of a child "capable of being born alive", a definition which depended on judicial interpretation of current medical science.

The Act treats abortion as a purely medical matter between a woman and her doctors. Fathers have no right in law either to insist on or prevent the abortion of their children.

The Human Fertilisation and Embryology Act 1990 reduced the time limit to twenty-four weeks to take into account changes in medical technology; the Act also decoupled the 1929 Act from the 1967 Act, allowing abortion to be carried out up to full term.

The unintended effect of this change was foreseen too late and an attempt to overturn it was unsuccessful; the law now permitted a child born, for example, with a hare lip to be destroyed during birth. In 2004, police chose not to prosecute two doctors who had approved the illegal abortion at twenty-eight weeks of a foetus suffering from a cleft palate. The Reverend Joanna Jepson, who had herself been born with a facial deformity, obtained leave to challenge the decision by judicial review. She disputed that a cleft palate constituted a "serious handicap" under Section 1(d) of the Act – the law does not define the term. Her challenge was unsuccessful.

The legalisation of abortion did *not* place an obligation on a doctor to abort a handicapped child, and a child born handicapped cannot sue the doctor (McKay v Essex [1982] HA).

A threat to kill an unborn child is *not* a threat to kill a third party (R v Tait [1990] CA).

A handful of men have engaged the courts to prevent an abortion: in Paton v BPS [1978] 2 All ER 987, a father, William Paton, argued that he had a right to a say in what happened to his child and that the mother was seeking the abortion out of vindictiveness in the context of a failing marriage. The Court disagreed; the law is clear: a foetus has no human right to life before it is born; there is no legal mechanism by which a father might prevent its abortion. Paton

4

took the case to the **European Court of Human Rights** – Paton v UK [1980] EHRR 408 – and again the Court rejected the notion that a father has the right to be consulted.

In C v S [1987] 2 WLR 1108, 1 All ER 1230, Robert Carver, president of the Oxford University Pro-Life group, failed to persuade the judges that abortion would be a crime under s.1(b) of the Infant Life (Preservation) Act given that the foetus was at a stage where it could survive outside the womb: such a prosecution could be brought only by the Director of Public Prosecutions and not by the father. Nevertheless, the pressure of the ensuing publicity forced the mother to abandon the termination and Carver raised his daughter himself.

In 2001, Stephen Hone went to the High Court in a bid to stop his former partner, Claire Hansell, aborting their child. He argued that only one doctor had been consulted instead of the two required by law and claimed a "partial victory" when the clinic said it would perform further medical checks before carrying out the termination, but Hansell's solicitors reported she had already aborted the child.

Abridged Notice

When an application is made for a hearing to be held at short notice but not **Without Notice.**

Abuse

Five categories of abuse were identified in the Government's 2006 guidance *Working Together to Safeguard Children*: **Physical Abuse, Emotional Abuse, Sexual Abuse, Neglect** and bullying. See also **Allegation.**

Access

An obsolete term, describing the relationship a **Non-Resident Parent** was allowed with his child; replaced in 1989 by **Contact.**

Achieving Best Evidence

ABE – a Home Office protocol developed to ensure that interviews of children are conducted in such a way as to produce evidence that can be used in court without leading the witness or otherwise influencing the result.

Guidance was introduced in 1992 and updated in 2002; it applies to the interviewing of all children under the age of seventeen and of other vulnerable witnesses. Children are categorised as "very young": up to five; "young": between five and eleven; and "older": between eleven and seventeen.

Interviews by CAFCASS, social services, medical practitioners, psychologists, the police or occasionally the judge are an ideal opportunity for a parent to groom their child to give the responses they want; confirming the story the parent is telling and avoiding anything contradictory. Another ploy is to give the child a "crib sheet" to take into the interview with him; perhaps containing drawings or diagrams of alleged incidents.

It is vitally important that where there are **Allegations** of physical or sexual abuse, children are properly interviewed; these interviews may affect whether the child has contact again, is properly protected from an abusive parent, or whether criminal proceedings are brought.

A correctly executed interview must be "phased": *Phase 1* involves establishing a rapport with the child and setting out ground rules; the aim is to obtain a fair, accurate and truthful account which is in the child's interests and acceptable to the Court. The pace of the interview is dictated by the age and ability of the child and he must leave the interview feeling he has been given the fullest opportunity to be heard.

Phase 2 allows the child to give a narrative account in his own words, spontaneously and with a minimum of prompting; the interviewer should act as facilitator, not interrogator. Where evidence is inconsistent or the interviewer suspects allegations to be false he should first allow the child to finish his account before investigating these issues more closely.

Phase 3 enables the interviewer to ask clarifying questions; they should be kept short and simple and asked only one at a time. Leading questions should be avoided and can result in the whole recording being ruled inadmissible. Research indicates that responses to leading questions are determined more by the manner of questioning than by what is accurately remembered. Leading questions can serve not merely to influence the child's answer but may also significantly distort the child's memory in the direction implied by the question.

The interview is closed in *Phase 4* by summarising to the child in his own language the evidence given, answering any questions he may have, and thanking him for his time and effort.

An interview which is not conducted according to these principles should not be accepted by a court as evidence, and a party should ask to have such evidence removed from the record.

Acknowledgement of Service

The form which the respondent must sign and return to the court, confirming receipt of a petition or application. Form C7 is used to acknowledge receipt of **Section 8** applications and D10 for a **Divorce** petition.

Activity Direction

A direction made by the Court under Sections 11A to H of the Children Act 1989 requiring a party to ongoing proceedings to undertake an "activity" intended to improve their involvement in the life of the child concerned.

These activities should be regarded not as sanctions with which to punish an intractable parent but as tools to help establish, maintain or improve the involvement in the life of the child concerned of the individual named in the order; the child's **Welfare** is paramount. An activity direction can form part of a final order, so the effect of the activity in facilitating involvement need not be monitored. There are three types of activity in which the Court may require parents to participate:

1. attending a **Mediation Information and Assessment Meeting**;
2. attending a **Separated Parenting Information Programme**;
3. attending a **Domestic Abuse Perpetrator Programme**.

The Court cannot require a party to undergo medical or psychiatric examination, assessment or treatment or mediation as part of an activity. See Re C (A Child) (Procedural Requirements of a Pt 25 Application) [2015] EWCA 539, in which an unrepresented father with limited English was ordered *Ultra Vires* both by magistrates and by the circuit judge to whom he appealed to "submit to a full psychological assessment"; Aikens LJ declared,

> [50] ...a mandatory order that the father should subject himself to a psychological assessment, a form of medical procedure, was unlawful. That, too, was not apparently appreciated by either the magistrates or Judge Scarratt.

Before making such an order the Court must consider the availability of the activity, the accessibility for the parent, the suitability of the parent, and the likely effect of participating. The person providing the activity must be named in the order. From April 2010, litigants have not had to pay for these programmes, to encourage their wider use.

Adjourn

To postpone a hearing to a later date. Enabled under Rule 3.4 of the **Family Procedure Rules 2010**.

Admissible

Describes **Documents** and **Evidence** which may be presented to the Court.

Adoption

An order made under Section 46 of the Adoption and Children Act 2002 which irreversibly transfers **Parental Responsibility** for a child to the adoptive parent(s) and *"extinguishes"* the PR of the natural parents, terminating all other existing orders. In Re X (A Child) (Parental Order: Time Limit) [2014] EWHC 3135, Lord Justice Munby said,

> *[54]* ...an adoption order ... has an effect extending far beyond the merely legal. It has the most profound personal, emotional, psychological, social and, it may be in some cases, cultural and religious, consequences... Moreover, these consequences are lifelong and, for all practical purposes, irreversible.

In non-consensual adoption (dubbed *forced adoption* by campaigner Ian Josephs), the consent of the parents is dispensed with, on the basis that the child's **Welfare** necessitates it, under Section 52(1)(b) of the Children Act 1989, or because the parent is believed to lack legal **Capacity**.

There are five steps involved in the adoption of a child:

1. The local authority (LA) applies for a **Care Order** to take the child into **Care**.
2. The LA gains the consent of one of the adults with Parental Responsibility for the child to be adopted; the child must be older than six weeks and the consent must be witnessed by a **CAFCASS** officer.
3. The LA applies to the Court for a **Freeing Order**.
4. If consent is not given freely, the LA must apply to the Court for a **Placement Order**. If the order is granted, the child becomes available for adoption.
5. After the child has been living with them for at least ten weeks the adoptive parents apply to the Court for an Adoption Order.

8

Thus, an LA may place a child for adoption only if it has the consent of those adults with PR for the child (Section 19, Adoption and Children Act 2002) or if it obtains a Placement Order from the Court (Section 21) by demonstrating the **Threshold** criteria have been met; so the consent of a father without PR won't be necessary, and he will need to make an urgent application for PR if he wishes to stop the adoption.

If the LA proposes to take a child from the resident parent and into care, it should issue the non-resident parent with notification of the proceedings and he should be **Joined**; LAs, however, do not always do this and claim, for example, that it cannot locate the father, that there has been insufficient contact between him and the child, or that there have been allegations of abuse. Again, he should also be joined when the LA commences placement proceedings.

Parents' final opportunity to oppose an adoption is when an application is made. The Court's paramount consideration remains the welfare of the child (s.1(2)ACA2002), and the **Welfare Checklist** therefore applies. By the time the application for the order is made, the child will have been living with the adoptive parents for at least ten weeks, and often for much longer. A new *Status Quo* has been established which the Court will not eagerly overturn.

Leave of the Court must be sought before applying to oppose an Adoption Order; the Court can only grant leave if there has been a significant **Change of Circumstance**. The Court's decision will be influenced by its assessment of the parents' prospects of success and how it predicts the decision of the application judge. In Re B (Adoption: Jurisdiction to Set Aside) [1995] Fam 239, Swinton Thomas LJ gave the standard judicial view,

> To allow considerations such as those put forward in this case to invalidate an otherwise properly made Adoption Order would in my view undermine the whole basis on which Adoption Orders are made, namely that they are final and for life, as regards the adopters, the natural parents and the child. In my judgment, (Counsel) is right when he submits that it will gravely damage the lifelong commitment of adopters to their adoptive children if there is the possibility of the child, or indeed the parents, subsequently challenging the validity of the Order.

In a notorious miscarriage of justice, three children were forcibly adopted from parents, Mark and Nicola Webster, believed to have caused non-accidental injuries to the middle child. When it subsequently emerged that the child had suffered from scurvy due to low levels of vitamin C in the formula milk given to him, the adoptions were not overturned (Webster v Norfolk County Council & Ors (Rev 1) [2009] EWCA Civ 59),

[149] Once Orders for Adoption have been lawfully and properly made, it is only in highly exceptional and very particular circumstances that the court will permit them to be set aside.

Few cases been successful, such as Re F (R) (An Infant) [1970] 1 QB 385, in which a mother hadn't been served with proceedings, Re RA (Minors) [1974] 4 Fam Law 182, in which the order was obtained by fraud and Re F (Infants) (Adoption Order: Validity) [1977] Fam 165, in which the adopters were not lawfully married. In Re K (Adoption and Wardship) [1997] 2 FLR 221, the adoption of a Bosnian child by an English couple was set aside because the procedure had been fatally flawed. In Re M (Minors) (Adoption) [1991] 1 FLR 458, a father had given consent to the adoption of his two daughters by their mother and stepfather, unaware the mother had terminal cancer. After her death, the girls came to live with their father and his new wife. The father successfully applied to have the adoption set aside.

The principles on which new evidence may be admitted to a case were established by Lord Denning in Ladd v Marshall [1954] 1 WLR 1489:

1. the evidence to be admitted could not have been obtained with reasonable diligence for use in the original trial;
2. the evidence must be such as would have a significant but not necessarily decisive influence on the outcome of the case; and
3. the evidence must be credible, though not necessarily incontrovertible.

The conditions for revisiting a judgment on the grounds of inappropriate procedure or fraudulent evidence were established in Taylor v Lawrence [2002] EWCA Civ 90, [2003] QB 528 (a boundary dispute): the applicant must show "significant injustice" has occurred by introducing new evidence, which must both be true and be accepted by the Court's **Discretion**. There must also be an effective remedy to the injustice.

Three recent cases were believed by some to indicate a shift in judicial thinking. Separate adoption orders had been made in respect of the two youngest of five children, the parents appealed so that the children could be raised by an aunt; the aunt's availability represented a **"Change in Circumstances"**, a fact Judge Sarah Watson had failed to consider. Watson's judgment said that the Court "*makes* an Adoption Order in respect of B ... to be made 7 days from today's date", so it wasn't clear whether the order had been made or not. She added as a condition that the child should be circumcised according to his parents' wish; in the Court of Appeal (Re W (Children) [2015] EWCA Civ 403) Munby LJ allowed the appeal and commented,

> *[58]* ...Paragraph 3 of the order is irretrievably flawed. It is in a form which is wrong as a matter of substance. No adoption order can be made expressed to be subject to satisfaction of a condition precedent.

In PK v Mr and Mrs K [2015] EWHC 2316, Mrs Justice Pauffley revoked an adoption order made in 2004; the four-year-old child, PK, had been removed from her mother and adopted by Mr and Mrs K. Two years later they gave her to relatives in Ghana who severely mistreated her. In 2014, she returned to England and was reunited with her mother and maternal grandmother. The respondents did not appear and were not represented, and the only argument against revoking the order was the "public policy" one,

> *[25]* If I were to decline to revoke the adoption order and refuse to allow PK to change her name back to that of her natural mother, it seems to me that there would be profound disadvantages in terms of her welfare needs.

In Re W (Adoption – Reunification) [2015] EWHC 2039, Mrs Justice Russell had to decide whether a girl should remain with her prospective adopters – with whom she had spent half her life – or live with her father and three siblings. Although judgment was in favour of the father, it was appealed, and the girl remained with the adopters. The case is remarkable for Russell J's criticism of the local authority for "case-building"; its evidence could "only be described as psychobabble... In short it voiced opinions which neither Ms Wilkinson nor Ms Alsop are [sic] qualified to make". A "misleading, damaging and inaccurate referral" had led to the father losing his job.

The guardian was just as incompetent; his report "was scant of any real analysis and... failed to set out the reasons for and against permanent placement outside her family". And, "the lack of any real child-centred analysis within these proceedings is inexcusable". His report was jargonistic and "empty of meaning"; his analysis, "lacking both depth and balance, bereft of objectivity and of little or no assistance". Russell was also concerned, ten years after *Mabon* (see **Joining a Child**) that the views of the three siblings, though important, had not been sought or put to the Court.

In *Cox and Carter*, the family court did not wait for the outcome of the criminal trial – which determined in October 2015 that there was no case to answer – and ordered the adoption of a boy found to be suffering from Von Willebrand disease and rickets. The parents launched an appeal to overturn the adoption.

Adoption of a Step-Child

A divorced or separated parent may want a new partner to adopt their child in order to cement his role as a fully committed parent.

This is a more complicated and bureaucratic procedure than merely acquiring **Parental Responsibility**. It is no longer necessary to be married but the couple must apply for joint adoption, even though one is already a legal parent. This means they will be assessed by the local authority for suitability as a couple and not as individuals. The relevant legislation is the Adoption Act 1976 and the Adoption and Children Act 2002; applications are made on Form A58.

The couple must contact their local authority first, before making the application; this will enable the LA to assess both parties. When a mother wishes her partner to adopt, the important question is whether the natural father has PR. If he hasn't and doesn't intend to acquire it (or cannot be traced), all is well; if he has, his consent will be required, and it won't be possible to complete the application until the Court has resolved this issue.

Under Section 16 of the Adoption Act, the Court can dispense with consent if the parent or guardian—

1. cannot be found or is incapable of giving consent;
2. is withholding consent unreasonably;
3. has persistently failed without reasonable cause to discharge his PR for the child;
4. has abandoned or neglected the child;
5. has persistently ill-treated the child; or
6. has seriously ill-treated the child.

The Court will ask the local authority to prepare a report on whether adoption is in the child's best interests.

An alternative to adoption is an application for a **Child Arrangements Order** naming the step-parent as someone with whom the child is to live; this would not necessitate the biological parent losing PR. The CAO will expire on the child's sixteenth birthday.

Adultery

Consensual sexual intercourse between a married person and someone of the opposite sex other than their spouse.

Adultery is organ-specific and requires that a penis be inserted into a vagina but, unlike **Consummation**, only demands some degree of penetration

(Dennis v Dennis [1955] 2 All ER 51). Infidelity without intercourse is not adultery; nor is any other sexual act.

If one spouse has committed adultery which is ongoing and the other finds it intolerable to live with him or her, then adultery can be used as one of the "**Facts**" upon which to base a **Divorce**. Only one occurrence is sufficient to deem the marriage destroyed. If the couple carry on living together for more than six months, the petitioner will not be able to use this as her fact. A petitioner cannot use her own adultery as grounds for divorce.

Adultery is proven either through the birth of a child, or by an established pregnancy, or through confession. Graphic photographs or videos may also be used as evidence, but social media and text exchanges or hotel receipts cannot. If the adultery cannot be proven and the adulterer won't cooperate, the petitioner will need to use a different fact, such as **Behaviour**, which need not be proved.

Even if they separated some time ago, if the couple are still married, intercourse with another is adultery, but this can only be used as the fact if it was the *cause* of the marriage breaking down; the criterion is that the petitioner finds it *intolerable* to remain married, not the adultery *per se*.

Consensual sexual intercourse between two people of the *same* sex is *not* adultery.

A couple in a civil partnership or same-sex marriage cannot commit adultery and thus cannot use it as their fact.

A married woman who is raped has not committed adultery as the act was not consensual (Stewart v Stewart [1914]), but a married male rapist *has*.

Believing one's spouse to be dead is not a defence (Hunter v Hunter [1900]).

In MacLennon v MacLennon [1958] SC 105, Lord Wheatley observed "the idea that adultery might be committed by a woman alone in the privacy of her bedroom, aided and abetted only by a syringe containing semen, was one with which the earlier jurists had no occasion to wrestle", concluding that adultery had to be "the physical contact with an alien and unlawful sexual organ". A wife who has had donor insemination without her husband's consent or knowledge has not committed adultery because no sexual intercourse has occurred.

In Scots law, there is no minimum period the parties must be married before a divorce action based on adultery may be started. If both parties agree to the divorce, the Court will usually need only statements and details of the adulterous sexual relationship. If the defender doesn't agree, proof will be necessary, and this may be difficult and expensive to acquire. Scots law allows two rarely used legal defences, *Lenocinium* and **Condonation**.

Adversarial System

A legal system described by Black's Law Dictionary as one "involving active and unhindered parties contesting with each other to put forth a case before an independent decision-maker".

Its weaknesses are the winner-takes-all outcome and the assumption that the result of hand-to-hand combat will inevitably be just; it is seldom the case in family disputes that one party is wholly right and the other wholly wrong, and more likely that the litigant with the deeper pockets will win. Today, many litigants must represent themselves, and those who are represented will, therefore, be advantaged.

The alternative is the inquisitorial system derived from Roman law which some reformers believe would better suit family litigation, particularly as **Litigants-in-Person** proliferate. It would certainly be cheaper: it is in part the high costs of an adversarial system which have led to the indiscriminate loss of legal aid.

Affidavit

(Latin: "he has declared upon oath") a written statement of evidence made under oath.

Many affidavits can be downloaded as forms from the Ministry of Justice website. The rules for completing and filing affidavits and witness statements are provided in the associated Practice Direction 22A. Although these rules are strict (prescribing paper quality and margin width), it is unlikely minor variations will result in the rejection of documents.

If any alteration is made to a statement or affidavit, it must be initialled both by its author and by the person before whom it is sworn. If the document has not been initialled in this way, it may only be used in evidence with the Court's consent.

At the end of an affidavit is a statement that the contents are true. This is called the "*Jurat*". The litigant must sign this; it must also be signed by the person before whom it is sworn, and he must print his name, full address and qualification beneath his signature.

There must be no space between the end of the affidavit and the *jurat*, and the *jurat* must not be on a separate page. This ensures that no one can add anything after it has been signed, sworn and witnessed. An affidavit may only be sworn before:

- a Commissioner for Oaths (Commissioners for Oaths Acts 1889 and 1891);

- another person specified by statute (Sections 12 and 18 of, and Schedules 2 and 4 to, the Legal Services Act 2007);
- certain officials of the Senior Courts (Section 2 of the Commissioners for Oaths Act 1889);
- a circuit or district judge (Section 58 of the County Courts Act 1984);
- any Justice of the Peace (Section 58 of the County Courts Act 1984); and
- certain officials of any County Court appointed by the judge of that court for the purpose (Section 58 of the County Courts Act 1984).

The person before whom it is sworn must have no other involvement in the case. If a litigant makes a false statement of truth, the Court may start proceedings against him for **Contempt**. The affidavit or witness statement must be filed in the court or court office in which the proceedings for which it will be used are taking place.

Affiliation

Literally, the adoption of a son, i.e., the obligation of a named father to take financial responsibility for a named child.

Affinity

Relationship through law (step-parents, parents-in-law, adoptive parents); see **Consanguinity** and **Void Marriage**.

Aliment

(Scots) periodical maintenance payments in support of a child or former spouse.

Under the Family Law (Scotland) Act 1985 there is a general obligation to provide support "as is reasonable in the circumstances" by a husband and wife to each other, a natural parent to their child or a person to a child who is accepted as a **Child of the Family**. This can apply equally when the husband and wife or parent(s) and child live together as when they are separated. A child is defined as a person under the age of eighteen or under twenty-five who is still in education or training.

Claims may be made in either the **Court of Session** or the **Sheriff Court** unless the Court considers it inappropriate in any particular case. In determining the amount of aliment, the Court must regard the needs and resources of the parties, their earning capacities and all circumstances of the case. On application by or on behalf of either party, an order or agreement for aliment may be varied, recalled or terminated if there has been a material

Change of Circumstances. It is not only a spouse who may make claims for aliment against the other, or on behalf of a child or children, but also children who may make claims in their own right against one or both parents.

While it is expected under Section 9(1)(c) of the Family Law Act (Scotland) Act 1985 that "any economic burden of caring after divorce for children under the age of sixteen years should be shared fairly between the parties", section 3(1)(b) makes allowances for claims of **Inlying Expenses**, such as educational expenses; any aliment awarded for this purpose can be paid directly to the school. When making its decision, the Court must factor in the needs and resources of both parties, their earning capacity and all other circumstances of the case, as set out in s.4. It is usually the wherewithal of the party who is to pay which is the determining factor.

Allegation

1174

An assertion by a party that the other has behaved illegally or inappropriately in some way.

Allegations can be used to limit or terminate **Contact**, to necessitate investigation and introduce **Delay** into proceedings, or be exploited to qualify for **Legal Aid**. Wrongful allegations of domestic or child abuse are damaging both to children's relationships with their parents and to the progress of cases; a new *status quo* can become established in which a parent will not have seen his children for many months.

In Re P and Q (Children: Care Proceedings: Fact Finding) [2015] EWFC 26, a mother and her partner concocted increasingly elaborate allegations against the father, none investigated by the lower court, culminating in the claim that he was the leader of a Hampstead-based satanic paedophile cult. Babies were bought from all over the world and delivered to London by TNT or DHL where they were abused, tortured and sacrificed before being cooked in the local McDonalds and eaten. Members of the 100-strong cult included teachers, priests, social workers and police. Mrs Justice Pauffley dismissed the entire edifice, "I am able to state with complete conviction that none of the allegations are true". She warned,

> [160] If there is one key message at the end of this inquiry it is that it is not and never will be sufficient to consider just one or two evidential features in isolation. It is always necessary to take account of all the material, not just a selection. Those who arrived at their own early conclusions on the basis of partial material were woefully misguided.

Allegation

Where an allegation is disputed, it is a fact in issue and should not be accepted by the Court or other professionals unless it is proven. In AS v TH (False Allegations of Abuse) [2016] EWHC 532, MacDonald J identified that professionals including teachers, CAMHS workers, police officers and social workers had interviewed two children with scant regard for the **Achieving Best Evidence** guidelines and treated allegations as "disclosures", concluding they had been abused where the Court found there was no such evidence.

MacDonald advised that a Court must rely on all the available evidence in a case, including that from the alleged abuser. It must first determine whether abuse has indeed taken place and then identify the perpetrator; MacDonald cautioned,

> Children's best interests are rarely served by precipitate action. Initial action in securing the widest possible information about the child's circumstances and family background is an essential pre-requisite to careful judgment and purposeful intervention.

In Re V (A Child) [2015] EWCA Civ 274, the trial judge's analysis of the allegations and parties' credibility was inadequate, and the appeal was allowed; McFarlane observed that there is often a knee-jerk reaction from CAFCASS that all allegations should be investigated and, if found proven, prevent all direct contact, but it is not for CAFCASS to dictate the progress of a case. He called for a re-reading of Butler-Sloss's careful balancing exercise in Re L (see **Finding-of-Fact**). McFarlane took the key factor from Practice Direction 12J to be the relevance of the allegations to the outcome of the case; that is, will the allegations, if proved, significantly influence the judge's decision?

Standard guidance on allegations of abuse was provided by Thorpe LJ's advice in Re M (Disclosure: Children and Family Reporter) [2002] EWCA Civ 1199. The relationship between the judge and the **Children and Family Reporter** is cooperative but independent; each has a function and a responsibility to perform and each must exercise their judgement and discretion:

a) The CFR's response will depend on whether the abuse,
    i.   has been observed by her or reported to her by the child; or
    ii.   has been reported to the CFR by someone else.

b) If the latter, the CFR must determine,
    i.   has the information already been relayed to social services or police?
    ii.   is there a history or pattern of past complaints?
    iii. how plausible is the report?
    iv. was the informant a party to the proceedings?

     v.   if yes, has he put this statement in evidence?

The CFR must also consider:

a) whether the abuse, if established, amounts to **Significant Harm** or the risk of significant harm within the meaning of Section 31.
b) whether there is a need for urgent action. What are the risks of delay?

The answers to these questions will determine the appropriate course of action. Second-hand reports need not be relayed to social services and are unlikely to be urgent. The judge will be consulted before further action is taken.

Thorpe warned CFRs to "be alert to the danger of being enmeshed in the strategy of the manipulative litigant". Both allegations and denials may be false: it is essential the CFR remains impartial and gives neither litigant cause to believe they have taken sides, compromising the exercise of justice. Where abuse is discovered by the CFR or reported to her directly she may report it to social services or police according to her discretion. The judge must be informed as early as possible, so he may consider any implications on the proceedings or the making of further directions.

In Re W (A Child) [2014] EWCA Civ 772, Ryder LJ warned, "Given the prevalence of false allegations made by parents against each other in private law proceedings, conduct at this level by a parent should be understood to be serious child abuse". Mr Justice Munby had given his view in Re D [2004] EWHC 727,

> *[54]* False allegations of misconduct are highly damaging and destructive... The court should grasp the nettle. Such allegations should be speedily investigated and resolved, not left to fester unresolved and a continuing source of friction and dispute. Court time must be found – and found without delay – for fact finding hearings... And allegations which could have been made at an earlier stage should be viewed with appropriate scepticism.

When allegations are first made, a simple written denial may be sufficient; the accuser should be challenged to produce corroborative material evidence to substantiate the allegations, and the Court should be asked to disregard allegations unless and until evidence is forthcoming.

When allegations are serious, however, the litigant must press for a **Finding-of-Fact**. If an allegation is not challenged when there is opportunity to do so, it will become accepted by the Court and cannot be removed later; in Re P (Children) [2008] EWCA Civ 1431, Ward LJ insisted,

> *[5]* I have to state to *[the father]* as emphatically as I can that he has to accept those findings of fact because they were not appealed by him, and the court will not go back and re-hear those matters. They have to be accepted.

Henceforth the allegations are taken as proven and the litigant is treated accordingly, regardless of his likely procedural ignorance and the fact that the balance of probabilities standard allows a degree of doubt. If the allegations are found to be unsubstantiated, further allegations will be looked upon with scepticism. This is one area in which judicial continuity is vital.

Alternative Dispute Resolution

The resolution of disputes outside of the adversarial court process. In April 2014, the word "alternative" was dropped to make resolution of disputes without litigation the default.

Ambush

A party "ambushes" the other by introducing into their oral evidence given in court something not contained in a **Position Statement** or **Affidavit**, or by making a new allegation. An ambushed litigant should request that the hearing be **Adjourned**.

Amending a Petition

There are circumstances in which a **Petitioner** may need to amend a divorce **Petition** after submitting it; for example, to reach an agreement with the other party or because the Court has rejected it for some reason.

An amended petition must be headed AMENDED PETITION and underlined in red ink; all amendments must also be underlined in red. Further amendments should be underlined in green and then in violet, then yellow; see Practice Direction 17. The amended petition is attached to the original Form D8 and re-served upon the respondent.

Amicus Curiae

(Or *Amica*, if female; Latin: "friend of the Court") one who volunteers to assist the Court on a point of law.

Analysis & Recommendations *Pro Forma*

(Latin: "for the sake of form") a tool adopted by CAFCASS in 2010 to replace the lengthy **Section 7** Template and to simplify reports and enable them to be completed more quickly at a time of growing pressure on the service.

It came under attack for producing inadequate and superficial reports and for omitting the **Welfare Checklist** which statute demands should be at the heart of everything CAFCASS does, thus exposing CAFCASS to sometimes unnecessary challenge through **Cross-Examination**, causing greater work and delay, contrary to the original intention.

Ancillary Relief

Financial settlement to a spouse on divorce.

The procedure for resolving financial matters can be confusing: applications can be made either for a "Financial Order" or for "**Financial Remedy**". Generally, a couple disputing finances during a divorce will need a Financial Order to be made; this can be for maintenance, for periodical payments, or for a lump sum. It can also be made to share a pension or to vary an order already made. An application for Financial Remedy would be made for financial provision or maintenance for a party or child, for financial relief following dissolution of a marriage or civil partnership abroad, for alteration of a maintenance agreement, etc. All applications are made on Form A.

It is vital to finalise this part of the divorce process as it will otherwise remain open indefinitely. In March 2015, Kathleen Wyatt made a claim against her former husband, Dale Vince, thirty-one years after their brief marriage had ended, by which time the former traveller had become worth £57m (Wyatt v Vince [2015] UKSC 14). Vince was unable to provide evidence of a settlement he claimed had been made twenty years before. Eventually, in June 2016, the parties agreed, with judicial approval, on an award of £300,000, much less than the £1.9million originally demanded.

The Matrimonial Causes Act 1973 enables a court to divide and apportion property, order its sale, and share out pensions; Section 25(2) of the Act provides a list of the factors a court should take into consideration when exercising its discretion; the welfare of any dependent children under eighteen is paramount, especially where the pot is limited.

Conduct is normally ignored by the Court, even if it has been very bad and a spouse has been consistently adulterous or abusive. These things are not considered relevant to the financial division and a party won't get extra money just because they are the victim. Consider, for example, MAP v MFP [2015] EWHC 627. Occasionally, financial misconduct which affects the total assets to be divided, such as gambling or fraud, will be taken into account.

The starting principle is that both parties keep whatever assets they brought to the marriage, while assets and property accumulated between the commencement of cohabitation (see McCartney v Mills-McCartney [2008] 1 FCR 707) and the **Separation Date** are divided *equally* unless there is good reason to do otherwise. This principle was established by Lord Nicholls in White v White [2001] 1 AC 596,

> *[24]* ...whatever the division of labour chosen by the husband and wife, or forced upon them by circumstances, fairness requires that this should not prejudice or advantage either party when considering paragraph (f) *[of section 25(2)]*, relating to the parties' contributions... If, in their different spheres, each contributed equally to the family, then in principle it matters not which of them earned the money and built up the assets. There should be no bias in favour of the money-earner and against the home-maker and the child-carer.

Nicholls concluded,

> *[25]* More often, having looked at all the circumstances, the judge's decision means that one party will receive a bigger share than the other. Before reaching a firm conclusion and making an order along these lines, a judge would always be well advised to check his tentative views against the yardstick of equality of division. As a general guide, equality should be departed from only if, and to the extent that, there is good reason for doing so.

In the later jointly-heard cases of Miller v Miller and McFarlane v McFarlane [2006] UKHL 24, Nicholls clarified that once the welfare of the children has been taken care of there are three strands to ensuring fairness:

1. the sharing principle established in *White*;
2. the requirement to provide adequately for the financial needs of both parties; and
3. to compensate for economic disadvantage, for example, where a wife has put a career on hold to bring up the couple's children.

"Needs" is interpreted broadly and generously; typically, it will include providing a home, daily living costs and a pension; as far as possible a spouse will aim to maintain their former standard of living; either party can claim entitlement to more than 50% if there are qualifying circumstances. Both parties should aspire to financial independence of each other – a **"Clean Break"**.

The contribution made by a spouse who has remained at home to raise the children is taken to be equivalent to that of the breadwinning spouse; this means

21

the starting point for the division of all assets accumulated during the marriage will be 50/50, though this is seldom the end point. This includes the proceeds of the sale of the house, furnishings and properties, any savings or investments, the family's liquid assets, any employment pension, and the value of all vehicles, etc.

A greater than 50% share may sometimes be justified if one party has made a "Special Contribution" to the marriage; in Cowan v Cowan [2001] 2 FLR 192, Thorpe LJ decided that "fairness certainly permits, and in some cases requires, recognition of the product of the genius with which one only of the spouses may be endowed", but in Lambert v Lambert [2003] 1 FLR 139, he reconsidered,

> the danger of gender discrimination resulting from a finding of special financial contribution is plain. If all that is regarded is the scale of the breadwinner's success then discrimination is almost bound to follow since there is no equal opportunity for the homemaker to demonstrate the scale of her comparable success.

Charman v Charman [2007] EWCA Civ 503 is one of – probably – only three cases since *Lambert* where the court has allowed the principle, but Sir Mark Potter called for parliamentary review of the law in this area, which has not been forthcoming. In Work v Gray [2017] EWCA Civ 270, Sir Terence Etherton MR provided a thorough chronicle of the concept, in a case where the husband failed to demonstrate that his "genius" merited special recognition, observing—

> [86] ...that recognition of a special contribution by a husband by virtue of a significant financial contribution risks commodifying the domestic contribution of a wife, that comparing the value of their contributions is comparing apples with pears, that what is relevant is the respective contributions of the husband and wife to the welfare of the family, and that fixing the level at which a financial contribution becomes a special contribution is purely arbitrary, as is the consequential unequal division of the matrimonial property.

The principle was rebutted in Sharp v Sharp [2017] EWCA Civ 408; the Court of Appeal reduced a 50% award to the husband in a short-lived and childless marriage.

The flowchart illustrates the typical progress of a case:

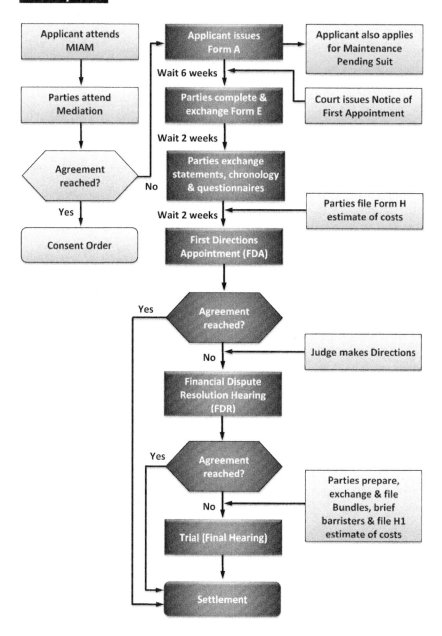

Flowchart 1: The Financial Resolution Process

Annulment

The declaration by a court that a **Marriage** was never valid. In circumstances in which a couple ought not to have married in the first place, it is better to seek an annulment than a divorce. Annulment is dealt with under the Matrimonial Causes Act 1973. A "Nullity Petition" must be presented to the Court on Form D8N within a reasonable time of the marriage, certainly within three years. The petitioner will also need to present a statement. Unlike divorce, it isn't necessary to wait a year before making an application for **Nullity**, but it is a complex process which requires the giving of oral evidence in court and involves a number of hearings and several affidavits.

Even if the parties are eligible and the case is uncontested (i.e., both parties agree to the annulment), it can end up costing more than a divorce – around £4,000 to £6,000 – and will take between six to nine months, whereas an uncontested divorce can take only four. An annulment is not, therefore, a suitable way of getting around the requirement to wait a year before filing for divorce.

Children who are born during the marriage, or whose births have been legitimised by the marriage, remain legitimate after annulment.

There are two types of annulment: of **Void Marriages** and of **Voidable Marriages**.

Answer

The document filed by the **Respondent** as part of the **Divorce** process, giving his response to allegations made in the **Petition**. It is filed on Form D8B, with a **Cross-Petition** if appropriate.

Anton Piller Order

A court order, known now as a search order, enabling the search of premises and seizure of evidence with consent but without prior warning. Named after Anton Piller KG v Manufacturing Processes Ltd & Ors [1975] EWCA Civ 12.

Apostille

(French: from the Latin *post illa* = "after these") the certification or authentication of a document.

Appeal

A complaint made to a higher court to correct a perceived error made by a lower one. Only an **Order** can be appealed; a judgment such as a **Finding-of-Fact** cannot be.

The **Court of Appeal** has power to interfere only if there is serious procedural or other irregularity in the proceedings of the lower Court, and if this irregularity caused the decision to be unjust. The Court must bear in mind that there is often no "right" answer in family cases, but a judge is nonetheless obliged under Article 6 of the **Human Rights Act** – the right to a fair trial – to explain his decision, especially if he rejects expert **Evidence** or a **CAFCASS** recommendation. If he does not, the appeal may well be successful. Section 55(1) of the Access to Justice Act 1999 allows appeals only where:

1. the appeal would raise an important point of principle or practice, or
2. there is some other compelling reason for the Court of Appeal to hear it.

Asquith LJ had said in Bellenden (formerly Satterthwaite) v Satterthwaite [1948] 1 All ER 343,

> *[345]* It is, of course, not enough for the wife to establish that this court might, or would, have made a different order. We are here concerned with a judicial discretion, and it is of the essence of such a discretion that on the same evidence two different minds might reach widely different decisions without either being appealable. It is only where the decision exceeds the generous ambit within which reasonable disagreement is possible, and is, in fact, plainly wrong, that an appellate body is entitled to interfere.

—which led to the following fundamental principles as expressed in G v G (Minors: Custody Appeal) [1985] 1 WLR 647; the appellant must show that the judge has:

1. "**Misdirected**" himself in law, or
2. failed to take account of a relevant factor, or
3. taken into account an irrelevant factor, or
4. made a decision which is "plainly wrong".

One should also consider the cautionary words of Lord Hoffman in Biogen Inc v Medeva Ltd [1997] RPC 1,

> *[54]* The need for appellate caution in reversing the trial judge's evaluation of the facts is based upon much more solid grounds than professional

courtesy. It is because specific findings of fact, even by the most meticulous judge, are inherently an incomplete statement of the impression which was made upon him by the primary evidence. His expressed findings are always surrounded by a penumbra of imprecision as to emphasis, relative weight, minor qualification and nuance... of which time and language do not permit exact expression, but which may play an important part in the judge's overall evaluation.

Judgments in the Family Court are made on the **Balance of Probabilities**, they may often be empirically wrong as a result, but cannot be appealed merely on that basis; consider also Lord Justice Ward's explanation in Re P (Children) [2008] EWCA Civ 1431,

[9] There is no appeal against that finding *[that the mother's version of events was to be accepted]* because *[the judge]* would not permit it, and rightly so, because it seems to me it is an unchallengeable finding made by the judge. He heard both parties, and it is the unfortunate task of a judge who has one witness come into the witness box and swear that the colour held up in front of him is white, then to hear the other side go into the witness box and the same piece of paper is held up before her and she swears that is black, and the judge has to choose whether it is white or black and sometimes may find it is actually grey. Here he accepted the wife's account, and it is beyond challenge in the Court of Appeal, for the father simply cannot show that the judge abused the great advantage he had of seeing and hearing the witnesses, judging their evidence, their demeanour and coming to a conclusion as he was duty bound to do. The Court of Appeal will not interfere absent the most compelling case that the judge had somehow egregiously come to the wrong conclusion.

The alternatives to appeal should be considered. Rather than appeal the order made, it is possible to apply for a retrial or a **Variation** on the order. If it is not claimed that the judge erred based on the evidence available to him, but that new evidence has come to light which undermines the earlier decision, it is better to ask for a rehearing than lodge an appeal. Such an application should be made on notice within fourteen days of the trial; an application to vary an order can be made on the same grounds. Alternatively, the litigant can apply to have the order discharged on the grounds that his circumstances have **Changed** for the better. This is an easier process to commence than an appeal. Under Section 34(9),

The court may vary or discharge any order made under this section on the application of the authority, the child concerned or the person named in the order.

Appeals Procedure

Until and unless an alternative order is made, the order appealed stands, and the parties are expected to **Obtemper** it. If a party does not intend to comply, he must apply for a **Stay** of order to prevent the order coming into force. If the child is separately represented by a **Children's Guardian** who is not happy with the order made by the Court, she also has the right to lodge an appeal.

A decision may be appealed only if it is appealable and fulfils one of the G v G criteria (see **Appeal**). If he is making a new application soon after a substantive hearing, the appellant will need to make clear why he is doing so and what his justification is, or the Court may consider him **Vexatious**. He will need to explain—

1. what information was not presented to the Court;
2. why it was not presented; and
3. what impact it will have on the case.

The appellant must abide by Rule 12.19 of the **Family Procedure Rules 2010** and not seek to introduce evidence by the back door for which the Court has not called: the Court is entitled to ignore such evidence. A judge can refuse permission to appeal without a hearing and refuse permission to hold a hearing if he considers the appeal to be without **Merit**.

The procedure for appeal is described in Part 30 FPR 2010. **Leave** to appeal must be requested at the end of the hearing. Appeals are always made to a more senior judge in the same court or in a higher court than the one which made the order being appealed. Orders made by—

- Magistrates – are appealed to a Circuit Judge or High Court Judge sitting in the Family Court where the appeal raises a point of principle or practice;
- a District Judge – as above, or to a High Court Judge sitting in the Family Court in financial remedy proceedings;
- a Costs Judge – are appealed to a High Court Judge sitting in the Family Court;
- a Circuit Judge or Recorder – are appealed to the High Court, with the exception of care, supervision and protection orders and orders made under the Adoption and Children Act 2002; and
- a High Court Judge – (or deputy High Court Judge) are appealed to the Court of Appeal.

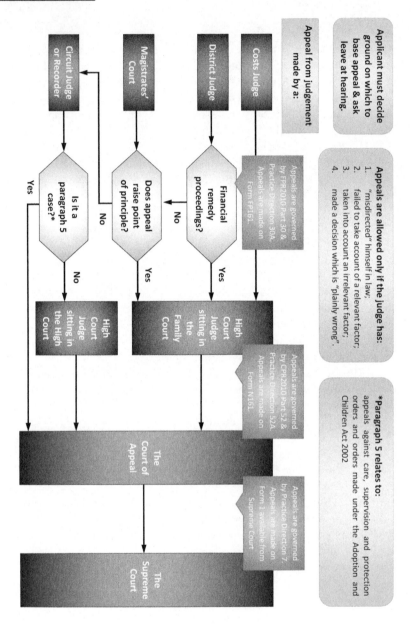

Flowchart 2: Appeals

28

Appeals to the Court of Appeal are governed by the Civil Proceedings Rules Part 52 and Practice Direction 52. Only if Leave of Appeal is refused by the Court of Appeal can it be appealed to the Supreme Court.

Leave will be granted only where the Court considers there is a reasonable chance of the appeal succeeding or where there is some other compelling reason to re-hear the case. The appellant must demonstrate the decision was wrong or unjust because one of the four grounds for appeal applies.

Applications, in which the appellant also states the grounds of his appeal, are made by means of an "Appellant's Notice" on Form FP161 for Appeals to the Family Division of the High Court or on Form N161 for all other appeals. At the same time, he must file a paginated and indexed appeal **Bundle**; this is a separate bundle of documents for the Court to use which includes a record of the reasons given for the decision being appealed. What the appellant must provide to the Court is explained in Leaflet 204 *How to Prepare an Appeal Bundle for the Court of Appeal*.

The bundle must be taken to the Court or posted to the Civil Appeals Office Registry, Room E307, 3rd Floor East Block, Royal Courts of Justice, Strand, London, WC2A 2LL. The appellant will be given a reference number and a receipt for the documents filed. The additional copies of the Appellant's Notice for the respondents will be sealed and returned for the appellant to serve. Unless the Court directs otherwise, a sealed copy must be served as soon as possible on all respondents and no later than seven days after the Appellant's Notice is filed; if leave to appeal has already been given or is not required, the appellant must also serve a copy of his appeal bundle on all respondents with his Appellant's Notice; if the Appellant's Notice includes an application for leave to appeal, copies of the bundle should not be sent to the respondent.

The Appellant's Notice must be served on all respondents, any **Children's Guardian**, welfare officer, or **Children and Family Reporter** and, where relevant, to the local authority.

A respondent may file and serve a Respondent's Notice if he wants leave to appeal or if he wants the Appeal Court to uphold the order for reasons different from or additional to those given by the trial Court. The Respondent's Notice (Form FP162) must be filed within fourteen days of service, or within such time as is specified by the Court. The respondent need take no action when served with the Appellant's Notice until notified that permission to appeal is granted, but changes to CPR 52 intended to relieve pressure on the Court of Appeal encourage him "to file and serve upon the appellant and any other respondent a brief statement of any reasons why permission should be refused, in whole or in part".

A judge will consider the application: the parties need not attend: if they do, the appellant will usually be allowed only twenty minutes to explain to the Court why leave should be granted. He will then be given an order setting out the judge's decision. If there is no hearing and permission to appeal is refused, he has seven days to request an oral hearing.

Leave to appeal may sometimes be granted only on certain issues. An appellant cannot raise any issue at the appeal hearing for which leave was expressly refused without the Court's permission. This he must seek as soon as possible after notification of its decision to give only limited permission. He must, at the same time, let the respondent know what he intends. His application will normally be dealt with at the outset of the hearing unless the Court instructs otherwise.

If leave to appeal is granted, the appellant will be given a date and time for the hearing. He has fifteen days to appeal a decision, however, he can apply for a "retrial" at any stage. He will need to make an *Ex Parte* application with the judge of the original hearing. Few retrials ever get off the ground and judges are not obliged to grant them as with appeals within time. If the appeal is allowed, the Court can return the case to the original court, transfer it to a higher court, or make a fresh order.

A second appeal is not usually possible; permission must be granted by the Court of Appeal and further fees will have to be paid.

Appellant

The party who lodges an **Appeal**.

Applicant

The party who applies to the Court for an **Order**.

Application

Family proceedings are commenced by making a formal application to the court via the appropriate form.

Most new applications for orders under **Section 8** of the Children Act will be made on Form C100. Where there are existing proceedings and an application is made for an additional order or where the applicant – such as a grandparent or sibling – needs the Court's consent to commence proceedings Form C2 is used.

The applicant will also need to provide the Court with evidence he has attended a **Mediation Information and Assessment Meeting** or is unsuited to attend. For C1, C2, C79 and financial applications a separate Form FM1 must be completed, but the new C100 application form now incorporates this. The form is simple to complete – it's just a matter of ticking some boxes. The applicant fills out Part 1; the mediator Part 2.

Applications for some s.8 orders, such as an order for Parental or Step-Parental Responsibility where agreement is impossible, are made on the older Form C1. Again, the applicant will need to complete Form FM1. Applicants for financial provision for children or variations thereof will need to complete supplemental form C10 with a **Statement of Means** on Form C10A.

The C100 form introduced some new fields such as parties' places of birth and previous surnames. The aim is to make identification of parties easier and to rule out "false positives" to reduce delay; it is, therefore, important to fill in all fields accurately. The new digital version inexplicably asks the applicant whether they have ever been sexually abused.

In Section 1, if the child's exact date of birth or name is not known – when, for example, the child has been born after separation, the child should be referred to as Baby X, where X is the presumed surname, and an approximate date will be given with "approx.; exact DoB not known" written in an empty box.

Section 2 concerns attendance at a **Mediation Information and Assessment Meeting** (MIAM). If there are existing or prior proceedings about emergency protection, care or supervision orders, it isn't necessary to attend a MIAM or complete Sections 3 and 4. If the applicant claims exemption, he must complete Section 3. If the mediator has determined that a MIAM is not appropriate, or a MIAM has been attended but mediation cannot proceed, they will tick the appropriate box in Section 4 and sign and date the form. If the applicant is not exempt and has not attended, he cannot make the application until he has.

Section 5b is where the applicant states his reasons for the application and the order he wants. The form asks only for a summary and the space available is limited; he needs to explain why he is bringing the application, what has gone wrong in the past, what explanations the respondent has given and what he wants the Court to do. That's a lot of information to cram into a small space, so it must be planned carefully. In the past, litigants have been advised to attach a more complete statement, but the **Family Procedure Rules** at 12.19 clarify that neither this nor any further documents should be submitted without **Leave** of the Court.

A **Parenting Plan** should be written and from that a draft version of the desired order should be prepared. This must be bullet-proof, and cover every aspect of the children's lives, with the relief sought clearly specified; see Bakir v Downe [2014] EWHC 3318.

If the applicant has ticked any of the boxes indicating concern about his children's welfare when in the care of the other parent and that they are at risk of domestic abuse, abduction, drug or alcohol abuse or any other harm, he will need to complete the supplemental Form C1A.

If the applicant wants his contact details or those of a child to remain confidential, he should not include them on the C100 form and should complete a Form C8.

The completed form must be taken or posted to the appropriate **Designated Family Centre** with the appropriate **Court Fee**, where it will be handled by a **Gatekeeping** team consisting of a Designated Family Judge (DFJ), a justices' clerk and as many legal advisors and **District Judges** as are necessary. If the gatekeeping judge is not satisfied mediation has been attempted, he can make directions for the applicant to attend. The gatekeeping team will decide what level of judge should determine the case; this will normally be a panel of **Magistrates** or a **District Judge**.

The Central Family Court in High Holborn has been experimenting with financial applications in PDF format submitted by email, with payment by telephone, though **Bundles** still need to be lodged with the court in the conventional way.

Arbitration

A form of **Alternative Dispute Resolution** in which the parties appoint an arbitrator to adjudicate their dispute and make a legally-binding award. The scheme is run by the Institute of Family Law Arbitrators. It was initially confined to financial disputes and was extended to child disputes in July 2016.

An arbitrator is an experienced family solicitor who has undergone specialist training and has power to make case management decisions, make interim orders and directions, appoint experts and make final and binding awards.

Arbitration is quicker than court and should be cheaper; parties are still advised to have independent legal representation, and this is, therefore, an option for the wealthier litigant.

Association

A particular form of legal connection; under Section 62 of the Family Law Act 1996 two adults are "associated" if—

1. they are or have been married to each other;
2. they are or have been civil partners;
3. they are cohabitants or former cohabitants;

4. they live or have lived in the same household (but not as an employee, tenant, lodger or boarder);
5. they are relatives;
6. they have agreed to marry one another (whether or not that agreement has been terminated);
7. they have entered into a civil partnership agreement (as defined by section 73 of the Civil Partnership Act 2004 and whether or not that agreement has been terminated);
8. they have or have had an intimate personal relationship with each other which is or was of significant duration;
9. they are a parent of the child; or have had **Parental Responsibility** for the child;
10. they are parties to the same family proceedings.

An adult is associated with a child if —

1. he is a parent of the child;
2. there are reasonable grounds for believing he is the father of the child;
3. he is a guardian of the child;
4. he is named in a Child Arrangements Order as a person with whom the child is to live; or
5. he has custody of the child.

Attachment Theory

A varied and fluid set of theories concerning how children develop and relate to their parents and to others. It borrows widely from other disciplines and provokes controversies and rivalries amongst its disciples.

In early attachment theory, John Bowlby proposed that a child is born programmed with a need to form attachments to others to ensure survival. Babies use behaviours called "social releasers", such as crying and smiling, to stimulate caregiving from the adults to whom they have attached and to maintain proximity to them. Bowlby's work was originally inspired by Konrad Lorenz, who studied how goslings imprint on the first moving object they see (like Lorenz's wading boots) and behave in such a way as to keep the mother nearby. Extending Lorenz's work to humans, Bowlby speculated (without evidence) that infants could attach only to one adult, generally their mother, and hypothesized that both infants and mothers have evolved biological needs to remain in close contact. This is called *Monotropy*.

Because this primary attachment forms the prototype for all the child's other relationships, Bowlby believed the attachment between mothers and infants could not be broken in the early, "tender", years without causing serious, permanent damage to the child's intellectual, social and emotional development; this is called the *Maternal Deprivation Hypothesis*. For Bowlby, the father had only indirect significance as a support to the mother; he had no direct emotional significance to the infant.

In the 1970s, psychologist Mary Ainsworth expanded on Bowlby's theory by assessing the nature of children's attachments using an evaluation tool called the "strange situation"; she concluded that there were three types of attachment; later researchers confirmed her conclusions but added a fourth.

In the years since Bowlby, attachment theory has developed, showing that children need attachments with both parents, not just one, and the doctrine of the **Primary Carer** has been exploded as a myth.

Attendance at Court

Refusing to turn up to court is foolish; the head-in-the-sand approach isn't a viable option and there's no excuse for not attending when the futures and protection of children are at stake. If either party has failed to attend an arranged hearing of which he has had reasonable notice, a court can respond in one of three ways: it can adjourn the hearing; it can issue a **Notice of Proceedings** to summon the parties together within forty-eight hours; or it can continue the hearing regardless (FPR 2010 12.14(6)).

If the applicant fails to attend, he risks having his application thrown out; if the respondent refuses to attend, the Court may make a decision she won't like (FPR 2010 12.14(7)), assuming that if she doesn't attend a hearing of which she has been informed she has little respect for their authority or concern for her child's welfare. She can apply to have the order set aside (FPR 2010 27.5), but will need to provide a convincing reason for not attending. If a party truly cannot attend, she must inform the court and the other party well in advance or as soon as possible afterwards. If the hearing takes place in her absence, she will need to find out what the outcome is as soon as she can so that, if necessary, she can appeal.

If the Court adjourns, an applicant should object, as any **Delay** is not in his child's interest; he will need to ask the Court to issue a Witness Summons and make an application for abortive costs. The summons is made using Form N20 and guidance is available in Leaflet EX342; the form must be filed at least seven days before the hearing and be served on the witness at least four days before. Two copies of the summons should be filed with the Court.

In Re P (A Child) [2006] EWCA Civ 1792, [2007] 1 FLR 1820, a resident mother refused to produce the child on four consecutive occasions; this breached a **Penal Notice** appended to the **Contact Order**. The father applied for **Committal**; the mother failed to attend and applied for an adjournment, citing childcare difficulties. The judge refused the adjournment and made a suspended committal order in her absence; further breach of the contact order would result in imprisonment. The mother appealed, but the **Court of Appeal** upheld the committal order: what was important was to ensure compliance with the contact order; the mother's reason for not attending was merely an excuse.

Avizandum

(Scots) (medieval Latin: "consideration") the time taken by a judge to consider his judgment.

B

Backsheet

The final page of a court document giving document title, court details, case number, parties' names, etc.

Bailiff

An officer of the court authorised to serve court documents on parties, execute arrest warrants and aid the **Tipstaff**.

Balance of Probabilities

See **Burden of Proof**.

Barder Event

A **Change of Circumstances** which occurs immediately after the making of a financial order, invalidating the basis upon which the order was made.

The principle is named after Barder v Caluori [1988] AC 20, in which a mother killed herself and her two children five weeks after the final order for ancillary relief. Her mother sought to enforce the order while her husband was granted permission to appeal; Lord Brandon detailed the four conditions such an application must satisfy:

1. New events have occurred since making the order which invalidate the basis, or fundamental assumption, upon which it was made, so that, if leave to appeal **Out-of-Time** were given, the appeal would be certain, or very likely, to succeed;
2. The new events have occurred within a few months of the order having been made and certainly not as much as a year;
3. The application for leave to appeal out-of-time is made promptly; and
4. The grant of leave to appeal out-of-time should not prejudice third parties who have acquired interests in property which is subject to the relevant order.

In Dixon v Marchant [2008] EWCA Civ 11, Mr Dixon applied to reduce his maintenance payments as he neared retirement; Mrs Dixon denied she was cohabiting or had any intention of remarrying and the parties negotiated a lump sum payment of £125,000 under Section 31 MCA1973. Mrs Dixon promptly remarried and became Mrs Marchant; Mr Dixon applied for the return of his money following what he claimed was a "Barder" event.

In the Appeal Court, Lords Justice Ward and Lawrence Collins decided the circumstances were not sufficiently *exceptional* to fall within the Barder criteria: the money was not returned. Wall LJ dissented and demonstrated that the first three criteria had plainly been met whilst the fourth did not arise.

In Myerson v Myerson [2009] EWCA Civ 282, it was initially agreed the wife would receive 43% of the couple's assets of £25.8million in the form of a property and a lump sum of £9.5million paid over four years. The husband's portion was in the form of shares in his company which subsequently dived in value by over 90%; the wife's portion as a percentage of the total rose to 105.2%. The husband appealed that the decision be **Set Aside** due to the change of circumstances; the Court refused, but accepted that because the sum due the wife was to be paid in instalments, the husband could apply to have both the timing and amount varied, following precedent set in the cases of Westbury v Sampson [2002] 1 FLR 166 and R v R (Lump sum repayments) [2004] 1 FLR 928.

In Critchell v Critchell [2015] EWCA Civ 436, Judge Black upheld Judge Wright's ruling that a husband's inheritance of £180,000 within a month of the consent order was a Barder event and extinguished his charge over the former matrimonial home, leaving both parties in roughly equal financial circumstances.

Barrell Jurisdiction

The Court's power to re-examine its decision in the light of new evidence at any time between the oral pronouncement and the **Perfected** order, when the judge becomes *Functus Officio*.

The jurisdiction allows a more extensive revision than is enabled under the **Slip Rule**, and the case of Re L and B (Children) [2013] UKSC 8 established that the circumstances need not be exceptional: the Court's overriding objective is to deal with the case justly. It is named after the case Re Barrell Enterprises [1973] 1 WLR 19.

In Quan v Bray & Ors [2014] EWHC 3340, Sir Paul Coleridge advised the mother —

> *[78(i)]* That process is designed to allow the court to look again at particular findings or conclusions where some particular fact or evidence has obviously been omitted, overlooked or has changed since the hearing. It does not afford a party the right to invite the court to start again from scratch and "have another go" at finding for them based on an entire re-arguing of the case. If that were a permissible approach it would result in litigation without end as one *Barrell* application would inevitably follow upon another and then another.

Barrister

A lawyer with greater **Rights of Audience** than a **Solicitor**, who specialises in courtroom advocacy. Barristers are not attorneys and cannot conduct litigation. They are more often engaged by a solicitor than a litigant, though increasingly litigants can **Instruct** barristers directly (see **Public Access**). The title is conferred by one of the four **Inns of Court**.

Behaviour

Section 1(2)(b) of the Matrimonial Causes Act 1973 allows a court to find that a marriage has broken down irretrievably if "the respondent has behaved in such a way that the petitioner cannot reasonably be expected to live with the respondent".

This is often abbreviated to "unreasonable behaviour" which creates confusion: it is not the **Respondent's** (or **Defender's**) behaviour that must be shown to be unreasonable, but the expectation that the **Petitioner** (or **Pursuer**) should continue to live with them. It is not even necessary to show that the behaviour led to the marriage breakdown.

"Unreasonable behaviour" is still the most popular fact used to prove **Irretrievable Breakdown** (45% of 2016 divorces) because it allows a petition for divorce after only a year and a day, and rarely requires factual confirmation (unlike **Adultery**).

Relevant behaviour can include physical and mental cruelty to the petitioner or the children, verbal abuse, dominating a partner, not letting the partner leave the house or speak to neighbours and friends, financial irresponsibility or domination, drunkenness or transmission of certain sexually transmitted diseases. The most usual behaviours cited are lack of communication, lack of an intimate relationship, an inappropriate relationship with a third person, spending time on hobbies or at work to the detriment of the marriage/family, etc.

It is necessary to cite five or six things which have made a spouse impossible to live with. These are summed up in a few short paragraphs in the **Petition**, including the first and most recent events, the most serious, and all dates, if they are known.

It isn't necessary to fabricate or exaggerate: the petitioner needs only to convince the judge the marriage has broken down irretrievably by showing it would be unreasonable to expect her to remain married and the threshold is set very low. She cannot use behaviour if the parties have lived together for six months or less following the most recent event adduced, and she cannot use her own behaviour as grounds.

Rare defended cases show the test is an objective one: "it is necessary to make findings of fact of what the husband actually did and then findings of fact upon the impact of his conduct on that particular lady" (Balraj v Balraj [1980] 11 Fam Law 110).

In 2015, Tini Owens petitioned for divorce. Her husband, Hugh, defended. Judge Tolson examined four of the twenty-seven isolated events Mrs Owens adduced as evidence and found they did not represent a "consistent and persistent course of conduct" and she had "exaggerated the context and seriousness of the allegations to a significant extent": she had not proved irretrievable breakdown and he dismissed the case.

Mrs Owens appealed (Owens v Owens [2017] EWCA Civ 182), but there were no grounds upon which the Court could overturn the decision, notwithstanding that this left her "locked into a loveless and desperately unhappy marriage which... has, in fact if not in law, irretrievably broken down".

A further appeal to the Supreme Court (Owens v Owens [2018] UKSC 41) also failed, though the Court deprecated the judge's use of the term "unreasonable behaviour" and his dismissal of the case based on limited examination of the evidence. The case raised a question for Parliament and the electorate whether the law remained satisfactory.

In Scotland, behaviour is used in only about 5% of cases and there is no minimum period. If the defender doesn't agree to the divorce, evidence and details will be needed; for example, from witnesses such as friends or medical evidence.

The wording "at any time" in the Divorce (Scotland) Act 1976 makes it clear that a single act or occurrence of misconduct is sufficient to seek a divorce; the behaviour must have occurred *after* the date of the marriage. Behaviour or conduct that has occurred after the date of separation *can* be used. A spouse who has been the victim of physical, sexual or verbal assaults may continue to live with the other through fear or because he/she has nowhere else to go (see Britton v Britton [1973], Bradley v Bradley [1973]) and this is not necessarily a barrier to a divorce.

Bench

The seat upon which the judge or magistrates sit and hence a symbol of their office and dignity.

Best Interests of the Child

BIOC – Article 3(1) of the UN Convention on the Rights of the Child requires of member states that—

> In all actions concerning children, whether undertaken by public or private social welfare institutions, courts of law, administrative authorities or legislative bodies, the best interests of the child shall be a primary consideration.

The best interests dogma enters UK law as the **Welfare** principle where it becomes *the* primary consideration of the Court. There is no agreed definition, so it is down to the **Discretion** of the individual judge and others to offer sometimes competing interpretations, not all of them child-focused.

The factors which best contribute to a child's development are not a mystery: most parents recognise the primary need of a child of separating parents is their continuing love and involvement in his life. Canadian academic Edward Kruk says,

> If it can be demonstrated that certain living arrangements, such as shared parenting, best address children's core needs... it is the responsibility of social institutions, including courts of law, administrative authorities or legislative bodies, to support such arrangements.

Children's needs are not well supported by an **Adversarial System** which undermines the very people with responsibility to serve those needs, and which creates those conditions – hostility and the separation from a parent – which are most predictive of poor outcomes.

The student should recognise the best interests principle is controversial and lacks universal approval: it overrides the Court's duty to observe due process, to presume innocence, to see justice done; and thus undermines the rule of law. It reduces parental authority by elevating children's welfare, but the arbiter of welfare is the Court, and thus it elevates the authority of the Court – and its officers – above that of parents. In so doing it turns welfare into a rights issue, pitting the child against his family, and excavating a chasm between children's interests and those of their parents. This, in turn, leads to the need for the state to represent the child and thus to a conflict between parents and state.

According to solicitor Oliver Cyriax, the best interests of the child —

is no more than a label affixed to the case retrospectively, irrespective of current research, irrespective of best opinion, irrespective of the facts of the case, irrespective of governing principles, irrespective of the merits of the case and irrespective of the outcome. This is an inevitability; all decisions (whatever they are) must by definition be in the best interests of the child since otherwise they would contravene the law. The definition of "the best interests of the child" is whatever decision the Court reached.

Beth Din

"House of judgment" – the rabbinical court of Judaism, based on religious precepts.

Beth Din tribunals have operated in the UK for centuries and can legally act as arbitrator in civil disputes, including divorces. Agreements achieved through arbitration are respected by the courts but are not binding; see AI v MT [2013] EWHC 100. Jewish divorce takes place only if the parties agree, and commences when the husband hands his wife a document called the *Get*. Orthodox Jews do not acknowledge a divorce obtained through the justice system and within her community a legally divorced woman will be regarded as an *agunah* – a chained wife.

Beyond Reasonable Doubt
See **Burden of Proof**.

Bird's-Nest Custody

A **Shared Parenting** arrangement first employed in the US and Canada. The child remains in one home while the parents alternate between their own homes and that of the child. The arrangement is expensive as it normally requires three properties, though it can theoretically be achieved with two.

The pattern, originating in the Virginia case of Lamont v Lamont, relies on the assumption that children suffer from being moved between two homes; it now appears that any harm children suffer from divorce is not the result of having two homes. It is probable that the disadvantages of birds-nest custody outweigh the advantages.

Birth Certificate

The record of a child's birth, showing where, when and to whom he was born. Controversy arises when a mother registers a birth without the father, or names the wrong father.

A man who wishes to be added to his child's birth certificate can do so at the register office with the mother; if she disagrees, he must apply to a court for a **Declaration of Parentage**; the Court will then inform the General Register Office.

A man who wishes to be removed from a child's birth certificate must first prove he isn't the child's father either through a legally recognised **DNA Test** or by means of a **Declaration of Non-Parentage** from a court. He will then need to send the appropriate application to the General Register Office.

Minor errors on a certificate can be corrected by contacting the office where the birth was registered; to change a child's **Name** requires completing a form and can only be done if all those with PR agree or via a court order.

Breach of an Order

The failure – deliberate or otherwise – to obey an order of the Court.

Court orders must be obeyed; in Re W (A Child) [2013] EWCA Civ 1177, Munby LJ referred—

> [51] ...to the slapdash, lackadaisical and on occasions almost contumelious attitude which still far too frequently characterises the response to orders made by family courts. There is simply no excuse for this. Orders... must be obeyed and complied with to the letter and on time. Too often they are not. They are not preferences, requests or mere indications; they are orders.

Breach of any order concerning a child is a serious matter which can put the child at risk. The best response may be a stern solicitor's letter to the child's other parent in the first instance, pointing out that they are in breach and advising that it will be necessary to proceed to court if the order isn't adhered to; the parent will, at least, be able to show he has tried to resolve the issue reasonably.

If this doesn't work and the breach continues, the next step is an application for **Enforcement**. Though the courts can enforce an order on their own initiative, it will almost always be necessary to make an application.

Breach of the following is **Contempt of Court** and a penal notice will be attached to the order:

- a **Child Arrangements Order**;
- an **Enforcement** Order;
- a **Domestic Violence Protection Order**;
- an **Occupation Order**;
- an **Undertaking**;
- Section 12 of the Administration of Justice Act 1960.

Breach of the following is an arrestable criminal offence:

- a **Non-Molestation Order**;
- **Section 97** of the Children Act 1989.

Breach of an order can result in committal to prison only if this is made clear to the respondent by attaching a **Warning Notice** to the order (older orders may already have a penal notice attached), informing the recipient that breach may result in a fine or committal to prison. There is no principle of "first free breach", and immediate **Committal** may be appropriate for serious breach; see Wilson v Webster [1988] 1 FLR 1097.

Breach of the Peace

The Queen's peace is the protection the monarch provides to her subjects; maintaining the Queen's peace is one of the duties of the Crown, exercised via the Royal Prerogative, advised by her Prime Minister who is, in turn, answerable to Parliament.

Responsibility for upholding the Queen's peace originally fell to volunteers from each shire known initially as Knights of the Peace, subsequently as Justices of the Peace (JPs) from 1361 and more recently as **Magistrates**. Many of the original responsibilities are now implemented by the police.

Breaching the Queen's peace is not itself a criminal offence but the police (and indeed any citizen) can arrest; a breach is defined in R v Howell [1981] as —

> an act done or threatened to be done which either actually harms a person, or in his presence, his property, or is likely to cause such harm being done.

Persons so detained will be taken before a magistrate who will "bind them over" to keep the peace, usually until they calm down or sober up. The charge of breaking the peace will not go on a person's criminal record, but a repeat offence within a specified time frame will result in imprisonment.

Brexit

The impact of the UK's withdrawal from the European Community is difficult to forecast; most family law will be unaffected, while areas such as **Brussels II** and **REMO** will change. Brexit will mean leaving the European Court of Justice but not the European Court of Human Rights, which is not an organ of the EU. The Government will seek to maintain close co-operation with the EU on matters of family justice and to retain a system for mutual recognition and enforcement of orders. It is likely there will be greater integration with international, rather than merely European, treaties, such as **Hague**.

Brussels II Revised

BIIR or Brussels II bis (Council Regulation (EC) No 2201/2003) – an agreement made between countries of the European Union.

BIIR brings together in a single regulation all provisions on parental responsibility and divorce. It excludes issues relating to paternity, changing a child's name and adoption. Under BIIR, orders made in one member country can be registered in another automatically and need not be retried. It is likely that after Brexit, while the UK will continue to honour orders made in member states, other states will not automatically recognise UK orders and will require that they submit to a recognition procedure. Without an effective framework in place in advance, lengthy and expensive *Forum Conveniens* disputes may ensue.

Brussels II takes precedence over the **Hague Convention**.

The first action of a parent with an order from another Member State should be to register it using the procedure in Part 31 of the **Family Procedure Rules 2010** and the certificate referred to in Article 39 of BIIR and detailed at Annex II (Article 42); he will be able to get this from the court from which he obtained the order he wishes to register and enforce.

This is a purely administrative process and the Court is required to handle it expeditiously. The Court has no jurisdiction to retry a decision by a fellow Member State save in exceptional circumstances. The lower courts don't always apply BIIR correctly (see, for example JRG v EB [2012] EWHC 1863) and it is wise to have a case transferred up.

In abduction cases, under Article 9 of BIIR, the country in which the child was **Habitually Resident** and from which the child was abducted continues to have jurisdiction for three months (though only to modify and not to enforce the order) and can issue an order for immediate mandatory return; the judgment must be made within six weeks. This doesn't always work as it should: in Re M (Children) [2017] EWA Civ 891, a father sought the enforcement of a contact order issued in Estonia, but the court declined due to the lack of cooperation from CAFCASS and the local authority.

Under Article 12, jurisdiction acquired in one country cannot be terminated by the decision of a court in another; see Re S-R (Jurisdiction: Contact) [2008] 2FLR 1741. This jurisdiction extends to all matters of **Parental Responsibility** and confers on the Court power in family proceedings to make an order under s.8 CA1989 even where no such application has been made; see AP v TD [2010] EWHC 2040.

Bundle

The file of relevant documents used by the Court for a particular hearing.

The current Practice Direction 27A was issued by Sir James Munby, as President, on the introduction of the **Family Procedure Rules 2010** in April 2011 and amended following the reforms introduced in April 2014; it applies to all family proceedings, made with or without notice.

PD27A should be complied with, *to the letter*; in Re L (A Child) [2015] EWFC 15, Munby lamented that it is "almost routinely ignored" and repeated Mostyn's suggestion in J v J [2014] EWHC 3654 for a special court where "delinquent" lawyers would be required to explain their failure to comply and be sanctioned accordingly.

Litigants must bring their bundles with them every time they attend court. The only exceptions are emergency *Ex Parte* hearings, and they will then have to bring the bundles to the subsequent *Inter Partes* hearing. For a brief hearing, it may not be necessary to provide the complete bundle, but it must still be agreed between the parties. For each hearing, the bundle must be updated with new summaries, statements of issues, chronologies, and skeleton arguments. The old ones should be removed and filed.

Responsibility for preparing the bundle is the applicant's if both parties are represented. If there are **Cross-Applications**, responsibility is with the applicant whose application was in first. If the applicant is a **Litigant-in-Person**, responsibility lies with the first listed respondent who is not an LiP. If all parties are LiPs, no one has to prepare a bundle unless the Court orders it, but even where both parties are, it is advisable to prepare a bundle and agree the contents with the other party. If a party objects to the inclusion of a document, it probably discloses something they want to remain hidden, so it should be included.

A solicitor is obliged to send only an index to the other party who is presumed to acquire copies of all relevant documents. Usually, a solicitor will supply the bundle for a fee (25p per sheet is typical). To avoid high costs, it is necessary to monitor closely what is going into the bundle. The judge should make directions regarding when the bundle should be prepared and when it must be agreed with the other side.

A litigant obliged to prepare the bundle must study the Practice Direction closely. He will need to produce an index which must be copied to the other side and provide any documents they don't have. We shall only cover the more salient points of the Practice Direction here.

It is important to be aware of what does NOT go into the Bundle in order to avoid duplication; these documents are filed separately in case they are needed:

a) correspondence, to include letters of instruction;
b) medical records;
c) bank and credit card statements or other financial records;
d) police disclosures.

Only documents relevant to the particular hearing and which it is necessary for the Court to read or refer to go in, so a different bundle is required for each hearing. There is a complete index at the front, and then six sections created by divider cards in each of which the documents are filed in chronological order:

a) Preliminary and case management documents; these should be kept short and succinct:
   i. a summary of the background to the case limited to four pages;
   ii. a statement of the issues (1) which are to be determined at the hearing and (2) which are to be determined at the final hearing;
   iii. a Position Statement from each party summarising the orders or directions sought (1) at that hearing and (2) at the final hearing;
   iv. if the summary at (i) is insufficient, an up-to-date **Chronology**;
   v. the **Skeleton Argument**;
b) a list of all the essential documents the judge should read prior to the hearing; copies of the authorities upon which the litigant is relying for his skeleton argument are provided in a separate bundle;
c) applications and court orders;

d) statements and affidavits, dated on the top right corner;

e) care plans (where appropriate);

f) reports from expert witnesses and any other reports, including those from the guardian, **Children's Guardian** and **Litigation Friend**;

g) any other documents as appropriate, or as directed by the Court (these may need to be further sub-divided). Statements, affidavits and reports, etc., must be photocopies of originals which have been signed and dated.

The Practice Direction is equally strict about format: the bundle is presented in no more than one lever-arch file, unless the Court directs otherwise. Each contains no more than 350 pages, printed on one side only in a legible 12-point font and in 1½ or double line spacing. Munby proposed further limits to the number of pages in each individual bundle document:

Case Summary	4
Statement of Issues	2
Position Statement	5
Chronology	10
Skeleton Argument	15
List of Essential Reading	1
Witness Statement or Affidavit (exclusive of exhibits)	20
Expert's or other Report	40
Care Plan	10

Bundles which exceed the maximum size will be refused; if they have been sent by post or courier, they will be destroyed.

Each page carries a page number using Arabic numerals (1, 2, 3, etc.). On the spine and front cover is written the title and number of the case, where the case is listed, the date and time of the hearing, the name of the judge and, where there is more than one file, they are numbered A, B, C, etc. The bundle is paginated so that all parties and the Court have the same documents in the same order.

An index is provided to all other parties not less than four working days before the hearing, and the bundle, excluding the preliminary documents, is lodged with the appropriate court office not less than two working days before. If bundles are lodged at the wrong court, they will be treated as not having been lodged and sanctions or **Wasted Costs** may be imposed. A receipt or proof of posting or dispatch must be obtained. Where the hearing is before magistrates, four copies must be provided to the Court. The preliminary documents are lodged not later than 11:00 on the day before the hearing.

Family litigation produces a great deal of paperwork, at least a large lever-arch file every year. When each is full another should be bought to save having to sort through what is still relevant – nothing should be thrown away before the child reaches sixteen and documents relating to a divorce should be kept indefinitely. The file should be efficiently organised with colour-coded dividers and indexing at the front to keep it all accessible. Losing an important document when it is most needed can be disastrous. There will be sections for:

1. the chronology;
2. applications to the Court and orders from the Court;
3. correspondence with the Court;
4. correspondence with the other parties and solicitors;
5. position and witness statements;
6. reports from CAFCASS and expert witnesses;
7. case precedents and research evidence;
8. miscellaneous.

Everything should be in chronological order, matching the Chronology. This is awkward when using a lever arch file, it's easiest to have the most recent documents on top, but if it is arranged with them at the end, it means everything is in the same order as the bundle. Documents should be printed on only one side of the paper as it is easy to miss something when searching through; "slippery fish" should be avoided: it makes getting a document out in court fiddly. Different coloured "Post-it" notes should be used to identify documents required at a particular hearing.

Burden of Proof

The imperative on a party to provide the evidence which proves their position. It translates the Latin *onus probandi*, often shortened to *onus*.

The burden is always on the party who makes the **Allegation**; the other party should not need to prove his case and is presumed innocent of the allegation until it is proved.

The courts act on facts, not speculation, assumption, worries or concerns (Re BR (Proof of Facts) [2015] EWFC 41). Evidence of these facts can be presented in a wide variety of forms. A disputed fact is "in issue" and must be adjudicated.

In England and Wales there are officially only two standards of proof: the criminal court *beyond reasonable doubt* standard, and the civil court *balance of probabilities* standard. In predicting **Future Harm**, the courts employ a third standard of "real possibility".

Acts of domestic and child abuse are rarely perpetrated in public, which means corroborative evidence is seldom available. The Court, however, must prefer the evidence of one party over the other and make its decision. Each piece of evidence must be considered in the context of the whole, and all possible explanations considered in light of the evidence; no explanation should be rejected merely because it is improbable. The Court must also consider that sometimes it is simply not possible to determine the truth.

The "balance of probabilities" principle was simply defined by Lord Nicholls in Re H and Others (Minors) (Sexual Abuse: Standard of Proof) [1996] AC 563:

> [73] The balance of probability standard means that a court is satisfied an event occurred if the court considers that on the evidence the account of the event was more likely than not.

Neither the seriousness of the allegation, nor the consequence of finding it proved, nor the inherent probability of an event affect this fundamental test; Lord Lloyd said in the same case,

> [30] In my view the standard of proof under that subsection ought to be the simple balance of probability however serious the allegations involved... It would be a bizarre result if the more serious the anticipated injury, whether physical or sexual, the more difficult it became for the local authority to satisfy the initial burden of proof, and thereby ultimately, if the welfare test is satisfied, secure protection for the child.

In Re B (Children) [2008] UKHL 35; [2008] 2 FLR 141, Lord Hoffman started a confusing trend explaining the courts' approach in terms of mathematics,

> [2] If a legal rule requires a fact to be proved (a "fact in issue"), a judge or jury must decide whether or not it happened. There is no room for a finding that it might have happened. The law operates a binary system in which the only values are 0 and 1. The fact either happened or it did not. If the tribunal is left in doubt, the doubt is resolved by a rule that one party or the other carries the burden of proof. If the party who bears the burden of proof fails to discharge it, a value of 0 is returned and the fact is treated as not having happened. If he does discharge it, a value of 1 is returned and the fact is treated as having happened.

Lord Justice Mostyn continued the analogy in AA v NA & Ors [2010] EWHC 1282, and again in A County Council v M & F [2011] EWHC 1804 (Fam),

The law sets a simple probability standard of 51/49, but the more serious or improbable the allegation the greater the need, generally speaking, for evidential "cogency".

This approach was rejected by the Court of Appeal in A (Children) [2018] EWCA Civ 1718,

With the greatest respect to the erudition of Mostyn J's arithmetical approach to the application of the 'simple balance of probabilities', I do not agree that it represents the appropriate approach.

They reiterated the approach taken by Baroness Hale in Re H which, rejected the escalating standard of proof and confirmed the "binary" standard,

[70] My Lords... I would go further and announce loud and clear that the standard of proof... is the simple balance of probabilities, neither more nor less. Neither the seriousness of the allegation nor the seriousness of the consequences should make any difference to the standard of proof to be applied in determining the facts. The inherent probabilities are simply something to be taken into account, where relevant, in deciding where the truth lies.

C

California Model

The theoretical model which arrived in this country in the 1980s and by which social workers, CAFCASS, therapists, police and others understand the workings of child abuse.

At its core is the discredited idea that children's minds block traumatic events, the memories of which must then gradually be teased out of the child – or the adult – over the course of numerous intensive sessions in a process of progressive disclosure, steadily exposing layer after layer of abuse.

Even an individual who has never alleged abuse should be understood as a victim who is suppressing memories and needs assistance to disclose, leading questions and deeply suggestive interviewing techniques are necessary to reveal the repressed memories, and the disclosure process is never complete: there are always further revelations to be uncovered.

Overlying this theory is the conviction that children never lie and must always be believed.

This model has obvious flaws: it is without evidential credibility; there is no research to suggest traumatic memories are suppressed, or that they can be exposed in a progressive manner through therapy; progressive escalation is exactly how false **Allegations** of abuse work. A 1995 American study by April Bradley and James Wood confirmed that, where there is genuine abuse, most subjects make full disclosure in the initial investigative interview.

In the US, cases based on the Californian model eventually collapsed, but by then it had already become securely established in the UK and was being proselytised by evangelical social workers; by the '90s it had become an article of faith amongst the police, who believed complaints of sexual abuse would not be brought to them directly, and that they had therefore to mount highly publicised "trawling" expeditions (often with the promise of lavish compensation) to encourage "victims" to come forward.

Capacity (1)

The intellectual ability to carry out certain functions such as to have sexual relations and marry, or to understand a case and **Instruct** a **Solicitor**.

A party lacks capacity in relation to a particular matter if, at the crucial time, he is unable to make a decision for himself about the matter due to an impairment of, or disturbance in the functioning of, his mind or brain. This impairment may be permanent or temporary. Lacking capacity is defined by reference to the Mental Capacity Act 2005.

Whether the party lacks capacity must be decided on the balance of probabilities and cannot be based on age, appearance, medical condition or an aspect of behaviour. The Court's assessment of his capacity will be based on:

1. whether he can understand the information relevant to the decision;
2. whether he can retain that information;
3. whether he can use and weigh that information as part of his decision-making process; and
4. whether he can communicate his decision through speech, sign language or other means.

Exceeding this understanding would involve "unnecessary paternalism and derogation from personal autonomy" (see IM v LM [2014] EWCA Civ 37). A party is presumed to have capacity; he will not be regarded as lacking it if he is able to understand the information via an explanation given in a way appropriate to his circumstances, through simplified language, visual aids, etc. Nor does being able to retain the information for only a short period necessarily mean he lacks capacity. He must, however, be able to understand the consequences both of his decision and of a failure to make a decision. Someone who lacks capacity through mental illness or learning disability may be aided by a **Litigation Friend**.

The leading judgment is Masterman-Lister v Brutton & Co (Nos 1 and 2) [2002] EWCA Civ 1889; Masterman-Lister v Jewell and another [2003] EWCA Civ 70 in which Chadwick LJ said,

> [75] ...the test to be applied... is whether the party to legal proceedings is capable of understanding, with the assistance of such proper explanation from legal advisors and experts in other disciplines as the case may require, the issues on which his consent or decision is likely to be necessary in the

course of those proceedings. If he has capacity to understand that which he needs to understand in order to pursue or defend a claim, I can see no reason why the law whether substantive or procedure should require the imposition of a next friend or guardian ad litem (or, as such person is now described in the Civil Procedure Rules, a litigation friend).

[82] ... a person is not to be regarded as unable to make a rational decision merely because the decision which he does make is one which would not be made by a person of ordinary prudence, so he is not to be regarded as having capacity merely because the decision appears rational.

Capacity (2)

The legal status enabling two parties to marry each other; i.e., that they are not already married, or not related to each other in a way that prohibits marriage, etc. See **Void Marriage.**

Care

The provision of accommodation, food, education, medical treatment, emotional support, etc., to a child to ensure that he develops to his full potential.

Section 31(2) of the Children Act allows the intervention of the state when "the care given to the child" is not "what it would be reasonable to expect a parent to give to him".

Does this represent an objective standard of care or that variety which can only be provided by a parent or parents? The test is given in the Adoption and Children Act 2002, which specifies at Section 31(10):

Where the question of whether harm suffered by a child is significant turns on the child's health or development, his health or development shall be compared with that which could reasonably be expected of a similar child.

In Re O (A Minor) (Care Proceedings: Education) [1992] 1 WR 992, Ewbank J held that a "similar child" meant one of equivalent intellectual and social development. This raises two controversies; first: should a child raised by Muslims, Rastafarians or Hassidic Jews, etc., be compared with a child from the same culture, or are there minimum standards of care which should be applied to all children regardless of culture? The latter approach was adopted by the Court of Appeal in Re D (Care: Threshold Criteria) [1998] Fam Law 656.

Second: the Court of Appeal warned in Re L (Children) (Threshold Criteria) [2007] 1 FLR 205 against the danger of social engineering where a child or his parents have learning difficulties and these factors are taken into account.

Care Order

A court order made on application by a local authority under Section 31 of the Children Act 1989 that a child be placed in its care.

The Court can also make an **Interim Order** for **Supervision** or care, where, for example, it is waiting for a **Section 37 Report** from the LA. Under Section 14 of the Children and Families Act 2014, proceedings are expected to be completed within twenty-six weeks, although the average in 2017 was twenty-eight.

If a court makes a Care Order, it obliges the LA to find accommodation for the child for the duration of the order. It then acquires **Parental Responsibility** and the power to limit the exercise of the parents' PR, provided it is necessary to protect the child's welfare. A supervision order does not confer PR. Even when it has PR, the LA cannot change the child's religion or name and cannot remove him from the UK for longer than twenty-eight days.

Under s.39 CA1989 the parents, the child or the LA can apply to discharge the order. If the child is in care and the parents have PR, they can apply to have the order discharged by making an application on Form C2, giving brief reasons for the application. Where a Care Order is discharged, the Court may put a Supervision Order in its place.

The only criterion for the discharge of a Care Order or the variation or discharge of a Supervision Order is the **Welfare** of the child concerned. The burden of proving that it is in the child's best interests for the order to be discharged or varied is upon the applicant; see Re B (Minors) (Contact) [1994] 2 FLR 1 and Re S and P (Discharge of Care Order) [1995] 2 FLR 782. Note, however, that the *Family Bench Book* warns judges "to guard against a discharge application being used as a back-door appeal against the original order".

An interim order must be appealed within seven days, as must a case management decision, unless the Court directs otherwise. If neither parent has harmed their child or has a criminal record, they have a good chance of winning. Even if successful, they will not be able to claim back costs against a local authority; in Re T (Children) (Care Proceedings: Costs) [2012] UKSC 36, the **Supreme Court** refused to order costs against an LA even though the allegations it had made turned out to be unfounded.

Case Conference

A meeting convened by social services and others to determine what intervention should be taken regarding a child.

Assuming there is no **Emergency Protection Order**, the Case Conference is the first step in removing a child; this can be followed by an application for a **Supervision** or **Care Order**. The meeting should include the child, all those with **Parental Responsibility** for him, the social services case manager and possibly their line manager, health services staff: health visitor, school nurse, GP, education services: teacher, education welfare officer, etc., and the parents' solicitor or **McKenzie Friend**, if they wish.

Others may be invited if they are professionals involved with the child (mental health services, domestic abuse advisor, etc.) but the best practice is to keep numbers to a minimum. If a key professional cannot attend, they may submit a written report. The purpose of the Case Conference is to:

1. collate and analyse information regarding the child's health and development and the parents' capacity to protect and promote these;
2. determine the risk of the child suffering future **Significant Harm**;
3. decide on the need for registration;
4. identify a Care Manager where registration is agreed; and
5. agree a child protection outline plan and its intended outcome.

Sometimes a parent may be excluded, but all parents with PR have a right to attend and research shows that parental involvement leads to better outcomes for the child. If social services call a Case Conference to which the resident parent, the school and other parties are invited, they must invite the non-resident parent as well. Parents should be given plenty of notice in writing of the time and location of the Conference. They should also be given in advance any reports by social workers or other evidence they propose to introduce unless it breaches the child's confidentiality or that of a third party, or is likely to interfere with a criminal investigation.

If it is considered that one parent's attendance will jeopardise the child, separate conferences can be held. Exclusion should be rare, and may only need to be partial, but there is a flexible range of justifications for excluding a parent, including the potential for his attendance to result in intimidation of another attendee, perhaps leading to their non-attendance, the possibility he will be disruptive or verbally abusive, or when there is a need to withhold certain information from him.

If a parent is excluded, he should be advised in writing and be given reasons; he must then be allowed to make representation through his solicitor or other representative.

Case Law

The body of law based on judicial decisions and **Precedent** rather than on **Statute**. Case law can be accessed either as **Transcripts** which are freely available online in *Family Law Week*, where new judgments will often appear first, usually with a summary, and in *BAILII*, the *British and Irish Legal*

Information Institute, or as **Law Reports**, which are available in subscription services such as *Westlaw*, *LexisLibrary*, *Justis* and *Casetrack*. Media reports of cases are selective, inaccurate and misleading and should be avoided.

Case Summary

A brief document, up to four pages, placed at the front of the **Bundle**, setting out the background to the case and limited to the matters relevant to the particular hearing and to case management. Where proceedings concern a child and are in front of magistrates, it should be anonymised.

Case Theory

See **Skeleton Argument**.

Cash Equivalent Transfer Value

(CETV) – the notional monetary value of a pension, used to calculate divorce settlements.

Certificate

The written guarantee from the Legal Aid Agency that they will provide a litigant with **Legal Aid**.

Certificate of Financial Complexity

A form which enables a particularly complex financial case to be transferred to the **Financial Remedies Unit**. Applicants must provide basic details of the marriage and divorce application, the potential complexities of the case, the scale of the sums involved and potential allegations that may arise.

Certificate of No Impediment

(CNI or *Nulla Osta*) – a certificate which may be required of a couple marrying abroad to prove that each party is single and otherwise able to marry. Couples should check with the authorities in the country where they propose to marry before they travel.

Chambers

A judge's office; the expression "in chambers" is used to translate the Latin *in camera*, referring to a hearing conducted in private. Also, a group of barristers and the premises they occupy.

Change of Circumstances

A relevant alteration in a litigant's personal situation sufficient to persuade a judge to revisit a case. The paramount consideration is the **Welfare** of the child.

Under Section 24(3) of the Children and Adoption Act 2002, a court can give leave for an application for a **Placement Order** to be revoked, and under Section 47(7) to oppose an **Adoption** order, but only if there has been a change in the circumstances of the applicant or, rarely, the child. The change need not be "significant" but must be "relevant" (Re T (Children) [2014] EWCA Viv 1369). In the words of Munby LJ in Re B-S (Children) [2013] EWCA Civ 1146, it must be "of a nature and degree sufficient, on the facts of the case, to open the door to the exercise of judicial evaluation". The test should not be set so high that parents are discouraged from bettering themselves or to prevent them from seeking to prevent the adoption of their child.

Chattels

Moveable personal property, usually items constituting the contents of a house and individually under the value of £500.

Child

A child only acquires independent legal status at birth.

Proceedings cannot be brought in the name of an unborn child (Paton v BPAS [1979], Paton v UK [1980]; see **Abortion**) and a foetus cannot be made a ward of court (Re F (*In Utero*) [1988] CA).

A woman has the right to refuse medical treatment of an unborn child which the Court can impose once the child is born (St. George's Healthcare NHS Trust v S [1998] 3 WLR 936). A foetus is a unique organism and neither a distinct person nor an adjunct of its mother and cannot be the victim of a violent crime (Attorney General's Reference (No 3 of 1994) [1998] AC 245). Similarly, a child damaged *In Utero* by his mother's excessive drinking is not the victim of an offence under Section 23 of the Offences Against the Person Act 1861 (CP (A Child) v First-Tier Tribunal (Criminal Injuries Compensation) [2014] EWCA Civ 1554).

Article 2 of the **European Convention on Human Rights**, which protects the right to life, does not apply to the unborn. In 2004, Thi-Nho Vo, whose pregnancy had been wrongly terminated in a French hospital, took her case to the European Court of Human Rights (Vo v France (2005) 40 EHRR 12) arguing that her unborn child had the right to life and the termination was manslaughter. The Court rejected her claim.

The relief available under the Children Act 1989 ends when a person reaches the age of sixteen. In exceptional cases – where a child has special needs, for example, the upper age limit is their eighteenth birthday. **Adoption** proceedings can apply to a person under the age of eighteen when proceedings commence (FAS v Bradford Metropolitan District Council & Anor [2015] EWHC 622), and **Hague Convention** proceedings to a person under the age of sixteen.

For the purposes of child support legislation, a person ceases to be a child when they reach their twentieth birthday and in many cases child support must be paid until the child completes full-time education.

Child Arrangements Order

CAO – an order enabled under Section 12 of the Children and Families Act 2014 which replaced and combined the old orders for **Contact** and **Residence** in Section 8 of the Children Act 1989, determining with whom and when a child will live or have contact and which apply to both parents equally.

The wording of the Act gives the courts considerable flexibility in the drafting of an order and is designed to eliminate any suggestion of winners and losers by conferring a status on the resident or custodial parent that the contact or access parent lacks. A CAO comes in two parts:

Part A regulates *with whom* a child is to live, spend time or otherwise have contact. This will state simply which adult(s) the child is to live with and which the child is to spend time with or otherwise have contact with, including indirect contact.

Part B regulates *when* a child is to live, spend time or otherwise have contact with any person. This part will set out the schedule showing when the child is living or spending time with each parent, and when any indirect contact is to take place.

Pre-existing **Contact Orders** became CAOs relating to with whom the child was to have contact and when, and **Residence Orders** became CAOs relating to with whom the child was to live and when.

An applicant will normally want to be named as a person with whom the child is to live – as with the old Shared Residence Orders. If he applies to be a person with whom the child is to have contact – as in an old Contact Order – and the other parent has a CAO making her the person with whom the child is to live, this will impose additional restraints on him – he will need her consent to take the child out of the country, for example.

Contact Orders imposed a requirement on the resident parent "to allow the child to visit or stay with the person named in the order". The new legislation imposes no such obligation, but it can be written into the individual order, and it is possible to enforce the order in the same way that Contact Orders were enforced. This resolves the difficulty which formerly existed in enforcing Residence Orders (pre-existing Residence Orders which have become CAOs cannot be enforced).

Child Arrangements Order; Application

Applications are governed by Parts 18 and 19 of the **Family Procedure Rules 2010**. Part 18 applies to making applications to start proceedings, making applications in proceedings already commenced and making applications in relation to proceedings already concluded. Part 19 applies to applications for permission to appeal and those not covered by Part 18.

A biological father (or a woman who is a parent by virtue of Section 43 of the Human Fertilisation and Embryology Act 2008) needs not have **Parental Responsibility** to apply for a CAO; when the Court makes such an order it must also make an order for PR.

Step-fathers and step-mothers can also acquire PR for their partner's children by applying to the Court for a CAO in which they are named as a person with whom the child is to live. If arrangements for step-children after a separation cannot be agreed, the Court's permission will be required before making an application.

The courts will use a **Template** (CAP04) to draft orders, which shows the kind of format a CAO will take:

> The child[ren] will live with the [mother/father/ mother and father] as set out in the schedule to this order (if extensive)/as follows...]

> The [mother/father] agrees to make the child[ren] available to visit/stay with/have indirect contact with the [mother/father] [as set out in the schedule to this order (if extensive)/as follows...]

The details of the CAO will be defined in a "schedule of contact"; this is referred to as "defined contact". The schedule must be detailed and include when and where the child is to be collected, by whom, how long the child is to stay, and when and where the child is to be returned and to whom. It is essential a CAO is written in clear terms so that both parties are in no doubt how to comply and will be aware if they are in breach. The order should be in injunctive terms to both parties.

The application is made on Form C100 and should only be made after the applicant has attended a **Mediation Information and Assessment Meeting** (MIAM), unless he is exempt or the application is urgent and to be made **Without Notice**. As evidence, the mediator will complete Section 4 of the form confirming the applicant's attendance or giving his reasons for not attending. If the other party would not engage in mediation or the case was unsuitable, the mediator will complete the form stating this and sign it. They will charge about £25 for this service which has largely become a box-ticking exercise. The Court must give the applicant:

1. a copy of the Application Form C100, together with Supplemental Information Form C1A if there are welfare concerns;
2. the Notice of Hearing;
3. the Acknowledgment Form C7;
4. a blank Form C1A;
5. the Certificate of Service Form C9; and
6. information leaflets for the parties (including the CB7 leaflet).

The completed application should be taken or posted to the appropriate Designated Family Centre, typically the one nearest the child.

When the court receives the forms, it must send to CAFCASS within twenty-four hours (or forty-eight hours in courts where applications are first considered on paper) copies of the C100 and C1A and Form C6.

Under the terms of the **Child Arrangements Programme**, the courts are expected to list the **First Hearing Dispute Resolution Appointment** (FHDRA) within five weeks of receipt of the application, or six at the latest. If that is not possible, a timetable must be drawn up between CAFCASS and the Courts Service.

Child Arrangements Programme

CAP – the procedure the courts must follow in family cases.

The CAP acts as a "road-map" to show both courts and litigants how a case should progress through the system and to keep cases on track. The measures to enable contact introduced by the Children and Adoption Act 2006 were incorporated into the Private Law Programme, the aim of which was to resolve most cases by consent at the **First Hearing Dispute Resolution Appointment** (FHDRA). Following its claimed success, it was streamlined into the Revised Private Law Programme.

Child Arrangements Programme

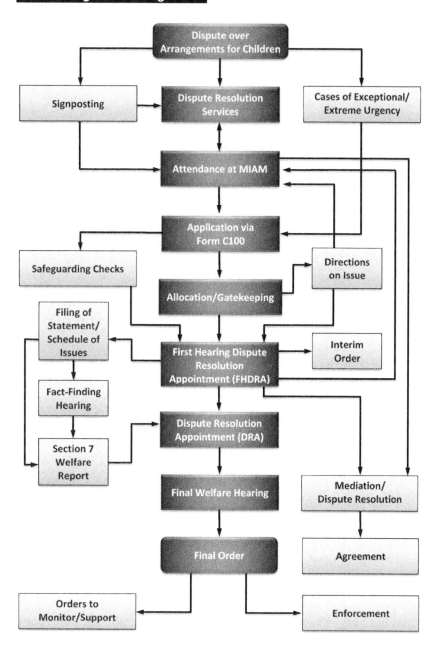

Flowchart 3: The Child Arrangements Programme

The CAP built further on these schemes and was designed to replace both the Pre-Application Protocol and the Private Law Outline. It is intended to keep couples out of court or to enable swift resolution where court proceedings are unavoidable. It recognises, as its predecessors did not, that most users of the family justice system will now represent themselves and it utilises simplified language and procedures.

Relevant family proceedings include private law proceedings involving children such as **Section 8 Orders**, or orders giving permission to **Change a Child's Name** or remove a child from the UK, and proceedings for financial remedies. They exclude consent orders, emergency proceedings, enforcement proceedings (where there will already have been court proceedings) and proceedings for financial compensation.

Child Assessment Order

An order made by the Court under Section 43(1) of the Children Act 1989, on application by the local authority, that a child be subjected to a medical, psychiatric or other assessment to assess whether he is suffering or likely to suffer **Significant Harm**.

The Court may make the order only if it is satisfied the LA has reasonable cause for its suspicion. A parent is then obliged to comply with the order and make the child available. The order lasts no longer than seven days and no further order may be made for six months.

Child Benefit

CB – an allowance paid to parents or guardians for the upkeep of their children from birth to the age of sixteen or the completion of full-time education or training. It is paid at a weekly rate of £20.70 for the first child and £13.70 for each subsequent child.

Receipt of CB is determined by the Social Security Contributions and Benefits Act 1992 which specifies that "between a husband and wife residing together the wife shall be entitled" and that "between two persons residing together who are parents of the child but not husband and wife, the mother shall be entitled"; note that this applies only when the parents reside together, though if they separate, the mother will take the CB with her.

The common belief that CB acts as a "gateway" benefit to Child Support is a myth: the assessment is unrelated; if, for example, a separated mother earns over £50,000 so that she does not qualify for CB, the father will still be liable for child support. When parents live apart, CB can be paid to either but cannot be split for a single child.

In 2002, one father, Kevin Barber, applied unsuccessfully to demonstrate that this perceived discrimination breached his human rights – R (on the application of Barber) v Secretary of State for Work and Pensions [2002] EWHC 1915 (Admin). The judge, Sir Richard Tucker, concluded,

> [43] The system must be kept simple and the costs of administering it must be kept low. So far these aims have been achieved.

> [44] I find that the present system works well and offers an efficient service at a relatively low cost... In my judgment there is no justification for a change in that system.

Child Contact Intervention

CCI – up to twelve hours of work with a local specialist resource, funded by **CAFCASS**, aimed at getting contact going again after it has broken down in a way that is safe and beneficial to the child. It might, for example, take the form of supervised contact followed by a feedback session.

Child Maintenance

Money paid periodically by liable parents to **Persons with Care** as a contribution towards the upkeep of their children.

If the **Child Maintenance Service** will not get involved or does not have jurisdiction – for example when a liable parent lives or works abroad, a parent or guardian of a child, or any person named in a **Child Arrangements Order** as a person with whom a child is to live can make a claim under Schedule 1 of the **Children Act 1989**.

These orders are to make or secure a periodical payment, to pay a lump sum, to make a settlement of property or to transfer property. Payment may be made either to the applicant for the child's benefit or to the child himself. The Court can also make an order for school fees, for the particular needs of a disabled child, for a "top-up" order if the maintenance that the CMS can order reaches a ceiling, or to vary an existing order. Claims for financial support can also be made under Section 22 of the **Matrimonial Causes Act 1973**. The orders have only a twelve-month shelf-life after which the CMS assumes jurisdiction.

The CMS has strict rules on how much money it can take from a liable parent; there are no such restrictions affecting the courts. An NRP is often better off, therefore, with an assessment from the CMS; a PWC will be advised that more money can be won through the courts.

An NRP can apply in the Magistrates' Court to overturn a maintenance order but an application cannot be made there again: once judged, the matter becomes *Res Judicata* unless a change of circumstances can be demonstrated.

The decision can be appealed to the High Court and, in the meantime, an NRP should pay the rate he would normally pay under the CMS. Appeals to reduce Maintenance Orders to the normal CMS rate are usually successful. If the Court considers he has made too many applications, it may make a **Section 91(14) Order** preventing more. While a variation application is pending, there should be a stay of execution of enforcement by bailiffs, etc.

Child Maintenance Service

CMS – the successor to the Child Support Agency (CSA), the government body responsible for the calculation and collection of statutory child maintenance. A related organisation, Child Maintenance Options, provides parents with support and advice. Both are run by the Child Maintenance Group within the Department for Work and Pensions.

Child of the Family

The biological child of a married couple or any **Child** treated by the couple as their child, including step-children and adopted children, but not a fostered child. The term is defined under the **Matrimonial Causes Act 1973**, Section 52.

Child Tax Credits

A means-tested benefit consisting of a family element worth up to £545 a year and a child element worth up to £2,780 a year. It is paid until a child reaches sixteen or completes full-time education. For new claims, only the child element is available for a maximum of two children.

In 2012, a disabled father of two challenged the rule that, unlike **Child Benefit**, Child Tax Credits cannot be shared between separated parents where there are two or more children (Humphreys v The Commissioners for Her Majesty's Revenue and Customs [2012] UKSC 18). The father had substantial contact, but was not the **Primary Carer**; he argued that, as a parent dependent on income support, incapacity benefit and disability living allowance, and responsible for the care of his children three days a week, he could not meet his children's needs when they were with him.

The question before the Court was not that the regulations were discriminatory, but whether discrimination was justified. In the **Supreme Court**, Brenda Hale ruled that the scheme had been introduced to tackle child poverty which was measured according to household income; government targets on poverty would be more easily met if financial support were given to single households and not split. Non-resident fathers' households were not included in the measurement of child poverty. Prior to the CSA, a court could have balanced the injustice by ordering the mother to make a payment to the father,

> Unfortunately, the advent of the child support scheme has removed the possibility of doing justice from the courts. To restore it would obviously be the more rational solution.

Child Welfare Hearing

(Scots) if there is a dispute in respect of children and the action is defended in the **Sheriff Court**, the first step in proceedings is a Child Welfare Hearing, convened under Rule 33.22A of the Ordinary Cause Rules. The Sheriff may also order such a hearing in other instances where it is considered appropriate.

If there is to be a Child Welfare Hearing, the Sheriff clerk must fix a date and time as soon as possible and not later than twenty-one days after the **Defender** lodges notice to defend or oppose an application for a **Section 11 Order** or makes their own application. The Sheriff can also order such a hearing at his own discretion or on the request of a party.

The Sheriff clerk must then inform the parties of the date for the Child Welfare Hearing using Form F41. Further applications to the Court can still be made after that date has been set.

A Child Welfare Hearing is an informal affair, intended to bring about the quick resolution of contact disputes, if at all possible. The hearing is usually held in private, with only the parties, their legal representatives and the Sheriff present; all parties are required to attend personally and are under a duty to provide the Sheriff with as much information as possible so that he or she can take whatever steps are necessary to deal with the matter. The child's welfare will be the Court's paramount consideration.

Child Witnesses

Traditionally, the courts would call a child to give evidence only in exceptional circumstances. In 2010, the **Supreme Court** overturned this presumption. A father of four children was accused by his step-daughter of sexually abusing her; all five children were taken into care with supervised contact with both parents.

The parents agreed to a fact-finding hearing in which the girl would give evidence by video link. The LA subsequently decided it no longer needed her evidence and the father's application that she be called was refused. His appeal was rejected (Re W (Children) [2010] EWCA Civ 57) and he appealed further to the Supreme Court (Re W (Children) (Abuse: Oral Evidence) [2010] UKSC 12).

The question remitted to her Honour Judge Marshall whether and how the daughter should give evidence. The existing presumption could not be reconciled with the balancing act between competing Convention rights: the Court had to weigh the potential harm to the child's welfare against the father's right to a fair hearing. The test was whether justice could be done without requiring the child to give evidence. As a precedent, Re W replaced the threshold test with a balancing one.

The Family Justice Council has issued two items of guidance: *Guidelines for Judges Meeting Children who are subject to Family Proceedings* (April 2010) highlights the Court's responsibility to enable children to comprehend the proceedings and be reassured the judge understands them; *Guidelines in relation to children giving evidence in family proceedings* (December 2011) emphasises the Court's primary objective to achieve a fair trial: it must weigh the advantages of a child giving evidence against the potential harm to the child in doing so; it must consider the **Needs, Wishes and Feelings** of the child, her understanding, the nature of the allegations, how to minimise harm to her while ensuring the quality of her evidence and corroborative evidence. Examination should be conducted in accordance with the **Achieving Best Evidence** guidelines to enable her to provide the best evidence of which she is capable. She should never be questioned directly by an alleged perpetrator. The Court should consider whether it is better to avoid cross-examination by compiling any questions and putting them to the child on a separate occasion before the substantive hearing.

A range of considerations should be made in advance, such as the use of video links, preparation of questions and the child's availability. Before the hearing, she should visit the court to be reassured of the arrangements made to prevent her having to meet an alleged abuser and shown where she will go and where she will sit. She should be able to meet lawyers, judges and magistrates and be encouraged to let the Court know if she wants a break.

In Re S, further contact between a married father and his two young sons was halted after his fifteen-year-old sister, K, made allegations of sexual abuse against him. After his arrest and again on the day he was due in court, she contacted police to withdraw the allegations. A guardian and solicitor were appointed, and a Section 37 Report ordered to determine issues including whether K would suffer **Harm** if called as a witness.

The guardian reported that K had lied and wanted the case dropped, but wished to give evidence in support of her brother; the social worker reported she had retracted her allegations only so she could see her nephews: K needed to express her views but giving evidence would be harmful; both the guardian and social worker suggested alternatives, such as a written statement. The father continued to deny the allegations, producing as evidence correspondence in which K said she wanted to help and offered to attend court, though in the event she did not.

Judge Judith Moir recognised the need for a fair trial and for cross-examination. She considered Re W and the FJC's Guidelines; she was concerned, however, that K would be emotionally damaged and queried the value of whatever evidence she might give; two friends, X and Y, to whom K had repeated the allegations, were also not called. Nevertheless, Moir accepted the allegations.

Unsurprisingly, the father appealed (Re S (Children) [2016] EWCA Civ 83). Lady Justice Black and Lord Justice Vos rejected his appeal, with the exception of Moir's unproven finding of anal abuse. Lady Justice Gloster, however, strongly disagreed:

> [69] ...the judge failed to give proper consideration to the fact that the burden of proof lay on the Local Authority. She had no basis for concluding on the balance of probabilities that K's serious allegations against the Appellant had been proved. In the absence of any opportunity afforded to the Appellant to challenge K's evidence that was not a conclusion which I consider she was entitled to reach. In my judgment, the Appellant did not have a fair trial in accordance with his rights under Article 6 of the ECHR and, as a result, his Article 8 rights and those of his infant sons, have been seriously infringed.

Children & Family Reporter

CFR – a **CAFCASS** officer who has been asked to prepare a **Welfare Report**.

Children Act 1989

The Act which pulled together, rationalised and codified the confusing jumble of private and public law. It abolished the rule of law that a father was the natural guardian of his legitimate child and replaced it with **Parental Responsibility**. It established the child's **Welfare** as the Court's paramount concern. It replaced orders for **Access** and **Custody** with ones for **Contact** and **Residence**. In public law, it imposed a duty on local authorities and courts to safeguard the welfare of children.

Children Act 2004

The legislation introduced following the Victoria Climbié inquiry which established the office of Children's Commissioner and coordinated all local entities under the statutory authority of the local Directors of Children's Services.

Children & Adoption Act 2006

The Act which introduced **Risk Assessments** and gave the Court further sanctions it could use to enable the **Enforcement** of breached orders.

Children & Families Act 2014

This Act finally made it mandatory for an applicant to attend a **Mediation Information and Assessment Meeting**, introduced the presumption of parental **Involvement**, replaced **Contact** and **Residence** orders with **Child Arrangements Orders** and imposed restrictions on the use of **Expert** evidence.

Children and Family Court Advisory & Support Service

CAFCASS – the controversial organisation tasked in the English and Welsh jurisdiction with protecting the interests of children during proceedings.

CAFCASS was established in 2001 under the Criminal Justice and Court Services Act 2000 with a duty under Section 12(1) of the Act to:

1. safeguard and promote the welfare of children;
2. advise the Court on any application in such proceedings;
3. make provision for the children to be represented in such proceedings; and
4. provide information, advice and other support to the children and their families.

CAFCASS staff provide various services to the courts, reflecting the diverse origins of CAFCASS, which was formed from 117 other organisations. One body replaced by CAFCASS was the Lord Chancellor's Department, and its function is now performed by CAFCASS Legal which acts as the child's solicitor in cases of legal or moral complexity which have not been resolved by the usual measures.

A CAFCASS officer's role is limited; in Re S (A Child) [2016] EWCA Civ 495 Keehan J clarified,

> *[28]* It is not the duty of a CAFCASS Officer, when preparing a report, to explore every aspect of a parent or a child's life or to investigate matters that are not in issue. The CAFCASS Officer will, aside from interviewing the parents and the child, usually make enquiries of the police, a child's nursery or school, health care professionals or social workers, if they have been involved with the family, but no more than that unless the court expressly requires other more extensive enquiries.

In F-D v The Children and Family Court Advisory Service [2014] EWHC 1619 (QB), a father sought damages from CAFCASS after he had been forced to withdraw his application for contact; CAFCASS had failed to attend court, to file reports on time and to deal with his complaint. The Court dismissed his case: CAFCASS had no particular duty towards a particular child; a duty of care to a particular father would hamper it in the exercise of its primary duty.

Children's Guardian

Formerly known as a Guardian *ad litem*; an officer from **CAFCASS** or CAFCASS Legal appointed by the Court whose duty is fairly and competently to conduct proceedings on behalf of the child independently of his parents.

The involvement of a Children's Guardian is enabled by Rule 16.4(1) of the **Family Procedure Rules 2010** which replaced Rule 9.5 of the Family Proceedings Rules 1991. Applications are made under Part 18 using an FP2 Application Notice. If a party wishes to change the Children's Guardian, he can do so under Rule 16.25, providing his reasons and evidence.

Only an officer from CAFCASS may act as a Guardian in "specified proceedings" or adoption and placement proceedings under Part 14. "Specified proceedings" are defined by section 41(6) CA1989 and include care and supervision orders and **Child Arrangements Orders** in respect of children who are already subject to care and supervision orders.

Where CAFCASS is unable to provide a guardian, or where they have failed or lost the confidence of the parties or the child, the involvement of a representative from **NYAS** can be requested and be appointed as a guardian under rule 16.4.

A Children's Guardian must have no interest in the proceedings adverse to that of the child and all steps and decisions they take must be in the child's **Best Interests**.

The Guardian must contact and seek to interview anyone they consider relevant to their investigation or whom they have been directed to contact by the Court. If necessary, they must contact appropriate **Experts**.

The Guardian must appoint a solicitor for the child unless one has already been appointed. They must advise the child, giving appropriate regard to his understanding, and **Instruct** the solicitor on all matters relevant to the interests of the child arising in the course of proceedings unless the child wishes to instruct a solicitor directly and the Guardian or the Court considers him to be of sufficient understanding to do so.

A Guardian or the solicitor must attend all directions hearings unless the Court directs otherwise. They must advise the Court orally or in writing on:

1. whether the child is of sufficient understanding, including the child's ability to refuse or submit to a medical or psychiatric examination or other assessment directed by the Court;
2. the child's wishes in respect of any matter relevant to the proceedings;
3. the appropriate forum for the proceedings;
4. the appropriate timing of the proceedings;
5. the options available to the Court in respect of the child and the suitability of each such option including what order should be made in determining the application; and
6. any other matter on which the Court seeks advice or on which the Guardian considers the Court should be informed.

Unless the Court directs otherwise, the Guardian must file a written report advising on the interests of the child in accordance with the timetable set; and notify the Court of any person who should be joined as a party to proceedings to safeguard the child's interests.

The Guardian must serve and accept service of documents on behalf of the child and, where the child has sufficient understanding, advise him of the contents of any document so served. If they are relevant to the determination of proceedings, the Guardian must make the Court aware of the documents.

The Guardian must relate the decision made by the Court to the child if she considers it appropriate and in a manner appropriate to that child's age and understanding.

Research by the University of Cardiff showed that representation is most beneficial in intractable cases but can impose too much responsibility and stress on the child if he thinks the judge's decision will be based substantially on his view. The report found that children can feel confused and manipulated by their parents, "repeating unfounded allegations or simply reciting the parent's view to the guardian".

It emphasised the need for haste and early assessment and the necessity that guardians are properly trained and trustworthy, with an aptitude to gain children's confidence. It stressed appropriate keeping of documentation and judicial continuity.

The researchers recommended there should always be separate representation before enforcement under the Children and Adoption Act 2006 (which enables sanctions for breached orders) and that the Guardian should ensure protection of the child from adverse repercussions from the resident parent following an Enforcement Order.

The primary precedent in applications for separate representation is Re A (Contact: Separate Representation) [2001] 1 FLR 715; the **President** considered that a Guardian can be effective at overcoming the initial hurdles in order to restore contact and facilitating **Handovers**, but this must be balanced against the additional delay introduced. A Guardian must not be allowed to take away from parents the responsibility of ensuring that contact takes place,

> There are cases when they do need to be separately represented and I suspect as a result of the European Convention for the Protection of Human Rights and Fundamental Freedoms 1950 becoming part of domestic law, and the increased view of the English courts, in any event, that the children should be seen and heard in child cases and not always sufficiently seen and heard by the use of a court welfare officer's report, there will be an increased use of guardians in private law cases. Indeed, in the right case I would welcome it. I hope with the introduction of CAFCASS in April of next year when the Court Welfare Service and the Guardian Ad Litem Service will be merged under one umbrella of a national organisation that it will be easier for children to be represented in suitable cases, but one ought not to assume that they will be separately represented in other cases that are less suitable.

However, to help CAFCASS clear its backlog, the President gave further guidance in 2009 that separate representation should be ordered only in cases which involved an issue of significant difficulty, and only after other alternatives had been explored. In cases requiring purely legal assistance rather than social work skills, the Court should consider appointing guardians from outside CAFCASS.

A party who wants a guardian removed must demonstrate clearly that she is guilty of substantial wrongdoing, or that one or both parties have lost confidence to the extent that proceedings cannot otherwise continue. The courts are reluctant to remove an FCA from a case and are unlikely to view a parent's request favourably. In Re N (A Child) [2009] EWHC 736, Sir Mark Potter rejected the father's attempt to have the guardian removed from the case, notwithstanding that she had been found in contempt,

> It is important to observe that, in many cases concerning children which come before the court, and in particular that category of cases described as "intractable", one of the parties will be critical and unaccepting of the views expressed, or actions taken, by the guardian on behalf of the child in whose interests she is bound to act. It is equally the position, that in such

cases, the criticisms of the guardian will give rise to an asserted loss of confidence on the part of that party which owes more to his or her subjective and inflexible views than to an objective and rational consideration of the interests of the child concerned. If that frequently encountered situation were sufficient to justify replacement of the guardian in every case where such loss of confidence is asserted, the progress of such cases would become yet further extended and the work of CAFASS impossible to organise.

Children's Solicitor

See **Joining a Child**.

Christmas Order

A consent order for **Child Maintenance** which automatically renews itself once a year just before the twelve-month expiration so that the Court and not the CMS retains jurisdiction.

Chronology

A list in chronological order of everything pertinent to a litigant's case.

It is the most important document he will need to prepare for family proceedings; it can act as an *aide memoire* and help clarify the course of events. It is vitally important to keep it up-to-date while events are fresh. It should include—

1. important dates, such as the date the parents met, when they married, when their children were born, incidents of infidelity or domestic abuse, dates of separation or divorce;
2. communications, including every letter exchanged by the parties, with a summary; letters to and from solicitors, **McKenzies**, etc.; meetings with legal advisors; telephone calls, with a summary of what was said; emails and text messages;
3. details of every period of **Contact**, including arranged contact which never happened, photographs and video should be provided where available; court hearings and subsequent orders; **Statements**, **Affidavits**, etc.

Everything should be cross-referenced and filed so that any document can be produced and any conversation recalled on demand. It should all be kept electronically, regularly backed up, so copies of documents can be produced easily. Hard-copies should be filed for use in court. It is vital to do this: at times of high emotion it is easy to forget things, and written records become essential. Increasingly, brief chronologies are being incorporated into **Position Statements**. Sometimes it is remarkable what emerges from a comprehensive **Chronology**: patterns can come to light which would not otherwise have been seen, and these can prove indispensable in fighting a case.

Circumcision

The ritual mutilation or wounding of a child's genitals for religious or cultural reasons.

All such wounding is illegal under the Offences Against the Person Act 1861 (see **Punishment of Children**) and female genital mutilation is specifically outlawed by the Female Genital Mutilation Act 2003 (though no successful prosecution has resulted), but male mutilation is tolerated by the courts in deference to Jewish and Islamic sensibilities, and is rationalised by claiming for it entirely specious health benefits; see for example Re B and G (Children) (No2) [2015] EWFC 3 (Family Court 2015).

Circuit Judge

Judges who are more senior than **District Judges** and can hear appeals from them. The "circuits" were replaced by "regions" in 2005. They can deal with leave-to-remove cases involving non-Hague countries; declarations under the Family Law Act 1986 as to marital status, parentage, legitimacy and adoptions effected overseas; orders preventing avoidance of child support; and parental orders under the Human Fertilisation and Embryology Act 2008 where the child's place of birth is in England or Wales.

Civil Partnership

An arrangement registered under the Civil Partnership Act 2004 which allowed same-sex couples to acquire rights and responsibilities similar to those of a married couple. In 2014, same-sex couples were enabled to marry, and it became possible to convert a civil partnership into a marriage. The marriage will be dated from the registration of the civil partnership.

In R (on the application of Steinfeld and Keidan) v Secretary of State for International Development [2018] UKSC 32, the Supreme Court declared it was discriminatory to deny Civil Partnerships to opposite sex couples. It remains to be seen whether the Government will extend the provision or abolish this now redundant arrangement entirely.

Clean Break

A one-off court order finally determining financial arrangements.

In its purest form, a clean break describes a divorce in which all financial aspects have been resolved, neither party has any claim against the other and both can carry on their lives, confident that no further claim is possible from either side. It was defined by Lord Scarman in Minton v Minton [1979] AC 593, [1979] 2 WLR 31, (1978) FLR Rep 461,

> The law now encourages spouses to avoid bitterness after family break-down and to settle their money and property problems. An object of the modern law is to encourage each to put the past behind them and to begin a new life which is not overshadowed by the relationship which has broken down. It would be inconsistent with this principle if the court could not make, as between the spouses, a genuinely final order unless it was prepared to dismiss the application.

A Clean Break **Consent Order** is a legally binding document which, in addition to setting out the division of matrimonial assets and liabilities, also contains a clause preventing either party making any future financial claim upon the other that could be made under the Matrimonial Causes Act 1973.

Where there are children, there will be a continuing liability to maintain them and there is thus a continuing financial link between the parties which ceases when the children become independent. Some people refer to that as a clean break between the parties. Where there is a liability on one former spouse to maintain the other, there can be no clean break. Where the maintenance is to be paid for a fixed term, that is often called a "deferred" clean break.

The alternative is a situation in which one party continues to pay the other indefinitely, often condemned as "a meal ticket for life". There is a shift away from this outcome, but in Mills v Mills [2018] UKSC 38, although the Supreme Court overturned the decision of the Court of Appeal that a woman who had mismanaged her divorce settlement should receive increased payments from her ex-husband, he was still left paying a "joint lives maintenance order" with no end in sight.

The "clean break" premise underpins Scots divorce law when it comes to financial agreements. Clean breaks are usually accounted for in capital although, when there is insufficient capital, deferred lump sum payments are a possibility. Seldom will a court decide the asset split and financial arrangements

– only about 3% of cases are decided in court; the majority are haggled out via solicitors or between the parties.

Closing Submissions

The concluding arguments usually made by the parties at a **Final Hearing** before judgment is given.

Each party carefully organises everything beforehand around his **Skeleton Argument**; he should prepare only an outline of what he wishes to say: reading a speech will sound stilted and awkward. The respondent speaks first, then the applicant. The parties then summarise the main points they have made, explain why the Court should make the order each wants, and outline their proposals for how parenting is to be shared.

After the closing submissions, the judge delivers the judgment, either extempore on the day after a brief break or "**Handed Down**" on a later day. If either party wishes to **Appeal** they do so after judgment is given.

Coercive Control

A term coined by feminist activist Evan Stark and a controversial element of the cross-government definition of **Domestic Violence**, incorporated in 2012. Stark defined it as—

> a pattern of domination that includes tactics to isolate, degrade, exploit and control [women] as well as to frighten them or hurt them physically.

It became a criminal offence under Section 76 of the Serious Crimes Act 2015 in an attempt to protect victims of psychological abuse not covered by other legislation.

An offence is proved if the offence is continuous or repeated, if it has a serious effect on the victim, if the perpetrator knew or ought to have known that it would have a serious effect, and if the perpetrator and victim are "personally connected"; that is, the parties must be in an intimate personal relationship or living together at the time of the alleged abuse, which rules out the use of this legislation in cases of obstructed contact.

Cohabitants' Property Rights

There is legislation to enable a court to regulate the financial affairs of married couples, but not of cohabitants. The starting and usually finishing point is that the person(s) named on the title deeds is the owner, but this comes without value. Owning an interest in the value of the house is termed beneficial or equitable interest. If the matrimonial home is owned jointly, it is relatively easy to divide up: the starting point is a 50/50 split unless there is a trust deed or declaration of trust which determines the proportion of the house each party owns and is usually binding.

If there is no written declaration and division is disputed, the Court will decide according to principles established by Baroness Hale in Stack v Dowden [2007] UKHL 17,

> *[69]* When a couple are joint owners of the home and jointly liable for the mortgage, the inferences to be drawn from who pays for what may be very different from the inferences to be drawn when only one is owner of the home. The arithmetical calculation of how much was paid by each is also likely to be less important. It will be easier to draw the inference that they intended that each should contribute as much to the household as they reasonably could and that they would share the eventual benefit or burden equally. The parties' individual characters and personalities may also be a factor in deciding where their true intentions lay. In the cohabitation context, mercenary considerations may be more to the fore than they would be in marriage, but it should not be assumed that they always take pride of place over natural love and affection... Having taken all this into account, those cases in which the joint legal owners are to be taken to have intended that their beneficial interests should be different from their legal interests will be very unusual.

In other words, if the parties have lived together in the property for the duration of their relationship, the inference is that ownership, both legal and beneficial, is 50/50; if, however, one of them is successful in convincing the Court the share of the property was to have been unequal, the Court must then determine what that share should be according to how much each party put into the original purchase, who pays the mortgage, who has paid for modifications or renovations and other household expenses, and all other relevant considerations. The significant phrase from Stack v Dowden – quoted from another case, Oxley v Hiscock [2004] EWCA Civ 546 – is "the whole course of dealing".

If the property is in only one party's name, then there is no automatic entitlement and the Court must determine whether it was the intention at the time of purchase that the other party should live in it. In some circumstances, it is possible to claim an interest if there was an intention to share and beneficial interest can be established: the other party may have a claim, but will need specialist advice to pursue it. It is better if they can agree to divide up any property but, if the separation is acrimonious, this may not be possible.

To contest a case, the party whose interest has been undocumented, owns part of the property or thinks she has a claim will have to go through the struggle of establishing that there was a joint intention for her to have an interest, using the Trusts of Land and Appointment of Trustees Act 1996 (ToLATA).

The Court will decide whether she has a claim, how much her share is and whether the property should be sold. Because such an application is not a family matter, if she fails, she may have to pay the other party's costs. This area of law is complex because it involves teasing out rights – beneficial interests – which have not been written down. There have been calls for new legislation such as already exists in Scotland, but there is also opposition to blurring this distinction between marriage and cohabitation. As expressed in the case of Lloyds Bank Plc v Rosset [1990] UKHL 14,

> The first and fundamental question which must always be resolved is whether... there has... been any agreement, arrangement or understanding... that the property is to be shared beneficially. The finding of an agreement or arrangement to share in this sense can only... be based on evidence of express discussions between the partners, however imperfectly remembered and however imprecise their terms may have been.

If the Court finds there *was* such an agreement, the claimant has only "to show that he or she has acted to his or her detriment or significantly altered his or her position in reliance on the agreement". This may be done by producing a written statement or recollection of conversations. Did they, for example, refer to the house as "our house"? The Court is invited to assemble a "constructive trust" arrangement to reflect the fact that each party intended the other party should own a share, and that he acted to his detriment in reliance. There is no need for a written agreement of deed, although it is much easier where there is such a document. A case can be based on recollections of discussions at the time.

If the party made a financial contribution to the property, this is known as "resulting trust", and her share will be proportionate to the amount contributed. The Court will then proceed to determine what the share should be by considering the discussions held between the parties, or, where these are absent, by considering "the whole course of dealing" between them. If the Court finds there is no evidence for such an agreement, the claimant invites the Court to accept a "resulting trust" on the basis of her financial contributions,

> *[132]* ...the court must rely entirely on the conduct of the parties both as the basis from which to infer a common intention to share the property beneficially and as the conduct relied on to give rise to a constructive trust.

> In this situation direct contributions to the purchase price by the partner who is not the legal owner, whether initially or by payment of mortgage instalments, will readily justify the inference necessary to the creation of a constructive trust... It is at least extremely doubtful whether anything less will do.

The situation was still not definitively settled by the long-awaited decision on Kernott v Jones [2011] UKSC 53 in November 2011. The Supreme Court's task was to determine whether the parties intended the property to be held in fair shares, or whether their beneficial interests altered upon separation.

In 1985, the parties had purchased a property in their joint names; Ms Jones paid the deposit and Mr Kernott built an extension. They never married but produced two children before separating in 1993. Mr Kernott moved out and Ms Jones remained with the children and took on sole responsibility for the mortgage and household expenses. In 1996, Mr Kernott bought a property for himself.

In 2006, Mr Kernott wanted to realise his 50% share of the property; as a first step, he severed the joint tenancy. The first instance court awarded him only 10% and the High Court agreed. He appealed and the **Court of Appeal** overturned the decision. The couple's agreement to continue the joint tenancy to this point was taken to "crystallise" his 50% interest. Ms Jones appealed to the **Supreme Court** which reinstated the original 10% decision.

Where there are children, it may be possible for a party who does not own the property but wishes to remain there and care for them to make a claim for financial provision under Schedule 1 of the Children Act 1989. This can be a capital sum or periodical payment or a temporary transfer of property. Any provision of capital reverts to the original owner on a triggering event such as the youngest's eighteenth birthday or completion of full-time education. This arrangement is effectively a **Mesher Order**. To qualify, the case must fall outside the Child Maintenance Service's jurisdiction, which means the liable parent must be earning at least £2,000 net per week (£3,000 gross for new claims) or be living abroad. The Court must consider the same factors it employs when dividing up the assets of a marriage.

If parties are renting property, one can end the tenancy without the other's agreement. To prevent this, an application should be made to the Court on Form D50B for a transfer of tenancy under Part IV of the Family Law Act 1996; once the tenancy has been surrendered, it is too late.

The case of Pamela Curran cannot but invoke some degree of sympathy. She and Brian Collins had been in a relationship for thirty years. Their home and valuable kennel business, which they had run jointly, were owned in the sole name of Mr Collins. When the relationship ended, Ms Curran owned nothing and applied to the Court for a share of the assets. In the County Court,

Hazel Marshall QC ruled she was not entitled to share in either the home or the business. She felt compelled to ignore her "human sympathies" and "apply the law". Ms Curran was allowed to appeal against the decision (Curran v Collins [2013] EWCA Civ 382), and Lord Justice Toulson recognised that "bluntly, the law remains unfair to people in the appellant's position". Had Ms Curran been married, she would have had claims by right to maintenance, pension sharing and capital (such as property transfers) under the Matrimonial Causes Act 1973. The case was re-listed (Curran v Collins [2015] EWCA Civ 404) but again failed: no evidence was proffered to counter the original decision.

Cohabitation; England & Wales

This once referred to a married couple who were living together but now usually refers to the arrangement in which an *un*married couple live together but do not enjoy the legal protections granted a married couple; it is also referred to as 'de facto' marriage. In many cases cohabitation will transition seamlessly into marriage.

It can be difficult to prove a couple are cohabiting; in England and Wales the criteria – not all of which need be satisfied – were established in the case of Kimber v Kimber [2000] 1 FLR 383 and employed in G v G (non-molestation order: jurisdiction) [2000] 2 FCR 638 and B v B [2012] EWHC 314:

1. the parties are living together in the same household and the living together involves a sharing of daily tasks and duties;
2. there are stability and permanence in the relationship;
3. the financial affairs of the couple are indicative of a mutually supportive relationship;
4. their sexual relationship is admitted and on-going;
5. they have children together or treat each other's children as their own; and
6. there is public recognition of the relationship and sufficient evidence that cohabitation exists in the opinion of a reasonable person with normal perceptions.

Couples who choose to cohabit have restricted rights compared with those who marry and do not enjoy the legal protections provided under matrimonial legislation. **Common-Law Marriages** simply do not exist and those couples who are in cohabitating relationships need to be aware they have no "rights" to each other's assets and properties should they end the relationship. Couples can draw up a legal agreement called a "cohabitation contract" or "living together agreement"; these are not legally enforceable, but they can remind a couple of their original intentions.

Cohabitants do not acquire rights, regardless of how long they live together; if they separate, each party retains the assets which are in each of their names, irrespective of whether that is the family home or the family business. They cannot claim maintenance or a share of their partner's income or pension; they will not inherit and, even if they have been paying the utility bills for years, can make no claim against a property.

Cohabitation; Scotland

In Scotland, a cohabiting relationship is defined by characteristics that are common for husbands and wives: i.e., shared mutual interests, shared social life, economic inter-dependence and being regarded as a member of the other's wider family. As the marital relationship is based upon sex, so living together as husband and wife requires the couples' relationship to be or to have been sexually intimate. The fact that a couple have a child together proves this last and important point.

Section 28(2) of the Family Law (Scotland) Act 2006 makes some financial provision and provides discretion to the Court both for the making of an award and for the amount to be awarded when cohabitation has ended otherwise than by the death of one of the parties,

> on the application of a cohabitant (the "applicant") the appropriate court may, after having regard to the matters in sub-section 3—
>
> a) make an order requiring the other cohabitant (the defender) to pay capital sum of an amount specified in the order to the applicant
> b) make an order requiring the defender to pay such an amount as may be specified in the order in respect of any economic burden of caring, after the end of the cohabitation, for a child of whom the cohabitants are the parents;
> c) make such an interim order as it sees fit.

The matters in Subsection 3 are:

> a) whether (and, if so to what extent) the defender has derived economic advantage from contributions made by the applicant; and
> b) whether (and, if so, to what extent) the applicant has suffered economic disadvantage in the interest of (i) the defender; or (ii) any relevant child.

These sections provide a basic set of rights and are also what the Court takes into consideration when a claim for financial disadvantage is made by a cohabitant whose relationship and co-habitation has ended:

1. the sharing of household goods bought during the time the couple lived together; this means that if the couple cannot agree about who owns any household good the law will assume they own it jointly and must share it or share its value;
2. an equal share in money derived from an allowance made by one or other of the couple for household expenses and/or any property bought out of that money; it is important to understand that this does not apply to the house in which the couple live;
3. financial provision when, due to the decisions the couple made together during the relationship, one partner has been financially disadvantaged; this means, for example, that if the couple decided one partner would give up a career to look after their children, they can ask the Court to look at the effect that decision has had on that partner's ability to earn money after the relationship has ended;
4. an assumption that both parents will continue to share the cost of childcare if they had children together.

Property in the name of one party only will remain in the sole ownership of that named party; property owned jointly by both parties (and where there is no Deed of Trust stating otherwise) is presumed in law to be equally shared and the Court will decide how it will be divided.

A claim for financial disadvantage under Section 28 of the Family Law Act (Scotland) 2006 must be made within twelve months of the relationship ending. Should the date cohabitation ended be disputed, the Court will require the matter to be proved. A **Pursuer's** entitlement to seek a capital sum from the **Defender** will depend on whether this is necessary to rebalance any contributions (i.e., mortgage payments) or disadvantages suffered for the benefit of the relationship or in order to share future child-care costs (if there are children from the relationship).

The Court will decide if any advantage has been offset by any disadvantage, and will specify the amount of the order, a date on which it should be paid, and whether it should be paid as a lump sum or as instalments.

A case brought before the Supreme Court (Gow v Grant [2012]) saw a successful application by Ms Gow for financial redress under the principle of "economic advantage, disadvantage or contribution". Usually, it is younger former cohabitants with young children who will seek to redress the financial burden of providing for those children, however Gow v Grant provided a precedent for those more mature cohabitants where one party is likely to have suffered a greater financial disadvantage by selling their home and losing at least a portion of their income.

Collaborative Law

A non-adversarial, non-competitive approach to resolving disputes cooperatively using specialist lawyers, introduced into the UK from America in 2003.

Both parties **Instruct** lawyers but, instead of fighting it out in court, meet to resolve matters face-to-face. Meetings are held in an informal and private setting in a dignified atmosphere of mutual respect and cooperation; the aim is to resolve problems through negotiation and establish a secure foundation for the future. Unlike a mediator who must try to remain neutral, a collaborative lawyer represents the interests of the paying party and can give legal advice.

All the facts, uncertainties, fears and differences are brought out into the open, discussed face to face and agreed before progressing further. Participants maintain respect for each other and self-esteem is preserved; they are in control at all times, and the process takes place at a speed which suits them both; they are not handing over their parental responsibilities to a judge. There are no exchanges of letters, no writing of position statements, no bundles, no affidavits.

Both parties, however, must want a dignified and cooperative resolution. If one abandons that approach, the whole process is wrecked: if one fails to act in good faith, or to disclose financial information, for example, under the Participation Agreement signed at the commencement of the process, their lawyer is disqualified and must withdraw. Under the same agreement either party can withdraw if they feel the other party or one of the lawyers is not acting in good faith.

Commissioner for Oaths

A person, usually a practising lawyer, with power to administer oaths or take **Affidavits** – this is a **Reserved Legal Activity**. A lawyer may not use this power in proceedings in which they are acting for any of the parties or in which they have an interest.

Committal

The act of sending a person to prison.

Committal is the last resort, used by a court only when no other option is appropriate. Committal may arise in both children's and financial proceedings.

Committal

The judicial approach to committal in parenting disputes was confirmed by Lord Justice Ormerod in Churchard v Churchard [1984] FLR 635,

> There is no doubt and it should be clearly understood... throughout the legal profession that an application to commit for breach of orders relating to access... are *[sic]* inevitably futile and should not be made. The damage which they cause is appalling.

In Thomason v Thomason [1985] FLR 214, Bush J agreed,

> The object of the exercise is to enforce the breached order for access in the sense of getting it working, or putting something more workable in its place. This is rarely achieved by sending a parent to prison or by fining them.

Imprisonment would infringe the human rights of a mother and her child and committal must be justified under Article 8(2) – the right to freedom from state interference: Re K (Children: Committal Proceedings) [2003] 2 FCR 336. Other remedies such as further orders, fines, family therapy and transfer of residence must all be tried first: Re M (Contact Order: Committal) [2004] EWCA Civ 1790.

In many cases judges have censured parties for flouting orders but have failed to do anything about it (for example F v M [2004] EWHC 727, A v A [2004] EWHC 142=20, C v C [2004] EWCA Civ 512); this is one judge's explanation,

> Once you've done that you've spent your powder as a court, really and in a way you've surrendered your jurisdiction to the mother. You've punished her but you haven't achieved anything; you've given her the power to control the case. I think it's a defeatist thing to do, quite honestly.

This judicial timidity has led to the perception that the courts are not prepared to enforce their own orders. No information is recorded to indicate the effect of committal on contact or on children, so the belief that it is ineffective or not in a child's best interests is not necessarily supported.

The reality for non-resident parents and their children is that the courts have never enforced contact with any enthusiasm and committal is rare; in the case of A v N (Committal: Refusal of Contact) [1997] 1 FLR 533, a mother had consistently flouted orders for contact; the judge imposed a six-week sentence suspended for six months, the mother again failed to comply, and the judge activated the sentence. Rejecting the mother's appeal Wall LJ said,

> The question which is before the court is whether there should be a committal for breach of orders of the court and in that inquiry the

upbringing of the child is not a paramount consideration. It is obviously a material consideration... *[The County Court judge]* was fully mindful of the distressing consequence of imprisonment on the child and indeed the other child of the mother, but he balanced against that the importance of this child knowing her father as she grows up and the long-term damage she will suffer.

Wall continued that the message should—

go out in loud and in clear terms that there does come a limit to the tolerance of the court to see its orders flouted by mothers even if they have to care for their young children. If she goes to prison it is her fault, not the fault of the learned judge who did no more than his duty to the child which is imposed upon him by Parliament.

In Re D [2004] EWHC 727, a father applied for contact; there were no fewer than forty-three hearings before sixteen judges producing 950 pages of evidence. The mother consistently obstructed contact, and the contact ordered, but never effectively enforced, dwindled away to nothing. The father had secured a penal notice added to his order, a year later a suspended sentence had been imposed, and after another year, the mother had at long last been committed. Judgment, by Munby J (as he then was), was given a full two years later. The mother had made numerous false allegations against the father and all proved groundless. Even when the father lost his temper, Munby excused him as a man "goaded beyond endurance". Finally, the father applied out of utter hopelessness to **Withdraw his Application**, Munby admitted, "We failed them. The system failed them",

[20] In this case it is mother who is overwhelmingly responsible for the predicament in which [D] and her father now find themselves. I simply refuse to accept that there is any equivalence – legal, moral, parental, or in any other respect – between a father who is "entrenched and rigid" in his desire to have the contact which everyone other than the mother thinks he should have with his daughter and a mother who is "entrenched and rigid" in her opposition to that contact.

[56] ...swift efficient enforcement of existing court orders is surely called for at the first sign of trouble. A flabby judicial response sends a very damaging message to the defaulting parent, who is encouraged to believe that court orders can be ignored with impunity, and potentially also to the child.

Note that a court will still make a committal order or suspended order even if the party to whom it applies refuses to attend court, see Re P (A Child)

[2006] EWCA Civ 1792, [2007] 1 FLR 1820. The preferable alternative to committal is an application for **Transfer of Residence** together with an application for a **Section 91(14) Order**.

In the long-running ancillary relief case following the divorce of Scot and Michelle Young, Mr Young claimed he had been left penniless, while Mrs Young claimed he had hidden his fortune and, in reality, owned assets in the region of £400m. Mrs Young made the first application for committal in 2009 on the basis that Mr Young had failed to respond to her **Questionnaire**, and when he eventually did, that the response was not sufficient.

A six-month committal order was made, suspended for ninety-two days to enable Mr Young to respond fully. He still failed to comply, claiming he had been detained under the Mental Health Act 1982, and was given further time. Eventually, he did produce some documents and an order for **Maintenance Pending Suit** was made, which included paying the children's school fees, as well as a monthly maintenance payment of £27,500. He did not appeal, but did not pay the maintenance and, by the time the new application for committal was made, had accrued approximately £1million of arrears.

When the matter returned to court (Young v Young [2013] EWHC 34), Mr Young was asked to explain how he had financially maintained his lifestyle over the last four years; he claimed he had been financed by generous friends but could produce no corroborative evidence. There was no proof he had even attempted to obtain evidence of the origin of the money and there was no doubt he had deliberately failed to comply with the order. He had also failed to provide evidence supporting his claim of significant financial losses.

Lord Justice Moor committed Mr Young for six months,

> [47] You are, at any stage, entitled to apply to me to purge your contempt. This will involve you finally complying with the orders for disclosure. If you do now comply, I would be very sympathetic to any application you make to purge your contempt. Whilst I recognise that this is more difficult to do so once you are in prison, you have brought this entirely upon yourself. You have had more than sufficient opportunity to comply with the various court orders. The court cannot go on giving further opportunities indefinitely.

The application for committal on notice is made on Form N78, which is obtained from the court. The applicant states the order which was breached with details of each individual **Breach**. The application should be made only if there has been a consistent refusal to comply with orders over a period of years and if all other remedies have been explored. Committal raises temperatures, leads to more litigation and ill feeling, and isn't necessarily effective.

It is important that the breach is such as can be proved, and such as, if proved, will justify committal. An application should not be made if the breach is trivial or a mere technicality; if the order has not yet been served on the respondent, the applicant will simply come across as petty and vindictive. If the breach is minor, it is unlikely the Court will commit, and more likely it will simply warn the respondent of the consequences of further breach. Should the applicant wish to withdraw his application, he must apply to the Court to do so.

The respondent must then attend court and argue why she should not be committed, using the same form N78; this appears to reverse the burden of proof. If the applicant or a witness is unable to attend, the hearing will be adjourned (though the Court may also dismiss the application), but if the respondent is unable to attend and the Court is satisfied she was informed of the hearing, it is likely it will still take place. The Court will take her absence as deliberate avoidance, and may issue a warrant for arrest. The respondent, therefore, is strongly urged to attend. If the Court decides to commit, it will defer sentencing until the respondent attends.

The purpose of a committal hearing is threefold:

1. to secure compliance with the orders of the Court (and in domestic abuse cases to protect the safety of the applicant);
2. to punish breaches of court orders;
3. to regulate the hearings of the Court and protect court users and staff.

The **Burden of Proof** is the criminal "beyond reasonable doubt" standard. It is important for both parties that serious allegations are proved to be either true or false; it is not desirable to have unproved allegations hanging around as they can prejudice a case.

If the matter cannot be dealt with at the initial hearing – perhaps medical reports are needed, the Court must issue directions regarding reports and the date of the next hearing. Orders must be drawn up on the appropriate Form N79 and the judge must sign it. He must state finding-of-fact for each breach proved, which witnesses are believed, and whether he found a party or a witness to have been lying.

Where the hearing has been convened following arrest for breach of an injunction, the Court can dismiss the application where,

1. no reasonable grounds are disclosed for alleging contempt; or
2. the application is an abuse of process; or
3. there has been a failure to comply with a rule, practice direction or court order.

Those accused of contempt cannot claim legal aid. Litigants who are represented in a family case should inform their solicitor that they have been charged or arrested.

The respondent – and any witnesses she calls – can still give oral evidence in court without first producing an affidavit; the applicant cannot. Thus, she is able legitimately to ambush the applicant.

Following concern about secret committal hearings, the Lord Chief Justice issued practice directions in the summer of 2013 and in March 2015 reminding judges that it is a fundamental principle of the administration of justice that committal hearings are heard in open court. Courts have a discretionary power to hear applications in private, but only in exceptional cases where it is necessary for the interests of justice. The Court must first hold a public hearing explaining why the full hearing will not be held in public. In such cases, the Court must still make public,

1. the name of the person;
2. in general terms the nature of the contempt in respect of which the committal order (including suspended orders) is being made; and
3. the punishment being imposed.

The direction cautions, "There are no exceptions to these requirements. There are never any circumstances in which anyone may be committed to custody or made subject to a suspended committal order without these matters being publicly stated". All judgments must be published on BAILII.

A party defending an application for committal should read the orders again carefully and check exactly what it is they oblige her to do or forbid her from doing and compare this with what she has actually done. Next, she should read the power of arrest carefully; does it make clear which paragraph of the injunction it applies to (see FPR 2010 10.9)?

If **Contempt of Court** is proved, the County or Magistrates' Court can impose a fine or commit the contemnor to prison for a period of up to one month; the High Court can commit for up to two years. For a first or minor breach of the order, it is likely committal will be suspended for a set term or indefinitely. Because it is not a criminal conviction there is no early release on licence and the party won't get a criminal record. Prisoners serving a sentence for contempt have privileges not granted other prisoners regarding clothing, letters and visits. No order can be made on a person under eighteen; persons between eighteen and twenty-one must be sent to a young offenders' institution.

Under the Civil Proceedings Rules 52.3(1)(a), permission of the Court is not required to appeal an order for committal. This applies to first appeals from a district judge to the circuit judge and first appeals from a circuit judge to the Court of Appeal. A second appeal still requires permission from the Court.

Common Law

Prior to the Norman Conquest, law-making was localised; thereafter a "common" law was developed, of uniform application throughout England and Wales. This process has been continued by judges through **Precedent** or **Case Law** which binds future decisions through the doctrine of *Stare Decisis*. Parties use existing precedents in an attempt to sway the Court to decide in their favour; if the Court decides that no precedent accurately suits the case it can create further precedent.

Common-Law Marriage

A marriage believed to be valid by the parties but not formally registered.

As usually understood, common-law marriage is a myth which continues to contribute to the rise in **Cohabitation** and illegitimacy: couples who reside together in an intimate relationship are either married or cohabiting, and cohabitation does not confer the same legal rights as marriage.

Confusingly, some legislation, such as the Inheritance (Provision for Family and Dependants) Act 1975 and the Jobseekers Act 1995, recognises unmarried couples. Sit-coms such as *Rings on their Fingers* in 1978 also helped propagate the misconception.

There are some very rare and specific exceptions where the common law will recognise a marriage that has not been conducted strictly according to the **Lex Loci Celebrationis**, for example where prisoners of war have been unable to marry formally.

Scotland has had four forms of "irregular marriage"; three were abolished under the Marriage (Scotland) Act 1939, and the final form, "irregular marriage by cohabitation with habit and repute" was outlawed by the Family Law (Scotland) Act 2006, by which time this was the last remaining common-law form of marriage in Europe.

Compensation

Where an order has been breached, such as a **Child Arrangements Order**, and a party has suffered financial loss, for example, through a wasted journey or cancellation of a holiday or flight, Section 110 of the Children Act 1989 enables him to apply for compensation from the defaulting party. The application is made on Form C79.

The Court may not make the order if the respondent has a reasonable excuse for the **Breach**. The **Burden of Proof** is on the applicant, and the standard is the balance of probabilities. The level of compensation is down to the Court's discretion but cannot exceed the applicant's financial loss. The Court must ascertain from CAFCASS the impact of compensation on the child's **Welfare**. The courts are reluctant to make these orders and make about four or five a year.

It is probable the applicant will make the claim at the same time as he makes an application for enforcement; the success of the claim will be contingent on the success of the enforcement application.

Competence

The mental **Capacity** required by a party to understand his case and instruct a lawyer (note that the word means different things in other areas of law).

If a child is of sufficient age and maturity to understand the nature and implications of a case and to make decisions accordingly, he has the right to take part in the proceedings and to give evidence under Article 12 of the United Nations Convention on the Rights of Children; this is sometimes referred to as **Gillick-Competence** in UK law. A competent child is a compellable witness and the Court may order a witness **Summons**, though a person under eighteen cannot be detained for contempt. See Re W (Children) (Abuse: Oral Evidence) [2010] UKSC 12 and Re S (A Child) [2016] EWCA Civ 83.

Conciliation

A form of **Alternative Dispute Resolution** which takes place in-court under the direction of the judge or CAFCASS.

An MoJ report into *The longer-term outcomes of in-court conciliation* in November 2007 showed disappointing results. The conciliation covered by the report was a brief, usually one-off session of guided negotiation within the court premises designed to prevent further litigation. The brevity and limited availability of this type of conciliation impose considerable pressure on parents to reach an initial deal, and an earlier report, *Making contact happen or making contact work?*, had shown high levels of short-term agreement.

Many parents reported that the period since conciliation had been "turbulent", 60% of agreements made had broken down, "a majority of parents had required further professional intervention and 40% had been involved in further litigation".

Most parents commence the court process to re-establish frustrated contact, and the report found conciliation had delivered a level of contact broadly comparable with the non-court population. Unsurprisingly, it found contact was more likely in cases which had been easy to start with, and was not taking place in more intractable cases, showing the limited ability of the courts to change family dynamics.

Levels of contact rose immediately after conciliation but then reverted to pre-court levels by the time of the follow-up. Most parents distrusted the other's parenting ability and reported children reluctant to transfer from one parent to the other. The median level of contact was still only half that recommended as a minimum and declined over time. Parents were in a state of "weary resignation" and didn't see further litigation as the solution. The main reason was "the sheer horror or the emotional and physical impact of being involved in court proceedings".

Coupled to this was the sense that litigation had been ineffective, and more of the same would be futile, "The underlying problem identified by parents was that court orders were not adhered to, either fully or in part... Little faith was placed in the court's ability to change the situation". Some parents found the court process so stressful they had been forced to seek alternative means to achieve solutions, and there was thus a "paradoxical assistance" from the courts.

The report reveals that conciliation can deliver a form of short-lived conflicted contact but does not offer the type of therapeutic intervention necessary to enable parents to parent cooperatively, "in contrast, mediation with a clearly therapeutic orientation and emotionally-informed content can have a profound and enduring impact on relationships".

Conclusions

(Scots) the first part of an application, specifying the order for which the **Pursuer** is applying, i.e., for **Residence** or **Contact**, dates and times, etc.

Condescendences

(Scots) the second part of an application, equivalent to the **Position Statement** made to an English/Welsh court, which supports the application and details the evidence.

Condition

A **Child Arrangements Order** can come with conditions, enabled by Section 11(7) of the **Children Act**. These apply to the final order made, in contrast to **Activity Directions** which are made while the case is ongoing.

Conditional Order

Conditional Order

A term introduced in 2007/08 to replace **Decree *Nisi***; it is still used in relation to **Civil Partnerships**.

Condonation

(Scots) the act of forgiving **Adultery**; under Section 1(3) of the Divorce (Scotland) Act 1976 where the **Pursuer** has knowledge or belief of the adultery and has continued to cohabit with the **Defender** for a period of more than three months, condonation may be used as justification to defend a divorce.

Conduct of Litigation

There is no clear definition of conducting litigation, and it may be taken to include any formal steps taken in proceeding, including acting as the litigant's agent, managing the litigant's case outside court, issuing proceedings before the Court and commencing, prosecuting or defending those proceedings, and the performance of any ancillary functions in relation to such proceedings, such as signing court documents, but not the provision of legal advice.

Conducting litigation is a **Reserved Legal Activity** and doing so without **Leave** of the Court is a criminal offence. **McKenzie Friends** must tread warily and if there is any doubt that what is intended is legal, the litigant must apply for leave. The right to conduct litigation is distinct from the **Right of Audience** and separate applications must be made, though the arguments and procedure will be the same; an application must be made as early as possible in proceedings, before the McKenzie has done anything which may amount to the conduct of litigation. It is for litigants to persuade the Court, on a case-by-case basis, that the grant of such a right is justified.

Conformed Copy

An official copy of a court document which carries the Court's **Seal** and any handwritten notes which may be on the original; it may or may not be guaranteed to be a true and exact copy of the original.

Connell Order

A form of maintenance order in which the Court orders a husband (usually) to pay a global amount for the maintenance of his wife and children, *less* whatever the **Child Maintenance Service** calculates he should pay. This ensures he is not made worse off if his wife goes to the CMS, and she is no better off because, if the CMS takes more, the husband pays less so the total remains constant. Whereas a **Segal Order** is short term, a Connell Order can last much longer, and even until the death of one of the parties.

Consanguinity

Relationship through blood (parents, grandparents, siblings, aunts, uncles, nephews, nieces). See **Affinity** and **Void Marriage**.

Consent Order

Any order made with consent between the parties; the term usually applies to the financial order made on divorce.

An agreement between the parties is not legally binding and does not remove the Court's power to make an order but, if both parties agree terms, the settlement arrangements can be written into an order which the Court will approve and seal and which will take effect with the **Decree Absolute**; the order then becomes legally binding. There must be full **Disclosure** and the Court will not make the order if there are circumstances into which it should inquire; see Sharland v Sharland [2015] UKSC 60 and Gohil v Gohil [2015] UKSC 61.

The petitioner drafts the order, agrees it with his or her spouse, then sends it to the Court together with a Statement of Information for a Consent Order on Form D81 and an Application for Financial Remedies on Form A (since the Court cannot finalise settlement until the application is made). Copies are enclosed for the respondent. It is not usually necessary to attend court unless the judge is unhappy with the terms.

Parties are advised to read the documents they receive from their spouses carefully and see if there is anything that can be agreed without court intervention. The more that can be agreed the better. This will be less costly, less stressful, less acrimonious and less protracted. The order should always be drawn up or at least checked by a solicitor or the Court may be unwilling to give it its **Seal**. The Court can then approve the financial arrangements which will prevent either party changing their mind later.

If terms cannot be agreed, it starts to get expensive. One party will still need to make an application on Form A for a financial order. The Court will set a timetable for the hearing, known as the **First Directions Appointment**, for filing and serving Form E and other documents.

Consent orders will often be drafted by the lawyer representing one side, or the judge will do it himself; it is not unknown for judges to make "consent" orders even where one party objects to the contents.

Consummation

The culmination of the marriage procedure through sexual intercourse.

A couple are not fully and legally married until the marriage has been consummated. A marriage which has not been consummated is **Voidable** and may be **Annulled**.

Sexual intercourse must be "ordinary and complete and not partial and imperfect" (D-E v A-G [1845] 163 ER 1039). This means that a sustainable erection must be achieved, there must be vaginal penetration to a significant depth and for a reasonable period of time, but there need be no "emission of seed", see W v W [1967] 1 WLR 1554; there needs to be only one incident. "Ordinary" was interpreted in Corbett v Corbett [1971] 2 All ER 33 to mean that a transgendered man's artificially constructed cavity could not be regarded as a vagina or ordinary and normal.

Non-consummation must be the result either of incapacity or refusal; see Potter v Potter (1975) 5 Fam Law 161, CA, Ford v Ford [1987] Fam Law 232 and A v J (Nullity) [1989] 1 FLR 110. For a party to be incapable, consummation must be a practical impossibility and the condition must be incurable, or only remedied by an operation involving an element of risk or danger (see S v S [1956]). Refusal is defined in Horton v Horton [1947] as a "settled and definite decision come to without excuse"; the expression "invincible repugnance" is sometimes employed.

As yet, there is no case law relating to consummation in same-sex marriages.

Contact

What Bob Geldof called "Life in an hour. Love in a measured fragment of State-permitted time".

"Contact" replaced "access" as part of the **1989 Children Act**; the intention was that these orders should be viewed from the child's perspective and not the parent's. In 2014 **Child Arrangements Orders** replaced Contact Orders, though the concept of contact was retained in the legislation.

Mr Justice Cobb opened Re A & B (Children) [2013] EWHC 2305 by quoting from Paragraph 41 of Baroness Hale's judgment in Re G (Children) [2006] UKHL 43, "Making contact happen and, even more importantly, making contact work is one of the most difficult and contentious challenges in the whole of family law".

Contact is generally held to be beneficial to the child; Lady Justice Macur set out the Court's general approach in Re M (a child) [2015] EWCA Civ 1296,

[22] ...The starting point should be that the welfare of the child requires ongoing and meaningful contact with both parents. This principle should only be displaced for compelling reasons on the clearest of evidence and only then when all reasonable avenues of promoting safe contact, both physically and emotionally for the child, have been considered and rejected.

McFarlane LJ expressed a similar view in Re A (A Child) [2015] EWCA Civ 910,

[43] ...It is and should be a given that it will normally be in the best interests of a child to grow up having a full, real and entirely ordinary relationship with each of his or her parents, notwithstanding the fact that they have separated and that there may be difficulties between the two of them as adults.

And Mr Justice Hedley affirmed in Re E (A Child) [2011] EWHC 3521,

Every piece of research that has ever been undertaken makes it clear that children with separated parents do best when they have a relationship with both their parents, and therefore, because there is a unanimous voice, the court approaches with the gravest caution any attempt to terminate or to abandon that relationship.

In Re C (Direct Contact: Suspension) [2011] EWCA Civ 521, Munby LJ considered the precedents and from them drew these important principles (Paragraph 47), repeating them in Q v Q [2015] EWCA Civ 991. They now represent the approved approach:

1. Contact between parent and child is a fundamental element of family life and is almost always in the interests of the child.
2. Contact is to be terminated only in exceptional circumstances, where there are cogent reasons for doing so, when there is no alternative, and only if contact will be detrimental to the child's welfare.
3. There is a positive obligation on the State, and therefore on the judge, to take measures to reconstitute and maintain the relationship between parent and child. The judge must grapple with all the available alternatives before abandoning hope of achieving some contact. He must be careful not to come to a premature decision, for contact is to be stopped only as a last resort once it has become clear the child will not benefit from continuing the attempt.

4. The Court should take a medium- and long-term view and not accord excessive weight to what are likely to be short-term or transient problems.
5. The key question, which requires "stricter scrutiny", is whether the judge has taken all necessary steps to facilitate contact as can reasonably be demanded in the circumstances of the particular case.
6. The **Welfare** of the child is paramount: "the child's interest must have precedence over any other consideration".

In Re H-B (Contact) [2015] EWCA Civ 389, a case which had run for six years, Munby reiterated the obligation a parent has to ensure contact takes place,

> [75] ...There are many things which they ought to do that children may not want to do or even refuse to do: going to the dentist, going to visit some "boring" elderly relative, going to school, doing homework or sitting an examination, the list is endless. The parent's job, exercising all their parental skills, techniques and stratagems – which may include use of both the carrot and the stick and, in the case of the older child, reason and argument – is to get the child to do what it does not want to do. That the child's refusal cannot as such be a justification for parental failure is clear: after all, children whose education or health is prejudiced by parental shortcomings may be taken away from their parents and put into public care.

> [76] ... what one can reasonably demand – not merely as a matter of law but also and much more fundamentally as a matter of natural parental obligation – is that the parent, by argument, persuasion, cajolement, blandishments, inducements, sanctions (for example, "grounding" or the confiscation of mobile phones, computers or other electronic equipment) or threats falling short of brute force, or by a combination of them, does their level best to ensure compliance. That is what one would expect of a parent whose rebellious teenage child is foolishly refusing to do GCSEs or A-Levels or "dropping out" into a life of drug-fuelled crime. Why should we expect any less of a parent whose rebellious teenage child is refusing to see her father?

Contact Centre

A facility in which contact may be ordered to take place when it is not possible in a parent's home or in another familiar and relaxing environment.

Contact in a contact centre may take two forms:

Supported; where contact is conducted under supervision by the centre staff with the parent and child in the same room as other families.

Supervised; where contact is conducted under supervision by the centre staff and where the parent and child are isolated from other families.

The purpose of contact centres is rather to allow social workers and CAFCASS officers to observe parents' interactions with their children than to enable meaningful contact. They are commercial enterprises and expensive to use, particularly when contact is supervised. Sessions are commonly limited to thirty minutes or an hour and can cost from £15 to £200, while there may be additional charges for "setting up" contact. A child will not be allowed to see his parent until payment has been received so the fees should be checked before making any arrangement.

In Re C (Abduction: Residence and Contact) [2005] EWHC 2205, Mostyn J ruled that under the Human Rights Act there must always be a presumption of unsupervised contact unless there are good reasons for supervision,

> *[28]* On the facts of this case it is clear to me that supervised contact would only have been appropriate if there was the most compelling evidence that in some way S's best interests would be jeopardised by unsupervised, normal contact. Given the terms of the Strasbourg jurisprudence *[the European Convention for the Protection of Human Rights]* to which I have referred, it is almost as if there is a presumption in favour of normal contact and it is for those who say it is inappropriate to prove by clear evidence why this is so.

Baker J defended their use in Re D (Children) [2016] EWCA Civ 89:

> *[39]* In most cases supervised contact is used as a short-term measure – a stepping stone on the way to unsupervised contact. There are, however, a minority of cases where the risks to the children are such that contact must remain supervised indefinitely. In such cases, an order for indefinite supervision of contact is not wrong in principle.

The only possible uses of contact centres are when contact cannot take place safely under any other circumstance (see Re S (Child Arrangements Order: Effect of Long-Term Supervised Contact on Welfare) [2015] EWCA Civ 689); when the relationship has already broken down entirely, perhaps because the parent has been in prison for a long time; or when a parent has finally tracked down an abducted child and the child has little knowledge or memory of him or her.

In Lord Justice Wall's report *Making Contact Work*, it was acknowledged that contact centres had "been seized upon by courts, lawyers and family court welfare services to accommodate their difficult contact cases". In turn, the Labour Government seized upon the report to justify an expansion of contact centres.

Contact centres are overused in more cases and for longer than is necessary, creating a shortage of places; many open only every other weekend for two hours on a Saturday or Sunday; many also share a venue with other associated services such as SureStart. This situation is not sustainable given local authorities' cuts in children's services. It can be necessary to wait four or five months for one to become available, on top of the nine months a parent may have had to wait before getting even to this stage.

Use of a contact centre must be for a specific purpose and for a defined period of time. *Both restrictions must be set out clearly in the order.* A contact centre should be used only as part of a long-term strategy; once it has served its purpose the parent will follow up with applications for **Overnight Staying Contact** and finally that parenting be shared. Any use of a contact centre to reduce contact should strenuously be opposed.

Contact Order

A court order, now obsolete in the English and Welsh jurisdiction, requiring a resident parent to allow the child to have **Contact** with the person named in the order.

The Children and Families Act 2014 replaced contact orders with **Child Arrangements Orders**.

There was controversy over whether a Contact Order could be made only once a **Residence Order** had been made identifying the resident parent. In Re S (A Child) [2010] EWCA Civ 705, the trial judge had ruled that a Shared Residence Order was not appropriate for two parents who lived more than 100 miles apart; he made an order, contrary to legislation, providing the periods during which the father would have "care of the child". The intention was probably to avoid the contentious word "contact", but it exceeded the Court's jurisdiction: in making an order the Court must remain within the statutory vocabulary.

On appeal Thorpe LJ quoted Ward LJ in Re B (A Child) [2001] EWCA Civ 1968 that it was necessary first to determine with whom a child lived before a Contact Order was made because the order required that parent to allow the child to visit or stay with the other parent (Paragraph 9). Thorpe interpreted this to mean that a Residence Order must first be made to which the contact was then attached. This was contrary to the **No-Order Principle** and was rejected by other authorities; Ward himself had already clarified the point in Re G (A

Child) [2008] EWCA 1468, arguably rendering Thorpe's ruling *"Per Incuriam"*. In Re H (A Child) [2011] EWCA Civ 585, Thorpe had the last word,

> *[13]* Of course what the statute requires is not in every case that there should be a residence order to which a contact order exists, but that there should be a person defined or capable of definition with whom the child lives. So if the parents agree that, say, the mother should be the primary carer, but do not trouble to get a Residence Order enshrining her role, still a Contact Order can be made against her as the person with whom the child lives.

The **Child Arrangements Order** eliminates this problem by enabling a child's living and contact arrangements to be defined within the one order. It should be obvious to a judge asked to make an order regulating when a child is to spend time or otherwise have contact with someone that he must also determine with whom the child is to live.

In the case of JDE v SDW 2014 in the Scots jurisdiction, the social worker had given the mother incorrect legal advice that she could prevent contact based on her "feelings". Sheriff George Jamieson emphasised that the Court had made a decision to order contact and it was not for the mother to interfere with that. He clarified her obligation to "persuade and encourage" using precedent set by Blance v Blance 1978 SLT 74, Brannigan v Brannigan 1979 SLT (Notes) 73 and Cosh v Cosh 1979 SLT (Notes) 72,

> The defender's duty in accordance with... case law was to "tell the child, if necessarily firmly, to go"; to "create a climate of opinion in which they view their father in a reasonable and well-disposed light"; not to leave it to the child to make the decision "without positive guidance and genuine encouragement" from the resident parent.

Contact Parent
The parent identified in a **Child Arrangements Order** as the parent with whom the child is to "spend time or otherwise have contact".

Contact with a Child in Care
While he is in care, the local authority must allow a parent regular contact with the child (Section 34 CA1989). In X Council v B & Ors [2004] EWHC 2015, Munby J said,

> [88] ... If the State in the guise of a local authority is to interfere as drastically with family life as it does when it separates a child from its parents before it has even established the grounds for seeking a final care order then it must provide and facilitate appropriate contact.

If necessary, the parent or child can apply to the Court for contact; the Court should not make a **Care Order** until it is satisfied with the arrangements for contact. The parent can apply to visit a child in care using Form C15 and giving his reasons. The Court can also make an order preventing him from having contact, either on application from the local authority or because the Court considers it necessary.

Children in care have the right to visit their parents in the afternoons, to make telephone calls and to email. Note, however, that to "induce, assist or incite" a child to run away, or prevent a child from returning to the care home, is an offence under Section 49 CA1989.

Social services are obliged first to arrange the return of the child by agreement; should they not believe the child is in immediate danger, they must notify the parent in writing of the actions they can take if he refuses to comply. If, however, they believe the visit puts the child at risk they can apply without notice to the Court for an Emergency Recovery Order under Section 50(8) and the police will take the child back. They have no power, however, to prevent the child visiting the next day, and after a few recoveries may give up.

Social services must demonstrate to the Court that the child has been taken away or is being kept away, has run away or is staying away.

The Recovery Order obliges the parent to hand over the child and empowers social services to remove him from his home. It authorises the police to enter the home and search it, using "reasonable force if necessary". The home must be identified in the order and there must be reasonable grounds to believe the child is there. A **Recovery Order** made in England or Wales has effect in Scotland.

Very often children are placed in care homes a great distance from their family homes in order to prevent them returning and to make visitation difficult or impossible.

Contact; Direct

Contact in which the child and parent are together in one place; it may either be "visiting" or "staying". Visiting contact is when the child comes to visit the parent at his address but does not stay **Overnight**. Staying contact is when the child does stay overnight.

The presumption in favour of direct contact is very strong, particularly since the introduction of the **Human Rights Act 1998**; in Re M (Children) [2013] EWCA Civ 1147 Lady Justice Macur reminded the Court,

> *[24]* There is no question but that an order that there should be no contact between a child and his non-residential parent is draconian. In this case, the order... can only be lawful within the meaning of Art 8(2) of the Convention if the order for no direct contact is necessary in a democratic society for the protection of the right of the mother, and consequently the minor children in her care, to grow up free from harm. In order to reach that conclusion the court must consider and discard all reasonable and available avenues which may otherwise promote the boys' rights to respect for family life, including, if in the interests of promoting their welfare during minority, contact with their father.

Contact; Indirect

Contact in which the parent and child are not able to see one another, and which is limited to letters, cards and emails only. Contact itself isn't defined in either the 1989 or the 2014 legislation, and the word "otherwise" allows for a broad interpretation. Telephone and **Skype** calls are often considered direct contact. No reasonable person pretends that indirect contact is anything but a sham; in V v V [2004] EWHC 1215 Mrs Justice Bracewell equated indirect contact with the judge "giving up"; it is a cowardly judicial response, not so much to the non-resident parent's inadequate parenting as to the resident parent's obstruction.

Indirect contact routinely means, for example, that a parent can send his child no more than a letter a month – which the resident parent need not acknowledge; or even that a parent receives just a photograph of his child every six months.

It is an article of faith amongst professionals that once a parent has been separated from his child for a period of time, there must then be a period of only indirect contact, followed by gradual reintroduction, preferably in a contact centre. This is why it is so important for obstructive parents to establish a *status quo* during which there has been no contact. This period does not have to be very long; just a few months will suffice.

There is no evidence to suggest this practice is necessary, or that it results in normal relationships being resumed and protected; it is based on unsupported opinion given in the Sturge and Glaser report (see **Parental Alienation**). No statistics are recorded on how often indirect contact is translated into direct: the courts do not use their power under Section 11H of the Children Act 1989 to impose monitoring orders. It is instead a means by which to kick an application into touch. Anyone who has ever been away from their child for a long period of time – in hospital, on military service, even in prison – will know that there is no need to be gradually reintroduced.

It is vital that indirect contact is converted to direct contact as soon as possible – even if supervised; otherwise it will remain indirect indefinitely. Indirect contact provides an ideal breeding ground for further contact problems. In Re P (Children) [2008] EWCA Civ 1431, Ward LJ emphasised that a "court should not terminate direct contact until every avenue has been explored, including counselling or therapy for the parents"; in Re W (Children) [2012] EWCA Civ 999, McFarlane demonstrated that, if direct contact is to be restored, three essential factors must be satisfied,

1. contact has been successful in the past;
2. the parent is committed to contact;
3. the parent has addressed the factors which led to the order for indirect contact.

Contact; Overnight Staying

It is important for a child to be able to stay overnight with both parents as this represents the beginning of a move towards a more complete "family life" for him.

His parents can bathe him, put him to bed, read him a story, deal with his night-time needs, get him up in the morning, make him breakfast, take him to school, etc. It is vital to effective **Shared Parenting** that children are able to stay overnight from as early an age as possible; once a child is of school age either parent should be able to collect him from school on a Friday afternoon and take him back on a Monday morning. This should be possible every other week, and certainly not less than once a month. If this doesn't happen, a *Status Quo* without overnight contact is established which becomes difficult to break.

This pattern has obvious financial implications, necessitating additional bedrooms, beds, bedding, clothing, toys, books and meals, for example. It is important that these items are seen as the child's and travel with him; insistence on "Mum's clothes", "Dad's clothes" or "Mum's home" and "Dad's home" tells the child that he has no clothes and no home to call his own.

Staying away from their mother at night may be more difficult for younger children than for older ones, especially if there has been a break in contact. Parents should try to do what their children are comfortable with: forming an attachment with one parent must not disrupt the attachment already formed with the other; remember, however, that a little homesickness now can avert a tragedy later.

Despite clear benefits to the child, allowing young children to stay overnight with their fathers has become controversial and the debate has been crudely polarised; the argument against is represented by self-proclaimed parenting "guru" Penelope Leach in her book *Family Breakdown: Helping children to hang on to both their parents,*

> *(p.7)* overnight separations from the mother are not only usually distressing, but also potentially damaging to the brain development and secure attachment of children under about four.

This sentiment, repeated throughout, derives from a study headed by Australian academic Jenny McIntosh. At its heart is the common belief (the **Primary Carer** fallacy) that infants can form only a single bond with a parent. Researchers Joan Kelly and Michael Lamb have demonstrated the lack of evidence for this view, and that it risks curtailing a relationship essential to the emotional and social development of the child. The importance of maintaining vital relationships with both parents gets lost in the emphasis on the "stability" offered by a single geographical home.

Bruce Smyth, one of the report's authors, says Leach misrepresented the study which does not support the claims she makes; other academics, such as Professor Linda Nielsen and Dr Richard Warshak, have criticised the report, and exposed deep flaws in its methodology.

Research by neuropsychologist Allan Schore has also been used to argue "that one primary caregiver needs to be the constant source of bedtime routines". Nielsen has demonstrated problems with this conclusion and with the small and unrepresentative samples.

Warshak spent two years analysing the reports of 110 of the world's top experts and concluded "the evidence shows that shared parenting should be the norm for children of all ages, *including sharing the overnight care for very young children"*.

There is further consensus amongst these experts that courts routinely order arrangements based on flawed science and damaging to children and that there is absolutely no scientific evidence to support postponing overnight stays for babies and toddlers or to substantiate the idea that overnight stays with a father may in any way be harmful.

All available research supports overnight staying for infants because it strengthens the child's relationship with both parents. There is no minimum age at which a child can stay overnight; for children under two or three the **Transitions** between parents need to be more rather than fewer in order to maintain the continuity of relationships and security. As children grow older they can cope with longer separations from each parent, and toddlers can manage two consecutive nights away without distress. There is some indication that girls benefit from overnight staying more than boys.

Where contact is day-time only it is more fragile and more likely to reduce over time; parents are pressurised into returning a child by a specific time and cramming a month's parenting into a tightly defined duration. Overnight staying is less pressured and more durable; children are encouraged to feel that both houses are their homes, and they are not merely visitors in one.

A child will not be distressed by overnight stays unless a parent deliberately or inadvertently causes distress by demonstrating her own anxiety. Fathers' parenting is vulnerable to maternal opposition, and where there is conflict fathers' involvement suffers. Opposition or rejection by mothers towards fathers' parenting is influential in driving fathers away. By contrast, conflict does not seem to impact mothers' relationships with their children.

Arguments against overnight staying are usually motivated by the desire to thwart contact. Sadly, there were accounts almost immediately following publication suggesting that Leach's book was being used in court to justify preventing overnight contact in cases which previously had been close to resolution.

Contemnor

A person who has been found guilty of **Contempt**.

Contempt of Court

Disobedience, disregard or disrespect to the authority of a court or its officers.

Contempt can take a variety of forms: "contempt in the face of the court" concerns behaviour in court which disrupts the course of proceedings; interfering with the administration of justice involves behaviour such as intimidating or bribing witnesses; civil contempt may be either the refusal to attend court or the failure to obey an order.

Where courts are required to and do make decisions, parents must obey. These decisions are enforceable. If a parent fails to obey the terms of a court order, he or she can be held to be in contempt and liable for punishment. Contempt is not a criminal offence, but it carries a sentence of up to two years.

Committal arises in family proceedings as the penalty for repeated refusal to obey an order or for disclosing confidential information, etc. In England and Wales, if breach of a court order is to result in committal, certain criteria must be satisfied:

1. First, there must be a "**Penal Notice**" attached to the original order. Penal notices can be attached only to "injunctive" orders, that is, an order which requires a party to do or not to do something.

2. Secondly, an order is only enforceable if it has been personally served on the respondent. If the respondent is deliberately avoiding **Service**, the order does not have to be served personally and can be put through his letterbox.

Re A (A Child) [2008] EWCA Civ 1138 established three further principles:

3. the contempt must arise through breach of the order and not from the event (abduction in Re A) which prompted the order;
4. the applicant must prove *beyond reasonable doubt* that the respondent knew about the order and that what they did breached it; and
5. the disobedience must be shown to be deliberate.

Wall LJ further clarified in Re S-C (Contempt) [2010] EWCA Civ 21 that the order which it is alleged the respondent has breached must be clear and unambiguous so that the respondent knows "with complete precision what it is they are required to do or abstain from doing". An application for committal must show what provision in the order has been breached and in what form. The application must be accompanied by an affidavit setting out these details.

This last criterion was employed by Munby LJ in Re L-W (Children) [2010] EWCA Civ 1253, which set the limits on the obligations of a parent subject to a **Contact Order** (now a **Child Arrangements Order**). The applicant must demonstrate that the letter of the order has been breached; it is not enough to show that its spirit has been. This can make contempt difficult to prove. It is also established, for example in Nicholls v Nicholls [1997] 1 FLR 649, that breach must have a significant or potential impact on the justice of the case.

Breach of the order does not result automatically in committal; the applicant must usually make a further application for committal to the Court. Alternatively, if there is a power of arrest attached to the order, the applicant can have the respondent arrested and brought to court. Hearings should be held in open court.

The case of JDE v SDW clarified the criteria to be satisfied in the Scots jurisdiction if contempt is to be determined: the pursuer must prove—

1. the defender is aware of the court order; and
2. she has refused to obey it; and
3. her refusal is wilful; and
4. she has no reasonable excuse for so doing.

Co-Respondent

The person named in the **Petition** as having committed **Adultery** with the **Respondent**.

Costs

The cost of family proceedings can vary greatly, depending on the complexity of the case and to what extent parties can agree.

The applicant or petitioner must pay **Court Fees** unless specifically exempted; that is, the Court can choose not to impose the fees if it thinks the litigant cannot afford them.

Costs rise rapidly if the litigant chooses to be represented, and litigants should always ask for an estimate of costs at the first meeting with a solicitor, but realise this figure will be a minimum and be prepared for it to change as the case develops. There may also be other fees which solicitors call **"Disbursements"**.

The petitioner to a divorce may be able to recover part of her costs from her spouse if both agree, or if the Court orders it; under the Legal Aid, Sentencing and Punishment of Offenders Act 2012 (LASPO), amendments were made to the **Matrimonial Causes Act 1973** which enable a court to order a spouse to pay towards the other's legal costs and even to order the sale of a property if necessary, but it is unusual for the Court to do this.

It is more likely that the respondent will have to pay costs, either directly, or indirectly through ancillary proceedings when the petitioner's costs will be added to the settlement. Generally, costs are paid by the party considered to be at fault, so the respondent who admits the petitioner's statement on the **Acknowledgement of Service** may have to pay their costs.

In children's proceedings, the general rule is that each party pays their own costs and there should be no order for costs where both reasonably present their case. Courts are reluctant to impose one party's costs on the other because of the implication that one is successful and the other not; costs orders are rare unless a party "goes beyond the bounds of what is appropriate" (Re F (A Child) [2008] EWCA Civ 938) or incurs unnecessary costs or otherwise causes the other party to suffer financial hardship. In cases where a resident parent paying their own costs might adversely impact the child's welfare, the other parent may be required to pay if able to do so.

In Re G (Children) [2013] EWCA Civ 1017, a father had brought proceedings in which there was "absolutely no merit" and had used them "as a vehicle for getting at the mother" and "abused the court process by using it as a vehicle to make the mother feel insecure and vulnerable". Costs were awarded against him despite the fact he was living on benefits and his appeal failed.

In HH v BLW [2012] EWHC 2199, costs were awarded against a father who, perversely, went ahead with an application for contact with his sixteen-year-old daughter, despite her clear objection to contact and the mother's declaration that she would seek costs. The appeal judge said the application was the only way the father could engage CAFCASS to determine the girl's wishes and feelings, but that the cost in dispute did not justify the cost of an appeal and permission to appeal was refused.

There is a provision in Schedule 1 of the Children Act for some of a litigant's capital to be released to the child and for that to be used to pay the other litigant's costs, particularly where failure to do this would result in only one litigant being represented and lead to an **Inequality of Arms**; see MG & JG v JF [2015] EWHC 564.

Bespoke **Finding-of-Fact** hearings are expensive and the result of serious allegations, and the courts often take a different approach. If allegations which are subsequently accepted by the Court are initially denied, it is not unreasonable that the party at fault should pay the other's costs. What is determinative is the seriousness of the allegations and the fact that the injured party's costs are "wholly referable" to the allegations and stand outside the general course of proceedings. In Re J (Children) [2009] EWCA Civ 1350, the costs the father had to pay – two-thirds – were calculated according to the proportion of the allegations – two-thirds – proved against him.

If a litigant is representing himself and the other side has a solicitor, every application he makes or letter he writes will cause them additional costs. This can be used as a tactic to wear down unreasonable opposition to contact, but it can also backfire if the Court thinks he is being vexatious.

Under the Litigants in Person (Costs and Expenses) Act 1975, a Litigant-in-Person has the right to recover "… sums in respect of any work done, and any expenses and losses incurred, by the litigant in or in connection with the proceedings to which the order relates".

An LiP can claim for the costs of legal work, for Disbursements (including fees paid to a direct access barrister), for payment for legal services relating to the conduct of the proceedings and for expert assistance in assessing the costs (Civil Procedure Rules 46.5(3)).

The LiP must demonstrate with evidence and on a balance of probability an actual financial loss; he must demonstrate both that he has worked during hours when he would otherwise have been in gainful employment and how much he would have earned during those hours. He may claim for the time spent researching his case, but in Grand v Gill [2011] EWCA Civ 902, the litigant claimed £15,000 but was only granted £707.77. An LiP cannot recover any fees paid to a McKenzie Friend.

If there has been no financial loss, or he cannot prove a financial loss, then a flat rate applies of £19 per hour (Practice Direction 46, Paragraph 3.4).

Typically, a claim may be a mixture of the two; the total maximum recoverable is two thirds of the amount to which he would have been entitled had he been represented (CPR 46.5(2)). A written claim must be served, together with the evidence relied on, at least twenty-four hours prior to the hearing.

Where a represented party makes a claim against an LiP, there is no maximum hourly rate.

If the Court allows costs, it will say so on the order. Most orders will say "No order as to costs, etc." in which case the other party – or her legal team – will not be able to claim costs. In Re F (A Child) [2008] EWCA Civ 938, a father made allegations in good faith against the mother's boyfriend which later proved to be unfounded and the mother made false counter allegations; the judge awarded all costs (£120,000) against the father, ignoring the mother's bad behaviour entirely. The father appealed, and his costs were reduced to £50,000.

Any party with a financial interest in the assessment of the full costs other than a funded party, may appeal against that assessment in accordance with the Civil Proceedings Rules Part 52 (Regulation 11(2) and CPR 47.20). A litigant may appeal either on a point of law, against the making of a costs order against the LAA, against the amount of costs the LAA is required to pay or against the Court's refusal to make such an order (Regulation 11(4)). He may also, in certain circumstances, re-apply to the Court for an increase in the sum payable on proof of a significant change in the other party's circumstances. Such applications cannot be made more than six years after the date of the first order under Section 11 (Regulation 12).

The costs of expert reports are usually split equally between the parties. If one is receiving legal aid, then that may cover half the cost, on the assumption the other party will pay half. If the child is represented and legally aided, the Legal Aid Agency will usually offer to pay a third. In JG v the Legal Services Commission [2013], the Commission (now the LAA) had refused to pay the whole cost of an expert and offered to pay only a third, insisting the parents should pay the rest. Mr Justice Ryder found in favour of the Commission.

In the Court of Appeal, however, Lady Justice Black overturned the finding (JG v The Lord Chancellor and Others [2014] EWCA Civ 656). The order for expert assessment had not been made as a "joint enterprise of all the parties" but on the instigation of the Children's Guardian and it should, therefore, be the child, through the funding certificate, who should pay; "the essential question was who was seeking the instruction of the expert".

The loss of legal aid has led to litigants being expected to pay what would once have been covered by the taxpayer. Even where failure to fund a case would lead to a serious breach of a litigant's Article 6 rights and where s.10 LASPO allows for exceptional funding, the LAA has still refused, resulting in some extraordinary cases.

In Q v Q [2014] EWFC 7, a **Risk Assessment** indicated it would be unsafe to leave a father with convictions for offences against young boys alone with his child and recommended no contact, direct or indirect. Public funding for his interpreter was cut and he was forced to represent himself.

The mother applied for the father's application to be dismissed and for a **Section 91(14) Order**. Munby LJ considered that, as the risk assessment relied on the mother's untested evidence, cross-examination was appropriate: the court had to deal fairly with the parties on an equal footing. There had to be an investigation into funding a cross-examiner and an interpreter – unfairness would disadvantage the child. Proceedings were adjourned, and the Ministry of Justice invited to intervene.

The MoJ responded that expert evidence was already available in the form of the risk assessment, "you will have to decide this issue in the absence of the cross-examiner you refer to in your judgment". In Q v Q [2014] EWFC 31, Munby observed, following Airey v Ireland (6289/73), that the Court was bound by Article 6 and would be in breach if it conducted the trial in a way it *knew* to be unjust; the words "cause to be put" in Schedule 10 of the Crime and Courts Act 2013 required the judge to direct that representation be provided at the expense of Her Majesty's Courts and Tribunals Service.

In Re K-H (Children) [2015] EWCA Civ 543, Judge Bellamy had ordered that the Court Service should pay for the cross-examination of a girl who had accused her stepfather of sexual abuse. The Lord Chancellor appealed, and the Master of the Rolls rejected Munby's Q v Q finding: "cause to be put" was merely a provision to enable magistrates' clerks to carry out some questioning; he ruled that Bellamy had had no power to make such an order and that he should have undertaken the questioning himself.

In Re D [2014] EWFC 39, in which lawyers of a father who lacked **Capacity** undertook the case *pro bono*, agreeing to pay the Official Solicitor's costs if a costs order were made against him, Munby observed,

> *[31(vi)]* ...the State has simply washed its hands of the problem, leaving the solution to the problem which the State itself has created – for the State has brought the proceedings but declined all responsibility for ensuring that the parents are able to participate effectively in the proceedings it has brought – to the goodwill, the charity, of the legal profession. This is, it might be thought, both unprincipled and unconscionable.

Counsel

One or more **Barristers** instructed on a particular case.

Counter Application

Application made by a **Respondent** against the **Applicant**.

Court

An institution with authority to decide legal disputes and dispense justice; also, the room or building in which this takes place.

We follow the convention that the body before whom cases are heard is capitalised, but the building, room and administration are not.

The **Children Act 1989** created the new unifying concept of "the Court", which comprised **Magistrates'** Courts, County Courts and the **High Court**. The new orders available under the Act could be made at any level within the Court. This meant that proceedings could be transferred with greater ease, and litigants no longer had to select a particular court for a particular remedy.

The unintended consequence was poor implementation of **Judicial Continuity**, and the resultant failure of judges fully to understand a case until it had appeared before them on a number of occasions. Section 31A of the Crime and Courts Act 2013 accordingly established a single **Family Court**, with a single point-of-entry via the Designated Family Centres, to replace the Magistrates' and County Courts.

Following the Crime and Courts Act 2014, there are now only two levels of court in which family proceedings may commence: the Family Court and the **High Court**. The Family Proceedings Court no longer exists and the Magistrates' and County Courts cannot accept family work. **Designated Family Centres** (DFCs) now represent the single point-of-entry to the family justice system. The Principal Registry of the Family Division ceased to be a divorce county court and became part of the High Court situated in the Royal Courts of Justice. Its judges were distributed amongst the three London DFCs.

The Family Court deals with all cases except those invoking the **Inherent Jurisdiction** of the High Court, whether in relation to children (wardship) or incapacitated or vulnerable adults, and international cases involving applications for relief under either the **Hague Convention** or **Brussels II**.

Court File

The documents a court retains on a particular case.

What a litigant has in his files at home won't necessarily represent everything that is in his court file: things like letters between his ex's solicitor and the court or CAFCASS may well be missing. He should, therefore, view his court file regularly so he can see exactly the same information the judge making decisions about his children has in front of him.

The file should be held at the court where the last hearing was held, though if the case has changed courts, there may be items missing.

Unless there is a specific court order preventing him, rule 29.12 of the Family Procedure (Amendment) Rules 2012 enables a litigant to view individual documents—

> A party to any family proceedings, or the legal representative, children's guardian or litigation friend for a party in any family proceedings, may have a search made for, and may inspect, and obtain a copy of, any document filed or lodged in the court office in those proceedings.

An application to view the whole file should be made in writing and an appointment made; many courts demand this. The letter will be passed to a judge who will make the decision. If court staff are obstructive, the litigant should ask to see the Court Manager. The litigant may need to make an application on Form FP1 under Part 19 of the Family Procedure Rules 2010 claiming it will further the "**Overriding Objective**" of doing justice by ensuring parties are on an equal footing.

If access is still refused, he must insist the judge puts his refusal in writing in the form of an order which he can appeal. Some judges will expect the litigant to specify exactly which documents he wishes to see, and won't sanction a "fishing expedition", but if he doesn't know what is in the file he won't be in a position to be specific.

On receiving the file, the litigant should inspect it and ask whether anything has been removed; if it has he must ask for it to be replaced. He should also ask for the judge's comments to be made available. There will be a fee for photocopying, though a smart-phone could be used to scan the documents. Technically this could breach Section 41 of the Criminal Justice Act 1925 which prohibits taking photographs in a court building. Legal certificates should be copied because these give an indication of costs which may need to be disputed later. The litigant will need access to the file regularly as things can be slipped in without notice by the other side.

Court of Appeal

The second most senior court in the English legal system sits in London at the Royal Courts of Justice hearing appeals from the County Courts and High Court. The Civil Division – which hears non-criminal cases – is presided over by the Master of the Rolls. Judges in the Court of Appeal are Lords Justices and Privy Counsellors. They are known as The Right Honourable Lord (or Lady) Justice X. Cases are heard by a group of (usually three) judges.

Court of Session

(Scots) the supreme civil court in the Scots judicatory. Located in Edinburgh, it consists of an Inner House, which deals with appeals, and an Outer House which deals with primary legislation, including family law. Cases are heard by three judges known as Lords Ordinary.

Court Room

Hearings will take place either in a more-or-less conventional courtroom or, especially for preliminary children's hearings, in the judge's office, known as his "chambers". Hence, these hearings are referred to as "in chambers", the Latin for which is "*in camera*".

Typically, there will be two tables arranged in a T shape; the judge will sit at the top of the T and the parties and their representatives on opposite sides of the second table, with whoever is to speak nearest the judge. The CAFCASS **FCA** will sit at the foot. Where the hearing is before **Magistrates**, the arrangement will be similar, but with the three magistrates sitting in a row together, and with their Legal Advisor sitting at a desk to one side. One of the court staff may be present to help the judge if necessary and will otherwise do administrative work on their computer. Everyone should be introduced before the hearing commences.

Crave

(Scots) the statement of the precise order sought in proceedings in the **Sheriff Court**.

Cross-Application

Where two parties make the same application simultaneously.

Cross-Examination

The questioning of a witness by a party other than the party who called the witness.

Once the direct examination of the applicant's witness is complete, the respondent, or their counsel, will cross-examine. The direct examination controls the cross-examination: the respondent cannot raise issues which were not covered by the direct examination.

To undermine the other side's case, it is necessary first to understand it. The litigant must present his case and evidence clearly, succinctly and forcefully, and expose the weaknesses and inconsistencies in the other party's case, to undermine the judge's confidence in it, using documentary evidence where possible, but without discourtesy.

As Sir John Mortimer's father, Clifford, said, "the art of cross-examination is not the art of examining crossly. It's the art of leading the witness through a line of propositions he agrees to until he's forced to agree to one fatal question". The litigant should ask no more than five or six questions and only one at a time, ensuring it is one the witness must answer, and referring to his **Skeleton Argument** to ensure each question is relevant. If a direct lie must be exposed, it should be done compellingly and without decoration or unpleasantness. Focus should be kept on the judge to see how he reacts to the points made; the presentation is adapted accordingly.

The Court will assume a litigant accepts anything the witness has said or written unless he has challenged it. He can't submit anything later he hasn't raised in cross-examination, so he needs to plan carefully in advance and write his questions down, with alternative routes to follow depending on the answers.

Partly because of the loss of legal aid, an ever-greater number of litigants are representing themselves, leading to a growing problem with alleged abusers cross-examining their accusers. This is increasingly regarded as intolerable and a relentless and mendacious campaign seeks to end the practice.

One option is for the litigant to apply in the **Directions Appointment** prior to the full hearing for **Leave** of the Court to allow his McKenzie **Right of Audience** to examine witnesses. The President, MacFarlane LJ, however, is not enthusiastic (Re: J (children) (contact orders; procedure) [2018] EWCA Civ 115),

> [Cross-examination] is a forensic process which requires both skill and experience of a high order. Whilst it will be a matter for individual judges in particular cases to determine an application by a McKenzie Friend for rights of audience in order to cross examine in these circumstances, I anticipate that it will be extremely rare for such an application to be granted.

Another option is for the judge to undertake the task himself, and guidance on case management where parties are self-represented was given by Ryder LJ in Re C (A Child) (Procedural Requirements of a Part 25 Application) [2015] EWCA Civ 539.

However, Hayden J issued alternative recommendations in an appeal following a case where a judge had abruptly barred a police officer accused of rape from cross-examining and had asked the questions himself with so little impartiality that it was necessary for the parties to start the case again (PS v BP [2018] EWHC 1987 (Fam)).

Hayden advised that before such a fact-finding hearing is held, a **Ground Rules Hearing** should be conducted by the same judge.

The judge will exercise his discretion regarding allowing the accused or some other to cross-examine, or whether he will undertake it himself, as well as which questions will be asked, remembering that cross examination is dynamic, and the answers will prompt further questions. Though adversarial, fact-finding is primarily investigative, and a conventional cross-examination may be less appropriate than a less adversarial one.

The burden of proof must be upon the accuser, and justice must be done, however distressed the accuser.

The court should consider joining the child as a party so that his advocate may undertake the cross-examination. Where there is no available advocate and cross-examination by the accused is not permitted, the questions should be asked in writing.

Until new legislation is forthcoming, an accused parent has the right under Article 6 of the **Human Rights Act 1998** "to examine or have examined witnesses against him"; under Section 6(1) it is unlawful for a court to deny a party these rights and he may insist if pushed.

Cross-Petition

Where a respondent to a **Divorce, Judicial Separation** or dissolution of a civil partnership accepts that the relationship has broken down irretrievably but does not agree to the allegations made, he may issue a cross-petition. This might also be appropriate where the petition is for judicial separation, but the respondent wants a full divorce. Cross-petitioning can result in complicated proceedings and increased costs and may only win a Pyrrhic victory; if the marriage has broken down irretrievably, the aim should be to divorce as painlessly and inexpensively as possible.

Curator ad Litem

(Scots) (Latin: "guardian to a lawsuit") a solicitor who prepares a **welfare** report and acts like an English **Children's Guardian**.

Custodianship

Prior to the Children Act 1989, the protective guardianship of a child, awarded by a court; replaced by the concept of **Residence** until 2014. The custodial parent is now the parent "with whom the child is to live".

D

Data

Under the Data Protection Act 1998, a litigant has a right to access personal information held on him by public authorities and private bodies, whether on paper or in electronic form. He may only access paper records if they are held in easily searched "structured files", or if they are health, social work, housing or school records.

To access records held by CAFCASS, the Social Services, the Child Maintenance Service or the police, he should make a written "subject access request" to the organisation's data controller, citing Section 7 of the Act. If his case is transferred to a different CAFCASS officer, he may need to make a subject access request to access the old file. CAFCASS and the CMS may well give him the run-around; they will certainly ask for proof of identity. He may have to pay a fee of up to £10, or £50 for access to health and educational records. He can only apply on behalf of a child if the child has given consent or is too young to understand the nature of the request.

The agency from which he is requesting information is obliged under the Act to respond within forty days; the countdown starts once they have received the fee and have all the necessary information to identify him and locate the data.

Some data are exempt, such as adoption records and reports. Where data contain the identities of third parties (children, witnesses, informants, CAFCASS or police officers) the data controller can blank out or remove their names; he is not obliged to release data which would reveal the identities of third parties without their consent. In the case of a child, this means CAFCASS would ask the other parent for consent to reveal data.

There is no right to be told if information has been removed or if the record given is complete or edited. This does not apply to health records. Information likely to cause "serious harm" to someone, especially a child, is also exempt.

If the information is not provided within the time allowed, a reminder should be sent first and it may then become necessary to commence the complaints procedure for the agency concerned. The matter can also be pursued through the office of the Information Commissioner: telephone: 01625 545 745; website: www.informationcommissioner.gov.uk.

De Bene Esse

(Latin: "of well-being") a phrase denoting a decision made provisionally or conditionally; often of *Ex Parte* proceedings where further proceedings must still be held.

Declaration of (Non)Parentage

See **Parental Responsibility; Removal.**

Decree Absolute

The final stage of the **Divorce** process, enabling the parties to re-marry. The application for the **Decree** *Nisi* to be made absolute is made on Form D36.

Decree *Nisi*

(Latin: "unless") the preliminary stage of the **Divorce** process: the parties are divorced *unless* some impediment is found.

Deemed Service

An order by which the Court declares that **Service** of the **Petition** has been made on the **Respondent**. The judge must be satisfied that service has been made: normally this will be through receipt of the **Acknowledgement of Service**; otherwise it may be necessary to have a **Process Server** serve the papers and file a statement of confirmation. The application is made on Form D13B and evidence of service must be provided by affidavit.

Defences
(Scots) the statement lodged by the **Defender** to a divorce in response to the **Pursuer's Condescendences**.

Defender
(Scots) the party against whom the divorce action is taken.

Defending a Divorce
The act of responding to a **Petition** in an attempt to prevent the divorce taking place and allowing the marriage to continue.

The words "defend" and "contest" are often used interchangeably. At Question 4 on Form D10, the **Acknowledgement of Service**, the **Respondent** is asked if he wishes "to defend the case".

There is a time limit of seven days within which the respondent must return his D10, and if he chooses to defend he must file his **Answer** within a further twenty-one days.

There is little point in defending a divorce if the intention is to preserve the marriage, but it can be a legitimate tactic to delay a divorce, refute untrue, fabricated or damaging allegations or to launch a cross-petition; the only legal justification for defence is that the marriage has *not* broken down irretrievably. A respondent must deny an allegation of **Adultery**, show that the examples of **Behaviour** do not amount to irretrievable breakdown or demonstrate that the parties have not been separated for two years.

Defending a divorce is time-consuming and expensive and few solicitors will be willing to take on the case. The Court will still take the view that ruling the marriage has broken down irretrievably is the only realistic outcome. The Court has only to find that the respondent has behaved in a way the petitioner cannot reasonably tolerate.

A successful defence, perhaps because of a technicality or a poorly written petition, becomes *Res Judicata*, meaning it cannot be tried again on the same evidence, making it necessary to base the divorce on a different "**Fact**" or on behaviour which has occurred since the date of the first proceedings. Though extremely rare, this is an awkward situation to be in – inextricably "locked" into the marriage – and is why petitions should be drafted carefully and be checked by an experienced advisor. See Owens v Owens [2017] EWCA Civ 182 and [2018] UKSC 41.

Defending a petition until it is amended ensures that the respondent is on record as having refuted disputed allegations and untruths do not become accepted as evidence. It is unwise to agree not to defend in return for an amended petition which may never materialise. The respondent has a statutory right to defend; the only reason he should not is if the amendments meet his objections, but he should not agree not to defend until he has the amended petition in his hands and has read it thoroughly. If he is refused leave to defend because he is **Out-of-Time** (because he has been misled), he must appeal the decision.

Defined Contact

A pattern of **Contact** defined by a detailed schedule in order to eliminate the chances of misunderstanding and dispute (see **Child Arrangements Order; Application**).

Delay

Delay is one of the most damaging aspects of the family justice process, and Section 1(2) of the Children Act specifically enjoins the Court to keep it to a minimum; this is the "No-Delay Principle":

> in any proceedings in which any question with respect to the upbringing of a child arises, the court shall have regard to the general principle that any delay in determining the question is likely to prejudice the welfare of the child.

Accordingly, the Court must, under s.11(1)(a), establish a **Timetable** for the proceedings and give details of this timetable in its orders.

Delay is a non-resident parent's worst enemy. The courts are predisposed to preserving the *Status Quo*; given that contact applications are made only once contact is obstructed, the *status quo* becomes the state of obstructed contact rather than the satisfactory contact which existed before. The longer this state continues, the more likely it is the Court will uphold it. Where an application is postponed, that lost time will never be recovered and, whatever the reason, the applicant will give the Court the impression he isn't really committed.

If CAFCASS becomes involved in a parent's case, there will be substantial delay both in allocating an officer and then in producing a report. If the case depends on that report, the parent realistically must be prepared for up to a year to elapse between enlisting the help of the system and receiving the report.

Parents sometimes dither for months before making their first application. This is destructive to a case and challenging to recover from. As soon as there is an issue which cannot be resolved without court intervention, a parent must make an application and thereafter remain proactive.

There will be rare circumstances where delay is a sensible course of action. In Re B (A Minor) (Contact) (Interim Order) [1994] 2 FLR 269, magistrates objected to an agreement between two parents that the father should have **Supervised Contact** in a **Contact Centre** with a review in four months, saying it would introduce delay. The appeal judge overturned the objection because it would have denied the child four months of beneficial contact.

Deponent

A person who gives evidence by **Affidavit**, affirmation or deposition.

Desertion

One of the "**Facts**" upon which a petitioner can base a **Petition** for **Divorce** but rarely used: the abandonment of a spouse for a continuous period of at least two years immediately preceding the petition without agreement and without good cause.

Designated Family Centre

DFC – the administrative hub to which initial applications are made and where hearings take place. All family proceedings within the Family Court are issued from the DFC and it is presided over by a Designated Family Judge (DFJ) under the overall supervision of a Family Division Liaison Judge.

A litigant's nearest DFC can be found by searching on Her Majesty's Courts and Tribunals Service website. The actual building is likely to be the local Magistrates' or County Court.

Dicta

See *Obiter.*

Diet

(Scots) the date set for a hearing and thus the hearing itself. From the Latin *dies* = day.

Direction

An instruction by a judge contained within an order for someone to do something; often a preliminary step to resolution, e.g., write a statement, prepare a report.

Directions Appointment

A hearing at which the judge makes **Directions**. The **First Hearing Dispute Resolution Appointment** is the first directions appointment.

Disbursements

Costs charged by a solicitor to cover payments to third parties such as court fees, service of documents, property valuations, barristers' fees or experts' reports.

Disclosure

The revelation of previously hidden evidence, information or documents to the Court and to other parties.

Parties have a duty of disclosure to the Court from which other parties cannot exonerate them. In return, what is disclosed to the Court remains confidential; the **Common Law** starting point in financial proceedings was expressed by Stanley Burnton LJ in Lykiardopulo v Lykiardopulo [2010] EWCA Civ 1315, [2011] 1 FLR 1427:

> *[76]* Parties to a matrimonial dispute who bring before the Court the facts and documents relating to their financial affairs may in general be assured that the confidentiality of that information will be respected... It is a general principle, applicable to both civil and family proceedings, that confidential information produced by those who are compelled to do so will remain so unless and until it passes into the public domain.

Disclosure in financial proceedings is controlled by the Civil Procedure Rules 1998; documents which are disclosed may be used only for the proceedings and for no other purpose (Rule 31.22). If a document has been read or referred to in court, it may be published.

Disclosure of information relating to children proceedings without leave of the Court is strictly controlled by Rules 12.72 to 12.75 of the **Family Procedure Rules 2010**. Changes to these rules reflect the changing approach to court privacy; the current rules took effect in April 2011.

Disclosure

Though the media may attend hearings, they have no right to receive or view documents relating to proceedings; if they wish to see any document they must apply to the judge and the judge may use his discretion to grant the application. The fact that a media representative has been allowed to see a document confers no right to publish.

Rule 12.73 determines to whom information may be disclosed. None may be disclosed to the public at large or to any section of the public or an individual not in the following list, unless the Court permits or directs it. Information may be communicated – whether or not contained in the court file – to:

a) a party;
b) the legal representative of a party;
c) a professional legal adviser;
d) a CAFCASS officer or a Welsh family proceedings officer;
e) the welfare officer;
f) the Legal Aid Agency;
g) an expert whose instruction by a party has been authorised by the Court for the purposes of the proceedings;
h) a professional acting in furtherance of the protection of children;
i) an independent reviewing officer appointed in respect of a child who is, or has been, subject to proceedings to which this rule applies.

Rule 12.75 determines the *purposes* for which information may be communicated. A litigant or a legal representative acting on his instructions may communicate information relating to the proceedings to any person where necessary to enable them:

a) by confidential discussion, to obtain support, advice or assistance in the conduct of the proceedings;
b) to engage in mediation or other forms of dispute resolution;
c) to make and pursue a complaint against a person or body concerned in the proceedings;
d) or to make and pursue a complaint regarding the law, policy or procedure relating to a category of proceedings to which this Part applies.

Where information is communicated for the purpose of support, advice or assistance, the person to whom it is communicated may not communicate it to anyone else. Where information is communicated for one of the other reasons it can be communicated to as many other persons as are necessary provided the litigant consents and provided the purpose of forwarding it is the same as the purpose he communicated it to the first person.

The rules as set out in Practice Direction 12G expressly permit the communication of "any information relating to the proceedings" by "a party" to a "lay adviser, McKenzie Friend, or a person arranging or providing *pro bono* legal services" "to enable the party to obtain advice or assistance in relation to the proceedings". The discussion must be confidential. If in doubt, a litigant should always check with the judge before disclosure.

A father had rejected four reports in his case: one by the child's Guardian, one by a social worker, and one each on the two parents by a psychiatrist; he considered the psychiatrist's methodology flawed and his reports to be biased in favour of the mother. Aware of his objections, the Guardian took advantage of his holiday to send the reports to a therapist who was to provide therapy to the parents.

The solicitor had advised the Guardian that, according to the table provided in the Family Proceedings Rules, the Court's consent for disclosure was unnecessary. She represented the child and was, therefore, a party; she believed the therapy provider was "a body providing counselling services for children or families" or a "mediator" for the purpose of "mediation in relation to proceedings".

On his return, the father sought the **Committal** for **Contempt** of the **Guardian** and the **Solicitor**. The solicitor conceded that these conditions did not apply: the therapy in question was to enable the parents to communicate better and did not constitute "mediation"; the provider did not qualify as a "mediator"; it would not "enable the party or any child of the party to obtain health care or counselling" since it was the parents of the party to whom the therapy would apply.

The solicitor relied on the old Family Proceeding Rule 10.20A which provided that: "(2) For the purposes of the law relating to Contempt of Court, information relating to the proceedings (whether or not contained in a document filed in court) may be communicated – (c) Where the communication is to, (vii) an expert whose instruction by a party has been authorised by the Court".

Sir Mark Potter ruled (Re N (A Child) [2009] EWHC 736) that the therapist was not engaged as an "expert" "instructed or intended to be instructed by a party to report for the purposes of participation in the proceedings" but rather "a body or individual consulted by the parties as providers of therapeutic services outside the confines of the proceedings or the control of the court". Thus, contempt had been committed but "unwittingly" and with "benign intention" and it would not be "appropriate or constructive to impose any penalty". The outcome was that the therapy ordered would be conducted by an alternative provider, one whose perception of the case had not been prejudiced by the four contentious reports, which were to be returned to the father.

The father wished to complain to the General Medical Council (GMC) concerning the psychiatric report: the expert had failed to gather sufficient information to make an assessment, showed bias towards the mother and disregarded concrete evidence. In order to make the complaint, it was necessary to disclose numerous documents in the case, including the reports on both parents, the letter of instruction, the father's statement, and the father's critique of the expert's methodology.

The original application to disclose had been made under the old rules; under the new rules the Court's leave was no longer required, but the father nevertheless made the application to provide the mother and the child's Guardian with the opportunity to oppose which, inexorably, they took.

Munby J provided a review of the legislation: Re N (A Child) [2009] EWHC 1663. He concluded that the new rule "imposes no limitation whatever" either on the subject matter or nature of the complaint, or the form the complaint may take, or the person, body or organisation to whom the complaint is made, or the persons or bodies about whom the complaint is made. He observed that, while the word "complaint" is intended to be limited to those made to disciplinary or regulatory bodies, there is nothing in the wording of the legislation to impose this limitation. Complaints may be made, therefore, to Members of Parliament, peers, the police, the media, campaign organisations, and anyone else. The only limitation is that the complaint must be against a person in some way "concerned in" the proceedings.

The other limitations imposed by the rules are that in order to make the complaint, the disclosure must be "necessary" (and Munby explored the legal implications of the word); that the recipient of the information is bound by rule 11.4(3); and that the information may not be put into the public domain.

Munby concluded that the father required no consent from the Court or from the other parties to disclose, nor did he need to inform them of disclosure. Accordingly, he made no order, other than to release the father from his earlier **Undertaking** not to disclose.

In Davies v Welch [2010] EWHC 3034 Admin, a father attempted to have his wife's solicitor found in contempt for disclosing personal information about him and his children to the CSA. The Court accepted that this was indeed contempt and noted that Madeleine Welch only apologised to Mr Davies once there were proceedings against her; it declined, however, to make an order for committal. The solicitor was left with a £4,000 bill for instructing counsel, and the judge's censure.

Re S-C (Children) [2010] EWCA Civ 21 was a wife's appeal against committal proceedings. She had breached a specific order forbidding disclosure by disclosing documents to her lawyer in Turkey. Wall LJ ruled that the committal criteria were not met: there was no **Penal Notice** attached to the order which did not specify such an action would be breach and a party had to be free to discuss any legal issue with her advisors. Wall found Judge Plunkett's committal order to be "manifestly unsound".

Dispense with Service
(See **Service**)

Dispute Resolution
The process of resolving disputes between parties who can't otherwise agree and facilitating them to come to a compromise and agree on a solution. This is what used to be called **Alternative Dispute Resolution.**

It is recognised that negotiated agreements are better for children, last longer and allow a separating or divorcing couple to remain in control of decisions relating to the division of assets or child arrangements. They are quicker, cheaper and less stressful. The word "alternative" has been dropped to convey the idea that this is what parties should be trying to achieve first, before resorting to court.

The Pre-Application Protocol for Mediation Information and Assessment introduced in April 2011 extended the existing requirement for legal aid claimants to try mediation to all couples wishing to litigate unless there were excepting circumstances such as bankruptcy or allegations of domestic abuse. It was governed by Part 3 of the **Family Procedure Rules 2010** and Practice Direction 3A. Section 10 of the Children and Families Act 2014 established this principle in law and obliges an applicant to attend a **Mediation Information and Assessment Meeting** before making any application.

Dispute Resolutions Appointment
DRA – by the time this hearing is held in children's proceedings, all the statements and CAFCASS or expert witness reports should be in. The Court will—

1. identify the remaining issues to be resolved;
2. identify which can be resolved at the DRA;
3. consider whether the DRA can be used as a final hearing;
4. limit or resolve issues by hearing evidence.

If agreement is reached, the process can stop. If matters aren't resolved, the Court will need to proceed to give **Directions** for a **Final Hearing**; it will—

1. identify the remaining unresolved issues and the evidence necessary to be heard;
2. give final case management directions including:
   i. filing of further **Evidence**;
   ii. filing of a **Position Statement** of facts/issues remaining to be determined;
   iii. filing of a witness template and/or **Skeleton Argument**;
   iv. ensure compliance with Practice Direction 27A regarding **Bundles**; and
   v. listing the **Final Hearing**.

The directions order will be issued on a Form **Template** CAP03 and will also include:

1. a statement of what issues, if any, have been resolved and which remain to be determined; and
2. any interim arrangements for the child.

Dissipation

The illegal or inequitable misuse of marital assets in order to reduce the other party's share of the marital pot. Evans v Evans [2013] EWHC 506 established that there had to be clear evidence of "wanton" dissipation to the extent that failing to compensate for it would result in an inequitable outcome.

District Judge

An officer of the court formerly known as a Stipendiary Magistrate – i.e., a magistrate who was paid a stipend.

They are appointed from the ranks of Clerks and are qualified solicitors and barristers. They include District Judges of the Magistrates' Court and District Judges of the County Court; they deal with applications to initiate children proceedings in which there is some complexity, such as serious allegations, disputed facts, matters of capacity, international cases, leave-to-remove, intractable cases and those where the child is joined as a party; all proceedings regarding divorce, nullity, etc.; applications for financial relief where the parties consent to permission being granted and to the substantive order sought; financial resolution under the Married Women's Property Act 1882; and financial provision for children.

Divorce

The final dissolution of a **Marriage**, sanctioned by a court.

For divorce procedure in Scotland, see **Ordinary** and **Simplified Procedure**.

Following a successful online, administrative divorce pilot run by the East Midland regional divorce centre, it is likely that this procedure for obtaining a divorce will be extended across the jurisdiction.

There is only a single *ground* for divorce in England and Wales: the **Irretrievable Breakdown** of the marriage. In Scotland, there is an additional ground that either party has been issued with an interim **Gender Recognition Certificate**.

Irretrievable breakdown must be demonstrated by one of five **Facts** in England and Wales or by one of three in Scotland.

In England and Wales, if the situation is simple, a "do-it-yourself" divorce is straightforward; the necessary forms can be obtained from the nearest **Designated Family Centre** or downloaded from the Ministry of Justice website. Alternatively, there are services which offer a fixed-price solicitor-managed divorce. It is essential that some steps are overseen by a solicitor or someone of equivalent experience.

All non-urgent petitions will be handled administratively at the appropriate **Divorce Centre** within forty-eight hours and will only be transferred to court and a District Judge when cases are contested.

Step 1: Initial Checks

The couple agree who is to be **Petitioner** and who the **Respondent**. It doesn't usually matter much, but the petitioner is less likely to have to pay costs. They must demonstrate three things:

- they have been married for at least a year and a day;
- the Court has **Jurisdiction**; and
- the **Irretrievable Breakdown** of their marriage.

In April 2018, it emerged that some petitions apparently dealt with administratively rather than judicially had been accepted without regard to the time requirement, invalidating the divorces granted and potentially leading some parties to enter into bigamous marriages.

Divorce

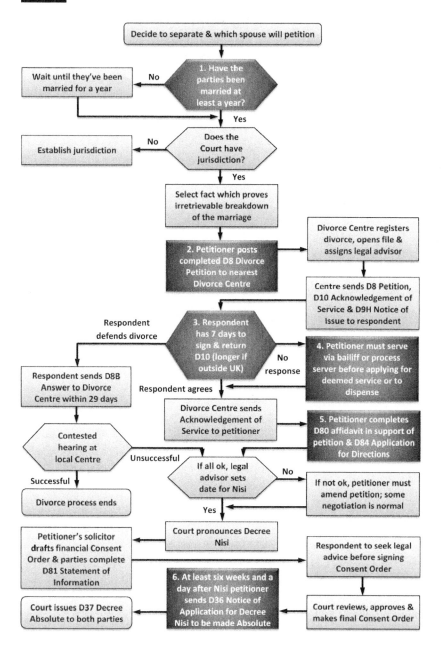

Flowchart 4: The Divorce Process

127

Step 2: Petition

The petitioner completes three copies of the divorce **Petition** on Form D8. Two copies (one for the court and one for the respondent) are posted recorded delivery to the nearest **Divorce Centre** with the marriage certificate and **Court Fee**.

Step 3: Responding

The Court "serves" on the respondent:

- a copy of the Petition, Form D8;
- the "notice of issue of petition", Form D9H, which confirms the documents have been sent; and
- the **Acknowledgement of Service**, Form D10, for him to return.

The respondent signs and returns the Acknowledgement of Service within seven days (or twenty-one if he lives outside the jurisdiction in Northern Ireland, Scotland or a Hague Convention country within Europe, or thirty-one days if he lives in a Hague country outside Europe) indicating he has received the petition. He must decide:

- Whether or not he intends to **Defend** the divorce;
- Whether or not he accepts the ground for the divorce: if the ground is adultery he will need to state whether he admits it; if so he can also complete a Confession Statement, though it isn't necessary (no one falsely accused of adultery should admit it just to get a divorce; it may be necessary to negotiate a change of wording in the petition);
- Whether he will accept the costs of the divorce.

The Court sends a copy of the Acknowledgement to the petitioner or to her solicitor.
If the respondent decides to contest or defend the divorce, he has twenty-one days to file an **Answer**. If the parties cannot negotiate an agreement, contested proceedings will follow.

Step 4: Failure to Respond

This may be the respondent's first indication that his spouse has been thinking in terms of divorce and it may take him longer than seven days to find a solicitor and respond appropriately. He must also provide an address for service.

If he does not respond, the petitioner will incur additional costs from her solicitor and from hiring bailiffs to serve papers, etc., and the Court is likely to rule he must pay these. If he doesn't attend court when summoned, he may be charged with **Contempt**.

If the respondent does not return an **Answer** within the specified period, the petitioner can proceed as if he has agreed. If she does not know the respondent has received the papers, she will need to have them served by a process-server (the respondent may end up paying), or by the court bailiff. The process can be hastened if she uses her solicitor as process-server.

If she knows the respondent *has* received the papers, she can apply for an order called **Deemed Service** which presumes service to have taken place. Alternatively, if she has made every reasonable attempt to discover her spouse's whereabouts, including newspaper advertisements and a Disclosure Order against HM Customs and they remain unknown, she can apply to the Court to **"Dispense with Service"**. Both applications are made on Form D13B.

Step 5: Decree Nisi

The petitioner next completes the Application for a **Decree *Nisi*** or (Judicial) **Separation** Decree (Form D84), and the appropriate D80 Statement of Truth form confirming the details on the Petition and Acknowledgement. These are the D80 forms:

- D80A – for petitions based on **Adultery**;
- D80B – for Unreasonable **Behaviour**;
- D80C – for **Desertion**;
- D80D – for two years' **Separation**;
- D80E – for five years' separation

It may be necessary to attach other relevant documents, such as a child's birth certificate as evidence of adultery.

If the petitioner has not applied for the Decree *Nisi* within six months, the respondent should contact the petitioner's solicitors and state that if there is no progress within a specified period – twenty-one days is not unreasonable, he will apply to the court on Form D11 for the petition to be dismissed on the grounds of "non-prosecution". He must then issue his own petition for divorce, ideally using as his fact "unreasonable" **Behaviour** which will get around the problem of the respondent failing to respond.

A District Judge will consider the petitioner's paperwork and, if it's in order, he'll grant a certificate and a copy will be sent to her with a date for Decree *Nisi* or Conditional Order for the dissolution of a Civil Partnership (see FPR 2010 7.25). If it is not in order, the petitioner may need to amend the petition or provide further evidence. Otherwise, the Decree *Nisi* will be pronounced in court on this date; the parties needn't attend – it's just a rubber-stamp. If they do wish to attend, they must notify the Court in advance.

Once the date for the *Nisi* has been decided, the parties should draw up a **Consent Order** detailing the division of marital assets – based on the agreement between the parties – this MUST be drawn up by a solicitor, and the other party should receive their own independent legal advice on the order. A Statement of Information (D81) should also be completed by the parties and submitted to the court along with the Consent Order. It may take a number of weeks for the Consent Order to be sealed by the court.

Step 6: Decree Absolute

Once the Decree *Nisi* is pronounced on the appointed day, the petitioner waits six weeks and a day before sending in her "Notice of Application for Decree Nisi to be made Absolute" on Form D36 – it isn't automatic. There must be a **Decree Absolute** or a Final Order for the dissolution of a Civil Partnership if either party is to re-marry. The respondent may, during this period, make an application (on Form D11) for the divorce not to be made absolute – usually because the finances have not been finalised. The Court will normally pronounce Decree Absolute within a few days, provided it is satisfied there are no applications or appeals that this should not be the case, and send a copy on Form D37 to both parties or their solicitors. If the petitioner does not make the application within three months and a day, the respondent may do so, and the roles reverse.

Parties are advised to wait until the Consent Order is finalised before applying for Absolute, especially if wealthy; if they should remarry before they have the Consent Order, they will forfeit the right to apply for **Ancillary Relief**.

A Decree *Nisi* has no expiry date but, if more than a year is allowed to elapse before the Decree Absolute application, the petitioner must lodge an explanation with the Court stating why she has allowed so much time to elapse, whether the parties have lived together in the interim and whether any child has been born and whether or not it is treated as a **Child of the Family**.

The respondent can also make an application for the *Nisi* to be made Absolute.

If further proceedings are necessary, for example because the divorce is defended or contested, they will be conducted under Rule 7.20 of the **Family Procedure Rules 2010** which determines what steps the Court can take and how it will manage the case, calling a case management hearing if necessary, setting a timetable and making directions so that the proceedings may be concluded.

There is no such thing as a **Quickie Divorce**, despite the media telling us otherwise. A party can get their Decree Absolute and be free to remarry, but still not have sorted out a financial settlement. The average divorce is now taking about eighteen months; a petitioner should take especial care that all forms are returned on time and correctly completed.

The total time depends on how quickly the parties – and their solicitors – complete the paperwork; the mandatory six-week delay between Decrees *Nisi* and Absolute accounts for some of the total but cannot normally be avoided. In exceptional circumstances, it is possible to ask the Court to expedite the decree, for example, if one party is expecting a child or is terminally ill; they must then make an application under Part 18 of the FPR 2010. Delay will be greater if the respondent decides to defend, or if the parties insist on resolving all financial matters before the Absolute.

Divorce Centre

One of eleven regional centres dealing with **Divorce** petitions.

Petitioners should post their petitions for divorce and applications for **Ancillary Relief** to the appropriate centre. Applications will be dealt with by a legal advisor. If a hearing is necessary, the applicant will be allowed to nominate a court. The centres are:

North East: Durham, Doncaster, and Bradford
North West: Liverpool
Wales: Neath, Newport and Wrexham
Midlands: Nottingham and Stoke-on-Trent
South West: Southampton
London and South East: Bury St Edmunds.

DNA Testing

A DNA test is directed by a court to determine whether or not a putative father is the biological **Parent** of the child subject to proceedings.

Since November 2015, there has been provision for CAFCASS to facilitate and fund testing by DNA Legal in applications for Child Arrangements Orders where the case cannot proceed without resolution of a dispute over paternity and the parties agree to the test.

Under Section 20 of the Family Law Reform Act 1969, amended by the Child Support, Pensions & Social Security Act 2000, the Court has discretion to direct a test of blood or other bodily samples on its own motion or on application by a party. The Court is able to make an order for a DNA test involving samples other than blood (usually cheek cells) by the Blood Tests (Evidence of Paternity) Amendment Regulations 2001, but consent must be given by all parties aged sixteen and over and the Court cannot force a party; the case of Mikulic v Croatia [2002] FCR 720 established that it may be a violation of one person's rights to compel him to undergo a paternity test simply so that another person can establish their identity.

If the child is under sixteen, consent must be given by someone who "has the care and control" of the child (the pre-1989 formula for **Parental Responsibility**). If consent is withheld, then the Court can order the test takes place if it considers it to be in the child's best interests. The child's **Welfare** is not the paramount principle (his development is not affected); the principle is provided by S v S; W v Official Solicitor [1970] 3 ALL ER 107,

> The court in ordering a blood test in the case of an infant has, of course, a discretion and may make or refuse an order for a test in the exercise of its discretion, but the interests of other persons than the infant are involved in ordinary litigation. The infant needs protection but that is no jurisdiction for making his rights superior to those of others.

The Court cannot order a DNA test other than in the context of other proceedings, so a party who wants a test ordered will either need to make an application for a **Child Arrangements Order** or request it through the **Child Maintenance Service**. It is almost always considered to be in the interests of justice to know the truth and not suppress evidence, and in the child's best interests to know who his father is. However, in L v P (Paternity Test: Child's Objection) [2011] EWHC 3399), the Court chose *not* to order the testing of a fifteen-year-old girl who had refused a test when her putative father requested it following a child support claim by the mother: the girl had understood him to be her father throughout her life and the evidence that he was not was very slight.

The courts will only accept test results obtained under supervision by CAFCASS or from an approved company; reputable companies will guarantee the data is secure and will not be passed to third parties, and they will destroy the DNA sample after three months.

For tests funded by CAFCASS, only the father and child are tested; the father must attend at a CAFCASS office and conduct the test himself; the parent with care must bring the child at a separate appointment. The test involves taking a swab from inside the cheek which is then transferred to a test card and sent to the laboratory. The laboratory then analyses the samples and sends the results out to the parents or to their solicitors.

For private testing, the parents first arrange an appointment with their doctors; the testing company sends each doctor a sampling kit; each parent has to take a passport-type photograph with them and complete and sign a form which then goes to the laboratory with the photograph and sample. This is to ensure the sample really comes from the named parent.

Testing is extremely accurate (inclusive tests quote a 99% accuracy, exclusive tests quote 100%) and is probably impossible to cheat.

If a man confirmed to be the father is not on the Birth Certificate, he can apply for a **Declaration of Parentage** under the Family Law Act 1986, and the Court can order the Birth Certificate to be amended if it is in the best interests of the child to do so. For child support cases, parents can apply for a Declaration of Parentage under Section 27 of the Child Support Act 1991.

If the result is negative, the putative father simply receives a letter with the two words "Paternity Excluded", plus a brief page of notes and a technical printout. No one can prepare him for the shock or dismay. Nor can they prepare him for the catastrophic consequences. We strongly advise lining up counselling for this eventuality.

There are no specific provisions for "mistaken paternity" or **Paternity Fraud** in the Children Act, and the definition of a father based on the *pater est* rule (see **Parent**) changes after a negative DNA test, leading to the loss of **Parental Responsibility**.

If the test excludes a man from being the father and a subsequent test shows that another man is, the latter then becomes the child's legal father, regardless of whether he wishes to be, and of the excluded man's involvement up to that point. The excluded man will then need to apply to the Court for a contested Child Arrangements Order naming him as a person with whom the child is to live, which is the only way he can re-acquire Parental Responsibility: he cannot apply for a Parental Responsibility Order. If his application is successful, he will gain PR; if it is ordered that the child will stay with him or otherwise have contact, the Court has discretion to decide whether or not he should acquire PR for the duration of the order, according to the child's best interests. He can only apply for a Child Arrangements Order, however, if the child has lived with him for a period of at least three years or if he was married and the child was regarded as a **Child of the Family**.

Domestic Abuse

The term increasingly used to replace 'Domestic Violence' in situations where there is no physical violence. The following definition has been proposed by the Government in the consultation on its Domestic Abuse Bill:

> Any incident or pattern of incidents of controlling, coercive, threatening behaviour, violence or abuse between those aged 16 or over who are, or have been, intimate partners or family members regardless of gender or sexual orientation. The abuse can encompass, but is not limited to psychological, physical, sexual, economic and emotional abuse.

In Yemshaw (Appellant) v London Borough of Hounslow (Respondent) [2011] UKSC 3, Lady Justice Hale clarified that violence signified not merely physical violence, but also "conduct which (rightly or wrongly) puts a person in fear of physical violence", and even "strength or intensity of emotion; fervour, passion" (Para. 19). Lord Brown's warning that the law must distinguish between actual physical violence and "verbal or psychological abuse" was scorned.

There are two fundamental and incompatible understandings of domestic abuse. The first, often referred to as the "feminist paradigm", is derived from feminist theory and holds that it is the means by which the "patriarchy" keeps women in subjugation. This makes abuse a deliberate, structured behaviour, predominantly perpetrated by men, and centred in "**Coercive Control**"; it is the basis of the Government's consultation.

The alternative view, described, for example, by the Partner Abuse State of Knowledge Project (PASK), shows that more women are perpetrators of DV (28.3% vs. 21.6%) and that most (57.9%) is reciprocal. Motivation includes revenge for emotional hurt, stress, jealousy, anger and attention-seeking. Witnessing mutual DV causes anxiety, depression and aggression in children.

As many as 85% of Family Court disputes involve allegations of domestic abuse; in Re: L, Re: V, Re: M, Re: H [2000] 2 FLR 334, the former president, Elizabeth Butler-Sloss, commissioned a report from two child psychiatrists, Claire Sturge and Danya Glaser. This led eventually to a controversial Practice Direction on how the courts should deal with this issue which was reissued in 2010 as *Practice Direction 12J on Domestic Violence and Harm* and rewritten in 2017 following successful campaigning by feminists. These are its essential points:

1. A child will be harmed by domestic abuse whether he is subjected to it directly, witnesses it, or lives in an environment in which it is perpetrated. He may also suffer harm where the abuse impairs the parenting capacity of either or both of his parents.

2. The court must always consider whether abuse is raised as an issue, either by the parties or by CAFCASS, and if so must—
    - identify the issues involved at the earliest opportunity;
    - consider the nature of any allegation, admission or evidence of abuse, and the extent to which it is relevant in deciding whether to make a child arrangements order and, if so, in what terms;
    - give directions to enable contested issues to be tried fairly and as soon as possible;
    - ensure that where abuse is admitted or proven, any child arrangements order protects the child and the parent with whom he lives, and does not expose either to the risk of further harm; and
    - ensure that any interim order is made only after following the guidance in the Practice Direction.

    In particular, the court must be satisfied that any contact ordered with a parent who has perpetrated abuse does not expose the child or other parent to the risk of harm and is in the child's best interests.
3. In all cases, it is for the court to decide whether a child arrangements order accords with the child's welfare; any proposed order, whether made by agreement or otherwise, must be scrutinised by the court. The court must not make an order by consent or allow an application for an order to be withdrawn, unless the parties are present, all initial safeguarding checks have been obtained, and an officer of CAFCASS has spoken to the parties separately, except where it is satisfied there is no risk of harm to the child or the other parent.
4. In proceedings relating to a child arrangements order, the court presumes that the involvement of a parent in the child's life will further his welfare, unless there is contrary evidence. The court must consider carefully whether this presumption applies, having particular regard to any allegation or admission of harm to the child or parent or any evidence indicating risk of harm.
5. In considering whether there is any risk of harm, the court must consider all the evidence available. The court may direct a report under Section 7 to be provided orally or in writing, before it makes its decision; in such a case, the court must ask for information about any advice given by the officer preparing the report to the parties and whether they, or the child, have been referred to any other agency, including children's services. If the report is not in writing, the court must file a note of its substance and a summary shall be set out in a Schedule to the order.

DV is not necessarily a bar to contact, contrary to campaigning by feminist groups. The Court must evaluate all the factors in the welfare check-list and weigh up both the detriments and benefits of contact to the child. This might seem reckless for one parent seeking to prevent the abuse of a child by the other, but the Family Court must balance the risks, and loss of contact with a parent can be at least as harmful as other forms of abuse.

Domestic Abuse Perpetrator Programme

An intensive intervention designed to challenge and address participants' violent and abusive behaviour.

They are commonly versions of the *"Duluth Model"* of intervention: an inter-agency, multi-disciplinary approach designed to enable local authorities to intervene effectively. It was developed in the early 1980s within the women's refuge community in the city of Duluth, Minnesota, and has spawned similar programmes such as Cecilia Lenagh's *AVERT* programme in Australia or Pat Craven's *Freedom* programme in the UK.

Duluth is based strictly on the feminist paradigm and the belief that women and children are vulnerable because of their claimed unequal social, economic, and political status. The model focuses solely on abuse perpetrated by men within a relationship and cajoles them to face their behaviour and change it. *Duluth* was developed by people who were political campaigners, not therapists, and ignores the typically reciprocal reality of intimate partner abuse. Only one party will be required to attend, if they have admitted abuse or been found through a **Finding-of-Fact** hearing to have been a perpetrator. Victims are offered support services.

Domestic Violence Gateway

Applicants using allegations of Domestic Violence (DV) to qualify for legal aid must pass through the "Domestic Violence Gateway" which demands evidence they have indeed been a victim.

The criteria are set out in Section 33 of the Civil Legal Aid (Procedure) Regulations 2012, amended by the Civil Legal Aid (Procedure) (Amendment) Regulations 2014 and Civil Legal Aid (Procedure) (Amendment) (No. 2) Regulations 2017. There are difficulties with these in that many do not directly constitute evidence and can reflect, or even encourage, false allegations. The Family Law Bar Association issued this warning,

> There will be an "inequality of arms" in cases involving domestic violence before the courts – where the alleged victim will be entitled to public funds, whereas the alleged perpetrator will not be so entitled. There is a real risk of a surge in the number of allegations, and possibly cross-allegations, of domestic violence in order to be able to qualify for public funds.

The Legal Aid Agency will not cover the cost of acquiring proof. Figures published in 2015 indicated that a third of claimed victims were being turned away, often because evidence was older than the requisite two years; a legal challenge was successful on appeal (Queen on the application of Rights for Women v The Lord Chancellor [2016] EWCA Civ 91). The Court found that the two-year threshold was invalid, and the rules were wrong to exclude victims of financial abuse; the LAA was obliged to allow evidence up to five years old and, from January 2018, the time limit was removed entirely, and the range of evidence extended.

Domestic Violence Protection Notice

DVPN – an alternative to the **Non-Molestation Order**, commonly known as a "Go Order': an injunction made by a police officer without a court's involvement to remove someone from their home for up to forty-eight hours.

These were introduced by the Labour Government in April 2010, shelved by the Coalition in September, and re-introduced by the Home Secretary, Theresa May, with a two-year-long pilot scheme trialled in the Greater Manchester, Wiltshire and West Mercia police areas through 2011 to 2013. They were part of the Home Office's campaign to end domestic violence against women and girls (VAWG) and were expected to apply only to men.

The scheme enables a police officer of superintendent rank or higher to remove a suspected perpetrator from his home for a period of fourteen to twenty-eight days where the police suspect abuse but would not otherwise be able to take action. The intention is to allow the putative victim to decide whether or not she wants to take the matter to court, but the forced removal of an individual from his home without the opportunity to be heard is a potential breach of his human rights.

Two criteria must be satisfied if a DVPN is to be issued:

1. the arresting officer must have reasonable grounds to believe the alleged perpetrator has been violent or has threatened violence to the alleged victim; and
2. the DVPN must be necessary to protect the putative victim from violence or the threat of violence.

The Notice must detail the molestation the alleged perpetrator is prohibited from doing, either generally or specifically. Molestation is not defined and can cover a range of behaviours. The written Notice served by the officer must state:

1. the grounds on which it is issued;
2. that breach will result in arrest without warrant;
3. that an application will be made for a Domestic Violence Protection Order (DVPO) within forty-eight hours;
4. that the Notice has effect until the application is heard; and
5. the provisions a court may make in such an order.

The officer will take down the alleged perpetrator's address so that a notice of the hearing may be served on him; this acts as a summons. If an address is not given, the hearing may be held in the alleged perpetrator's absence.

The alleged perpetrator must be given a leaflet providing advice on how to cope with enforced homelessness and be given a single opportunity, supervised by police officers, to enter the premises from which he is excluded so that he can collect essential items. Removal of non-essential items may constitute breach. The Court – preferably a Specialist Domestic Violence Court – can make an order if it is satisfied on the balance of probabilities—

1. the alleged perpetrator has been violent or threatened violence against the alleged victim; and
2. making the order is necessary to protect her.

Once made, the Court cannot vary or revoke the order and it must run its course. A constable who has reasonable grounds to believe that either the Notice or the Order is being breached can arrest the alleged perpetrator without warrant and must bring him to a Magistrates' Court within twenty-four hours. There is no power of entry and officers will need to use other legislation.

The evaluation of the pilots disregarded the human rights perspective on the ground that none of the alleged perpetrators in the study launched a legal challenge; only two were interviewed. Nevertheless, they remain unpopular and rare orders.

Domicile

The legal **Jurisdiction** in which a party is deemed to have his permanent home.

Following the Domicile and Matrimonial Proceedings Act 1973, a woman does not necessarily have the same domicile as her husband. An individual cannot normally be without a domicile, though he may never have more than one.

There are three types:

1. The *domicile of origin* is the domicile an individual is born into; if he is legitimate it is his father's, if illegitimate his mother's. This is his default domicile throughout his life, though it can be superseded by another.
2. Up to the age of sixteen, he has a *domicile of dependence*: if his parents move abroad and their domicile changes so, too, will his.
3. If, after the age of sixteen, he moves abroad with the intention of living there permanently, or at least indefinitely, this then becomes his *domicile of choice*. He must take up **Habitual Residence** there – the mere intention to move is not sufficient. Living somewhere for a long time – for example, because he works there – does not confer a new domicile of choice. Should he move again, with the intention of making the new country his permanent residence, he will lose his old domicile of choice and acquire a new one; he will also lose his domicile of choice if he goes travelling with no clear idea where he will finally end up.

Draconian

A word favoured by judges to indicate a decision more severe than the circumstances of the case justify.

Draco was a 7th century BC Athenian legislator who became notorious for the harshness of his laws. According to Plutarch, when asked why he punished most offences with death, Draco answered that he considered lesser crimes deserved it, and regretted he had no greater punishment for more severe ones.

In Re G (A Child) [2013] EWCA Civ 965, McFarlane LJ warned,

> [53] Since the phrase was first coined some years ago, judges now routinely make reference to the "draconian" nature of permanent separation of parent and child and they frequently do so in the context of reference to *"Proportionality"*. Such descriptions are, of course, appropriate and correct, but there is a danger that these phrases may inadvertently become little more than formulaic judicial window-dressing if they are not backed up with a substantive consideration of what lies behind them and the impact of that on the individual child's welfare.

Drug & Alcohol Testing

Nearly a quarter of applications for Child Arrangements Orders trigger an allegation that a party habitually takes drugs or abuses alcohol. The Court will need to deal with the allegation before proceedings can continue.

Accordingly, the Court may make a direction for a hair-strand test; this involves taking about fifty hairs from the head (or elsewhere on the body if there are none on the head) and testing them for evidence of drug or alcohol consumption. The advantage of such a test is that whereas a urine test will reveal drug use only over the last forty-eight to seventy-two hours, a hair-strand test will reveal use over up to twelve months, though six is typical (depending on the length of hair). It can, therefore, distinguish between recreational and habitual drug users. It will also provide conclusive proof if the party has *not* been taking drugs, and this will cast doubt on the veracity and motivation of the party making the allegation.

Note that testing is based on the average 0.6 to 1.4cm per month hair growth of Caucasian hair; because Afro-Caribbean hair grows more slowly (as little as 0.5cm per month), results will be distorted.

Most such tests are performed as part of family law disputes, and the majority reveal the allegations behind them to be false. It is common that the Court will make other **Directions** as well at this stage, such as a **Welfare Report**. Refusing the test looks as if the party has something to hide, but he might suggest that whoever makes the allegation would like to pay for the test or undergo the same.

Hair-strand tests can detect up to sixty-three different drugs and metabolites (the chemicals produced as a result of drugs being metabolised). It is tempting to get a haircut if a hair-strand test is ordered and the party is worried about what it will reveal, but the Court will be unimpressed. If he has shaved his entire body, he may be ordered to provide observed urine tests twice a week for three months. Some companies and internet sites offer cleansing solutions which are claimed to remove the evidence from hair. There is some indication that they work for alcohol but not for other drugs. The testing company will wash the hair anyway, to eliminate contamination.

The public law case London Borough of Richmond v Others [2010] EWHC 2903 established the limitations of hair-strand testing (Para. 22),

1. A hair-strand test should be used only as one element of the evidential picture. Where alcohol consumption is shown to be high, the test might form a significant part of the evidence but, generally, a hair-strand test should not be used in isolation to justify a significant decision about a child.
2. The two tests used – ethyl glucuronide (EtG) and fatty acid ethyl esters (FAEEs) – can produce conflicting results, therefore, both tests should be used. The tests must be performed to the ISO 17025 standard.
3. In 2009, the Society of Hair Testing established a minimum level – based on a 3cm segment of hair closest to the head – above which alcohol consumption is considered chronic and excessive; the tests should only be used to determine whether or not results are consistent with excessive alcohol consumption. Below that level, it is not possible

to determine whether the results indicate social drinking or abstinence. As many as 10% of results will return a false positive.

4. The 3cm segment may be divided into three 1cm segments to indicate a trend in drinking, but there is insufficient published data to establish peer-agreed minimum levels.
5. Results will be skewed by changes in metabolism, changes in frequency of hair washing, or changes in hair-care products.

Since February 2013, a new method of alcohol testing has been available: Transdermal Alcohol Continuous Testing (TACT) measures current consumption using an ankle bracelet to take samples at thirty-minute intervals of alcohol eliminated through the skin. Data is sent to a base-station in the home and thence via the internet for analysis. Costs of a month's monitoring are about £650 plus VAT compared with £720 for a hair strand test. TACT can detect about one unit of alcohol consumption.

If a test indicates the party has been taking drugs when he hasn't, he must demand a second test by another company. In 2011, a test by *Trimega Laboratories* indicated that a mother in care proceedings had been using increasing amounts of cocaine and opiates; she vehemently denied that this was the case and a second test ordered from *Concateno Cardiff* showed she had not used drugs as described or at all for the previous four months. *Trimega* conceded that they had made an error but did not specify what the error had been. They subsequently went into receivership. In 2017, the Government offered free case reviews to more than 34,000 families who may have been affected.

In Bristol City Council v A and A and Others [2012] EWHC 2548, Mr Justice Baker repeated four propositions put forward by counsel for *Concateno*, Robin Tolson QC,

1. the science involved in hair strand testing for drug use is now well-established and not controversial;
2. a positive identification of a drug at a quantity above the cut-off level is reliable as evidence that the donor has been exposed to the drug in question;
3. sequential testing of sections is a good guide to the pattern of use revealed; and
4. the quantity of drug in any given section is not proof of the quantity actually used in that period but is a good guide to the relative level of use (low, medium, high) over time.

Duress

A party has married without his consent if he has been forced to marry under duress. Duress is defined in Szechter v Szechter [1970] 3 All ER 905 as a "genuine and reasonably held fear caused by the threat of immediate danger (for which the party himself is not responsible) to life, limb or liberty, so that the constraint destroys the reality of consent". Such a marriage is **Voidable**.

Duxbury

A "Duxbury Fund" is a capital payment to a former spouse to provide a dwelling and annual income; named after the case Duxbury v Duxbury [1992] Fam 62. A "Duxbury Calculation" is made using "Duxbury Tables" which take into account factors such as inflation and life-expectancy. It gives rise to the so-called "Duxbury paradox": that, following a longer marriage, an older wife will require a smaller fund than a younger wife.

DX Number

A law firm's unique identifying number for the Document Exchange: a service which stores and distributes legal documents.

E

Early Intervention

EI – a scheme devised by a team led by solicitor Oliver Cyriax to improve the outcomes for parents and children involved in divorce and separation.

EI sought to intervene early in cases to steer parents away from litigation; its basis was "predictability": the principle that if parents knew in advance what order the Court was likely to make, there would be less point in continuing to litigation; after more than a million cases since the Children Act 1989, the courts should have been in a position to know what would be in the child's best interests, making it unnecessary to litigate from first principles each time.

Instead, parents would be able to construct a **Parenting Plan** from a "box" of pre-formulated parts devised to apply to different situations and ages of children, etc., with the caveats that the child must have frequent and continuous contact with both parents, the parents must not seek to exclude each other and that litigation is bad for parents and for children. The attraction of the scheme was that it was purely procedural and required no new legislation.

There were flaws, however: couples could still demand their "day in court" and, despite now having made around two million orders for contact, the courts have still gathered no evidence on their outcomes.

EI nevertheless had unprecedented support from government departments, the judiciary, lawyers' representatives and parenting groups. A pilot was launched in October 2003, but was hijacked by two civil servants, Bruce Clark and Brian Kirby, who substituted a failed CAFCASS programme. Only twenty-nine couples completed the project and it sank without trace.

Edgar Agreement

A financial agreement entered into prior to divorce in which one party agrees to the settlement offered and undertakes not to make further demands after divorce.

In the eponymous Edgar v Edgar [1980] EWCA Civ 2, although the wife's settlement was a relatively small proportion of her husband's fortune and she subsequently asked for a larger settlement, the Court held that she was bound by the agreement,

> Men and women of full age, education and understanding, acting with competent advice available to them, must be assumed to know and appreciate what they are doing... One may, of course, find that some unfair advantage has been taken of a judgment impaired by emotion, or that one party is motivated by fear induced by some conduct of the other or by some misapprehension of a factual or legal position, but in the absence of some such consideration as that – and these are examples only – the mere strength of one party's desire for a particular result or the mere fact that one party has greater wealth than the other cannot... affect the weight to be attributed to a freely negotiated bargain.

Emergency Protection Order

EPO – an order made under Section 44 CA1989 if the Court is satisfied that not removing the child to local authority accommodation or not keeping him there will cause him **Significant Harm** or if enquiries made in respect of the child under **Section 47** are unreasonably frustrated. *Anyone* may make the application. An EPO—

1. gives the LA **Parental Responsibility** for the child;
2. obliges anyone in a position to do so to comply with a request to produce the child to the LA; and
3. authorises the removal of the child to LA accommodation or the prevention of the child's removal from any hospital, or other place, in which he was being accommodated immediately before the making of the order.

There is no right of appeal and no written justification need be given for two days; no steps to set aside the order may be made for three days.

The leading case is X Council v B & Ors [2004] EWHC 2015 in which Munby J established (at paragraph 57) the criteria which must be considered by a court to which application has been made. An EPO is **Draconian** and both LAs and courts must have an "anxious awareness of the extreme gravity of the relief being sought"; the PR granted the LA is strictly limited to what is necessary to ensure the child's safety.

Evidence offered by an LA to justify an EPO must be "full, detailed, precise and compelling". Exceptional circumstances are required to justify an *Ex Parte* application; disclosure of all relevant facts to the parents must be full, candid and frank.

The order itself must be the least interventionist solution and must apply for no longer than necessary; it normally lasts up to eight days but can be extended once for no more than seven. The order must be made only where it is proportionate and essential for protection of the child's safety. Even when granted, the LA has an obligation to consider alternatives to removal. It must enable contact between the child and his parents and return a child when circumstances have changed sufficiently to make return safe.

> [93] ...The summary removal of children from their parents in circumstances such as this is bound to be traumatic for all concerned. It needs to be handled with great care and sensitivity. Otherwise lasting damage may be done, both to the children and to their parents. And heavy-handedness is likely to be totally counter-productive, making it impossible for parents and local authority to 'work together' productively in future.

The order served on the parents must be "conformed" by bearing both the signature of the judge and the **Seal** of the court. If it is not, the order has not been served. Parents need to read it thoroughly before admitting anyone into their home. They must also check the identification of the police and any persons claiming to be social workers or court officers, tipstaffs, etc. If they are in any doubt about the legitimacy of the order, they must phone the court using the number on the order. A draft of an order has no legitimacy and a copy is not a legal document; if they are shown a copy, the original must be sent to them as soon as possible.

Emotional Abuse

The Government guidance, *Working Together to Safeguard Children 2013*, defines emotional abuse as—

> the persistent emotional ill-treatment of a child such as to cause severe and persistent adverse effects on the child's emotional development. It may involve conveying to children that they are worthless or unloved, inadequate, or valued only insofar as they meet the needs of another person. It may feature age or developmentally inappropriate expectations being imposed on children. It may involve causing children frequently to

feel frightened or in danger, or the exploitation or corruption of children. Some level of emotional abuse is involved in all types of ill treatment of a child, though it may occur alone.

This was the definition employed by Mr Justice McFarlane in Re X (Emergency Protection Orders) [2006] EWHC 510: a case can still proceed without a court considering a definition of emotional abuse necessary or helpful. In Re C-R (Residence and contact) [2014] EWCC B29, a father pushed an expert witness, Dr Gary Wannan, who had accused him of emotional abuse, to produce a definition. Wannan admitted there was a range of accepted definitions but that he had not come to court prepared with one; the judge concluded that the expert was—

> [199] ...clearly aware of other, longer, more comprehensive definitions but had not memorised them. There is no evidence... that Dr. Wannan relied on a definition that is not supported by peer review or widely used by his colleagues. He produced in court, without notice, a short definition while making it clear that he was aware of other longer, more comprehensive definitions. That there are other definitions is clear, but the fact that Dr. Wannan could not produce one, without notice, does not in my view detract from his assessment in this case.

Emotional abuse must be persistent or frequent; isolated incidents do not satisfy the definition, nor does behaviour which does not cause "severe and persistent effects on the child's emotional development". If it cannot be demonstrated that a parent has abused his child according to this definition, the allegation must be challenged. Most such allegations are too vague to be substantiated. The accused parent must state in his position statement and in his evidence to the Court that there is no evidence to show his child has ever suffered or been at risk of suffering emotional abuse.

Enforcement

Further intervention by the Court to compel compliance with an obstructed order.

In Re C (Contact Order: Variation) [2009] 1 FLR 869 CA, Thorpe LJ had emphasised,

> Where a contact order is not operating smoothly, the court that made the order has a continuing responsibility to strive to make it work, and that responsibility is all the greater where a litigant in person is before the court and plainly frustrated by the obstruction.

Enforcement

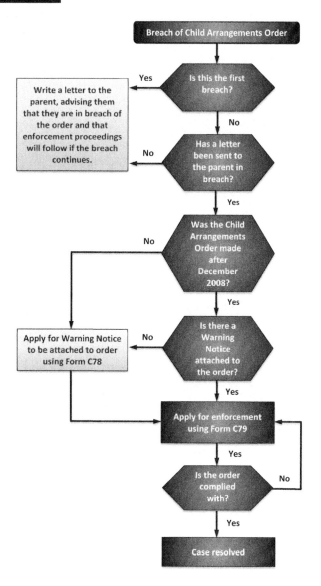

Flowchart 5: The Enforcement Process

The problem had been examined by Mr Justice Munby in 2004, "Efficient enforcement of existing court orders is surely called for at the first sign of trouble", while Lord Filkin, Minister for the Family Courts, had expressed what thousands thought, "Any court that does not enforce its own orders is a sham". In V v V [2004] EWHC 1215 at Paragraph 10, Mrs Justice Bracewell listed the four options then available for dealing with **Breach**:

1. **Committal** of the parent to prison for up to two years or the making of a suspended order for imprisonment;
2. the imposition of a fine;
3. **Transfer of Residence** to the other parent;
4. giving up: making an order for **Indirect Contact** or no order at all.

Most judges refuse the first three options because, they say, they are not in the best interests of the children and where respondents are implacably hostile to the idea of contact even committal is not necessarily effective. In too many cases judges resort to the fourth option. A 2008 survey of legal professionals by law students at Cardiff University (*Enforcement of Contact Between Children and Non-Resident Parents*) showed overwhelming support for the view that orders were not adequately enforced; enforcement was dismissed as "an absolute joke". One solicitor with over twenty-seven years' experience had seen only two enforced. Family law judges long excused this situation by complaining they had no sanctions beyond fines and committal with which to enforce compliance.

The Children and Adoption Act 2006 was designed to rectify this problem by introducing more flexible powers to facilitate contact and enforce orders made under the Children Act 1989; since 2008, the implementation of Part 1 of the Act has provided the courts with the additional sanctions for which they had long been clamouring. Half of the lawyers surveyed in the Cardiff study regarded the proposals with pessimism, however, and were not convinced the courts would make use of the available measures.

A 2013 evaluation (Trinder, L., McLeod, A., Pearce, J., Woodward, H. and Hunt, J., *Children and Families Bill: Memorandum of Evidence*) confirmed the sanctions were not being used and that the most common court response – in 62% of cases – was to make another contact order similar or identical to the original. Despite the repeated rhetoric (see **Order**), however, nothing actually changed, and breached orders remain unenforced.

An application can be made only where there is an existing order; a private agreement cannot be enforced. The application for enforcement or for **Compensation** for financial loss is made on Form C79 and is dealt with under Section 11J of the Children Act. The applicant must prove beyond reasonable doubt that the other party has failed without reasonable excuse to comply with a provision of the order. The application may be made only by a parent of the child, another adult with PR for the child, an adult with whom the child is living, or the child himself. It is likely the Court will give directions for serving the application on the respondent(s) but, given the nature of the application, it is advisable to have it served by a **Process Server** rather than risk causing distress or a **Breach of the Peace**.

Form C79 can also be used by the respondent to request a reduction in the hours in the order, or an extension on the time allowed.

Proceedings should be heard within twenty days and concluded without delay. The Court must consider:

1. the **Welfare Checklist**;
2. whether the allegation of non-compliance is agreed, or if a hearing is necessary to establish the facts;
3. the reasons for non-compliance: why the order isn't working;
4. how the child's **Wishes and Feelings** are to be ascertained;
5. whether CAFCASS can advise on the way forward;
6. whether there are risks involved in making a further Child Arrangements Order;
7. whether it is appropriate to send the parents to a **SPIP** or other dispute resolution; and
8. whether enforcement is necessary.

The Court's response can include:

1. further mediation or referral to an SPIP;
2. variation of the existing Child Arrangements Order;
3. a Contact Enforcement Order (which may be suspended) under the Criminal Justice Act 2003, imposing an **Unpaid Work Requirement** on the party;
4. a Financial Compensation Order under s.11O;
5. a fine; or
6. **Committal**.

A court cannot make an order for enforcement on the same occasion it makes an order for Child Arrangements.

The Court must be satisfied that there is no reasonable excuse for failing to comply. "Reasonable" means that it was within the respondent's power to comply, but she had a reasonable excuse not to, such as a sudden medical emergency necessitating taking the child to the doctor rather than to contact. The burden of proof is on the respondent to demonstrate to the balance of probabilities the truth of her excuse.

Enforcement

The Court must satisfy itself that the Enforcement Order is necessary to ensure compliance and has a reasonable chance of success. The unpaid work must be available locally and not interfere with the person's work, education or religious observance. How the unpaid work impacts on the welfare of the child must also be considered, but the child's **Welfare** is not the paramount concern.

The Court will attach a **Warning Notice** to the Enforcement Order advising of the consequences of breach; if the order is not carried out, it can be increased to a maximum of 200 hours and a fine can be imposed. Continued breach may result in prosecution for **Contempt of Court**.

If the original order is more than three months old, CAFCASS will be engaged again for further safeguarding checks. The Court will ask the FCA to monitor compliance with an order for unpaid work and failure will be reported to the Court. The work requirement itself must be monitored by a reporting officer who will warn a party in breach of an Enforcement Order without reasonable excuse. She may also report first-time breaches to CAFCASS.

If the breach is *not* the first within the previous twelve months, she *must* report it to CAFCASS. If it sees fit, the Court can also order the parties to attempt **Mediation** to resolve their differences. If in the substantive proceedings the child was represented by a **Children's Guardian**, the guardian is not automatically served with the application to enforce. However, an application for a fresh appointment may be made to the Court.

Applications for enforcement must be treated as family proceedings and are held in **Chambers**, but any committal proceedings that follow must be held in open court.

The Court's objective is not to punish an uncooperative parent but to get contact working. If involvement starts again while the unpaid work is being carried out, the Court is likely to end the order, provided it thinks contact will continue.

In Scotland, a litigant who already has an English/Welsh, or Northern Ireland court order will need to have it registered under Section 27 of the Family Law Act 1986; the clerks at the court which made the order will tell him what to do. Because the Hague Convention on child abduction failed to include Scotland as a jurisdiction separate from England/Wales or Northern Ireland, he will then have to make a further application to the **Court of Session** in order to enforce it.

An order made in Scotland can also be registered elsewhere in the United Kingdom under the same act when the children are resident in England or Wales.

Enforcement; Role of CAFCASS

Under the amended Section 11E of the **Children Act**, the Court may ask a **CAFCASS** officer to provide information in the process of making an **Activity Direction**.

Before the Court can order the activity, it must first determine from CAFCASS that the proposed activity is appropriate to the circumstances, that the person named as the provider is suitable to provide the activity, and that the person to whom the order applies can reasonably be expected to travel to the activity. CAFCASS must also advise the Court of the likely effect making the direction or order will have on the person affected, including possible conflicts with religious beliefs and interference with work or educational commitments.

CAFCASS must also advise the Court on the local availability of unpaid work which is administered by the National Probation Service (NPS). The CAFCASS officer may be required to discuss aspects of the case with an officer from the NPS but must not disclose details without leave of the Court. If an Enforcement Order is made, CAFCASS must liaise with the NPS who will monitor it to ensure the work requirement is carried out. If the order is not complied with, or the party is for any reason unable to carry out the requirement, the NPS will report this to CAFCASS who will report back to the Court. Practice Direction 12N ensures the Court will give leave accordingly for disclosure in order that the officer will not potentially be in contempt.

Under Section 11G CA1989, the Court may ask a CAFCASS officer to monitor compliance with activity directions and conditions. They will be expected to monitor the programmes and report back on the effects, whether beneficial or not.

The Court may also ask the officer to monitor compliance with a **Child Arrangements Order.**

CAFCASS will be expected to make the initial suggestion that an activity is appropriate and to incorporate the recommendation into the assessment it makes.

It has been agreed with the President of the Family Division that the provisions should not be used in "consent order" cases where proceedings have ended. Instead, their use will be limited to those cases where parenting has remained in dispute during proceedings and where a trial and judicial determination have taken place. For example, where one party remains resistant to contact, the Court may consider the imposition of a monitoring requirement is appropriate. Unlike the situation with **Family Assistance Orders**, the consent of the parties is not required. CAFCASS may also transfer this duty to a Family Support Worker.

Under Section 11H CA1989, if it deems it appropriate, the Court may set a further date for a review hearing, preferably before the same judge. CAFCASS will be expected to monitor compliance with the Child Arrangements Order by means of phone calls to the adults and interviews with the children if they are **Competent**.

CAFCASS should make recommendations to the Court on how involvement is to be monitored so that this can then be incorporated into the order. If CAFCASS fails to monitor the involvement, they will be in breach. Where compliance is satisfactory, it may be possible for CAFCASS to reduce the frequency of monitoring. The Court may not order CAFCASS to monitor compliance for longer than twelve months.

The Court can instruct CAFCASS to provide a written report on the outcomes of the order either at the end of the monitoring process or before if compliance is not satisfactory. If the respondent is not complying, or is introducing minor or petty infractions, the applicant should return to court before this becomes a pattern and not let CAFCASS persuade him that anything less than complete compliance is acceptable. The Court may then decide it is necessary to bring forward the review hearing, and CAFCASS will need to inform both parties and the judge how best to monitor any compliance which *is* taking place while the Court considers how best to proceed.

Some applications will be made as a result of a non-compliance notification from CAFCASS, while others will arise in cases where CAFCASS has not recently been actively involved. In either case, CAFCASS must notify the Court promptly as to the outcome of the checks, together with any other information they request. The Court has discretion to **Join** the child as a party to enforcement proceedings; the child is not automatically a party even if he was a party to the original proceedings which led to the making of the breached order. CAFCASS may be asked to advise the Court on whether the child should be joined. In practice, it will seldom be necessary, and CAFCASS Legal can advise in difficult cases.

Equalisation of Assets

The act of dividing assets or the estate equally between a couple in order fully to exploit the tax exemptions available to each.

Equality of Arms

The principle in human rights law, as expressed in Kaufman v Belgium (1986), which "entails a party shall have a reasonable opportunity of presenting [its] case to the court under conditions which do not place [it] at a substantial disadvantage vis-à-vis its opponent".

It is protected by Article 6 of the **Human Rights Act** which entitles the individual to a fair trial and can be traced back at least to the medieval principle that champions should be evenly matched. In family law, it ensures that parents contesting an application by a local authority should have legal representation. See Re D (A Child) [2014] EWFC 39,

> *[26]* It is, however, the responsibility – indeed, the duty – of the judges in the Family Court and the Family Division to ensure that proceedings before them are conducted justly and in a manner compliant with the requirements of Articles 6 and 8 of the Convention. That, after all, is what Parliament determined when it enacted section 6 of the Human Rights Act 1998, declaring, subject only to section 6(2), that it is "unlawful" for a court to act in a way which is incompatible with Articles 6 and 8.

European Convention on Human Rights

The European Convention for the Protection of Human Rights and Fundamental Freedoms is an international treaty. It was drafted in 1950 and came into force in 1953; member states of the Council of Europe are party to the Convention and new members are expected to ratify it.

The eighteen Articles of the Convention were integrated into UK law through the **Human Rights Act 1988** which remains independent of the ECHR and of the EU; the Government has committed to reforming the Act following the UK's exit from the EU.

European Court of Human Rights

ECHR – an instrument of the Council of Europe and independent of the EU; even if the Human Rights Act is repealed, the Court could still impact UK law.

Decisions made by a court in England and Wales which are alleged to breach one or more articles of the **European Convention on Human Rights** can be appealed in the ECHR. Taking an appeal to the ECHR is seldom to be recommended: it takes four to five years to get a ruling and in apparently successful cases like Hokkanen v Finland the parents involved didn't actually get meaningful relief, they received only monetary compensation. A case must satisfy three criteria:

1. the party must be the victim of a violation of one or more articles of the European Convention on Human Rights, or demonstrate that he is likely to be a victim because he belongs to a group deemed vulnerable, such as gay men;
2. he must exhaust all possible legal remedies in the UK; and

3. he must make his application within six months of the conclusion of proceedings in the UK or, if there are no proceedings, within six months of the alleged violation.

Cases such as Glaser v UK [2000] 3 FCR 193; [2000] 1 FCR 153 ECHR, Hansen v Turkey [2004] 1 FLR 142, or Zwadaka v Poland [2005] 2 FLR 897 established that states have a duty to allow access, to engage social services or child psychologists and to apply reasonable coercive measures to custodial parents who consistently refuse to comply with court orders, as long as it is in the **Best Interests of the Child**. The failure of parents to cooperate does not absolve states of their Article 8 responsibilities, yet the courts remain equivocal.

In Sommerfeld v Germany, the Court concluded there had been a beach of Article 14 (discrimination) taken together with Article 8 (respect for family life): an unmarried father had been treated less favourably than a divorced father would have been; such difference in treatment constituted discrimination (the differential treatment of fathers and mothers under German law was not considered discriminatory). Manfred Sommerfeld received compensation of €20,000 and costs of €2,500.

The Court considered that a child's birth parents constitute his family regardless of their married state, his right to his family life endures beyond the breakdown of his parents' relationship, and measures hindering such enjoyment "amounted to an interference with his right to respect for his family life, as guaranteed by Article 8(1)".

The Court then considered whether interfering in the applicant's human rights by denying him access to his child was justified. The Court concluded that the intervention in his family life by the German court had been made in order to protect the child's "health or morals" and his "rights and freedoms", and was, therefore, legitimate. The Court must strike a balance between the rights of the child and those of his parents, but there are circumstances where the best interests of the child will override the parents'.

The purpose of the ECHR was not to usurp the role of the domestic court but to review that court's decisions in light of the Convention. The ECHR considered that the German court should not have been satisfied only with the child's wishes and had failed to involve the applicant in the decision-making process by failing to order a psychological report; the German court had thereby violated the applicant's Article 8 rights.

The German Government had argued (without evidence) that the father of a child born out of wedlock was less likely than a divorced father to take responsibility for the child and it was, therefore, justifiable to discriminate against such a father. The ECHR disagreed and ruled that Article 14 had been breached: placing unmarried fathers in a "less favourable" position than divorced fathers without an automatic right of access was discriminatory,

The crucial point is that the courts did not regard contacts between child and natural father prima facie as in the child's interest, a court decision granting access being the exception to the general statutory rule that the mother determined the child's relations with the father... the court is not persuaded by the Government's arguments, which are based on general considerations that fathers of children born out of wedlock lack interest in contacts with their children and might leave a non-marital relationship at any time.

Evidence

The proof a litigant must provide to support his position. **CAFCASS** defines two fundamental categories:

Hard Evidence

Hard evidence is factual evidence presented in the form of DNA and hair-strand test results, hospital and medical records, letters from GPs. Other factual evidence may also be presented such as video and audio recordings, print-outs of text messages and emails or from social websites.

Soft Evidence

Soft evidence is non-factual evidence which takes the form of written opinions and reports from CAFCASS, social workers, child psychologists and other "experts". These people may also be called upon to give oral evidence. Most evidence of this kind will be in the form of written witness statements and affidavits. Letters from the children involved may also be given in evidence. Parties and witnesses can give oral evidence which gives other parties the opportunity to challenge their written evidence.

Evidence in the Family Court is assessed not to the "beyond all reasonable doubt" standard of the criminal courts but to the civil court "balance of probabilities" standard. Hard evidence is inconsistent with this standard and may be rejected. Incontrovertible evidence presented to the Court which has been obtained by recording a conversation or a CAFCASS interview, for example, or through the services of a private investigator, may be considered underhand and inappropriate.

Rules under Section 13 of the Children and Families Act 2014 enable the Court to exercise complete control over what evidence can be presented and in what manner. Evidence can be presented only if the Court has requested it: unsolicited evidence is not, at least in principle, admissible. A litigant must seek the Court's permission to introduce evidence and, if the other party objects, the Court will have to resolve this dispute first. If the Court chooses, it can exclude evidence which a litigant thinks should be admissible (Rule 22.1 FPR 2010).

Case law presented to support an argument must be clearly referenced and the paragraphs numbered. Documents presented as evidence must be filed in a separate **Bundle** and referenced within it. Each document is an "exhibit" and must be numbered.

A document attached to an affidavit must remain separate and not be printed on the same sheet of paper. It must be shown to the person before whom the affidavit is sworn, and he must identify it through a written declaration headed with the title of the proceedings and identification of the parties.

At the top right-hand corner of the first page there should clearly be written the party on whose behalf it is made, the initials and surname of the maker, the number of the affidavit/statement in relation to its maker, the identifying initials and number of each exhibit referred to (i.e., [AB1], [AB2], etc.) and the date on which it was made. This information is repeated on the **Backsheet**.

If more than one statement or affidavit is made to which exhibits are attached, the numbering of the exhibits must be consecutive. So, if there are two exhibits attached to the first affidavit – AB1 and AB2 – the first exhibit attached to the second affidavit must be numbered AB3, and so on.

Photocopies of documents can be exhibited as long as the originals are made available for inspection by the other parties in advance of the hearing and by the judge at the hearing. Court documents should not be exhibited.

Where exhibits contain more than one document or letter, a front page must be attached listing and dating them; they must not be stapled together but be fastened in a way which does not hinder reading (such as treasury tags). The pages should be numbered consecutively at bottom centre. If any documents are hand-written or otherwise difficult to read, a clearly typed transcript should be provided, carrying the same page number as the original, but with an "a" beside it. Refer also to the Practice Direction on **Bundles**.

These rules may seem pedantic but following them will provide the judge with all the information he needs to decide the case, arranged in a format and order with which he is familiar, in such a way that no court time is wasted trying to hunt down a vital page of evidence. A litigant should do all he can to keep the judge on side, and a neat, well-presented bundle is essential.

All evidence must be **Filed** (a copy to the Court) and **Served** (a copy to all other parties). The Court will not allow evidence introduced on the day to wrong-foot the other party – "**Ambushing**"; the case may be postponed, and costs ordered: all parties must be given time to read all documents and consider them properly.

Evidence will not be requested for brief directions hearings or conciliation appointments. Evidence is most likely to be requested for a final hearing or, rarely, for a **Fact-Finding** hearing.

Ex Parte

(Latin: "by a party") a hearing at which only one party is present; usually because the application has been made **Without Notice**. The opposite is an *Inter Partes* hearing.

Examination

The questioning of a party's witness. **Cross-Examination** is the questioning of the other party's **Witness**.

When examining a witness, a litigant will begin with some background explaining who the witness is, and their relationship to the case; he will then move on to the evidence: where they were, and what they saw.

If relevant, **Exhibits** will be introduced: photographs indicating abuse, for example; these must include the child's face for identification. Lastly, the litigant will question the witness, phrasing the questions in a way to encourage the witness to elaborate on their story; questions which simply produce a "yes" or "no" answer should be avoided. These questions should be prepared and discussed with the party's solicitor or **McKenzie** before the hearing.

Exemption

See **Court Fees**.

Exhibit

A document attached to an **Affidavit** and referred to by a letter of the alphabet. Items other than documents can be exhibited; they must be labelled securely so the label cannot come off. Small items can be placed in a labelled container.

Expert Witness

In the words of the British Psychological Society—

> a person who, through special training, study and experience, is able to furnish the court, tribunal or oral hearing with scientific or technical

information which is likely to be outside the experience and knowledge of a judge, magistrate, convenor or jury.

There will be situations in a case in which one or other side will need to call on the services of an expert witness. This may be a medical practitioner, for example where there are abuse allegations, a clinical psychologist, an expert on parental alienation, an expert on the law in a foreign jurisdiction, and so on.

An expert witness will produce a written report which will assist the Court to:

1. identify, narrow and, where possible, agree the issues between the parties;
2. provide an opinion about a question that is not within the skill and experience of the Court;
3. encourage the early identification of questions that need to be answered by an expert; and
4. encourage disclosure of full and frank information between the parties, the Court and any expert instructed.

A 2012 report on experts by Jane Ireland, *Evaluating Expert Witnesses Psychological Reports: Exploring quality*, showed that 90% of her sample weren't engaged in current practice, 20% lacked relevant qualifications, another 20% made findings and recommendations beyond their area of expertise and that 65% of reports were either "poor" or "very poor". Ireland was accused of misrepresenting the data, but the allegations were dismissed by a 2016 disciplinary hearing.

Litigants should be careful before **Instructing** an expert: the well-known cases involving Angela Cannings, Sally Clark and Trupti Patel show that it can be dangerous to rely on the evidence of a single expert. Some widely-used experts, including Professor Sir Roy Meadow, Professor David Southall and Dr Marietta Higgs have subsequently been discredited. Experts are open to disciplinary action by their regulatory medical bodies, though a complaint will take eighteen to twenty-four months and probably result in a slap on the wrist at best.

The rules on the instruction of experts are given in Section 13 of the **Children and Families Act 2014** and Part 25 of the **Family Procedure Rules 2010**, revised in January 2013; guidance is given in Practice Direction 25B. Failure to follow the rubric may lead to a successful appeal. The Court's permission *must* be sought to call and instruct an expert, to examine a child medically or psychiatrically and introduce the report as evidence (s.13(3) and Rule 12.20). Evidence obtained in contravention of the rules will be inadmissible.

See Re C (A Child) (Procedural Requirements of a Part 25 Application) [2015] EWCA Civ 539, where counsel for the mother ignored the rules entirely:

> *[9]* ...The expert was not identified. There were no CVs for the Court to consider, no timetable, no issue identification, no draft letter of instruction and no costings. Father's only notice of the application was in an informal discussion before the proceedings and he says that he did not understand that the application was going to be made in the face of the court.

> *[50]* ...It is the duty of all family law practitioners and the courts to learn, mark and digest these provisions and ensure that they are applied rigorously. They were completely ignored in this case by both the magistrates and, I fear, by Judge Scarratt.

The Court cannot order a competent adult to undergo a medical procedure, which includes psychological evaluation, but it can give parties permission to instruct a relevant expert and add a warning that the Court may draw negative inferences if a party fails to co-operate.

The Court may give its consent only if is of the opinion that the expert evidence is *necessary* to assist the Court to resolve the proceedings justly. Formerly an expert had only to be reasonably required. In Re H-L (A Child) [2013] EWCA Civ 655, Munby emphasised that "necessary" is "an ordinary English word" and means "necessary", and cited Re P (Placement Orders: Parental Consent) [2008] EWCA Civ 535, [2008] 2 FLR 625, in which the Court said the word "has a meaning lying somewhere between "indispensable" on the one hand and "useful", "reasonable" or "desirable" on the other hand", having "the connotation of the imperative, what is demanded rather than what is merely optional or reasonable or desirable".

Where a party wants the involvement of an expert in their case they must make a formal, written application to the Court no later than the **First Hearing Dispute Resolution Appointment**. Before so doing, they must identify the relevant expert and ascertain their availability and charges.

Expert reports are expensive; the expectation is that **Costs** are split equally if the parties are jointly instructing and it is imperative to ascertain if the other party can afford this. If one party refuses to pay for the report, it may not be possible to produce it, making the Court's assessment of the case that much more difficult; in some disputes, the party requesting the expert report has had to pay the full cost. Where a party is legally aided, the Legal Aid Agency (LAA) must be approached; where a child is represented, the LAA will not normally cover more than a third of the costs.

The application must:

1. specify the precise issues the expert is to be engaged to resolve;
2. explain how resolution of these issues will further the case;
3. explain how involvement of the expert will resolve these issues;
4. identify the expert to be engaged;
5. identify the field in which the expert is competent;
6. provide a copy of the expert's CV;
7. include a timetable showing how the expert will conduct their enquiry and when they will produce their report;
8. provide a draft letter of instruction;
9. provide a draft order the Court will make if it approves engagement of the expert (guidance is provided in Practice Direction 25C); and
10. provide an estimate of costs.

Evidence that the expert's involvement is *necessary* must be filed, explaining why the information cannot be obtained in any other way; justification for the inevitable delay the report will involve must also be given; the onus of proof is on the party requesting the expert. All parties must be served with a copy of the application. If the Court approves, it will make directions accordingly.

Like a solicitor or barrister, an expert's overriding duty is to the Court and not to a litigant; expert witnesses must be independent of the parties. It is preferable – though not always possible – to instruct a single joint expert via a letter of instruction agreed between the parties; having one representing each side is likely to increase time, costs and conflict. The **Children's Guardian's** solicitor will almost always instruct the expert in cases where a Guardian has been appointed.

Disclosure of information about a case to others is governed by the FPR 2010 which permit communication of information to an expert witness only if the Court has authorised their instruction. The party must also have the consent of the Court if his child is to be examined or assessed by an expert witness. He must seek consent by or at the **FHDRA**. In an emergency or urgent case, he must make an *Ex Parte* application to the Court for directions on what steps he should take. If the Court makes an order requiring a report or assessment from an expert, he must serve them with a copy of the order as soon as he receives it. If he is representing himself and both sides are jointly instructing the expert, the Court will designate the other side's solicitor the "nominated professional".

Whether the judge takes an expert's testimony into account is at his **Discretion**. If he doesn't take into account testimony on which a party is relying, an appeal will be necessary. In particularly difficult High Court cases, the judge may call his own expert witness to sit in and monitor the actions and behaviour of the parties and report. This is pursuant to Section 70(1) of the Supreme Court Act 1981.

Any party is allowed to put written questions to the expert for the purpose of clarification within ten days of receipt of the report; copies of the questions must be served on the other parties. The expert's answers become part of the report.

The Court will normally follow the guidance of an expert witness or CAFCASS officer unless either party can provide a good reason why it should not. If a party objects to the report produced, it still goes into the **Bundle** as evidence. A party who does not agree with the expert's findings must inform the Court so that, if necessary, the expert can be summonsed for cross-examination. If the opinion is not challenged, the Court will accept it and make a decision accordingly. The Court must be provided with a good reason not to accept the report.

It is rare for an expert to be called to court, but if the Court directs attendance, the "nominated professional" must ensure that a date and time are fixed for the expert to give oral evidence and an indication of duration of the attendance; if he is not required to give oral evidence, he must be notified as soon as possible. To minimise costs, the expert may attend via telephone or video link.

Challenging an expert witness's evidence will be difficult: he has been paid for his expertise which is likely to be greater than that of the parties, and if they disagree with his opinion it will always count more with the Court than will theirs. When a party counters, for example, an adverse psychiatric assessment in court, he can only do so on the grounds that he questions the psychiatrist's methodology.

To do that, he will need to write a document showing exactly where in his evidence the psychiatrist broke the rules he should have been following, he will also have to cross-examine him in court. To do that, he will certainly need qualified assistance. He will need to read the Practice Direction in full and read up on the expert's field of expertise, paying careful attention to any controversies. He will then have to apply to the Court for leave to present the documents of the case to the professional body which represents the expert so that he can bring an official complaint against him. Without leave of the Court, he will be in contempt.

Extempore

(Latin: "out of the moment") a **Judgment** delivered *extempore* is delivered by the judge on the day, after the parties have presented their arguments. It will be read out by the judge in court, copied down in shorthand by the court stenographer, transcribed, and then given to the judge for approval, before being made available to the parties.

F

Fact

An event or circumstance which must be proved through the presentation of sufficient **Evidence**. An issue in dispute is not a fact until it has been proved to the satisfaction of the Court.

In children's proceedings, a fact may be determined by the Court ordering a **Finding-of-Fact** hearing. In **Divorce** petitions, it usually refers to one of the legally recognised justifications; in England and Wales, under the Matrimonial Causes Act 1973 (s.1(2)), these are:

- **Adultery**;
- "Unreasonable" **Behaviour**;
- two years' **Desertion**;
- two years' **Separation** with consent; or
- five years' separation without consent.

In Scotland, under the Divorce (Scotland) Act 1976 (s.1(2)), they are:

- Adultery;
- Unreasonable Behaviour; or
- **Non-Cohabitation** (one year's separation with consent or two without).

Facts & Reasons Report

A report written by **Magistrates** to provide a rationale for a decision to order a child to be taken into **Care**. It is customary, however, for these to be written by the applicant local authority and given to the magistrates for rubber-stamping, a custom denounced by Mrs Justice Pauffley in Re NL (A child) (Appeal: Interim Care Order: Facts and Reasons) [2014] EWHC 270.

Family Assistance Order

A relatively rare order made by the Court under Section 16 of the **Children Act 1989** which orders **CAFCASS** or social services to "advise, assist and befriend" families caught up in family breakdown. A court may not extend this definition. It is made only in circumstances such as,

1. a major change in a child's circumstances;
2. when contact begins again after a long period without;
3. when the Court decides contact with a parent must end;
4. when parents cannot reach agreement.

Its purpose is to promote the continuation of a child's relationships with both parents and prevent **Alienation**; it may be used, for example, to allow CAFCASS a period of time to monitor a situation before making a recommendation on the final order. CAFCASS must first carry out an assessment and recommend to the Court that such an order is necessary and practical. Before making the order, the Court must allow the parties to comment on the recommendation. The order cannot be made without their consent.

A Family Assistance Order may not remain in force for longer than twelve months in the first instance.

Family Court Advisor

FCA – the **CAFCASS** officer who interviews the parties and children before advising the Court on the appropriate decision to make.

Family Division

Together with the Queen's Bench and Chancery Divisions, one of the three divisions of the High Court of Justice of England and Wales. It deals with children cases, divorce, probate and medical disputes. It was formed in 1971 from the Probate, Divorce and Admiralty Division (when Admiralty was absorbed into the Queen's Bench) which had been the improbable result of combining in 1875 the Court of Probate, the Court for Divorce and Matrimonial Causes and the High Court of Admiralty and had been nick-named the Court of Wills, Wives & Wrecks.

Family Drug & Alcohol Court

FDAC – a court established in 2008 to address the drug or alcohol dependency which often results in mothers having a succession of children taken into care. FDAC is exempt from the 26-week rule to enable parents to demonstrate the motivation and ability to change within their children's timescales.

It engages parents in an intensive programme of intervention and assessment, presided over by a judge with the authority to remove the child if necessary. An evaluation by Professor Judith Harwin of Brunel University showed that FDACs achieved higher rates of rehabilitation and family reunification and lower rates of child neglect and abuse.

Family Life

Article 8(1) of the **Human Rights Act 1998** protects one's right to "family life" but, as the Family Court interprets it, a father's right is only engaged where his "family life" has already become established. If he has or has had a meaningful relationship with his children, then he has a "family life" but, if that relationship has been slight or non-existent – perhaps because his child was born after separation, then he has no "family life" and no right which can be violated. A child's right to family life endures beyond the breakdown of his parents' relationship.

In Re G (A Child) (Adoption; Disclosure) [2001] 1 FLR 646, the Court concluded that a putative father had no right to be informed of his child's birth: the parents had never cohabited, and their relationship had never constituted a "family".

In M v F and Others [2011] EWCA Civ 273, 1 FCR 533, the **Court of Appeal** upheld the High Court's decision to refuse the application of a mother who wanted to place her child for adoption and keep its existence a secret from the father; the local authority believed the father should be informed. The critical factor was that the parents had children, a full family life already existed, and so the father's Article 8 rights were engaged. His Article 6 rights were also engaged as he had the right to be involved in and to challenge any legal process which would have taken the child out of the family.

Article 8 can also be used to argue for the preservation of the relationship between parent and child and to argue for regular contact; in Re C (Abduction: Residence and Contact) [2005] EWHC 2205, Article 8 was interpreted to mean that there must be a presumption of unsupervised contact unless there are good reasons for supervision.

If ever there is conflict between the child's and the parent's Article 8 rights the child's right is paramount; see Yousef v Netherlands [2003] 1 FLR 210 and Hoppe v Germany [2003] 1 FCR 176.

Family Procedure Rules 2010

A piece of legislation known as a Statutory Instrument which is susceptible to constant revision – sometimes several times a year. The Rules and their associated **Practice Directions** determine the manner in which the courts must deal with cases. Some proceedings such as committals come under the Civil Procedure Rules 2010.

Fees

There are fees to be paid for most court applications. They are subject to change and an LiP should ensure the correct fee is paid. Fees may be paid at the court by card or cash, or by cheque or postal order. At the time of writing the fees are:

Divorce

Filing a petition for divorce, nullity, or civil partnership dissolution:	£550
Filing an application for judicial separation:	£365
Filing a second or subsequent petition with leave granted under FPR 7.7(1)(b):	£95
Filing an answer:	£245
Filing an amended petition:	£95
Filing originating proceedings where no other fee is specified:	£245
Application to make a decree nisi, absolute (divorce), or a conditional order, final (dissolution), only if original application was filed before 1st July 2013:	£50

Ancillary Relief

Application on notice for ancillary relief, other than by consent:	£255
Filing a notice of intention to proceed with an application for ancillary relief:	£255
Application by consent for a financial order:	£100

Applications for injunctive orders

Application for a non-molestation order:	No fee
Application for an occupation order:	No fee
Application for forced marriage protection order:	No fee

Applications under the Children Act 1989

Any new applications under the Children Act 1989 to request permission to issue proceedings or for an order or directions to be made concerning the child(ren) - with the exception of applications for care and supervision orders, applications for breach of or for revocation of an enforcement order: £215

Application for breach of or for revocation of an enforcement order: £95

Adoption and wardship

On an application for permission, or an order, made under any provision in Part 1 of the Adoption and Children Act 2002, except s.22: £170

Application for placement order: £455

Parentage

Filing a petition for declaration of parentage or non-parentage: £365

Maintenance orders

Application for a maintenance order to be registered: £45

Application for a maintenance order to be sent abroad for enforcement: £45

Applications within proceedings

Application on notice where no other fee is specified: £155

Application by consent or without notice where no other fee is specified: £50

Appeals

Filing a notice of appeal of any decision in family proceedings made by a district judge, by one or more lay justices, a justice's clerk or an assistant to a justice's clerk, except appeal against decisions under the Children Act 1989: £125

Filing a notice of appeal of any provision of the Children Act 1989, except in relation to appeals for breach of or revocation of an enforcement order: £215

Appeals to the Court of Appeal

Appellant's notice if permission not already granted (N161):	£528
Appellant's notice if permission granted (N161):	£1,199
Application notice (N244):	£528
Respondent's notice (N162):	£528

Appeals to the Supreme Court

Application for permission to appeal	£1,000
Respondent's acknowledgement	£320
Filing statement and index	£4,820

Copy documents

For between 1 and 10 pages of any document:	£10
For each subsequent page of the same document – per sheet:	50p
For copies of documents provided on computer disk or other electronic form:	£10

Bailiffs

To have any document process-served by a bailiff: £115

Fees in the Scots Courts	Sheriff Court	Court of Session
Application for ordinary divorce or dissolution of a civil partnership application:	£150	
Application for simplified divorce or dissolution (no children or financial matters):	£113	£125
Application to start a family action:		£166
Defences, answers or other writ:		£166
Lodging of affidavit:	£66	£70
Petition for adoption:	£96	

Fee for court hearing before single judge per half hour:	£96
Fee for court hearing before 3 or more judges per half hour:	£239
Registering copy of English or Welsh order:	£18

A litigant on a low income or in receipt of certain benefits and with savings of under £3,000 if he is under 61 or under £16,000, if over, may qualify for fee remission to reduce the fee, or exemption which means he won't have to pay anything.

If he is over the threshold, he will have to pay in full; he will also have to pay if the Court considers him a **Vexatious Litigant** or he is bound by a civil restraint order. Some fees can be partially remitted if the applicant will suffer hardship or is a serving or remand prisoner. He may have to pay a contribution on a sliding scale.

Fees cannot be remitted retrospectively, and before submitting any petition or application to the court he must apply for remission using Form EX160, which is attached to the guidance leaflet EX160A, return it to the court (or to his solicitor), together with original documentary evidence (not copies) of proof of his means-tested benefits – this will be an original, recent letter or entitlement notice signed by a named member of staff from his provider containing his full name and address and proof of his income.

If successful, the exemption certificate is then submitted with the application. Civil and Family Court fees are detailed in the leaflet EX50; Magistrates' Court fees are given in the Magistrates' Court Fees (Amendment Order) 2007.

File

To deliver a document by post or otherwise to the court office.

Final Hearing

The hearing at which the judge makes his final decision.

If no agreement can be reached at any of the previous stages the Court can progress to a "full" or "final" hearing at which all contentious issues of the case can be discussed and, if possible, finally be resolved.

Due to its probable complexity, a full hearing in children's proceedings is scheduled to last several days – three is typical, five not uncommon. It is important, therefore, to follow the timetable set by the judge; delay at this stage can mean having to wait for another five consecutive days to become available, which could be many months away.

In a very complex case, the full hearing may be one of several; some cases run to numerous "final" hearings.

The judge will consider the **Family Court Advisor's** report, the parents may call witnesses and examine them, and the judge will decide on the case.

The hearing will probably take place in a conventional court rather than in chambers. It will be more formal than earlier hearings. If the other side has been using a solicitor thus far, it is likely they will now be represented by a **Barrister**. A **Litigant-in-Person** can also directly instruct a barrister (see **Unbundling**), or his **McKenzie** may be allowed **Right of Audience**.

The **Position Statements** prepared for this hearing must be more comprehensive and detailed than before and will contain all the relevant evidence. They should be clear and concise and be written in a logical sequence. Litigants should include the order(s) they wish the judge to make using the CAP02 **Template**.

At the end of the hearing, the judge will record the outcome on Form CAP04. It will include:

1. any agreement reached;
2. any undertakings offered to the Court;
3. any orders made for **Child Arrangements**; and
4. any orders made in relation to **Parental Responsibility**, **Activity** conditions, **Prohibited Steps**, **Specific Issues**, **Contact Centre** directions, monitoring of Child Arrangements Orders, or **Family Assistance Orders**.

In financial proceedings, a Final Hearing takes place where no agreement has been reached at the **Financial Dispute Resolution** (FDR). It will be a much longer hearing and involve a different judge. The judge who presided over the FDR cannot deal with the final hearing because he/she will be aware of the **Without Prejudice** offers which cannot be disclosed to the trial judge.

A **Bundle** will need to be produced prior to the hearing. It is important the bundles used by both parties and the judge are identical. An LiP will only have to produce a bundle if the Court specifically directs it, but we would advise him to prepare one anyway and try to agree the contents with the other party. It is much better to go to court with one and find it isn't needed than to go to court without and find that it is.

At the start of the hearing the solicitor or barrister for the applicant will make an opening speech explaining what the hearing is about. Both of the parties and any witnesses then give evidence and are cross-examined: the applicant going first, followed by his witnesses, and the respondent and her witnesses giving evidence second. Each lawyer makes a closing speech.

Depending upon the complexity of the case and time constraints, the judge will either retire to consider the judgment or indicate a time when it will be available. If the former, the judge will then give judgment and make whatever order is appropriate; if the latter, a date will be arranged for the handing down of the judgment. After the order has been made there will be more arguments presented on the question of **Costs** and a corresponding order may be made.

Final Order

A term introduced in 2007/08 to replace **Decree Absolute**; it is still used in relation to **Civil Partnerships**.

Financial Arrangements

(Scots) it is rare in Scots litigation for financial disputes to be decided by the courts. There are four steps which should be considered before making a decision about the financial arrangements on separation. Note that matrimonial property is that which is accrued between the date of marriage and the agreed **Separation Date** (otherwise known as the relevant date):

1. Establish the **Separation Date** on which the married couple ceased to cohabit as man and wife.
2. Identify all assets over the value of £500 owned jointly or individually by the couple at the separation date including the house, furnishings, car, pensions, savings and investments and any outstanding liabilities (mortgage, car finance, personal loans, credit card debts etc.). Property and other assets acquired after the agreed date of separation are not matrimonial property.
3. Determine any non-matrimonial property by looking at the circumstances in which individual assets were acquired. Assets owned by either party before the marriage or those gifted or inherited are not matrimonial property. However, gifted or inherited property or assets must remain substantially in the same form; where gifted or inherited property is sold, and other property is acquired, or where property is acquired using gifted or inherited money, the acquired property is matrimonial property. The Court may take into account the source of the funds used to purchase the property in order to justify dividing the property unequally.

The exception to property owned prior to the marriage is that, where the matrimonial home has been purchased before the marriage with the intent for use as the matrimonial home, it will be included as a matrimonial asset, as will any furnishings and other items purchased for the home prior to the marriage.

4. Matrimonial assets should be valued at the date of separation; for example, by providing statements of savings, asking insurance companies for surrender valuations of endowments and pension providers for the **Cash Equivalent Transfer Value**. Endowment policies and pensions started before the marriage are apportioned for the years of the marriage. It's best to have agreement before having the house valued by a chartered surveyor. The liabilities are deducted from the assets to provide the net value of matrimonial property.

The principles the Court applies in deciding what order for financial provision, if any, to make are that—

1. the net value of the matrimonial property is shared fairly between the parties to the marriage;
2. fair account is taken of any economic advantage derived by either party from contributions by the other, and of any economic disadvantage suffered by either party in the interests of the other party or of the family;
3. any economic burden of caring, after divorce, for a child of the marriage under the age of sixteen years is shared fairly between the parties;
4. a party who has been dependent to a substantial degree on the financial support of the other party is awarded such financial provision as is reasonable to enable him or her to adjust, over a period of not more than three years from the date of the decree of divorce, to the loss of that support on divorce; and
5. a party who at the time of the divorce is likely to suffer serious financial hardship as a result of the divorce is awarded such financial provision as is reasonable to relieve him or her of hardship over a reasonable period.

"Economic advantage" means advantage gained whether before or during the marriage and includes gains in capital, in income and in earning capacity, and "economic disadvantage" is to be construed accordingly; "contributions" means contributions made whether before or during the marriage, and includes indirect and non-financial contributions and, in particular, any such contribution made by looking after the family home or caring for the family.

It is reasonable (and advisable) to apply these principles when making an agreement between the two parties, whether or not they use solicitors to negotiate on their behalf.

If a financial order is applied for on behalf of a child, or to redress the balance of burden of caring for a child, the Court shall give regard to:

1. any decree or arrangement for **Aliment** for the child;
2. any expenditure or loss of earning capacity caused by the need to care for the child;
3. the need to provide suitable accommodation for the child;
4. the child's age and health;
5. the child's educational, financial and other circumstances;
6. the availability and cost of suitable child-care facilities or services;
7. the needs and resources of the parties; and
8. all the other circumstances of the case.

If a financial order is sought on the basis that one party has been dependent to a substantial degree on the financial support of the other, then the Court shall give regard to:

1. the age, health and earning capacity of the party who is claiming the financial provision;
2. the duration and extent of the dependence of that party prior to divorce;
3. any intention of that party to undertake a course of education or training;
4. the needs and resources of the parties; and
5. all the other circumstances of the case.

The above considerations are regarded by the Court for all other financial order applications. An order for financial provision must be justified by one or more principles in Section 9 of the Family Law (Scotland) Act 1985 and the order must be reasonable having regard to the resources of the parties.

Financial Dispute Resolution

FDR – in financial proceedings, a hearing in which the judge gives his opinion and encourages settlement.

If agreement cannot be reached at the initial hearing, it will be necessary to proceed to the FDR. This is likely to be listed at least two months later, by which time both parties should have available all relevant facts and documents. The appointment is led by the **District Judge**, with a view to encouraging the parties to settle. Proposals are usually made on both sides; these are considered by the judge and (if the parties are represented) each of the legal representatives explains their respective positions. The judge is likely to give a view as to which arguments will find favour and may provide an indication of what kind of order he or she would make if the case were to go to trial.

Each party is invited to give their position before the judge gives his or hers. The aim is always to reach agreement, and the judge may be able to suggest a resolution which has not occurred to either party. The parties and their lawyers are then invited to go outside the court to negotiate, and to return to present the outcome to the judge. If the parties are represented, the bulk of the negotiation will be dealt with between the lawyers. This process can be repeated.

The Court cannot impose an outcome on the parties at an FDR, but if agreement is reached it can be drawn up into a consent order then and there, but it is quite usual for the parties to draft a summary of what has been agreed – a **Heads of Agreement** – which the applicant's solicitor can work up into a full order to be sent back to the Court for approval.

If agreement cannot be reached, the judge will issue further directions accordingly and set the case down for a final hearing. The directions will include the date and time of the trial, further documents required (including **Position Statements**) and the preparation of a **Bundle**, the calling of necessary experts, etc.

If there are complicated issues (such as substantial assets owned abroad, joint ownership of properties by third parties or trust funds), a party may wish to seek legal representation at this stage, even if eventually he decides to represent himself.

If agreement cannot be reached at the FDR, the case will have to go to **Trial**. Each party will present evidence and be cross-examined. The Court may also hear evidence from an expert, for example regarding the value of property or assets.

The process will end with the Court making an order which can then be appealed within fourteen days. The parties pay their own costs. If the order is not obeyed by the other party, the applicant will need to start action for **Enforcement**.

Financial Provision Order

While the **Child Maintenance Service** can demand only regular contributions from a liable parent based on income, the Court can order the payment of lump sums from his capital.

Section 15 of the **Children Act 1989** gives the Court jurisdiction to make one of a number of orders under Schedule 1 of the Act in respect of the child on application by anyone who is named in a **Child Arrangements Order** as a person with whom the child is to live:

1. an order requiring one or both parents to make or secure to the applicant or the child periodical payments or a lump sum;
2. an order requiring a settlement of property to be made for the child's benefit;
3. an order requiring either or both parents to transfer property to the applicant or to the child.

In Phillips v Peace [1996] 2 FLR 230, although the Child Support Agency had assessed a father as having no income and, therefore, no liability for child maintenance, the Court made a Schedule 1 order for him to provide the mother with a house for the child's benefit. In 2005, the same mother returned to court (Phillips v Peace [2005] 2 FLR 1212) to argue that she, the child and another child by an unknown father had outgrown the house provided in 1996 and required further capital provision. The Court cited the prohibition in Schedule 1 at 1(5)(b) on the making of more than one order in respect of the same child and held that there was no power to review or vary a property order (Schedule 1 at 1(4) allows variation only of an order for periodic payments).

In W v J (Child: Variation of Financial Provision) [2003] EWHC 2657, a mother sought an increase in financial provision to provide an element for legal fees for proposed future litigation over the child. The Court ruled that Schedule 1 provided no jurisdiction for a payment which would be for the benefit of the parent and not of the child.

Financial Remedies Unit

FRU – a specialist unit within the Family Court comprising seven full-time courts dedicated to the efficient handling of cases of financial complexity.

Financial Remedy

Financial settlement to a spouse on divorce; see **Ancillary Relief.**

Financial Statement

Form E, on which parties to a divorce must disclose their financial details if they wish the Court to make a financial order.

Financial disclosure must be full and frank. Parties cannot keep important items of financial information from their ex or from the Court. If a party is about to receive a pay rise, is about to be made redundant or has spent all the family savings, he must declare it.

The duty of full and frank disclosure lasts until the case is completed; if anything changes after the Form E has been filed, the Court and the other party must be notified.

Before a party sits down to fill out his Form E, he will gather together every item of information regarding his financial situation; corroborative copies – not originals – are then attached to the form and the appropriate boxes are ticked. There is a list towards the end of the form showing what should be included. If any of the requested documentation is not available, letters from an accountant or evidence that the information has been requested must be provided. Failure to provide information will result in additional delay and expense and the information will have to be provided eventually, so it is advisable to do it early, otherwise it will appear that the party is being evasive. The party must then file with the Court and serve on the other party(ies):

1. The fully completed Form E.
2. A statement of the issues in dispute – such as the parties' income and earning capacities, their housing needs, sale of the family home, lump sum payments, maintenance, pensions.
3. A brief **Chronology** of the dispute, including dates of marriage and separation, date of divorce application and any orders, the parties' and children's dates of birth, purchase of property and any other key dates.
4. A **Questionnaire** setting out further information and documents required from the other party, anything he or she has omitted from the Form E, and clarification of anything in the form which seems fishy. Again, things must always be kept relevant. If the Questionnaire is not satisfactorily answered, a more specific version can be sent, referred to as the **Schedule of Deficiencies**.
5. A copy of Form G (this will have to be obtained from the court; it isn't available online), indicating simply whether or not it will be possible to proceed with a **Financial Dispute Resolution** at the **First Directions Appointment**.

Each spouse should check thoroughly the copy of Form E received from the other and, where possible, attempt to verify the information in it. It is possible that they will misrepresent their wealth and downplay their income, while at the same time over-represent their outgoings.

The evidence a party is required to produce on Form E cannot be used by the other party without leave of the Court; however, other evidence provided voluntarily can be used, regardless of the hearing being in chambers. Orders of the Court certainly can be used. The question of confidentiality in ancillary relief (financial remedy) was gone into by Thorpe LJ at some length in Clibbery v Allan [2002] 1FLR 565 CA, and this should be consulted.

Finding-of-Fact

A hearing convened to determine on the **Balance of Probabilities** whether some alleged but disputed **Fact** is really true.

A litigant who wants a Finding-of-Fact hearing must make a written application to the Court of the findings he wishes to be made; he should include the **Evidence** which will support his case and details of any witnesses he intends to call. If the judge decides a Finding-of-Fact is unnecessary and merely uses his discretion to decide the veracity of the allegations on the balance of probability, the decision must be appealed.

Where the applicant admits the allegations or already has a criminal conviction for the abuse alleged, it will be taken as evidence and a Fact-Finding won't be necessary; such a conviction cannot be challenged in the Family Court, even if unjust. If he was found not guilty, the Court will take that as merely not proven and still hold the Fact-Finding because the lower standard of proof means the Court may consider the allegations are warranted. Similarly, if the police decide to take "**No Further Action**" on an allegation, this is not evidence of innocence.

The fundamental precedent is set by Re L, V, M & H (Contact: domestic violence) [2000] EWCA Civ 194, 2 FLR 334/404, in which the Court of Appeal stated that, where allegations of domestic violence might affect the outcome of a Section 8 application, they must be adjudicated upon and found proven or not proven (Fact-Finding hearings are sometimes called "Re L" hearings). Re L also presented an exhaustive analysis of the issue of domestic violence and contact and included a valuable review of the current state (as at 2000) of psychiatric opinion on this topic.

The criteria which should decide whether or not a Finding-of-Fact hearing is appropriate are given in Mr Justice McFarlane's judgment in A County Council v DP, RS, BS (By the Children's Guardian) [2005] EWHC 1593, [2005] 2 FLR 1031 at paragraph 24,

    a) the interests of the child (which are relevant but not paramount);
    b) the time the investigation will take;
    c) the likely cost to public funds;
    d) the evidential result;
    e) the necessity or otherwise of the investigation;
    f) the relevance of the potential result of the investigation to the future care plans for the child;
    g) the impact of any fact-finding process upon the other parties;

h) the prospects of a fair trial on the issue;
i) the justice of the case.

The current *Practice Direction: Residence and Contact Orders: Domestic Violence and Harm [2009] 2 FLR 1400* makes these further points:

i. the decision to hold a Fact-Finding hearing is a judicial one, and not one for CAFCASS or the parties to make or influence;
ii. a Fact-Finding hearing will be necessary only if the fact of the allegations being true or not has a bearing on the order applied for and the case cannot properly be decided without;
iii. if a Fact-Finding is necessary, consideration must be given as to whether it needs to be a **Split Hearing** or should form part of the substantive hearing;
iv. in domestic abuse cases, this means allegations of harm put forward as a reason to deny contact do not automatically require a Fact-Finding; instead, the Court should rigorously apply the guidance in the Practice Direction in considering whether the outcome of any Fact-Finding would affect the decision of the Court, and to what extent.

In the case of Hampshire County Council v Mother & Ors [2014] EWFC B126, mental health workers, a psychotherapist and even the vicar were persuaded to accept a delusional and drug-dependent mother's false allegations at face value despite the lack of evidence. Professionals who should have enabled the mother to care appropriately for her daughter by challenging her delusional thinking instead reinforced it. A Fact-Finding found the allegations to be false, threshold was proved in respect of the mother, but she had made no progress in accepting the findings against her. Residence was transferred to the father with supervised contact.

At the hearing, the Court must make findings-of-fact as to the nature and degree of any domestic abuse alleged and as to its effect on the child and any other relevant person. The findings must be recorded in writing and copied to the parties and to CAFCASS. The Court may then reconsider its earlier directions regarding the Section 7 report, including the necessity for expert witnesses. If the allegations are accepted, the Court should consider the possibility and availability of supervised contact and whether any party should seek advice or treatment (such as a **Domestic Abuse Perpetrator Programme**) as a precondition to any **Child Arrangements Order** (CAO). If evidence is available from the police or a hospital, this must be obtained, and the Court make an order for disclosure. This can take up to twenty-eight days.

The order must be made with regard to the welfare of the child and with the parties present. **Contact** should be ordered only where the safety of the child and the resident parent can be secured. In ordering contact, the Court should direct whether contact is to be **supervised** and, if so, where and by whom, whether any conditions – such as treatment – should be imposed on the applicant, whether contact should be for a specified period and whether the order needs to be reviewed; if so, a date should be set. If the Court considers **Direct Contact** is inappropriate, it should consider **Indirect Contact**. The Court must spell out in its judgment how its findings on the allegations have influenced its decision, and explain, if it has made a CAO, why it takes the view that it is in the best interests of the child to do so.

Typically, the hearing will take a day, and there will then be a wait of some weeks for the judge's report and a further hearing for determination of the application, i.e.: whether or not the applicant will be granted an order in his favour. This is a called a **Split Hearing**. Opportunity must be given to challenge the allegations, which means the party who has made the allegations must take the stand to be cross-examined. If this doesn't happen, the applicant must appeal.

If the allegations are neither admitted nor proven by Finding-of-Fact or a pre-existing conviction, the accuser may not continue to rely on them. If the accuser refuses a Finding-of-Fact, the Court should dismiss the allegations.

Appealing a finding-of-fact is unlikely to succeed. Once a Finding-of-Fact is made, it is difficult to challenge or overturn; only orders, not judgments, can be appealed. In Re V (A Child) [2015] EWCA Civ 274, a father appealed against a fact-finding concerning allegations of domestic violence which had occurred before the child's birth. McFarlane LJ countered that the trial judge "has had the privileged position of seeing the protagonists and using that privileged perspective to inform a conclusion on credibility": the Court of Appeal should not lightly overturn that judgment. The trial judge must still give his reasoning, though "there is no need for an elaborate distillation of each and every point".

Finding-of-Fact hearings are rare – one study of court outcomes didn't find a single one – and there is concern that there are cases where the courts are failing to hold one when it is called for; this is attributed largely to the failures of CAFCASS to manage its workload effectively. Instead of a proper Finding-of-Fact we are seeing CAFCASS carrying out **Risk Assessments**. The Practice Direction should ensure that Finding-of-Fact hearings do take place.

First Directions Appointment

FDA – in financial proceedings, the first meeting with the judge.

This is relatively informal and usually listed for no more than thirty minutes with no evidence examined. The Court will make directions rather than an order so that at the **Financial Dispute Resolution** stage the dispute can be resolved.

Directions will include providing information still outstanding, such as the completed **Questionnaire**, valuations of property, etc. This is why it is important to get all this information together early. If the information is all available, it may be possible to treat the FDA as an FDR and avoid further expense to the parties and taxpayer.

First Hearing & Dispute Resolution Appointment

FHDRA (pronounced F'hydra) – in children proceedings, the first meeting with the judge in which the tone is set for all subsequent proceedings.

A date for the FHDRA should be given in the fifth week – and certainly no later than the sixth – following application. This hearing is also known as the "Directions Hearing" or sometimes the "Conciliation Hearing".

The respondent should be given ten working days' notice, but the Court may abridge this time; the respondent must respond no later than ten working days before the hearing on Form C7, and on Form C1A where there are welfare concerns. All parties attend, with their **Solicitors**, **Litigation Friends** or **McKenzies**; the CAFCASS FCA must attend the hearing even if there are no safeguarding concerns, and speak separately to each party outside the courtroom beforehand.

The hearing will typically be brief – perhaps only thirty minutes – on the assumption that agreement won't be reached so soon. Parties must be organised and have a written list of the directions they want the judge to make to keep him focused and prevent him introducing unnecessary directions or delay. The Court should have before it:

1. the application on Form C100;
2. the applicant's Form C1A (if one has been completed);
3. the respondent's Acknowledgement of Service on Form C7;
4. the respondent's Form C1A (if one has been completed);
5. the Notice of Proceedings on Form C6; and
6. the **Safeguarding Letter** from CAFCASS.

The **Child Arrangements Programme** intends that this hearing will provide the parties with a forum in which they can be helped towards "agreement as to, and understanding of, the issues that divide them. It recognises that, having reached agreement, parties may need assistance in putting it into effect in a co-operative way". At the FHDRA the Court must consider:

Mediation

How many of the issues can safely be resolved through the assistance of the FCA or a mediator and in collaboration with the Court? If a **MIAM** has not taken place or becomes appropriate during the case, the Court may stop proceedings at any point and order the parties to attend.

In **Section 8** applications, once the issues have been stated, and the CAFCASS report produced, the parties will be encouraged, with the support of the FCA, mediator and judge, to explore the possibility of reaching agreement on some or all of the disputed matters. Court time is expensive and should be kept to a minimum. Other options will be considered such as further intervention by CAFCASS, the use of **Collaborative Law** or a **Parenting Plan**, or the Court may send parents to a **Separated Parents Information Programme**.

Safeguarding

The Court will inform the parties of the safeguarding letter and its contents unless to do so would expose the child or a party to harm. If either party has completed a C1A Form alleging domestic abuse, the judge can order a **Risk Assessment** or **Fact-Finding Hearing** to determine the truth or nature of such allegations, though this may need to be requested and such hearings are rare.

The Court can also direct the local authority to undertake an investigation under **Section 47** of the Children Act where there is reasonable cause to suspect a child is suffering or likely to suffer **Significant Harm**. In extreme cases, where the Court considers it may be appropriate to take a child into care, it will direct the local authority to undertake a **Section 37** investigation into the child's circumstances.

Consent Orders

The majority of cases are resolved through mutual agreement or mediation and the judge making a **Consent Order**, that is, one to which both parties consent. A consent order is made only under the Court's scrutiny and cannot be approved unless it is confirmed that safeguarding checks have been completed or the safeguarding duty of CAFCASS under Section 16A CA1989 is not required.

If further assessments or reports are necessary, proceedings must be delayed for no longer than twenty-eight days to a fixed date, but CAFCASS must provide written justification. If the evidence supplied to the Court is satisfactory, the order can be made without the parties present.

Reports

In **Section 8** applications, the judge may order a welfare report under **Section 7** of the Children Act. Full welfare reports should be ordered only where there are welfare concerns and other measures such as mediation or parenting classes have been tried, though they are often ordered where there are no such concerns. They introduce considerable delay: it can take a couple of months to find an FCA to undertake the report, and another three to nine months for them to complete it. **Delay** within CAFCASS is so severe in some areas that judges no longer order s.7 reports even where there are welfare concerns.

The Court must direct in the order that the report be limited to the specific factual and other issues still in dispute. The Court can direct CAFCASS to prepare:

1. a **"Needs, Wishes and Feelings"** report within six weeks;
2. a single-issue report within six weeks;
3. a report covering more than one issue within six to twelve weeks depending on complexity;
4. a risk assessment within six to eight weeks.

All of these reports are enabled under Section 7 CA1989, but only 3 is recognizably a Section 7 report. They must be prepared according to the **Welfare Checklist**.

It is also at this hearing that a party who wants an expert witness called should invite the judge to make appropriate directions. The Court will then consider whether obtaining expert evidence is necessary.

Wishes & Feelings

The CAP expects the child's wishes to be taken into account and the child to be informed of the proceedings and their outcome. The Court must consider how the child's view will be incorporated into proceedings and whether the child should be joined as a party to the application. If the Court is considering whether it should appoint a **Children's Guardian**, it must first discuss this with CAFCASS to determine how long it will take for one to become available and how much this will delay proceedings.

Case Management

It is vital the Court manages the case effectively to ensure identification of the issues in dispute and that only they should then inform proceedings. The Court must move swiftly to the directions it will make before further resolution can be achieved and make interim orders where it can while awaiting the reports it has directed. The **Final Hearing** must be listed as soon as practicable. At the end of the first hearing, the Court will set a date for the next. This is supposed to prevent the delay which so often blights proceedings but, unfortunately, the process rarely runs smoothly and there will be cancelled, delayed and additional hearings.

Allocation

The Court should observe **Judicial Continuity**, allocating the case to a judge who can preside over it from FHDRA through to final hearing. If the Court decides to re-allocate or transfer proceedings to another court (though this is not always possible), it must give its reasons and make directions.

Orders

If no final order is made, the Court must make case management directions regarding the future progression of the case and record them on Form CAP02. The parties should not leave court without a copy. It will record the following:

a)   whether the MIAM requirements have been complied with;

b)   where a claimed MIAM exemption is not valid, a direction to attend, unless the Court considers it inappropriate;

c)   that non-court dispute resolution has been considered;

d)   timetabling and case management, including listing the next hearing, which is normally the **Dispute Resolutions Appointment** but could be the final hearing;

e)   the issues about which the parties are agreed;

f)   the issues which remain to be resolved;

g)   the steps the Court plans to resolve the issues;

h)   any interim arrangements pending such resolution, including, in Section 8 applications, arrangements for the involvement of children;

i)   the timetable for such steps and, where this involves further hearings, the date of such hearings;

j) a statement as to any facts relating to risk or safety; in so far as they are resolved the result will be stated and, in so far as not resolved, the steps to be taken to resolve them will be stated;

k) whether the parties are to be assisted by participation in mediation, SPIPs, or other types of intervention, and to detail any activity directions or conditions imposed by the Court;

l) the date, time and venue of the next hearing.

Forensic

Pertaining to or taking place in open court.

Forum Conveniens

(Latin: "the convenient or appropriate forum"); the question of which jurisdiction should hear a case so as to best serve the interests of the parties and of justice.

The corresponding rule of *Forum Non Conveniens* grants a court discretionary power to decline jurisdiction if the parties are aliens and there is an alternative and more appropriate jurisdiction in which litigation will achieve the ends of justice.

The doctrine originated in 17th century Scotland and spread to England in the 19th century. The European Court of Justice ruled in 2005 that the Brussels Convention prevented a court from declining jurisdiction and the rule was superseded by the European "first in time" rule which meant the party who petitioned first secured jurisdiction.

Foster-to-Adopt

A fast-track procedure enabling a local authority to make a placement of a child with an approved prospective adopter.

It is made under Section 2 of the Children and Families Act 2014 even where no **Placement Order** has been made when the LA is either considering the child for adoption or satisfied the child should be placed for adoption. No proceedings are necessary, and the parents have no opportunity to take legal advice.

The legislation also repealed the requirement to give due consideration to a child's religious persuasion, racial origin and cultural and linguistic background when placing him or her for adoption. This was intended to speed up the adoption process but was a controversial development.

It means that if the child does need to be adopted, it is already placed with the adopter and needs not be moved again nor risk forming a relationship with a foster carer which will later be lost. It reassures the Court that a secure placement has already been found and enables the adopters to get to know the child before making a final commitment.

But it also persuades everyone involved that the adoption is already a *fait accompli*, merely awaiting the rubber-stamp of the Court's approval; it encourages the Court to make an inappropriate comparison between the child's life at home and with the adopters; it enables the child to bond with the foster carers so that removal and return to its family seems unworkable; by eliminating delay it risks an unsuitable placement which will later break down or emotional devastation to the foster carers if the adoption isn't finally approved.

Concerns raised about this legislation were dismissed, but opponents say it gets the balance wrong between reducing delay and serving the interests of justice. It bypasses legal process and denies parents the opportunity to seek legal advice. By the time the case reaches court, the child is settled in the new home. It also bypasses the requirement on an LA to consider placement with a suitable relative, and removes the usual safeguards designed to keep siblings together, place children near to their family home, avoid disrupting education and provide accommodation suitable for disabled children.

Freeing Order

The court order which frees a child for **Adoption**.

Applications to revoke a Freeing Order are made to the same court which made the order using Form A4 on which the applicant must set out the reasons she wishes to resume **Parental Responsibility** for the child. She cannot make the application sooner than twelve months from the original order.

Freemen on the Land

A legal cult which began in Canada in 2008, spreading to the US and Britain soon thereafter; its members imagine that western democracies such as Britain and the US operate, not under Civil Law, but under Maritime/Admiralty Law which operates as a form of contract, binding them only if they consent, and that they themselves are bound only by **Common Law**; they consider themselves independent of governmental jurisdiction and lawfully entitled even to refuse arrest.

A Freeman believes that, in common with all legal documents, a birth certificate robs him of his personal liberty, but only if his name is in capital letters; his name in lower case letters represents the real man. Because the birth certificate is imposed on an infant, the contract thus formed between the infant and the state is illegitimate.

Freemen believe that in all legal dealings, the state engages only with this persona – referred to as the "Straw Man" – represented by the birth certificate. Freemen have a distinctive way of expressing themselves using quaint turns of phrase and extravagant use of capitalisation.

In Doncaster Metropolitan Borough Council v Haigh [2011] EWHC B16 Vicky Haigh, a trainer of race horses, had alleged that her daughter was being abused by the girl's father. Vicky fell in with a Freewoman called Elizabeth Watson who encouraged her not to engage with the legal process and used Haigh to further her own agenda. The result was that Haigh lost contact with her daughter entirely and was banned for two years from making further applications; she was eventually gaoled for three years by Lord Justice Wall, following a chance encounter with her daughter at a petrol station, though she was later released early and reunited with her second child. Watson was imprisoned for nine months for contempt but released after ten days (Doncaster Metropolitan Borough Council v Watson [2011] EWHC B15).

In Re A Child [2015] EWFC B34, the parents apparently believed that not giving their child a name would ensure she had no legal existence and deny the Court any jurisdiction over her; they had placed her, they believed, into a Private Trust. They were mistaken: had they engaged properly with the legal process they might very well have kept their daughter; by considering themselves beyond the law, they lost her.

Freezing Order

An order which freezes a party's assets and prevents their removal from the jurisdiction.

Full Hearing

See **Final Hearing**.

Functus Officio

(Latin: "having performed his office") the status of a judge who has done his job and fulfilled his office; it is related to the doctrine of **Res Judicata** which applies to a case that has been judged. Once the order of the Court has been drawn up and sealed, the judge has no jurisdiction to reopen the case or change his mind; should he change his mind before then, he should give the parties opportunity to make further submissions.

G

Gaslighting

A form of domestic abuse in which the victim is made to doubt her own memory and sanity – named after the 1944 film *Gaslight*, starring Ingrid Bergman.

Gatekeeping (1)

All applications to the family justice system are passed to a "gatekeeping team" consisting of a Designated Family Judge, a justices' clerk and as many legal advisors and District Judges as are necessary. They are expected to consider the application within one working day of receipt.

Their role is to ensure the application is satisfactory and that the case is handled throughout by the most suitable court; this will normally be the Magistrates' Court unless the case is complex. There may also be a case-management judge who oversees the case. The team will consider the following criteria:

1. the need to make the most effective and efficient use of local judicial resources, given the nature and type of application;
2. the requirement to minimise **Delay**;
3. the need for **Judicial Continuity**;
4. the location of the parties and any child subject to proceedings; and
5. the complexity of the case.

If the gatekeeping judge isn't satisfied that mediation has been attempted, he can make directions for the applicant to attend a **MIAM**. If he thinks it required, he may give directions for an accelerated hearing. He may also give directions for further evidence. Directions on Allocation will be given on Form CAP01.

Gatekeeping (2)

The behaviour of a parent who believes she has the right to control the other parent's access to his child.

Common tactics by parents who think contact is unimportant can include claiming that a child is ill or making other arrangements – for a children's party, football practice, to see grandparents, etc. Some parents will arrange after-school activities every day of the week and throughout the weekend; as a consequence, children become exhausted and their school work deteriorates.

Perhaps the most common obstacle is the self-appointed **Primary Carer** who seeks to control contact, dictating not only times but also what the other parent does during those times, insisting they be told where they are and where they are going, and demanding regular telephone calls with the child. This behaviour is unhealthy and likely to result in conflict and, eventually, litigation.

The reasons for gatekeeping are complex. Some derive from cultural norms: the belief that a mother is rightly the primary carer of a child; some mothers, having carried a child for nine months, given birth and breast-fed, tend to see their child as an extension of their own bodies and cannot imagine that anyone else can love or care for their child as they do:

> My children are little bits of me walking this earth; always will be mine and mine completely and nobody will ever be able to love them, understand them, care for them and spoil them to the core as I do... I'm the one who had a VERY hard time letting go of the control that I have on every aspect of their life, as the primary care giver.

Some motives are more reasonable: the mother may believe, rightly or wrongly, that the father will not return the child on time, or even at all, that his home isn't suitable or that it's inappropriate for the child to meet his new partner. A **Non-Resident Parent** needs to understand why contact is being impeded and the concerns – sometimes legitimate – the resident parent may have. A father who left the relationship early in his child's life, or who has limited contact following separation, has little experience of hands-on parenting. It takes a leap of faith for an over-protective mother to hand her child over. If she feels abandoned or blames him for the break-down of the relationship, it is understandable there should be difficulties with contact.

The father should tread sensitively, while at the same time focusing on his child's need for a meaningful relationship with him. It is important for him to understand why the mother is unwilling to share parenting; it is easy to allege **Parental Alienation** or **Implacable Hostility** and make heavy-handed applications when empathetic mediation would be a more constructive approach.

The first response should be to express surprise that more notice wasn't given and to agree to change the contact to another date. If a child is genuinely ill, the non-resident parent should be kept informed. He should say simply how sorry he is to hear it, how disappointed he is not to be able to see his child, and how he respects the decision; a get-well card is a good way to show he is thinking of his child. He should telephone regularly to enquire after the child's health and suggest a new date for contact, such as the following weekend. Any agreement should be confirmed by letter.

If the practice becomes a habit and the child's health, development and educational progress start to suffer, a more robust approach will be necessary and a return to court may be called for. The resident parent must understand the child's developmental needs and not burden the child with her own insecurities. Both parents must learn to respect that each other's parenting time is their own, to use as they see fit. Parents often have very different ideas about appropriate parenting, but neither should make any attempt to control the other or interfere.

Gender Recognition Certificate

The Gender Recognition Act 2004 makes provision for transsexual persons to submit an application to the Gender Recognition Panel to enable them to be legally recognised in their adopted gender. Successful applicants receive a Gender Recognition Certificate or, in cases where the individual is married or in a civil partnership, an interim Gender Certificate.

As part of the evidence currently required, individuals must demonstrate to the Panel that they have been living in their acquired gender for two years or more. It is not necessary for the individual to have undergone surgery.

The certificate is valid for a period of six months from the date on which it is issued and in Scotland under Section 1(1)(b) of the Divorce (Scotland) Act 1976 may be used by an individual's spouse or civil partner as grounds for **Divorce**. The Interim Certificate is lodged with the local Sheriff Court together with an initial **Writ** drafted by the solicitor. The Court then clarifies with the Gender Recognition Panel that the Certificate is genuine and thereafter the divorce is granted, provided the Court is satisfied suitable arrangements are in place for any children of the marriage or civil partnership.

Gillick Competence

The capacity of a child to understand his own case, named after the case Gillick v West Norfolk and Wisbech Health Authority [1986] AC 112, which concerned the prescription of contraceptives to a minor without her parents' knowledge or consent.

The basis of Gillick Competence is a child's intellectual development; thus, one child might be adamant at eight-years-old about her wishes, whilst another child of thirteen or fourteen might not. The "Gillick Principle" reads as follows,

> In the Health realm, children are considered competent to make decisions on their own behalf when they are capable of understanding fully the nature of what is proposed. A competent child's refusal should not be overridden, save in exceptional circumstances. The decision as to whether a child is Gillick Competent will usually be taken by health care professionals involved in the child's care, sometimes with input from clinical psychologists, teachers etc.

In practice, Gillick Competence is a redundant concept because a child under sixteen cannot be expected to understand complex legal or medical matters. Where a child lacks competence and a parent gives him medical treatment while in his care, he is required to consult with the other parent; if the treatment is an emergency, he needn't consult, but must still tell the other parent afterwards. Where a medical decision must be made, the law requires the consent of all those with PR. In Re J [2000] 1 FLR 571 (a **Circumcision** case), Butler-Sloss established the principle,

> *[31]* There is in my view a small group of important decisions made on behalf of a child which, in the absence of agreement of those with parental responsibility, ought not to be carried out or arranged by one parent carer... Such a decision ought not to be made without the specific approval of the court.

The case confirmed that a court would not in any circumstances order an unnecessary medical procedure on a child too young to consent.

Once a child reaches the age of sixteen, Section 8 of the Family Reform Act 1969 provides that a minor's consent to any surgical, medical or dental treatment "shall be as effective as it would be if he were of full age", though it can still be overruled by a court having regard to the paramountcy of his welfare.

In Re E (A Minor) (Wardship: Medical Treatment) [1993] 1 FLR 386, the Court found that the fifteen-and-a-half-year-old child of Jehovah's Witnesses who was refusing a blood transfusion could not be Gillick Competent because he had no realisation "of the full implications which lie before him as to the process of dying". When he reached eighteen, the courts could no longer intervene and were obliged to let him die.

If one parent objects to medical treatment, such as vaccination, the treatment will not go ahead until the Court has ruled otherwise. To prevent treatment, a parent should apply for a **Prohibited Steps Order**; if he wants treatment opposed by the other parent he should apply for a **Specific Issues Order**. The Court will rule according to the child's welfare, so case precedent must be used or an expert witness to put the case.

In Re C & F (Children) [2003] EWHC 1376 (subsequently heard as Re B (Child) [2003] EWCA Civ 1148 by the Court of Appeal) Sumner J undertook a detailed and comprehensive analysis of the competing scientific arguments surrounding vaccination, but in F v F [2013] EWHC 2683, and again in Re SL [2017] EWHC 125, no medical evidence was heard because it all pointed to the benefits of vaccination and the children's welfare was the paramount consideration.

Grandparents

Grandparents are often caught in the fallout from relationship breakdown and can lose contact with a grandchild, particularly when their own child is being excluded. If that parent's contact can be restored then the grandparent's contact will, in most cases, automatically follow.

A grandparent should be wary of getting too involved and making the situation worse; it can be best to take a step back, remain neutral and offer support. Very often the best thing she can do is to support her son or daughter's application for **Child Arrangements** and give them all the emotional support and love she can at what is a traumatic time for the family. If she is able, she can also provide practical and financial support; a grandparent can provide valuable assistance facilitating handovers or even supervising contact.

A court application should be the last resort: it is always best to resolve disputes out of court and **Mediation** should be attempted first. Grandparents are at a disadvantage because they have no formal legal right to contact with their grandchildren and it is necessary for them to apply for **Leave** from the Court before making a **Section 8** application. The parent may object, in which case the Court must be persuaded, usually by way of a hearing, that the grandparent has had a meaningful and ongoing relationship with the grandchild and it is in his best interests for this relationship to continue.

Even when courts allow grandparents contact they commonly order that their contact runs concurrently with the parent's; obviously, if the parent is getting minimal contact, that will impact the grandparent, so it is worthwhile applying for separate contact, bearing in mind the Court may suspect her of trying to win contact for her son or daughter through the back door. If she does decide to pursue an application, she will need to accept it will be an unpleasant, prolonged and stressful experience.

The application for leave is made on Form C2. Under Section 10(9) of the Children Act, the Court must consider:

1. the nature of the application;
2. the grandparent's connection with the child;
3. any risk that the application may disrupt the child's life to the extent that **Harm** is caused; and
4. where the child is in local authority care, the authority's plans for the child's future and the wishes and feelings of the parents.

If court proceedings are already on-going in respect of the child, the grandparent can also request at Question 6, with the leave of the Court, to be made a party to them. She must attach to her application a completed Form C100. At Question 3 she must give details of both parents, and at Question 7 detail the **Child Arrangements Order** she wants the Court to make.

At some stage in the process she may be interviewed by a CAFCASS case worker. She will need to present her family as close-knit and normal, and her child as a loving and committed parent, emphasising the close bonds between herself and her child and her involvement in the life of the grandchild.

There are situations in which a grandparent may apply to be the main carer for a child; there are a number of precedents which can be used.

In Re J (A Child) (Leave to issue application for Residence Order) [2002] EWCA Civ 1346, the mother was a psychiatric in-patient and the local authority wanted to place her eighteen-month-old daughter for adoption. An older child had largely been raised by the paternal grandparents and, to a lesser extent, by the maternal grandmother and was about to go to university. The local authority had rejected the grandmother as a possible carer due to her volatile relationship with her daughter and her age, fifty-nine. It said the application did not merit judicial consideration. Nevertheless, the grandmother applied to be **Joined** as a party and for leave to apply for residence; the mother supported the application as had the father prior to the LA's objection.

The lower Court had not adequately considered the Section 10(9) checklist; the question for the Court (at Paragraph 18) was, "has the applicant satisfied the court that he or she has a good arguable case for the criteria that Parliament applied in section 10(9)?" The Court allowed the application, accorded the grandmother party status and allowed her to make an application for residence.

In Re C (A Child) [2009] EWCA Civ 72, a CAFCASS guardian appealed against a decision to place a five-year-old child with his seventy-year-old paternal grandmother rather than send him for adoption. The appeal was dismissed because (Paragraph 19),

1. the law was biased in favour of placements with the child's wider family;
2. the grandmother had demonstrated her commitment to the child and had a good relationship with him; and
3. the grandmother wanted to promote continuing contact between the child and his half-sister with whom he had spent his life.

The first case to be reported from the new **Supreme Court**, Re B (A Child) [2009] UKSC 5, overturned a decision from the **Court of Appeal**, Re B (A Child) [2009] EWCA Civ 545, which itself had reversed a decision of the Family Proceedings Court in the grandmother's favour. The case confirmed residence of a four-year-old boy with his grandmother rather than transfer to his father.

The grandmother had been the primary carer for most of the boy's life, while the father had served time for assault. The FPC ruling had not been "plainly wrong" and the Court of Appeal had erred in overturning it; it had also misinterpreted Re G [2006] UKHL 43: biological parenthood was a contributor to a child's welfare but there was no presumption in its favour and the child's welfare remained paramount. The boy's current stability depended on the bond with his grandmother.

Many grandparents are their grandchildren's primary carers but haven't formalised the relationship and find they have difficulties with schools and medical authorities, etc. Although they don't have **Parental Responsibility** they are advised to apply for a **Special Guardianship Order** which will place them in a much stronger position with regard to schools and doctors. If the Court refuses, using the **No-Order Principle**, B v B (A Minor) (Residence Order) [1992] 2 FLR 327 can be used, which showed such an order to be in the child's best interests.

Grepe v Loam Order

A civil restraint order preventing a **Vexatious Litigant** who has made a number of financial applications without **Merit** from making further applications. Named after the case Grepe v Loam (1887) 37 Ch D 168; see K v K [2015] EWCA Civ 583,

[37] This further attempt by the father to re-litigate, yet again, matters which have already been concluded against him, demonstrates not merely the continuing need for the Section 91(14) Order but also the need for a corresponding order to prevent him making further applications without permission in relation to the financial matters... In relation to that I propose therefore to make a Grepe v Loam order... The Grepe v Loam order should provide, and the section 91(14) order should be amended to provide, that

all future applications, including any applications by the father for permission to apply, are reserved to the President of the Family Division unless released by the President to a judge of the Division.

Ground Rules Hearing

A hearing to determine whether a witness is vulnerable and if so what support or adjustments they need (e.g., use of a video link) to be able to give evidence without inhibition.

Guardian

A person with the legal authority and duty to care for the person and property of a "ward".

Historically guardianship of legitimate children lay with fathers and of **Illegitimate** children with mothers. It combined legal authority over a child with a duty of care. A father could appoint another man to acquire guardianship on his death and, in 1886, the Guardianship of Infants Act allowed a mother to become her child's guardian, but only jointly with whomever the father had appointed. The Court became "the guardian of all infants, in the place of a parent, and as if it were the parent of a child, thus superseding the natural guardianship of the parent", Regina v Gyngall [1893] 2 QB 232.

The 1925 Guardianship of Infants Act gave married women powers equal to their husbands' over their legitimate children to apply to the Court over any issue regarding their children, equal rights to appoint guardians after their deaths, and the right to receive maintenance from fathers. The Act drew the line, however, at making mothers "joint guardians" and a father remained sole legal guardian of his legitimate children, while such equality as it gave mothers depended on their making an application to the Court.

Under Section 2(4) of the **Children Act 1989**, the centuries-old rule of law that a father was the natural guardian of his legitimate child was finally abolished.

If a child has no living parent with **Parental Responsibility** or, if a parent named in a **Child Arrangements Order** as the parent with whom the child is to live dies while the order is in effect, another adult may apply to the Court under Section 5 CA1989 to be made a guardian of that child. A parent with PR may nominate in writing another adult to be guardian in the event of the parent's death; the document must be signed and dated. A person appointed as guardian will acquire PR for the child.

The **High Court** has an ancient power under its **Inherent Jurisdiction** to place a child under its protection as a "ward of court" if it is proportionate and necessary, so that no important decision may be made on behalf of the child without the Court's consent. In particular, it may concern children who have been abducted or who have been ordered to be returned from a foreign state, or children subject to disputed medical treatment. It can be a useful tool in especially complex or conflicted private law cases, see T v S (Wardship) [2011] EWHC 1608, [2012] 1 FLR 230. Custody of the child becomes vested in the Court, while day-to-day care becomes the responsibility of the local authority. The Court's powers are restricted under Section 100 CA1989 and it cannot use wardship to place a child into the care of the local authority or where a power under the Act could achieve the same objective.

Application supported by an **Affidavit** can be made by any person "with a genuine interest in or relation to the child", such as an LA, with **Leave**, where **Significant Harm** would otherwise result; a parent – usually where there is a fear of abduction; or a hospital trust. The child becomes a ward as soon as the application is made, and the respondent(s) must be served and return an acknowledgement of service; a hearing must be held within twenty-one days to confirm wardship or it will lapse. See Practice Direction 12D.

Guardian *ad Litem*

See **Children's Guardian.**

H

Habitual Residence

The jurisdiction in which someone voluntarily lives for his work or education and where he conducts his family life.

Normally it will be where he has lived for the previous twelve months. Holidaying abroad does not change his habitual residence.

Identifying a child's habitual residence is vital in many cases in order to determine which court has jurisdiction to make decisions on the child's behalf and apply the legal protections provided by the 1980 **Hague Convention** on the Civil Aspects of International Child Abduction (which does not define the term). Recent case law has introduced significant changes in how the courts approach these matters; the traditional position was described in Dickson v Dickson [1990] SCLR 692:

> A person can, we think, have only one habitual residence at one time and in the case of a child, who can form no intention of his own, it is the residence which is chosen for him by his parents. If they are living together with him, then they will have their residence in the same place. Where the parents separate... the child's habitual residence cannot be changed by one parent unless the other consents to the change.

The principle of consent was shown to be wrong, however, in Re R (Children) [2015] UKSC 35; [2016] AC 760. Similarly, Re LC (Children) [2014] UKSC 1; [2014] AC 1038 confirmed the European position that a child's habitual residence does not automatically follow that of the parent with whom he lives.

When a child is removed from his habitual residence by a parent who has no intention of returning him, he has traditionally been considered immediately to have lost his habitual residence.

It is reasonable to suppose that in order for the child to acquire a new habitual residence there must be a degree of integration into the new country. In Feder v Evans-Feder, 63 F3d 217, 224 (CA 3, 1995), for example, the US Appeal Court held that "a child's habitual residence is the place where he or she had been physically present for an amount of time sufficient for acclimatization and which has a degree of settled purpose from the child's perspective". Lord Brandon noted in Re J (A Minor) (Abduction: Custody Rights) [1990] 2 AC 562,

> A person may cease to be habitually resident in country A in a single day if he or she leaves it with a settled intention not to return to it but to take up long-term residence in country B instead. Such a person cannot, however, become habitually resident in country B in a single day. An appreciable period of time and a settled intention will be necessary to enable him or her to become so.

The flaw in this approach was that it potentially left a child for a time in a "jurisdictional limbo" in which he was not protected by the provisions of the Convention. In Re T (A Child: Article 15 of B2R) [2013] EWHC 521, Nicholas Mostyn rejected the convention that a child automatically acquired his mother's habitual residence on the grounds that the child had never spent a day of his life in his mother's country and that actual physical presence was a prerequisite. T had not acquired habitual residence in the UK either, and Mostyn concluded that he therefore had *no* habitual residence.

The steady rise in cases involving parents of different nationalities and sometimes complicated international issues has created a need to harmonise the law in different jurisdictions. With the adoption of the European concept of habitual residence into English/Welsh law it has been necessary for the courts to reconsider the point at which habitual residence is lost, illustrated by a number of cases in the Supreme Court, which has grappled with the argument over whether habitual residence is a matter of fact or of law.

In the case of A v A, the High Court ordered the return to the UK of three children born in England and a fourth, Haroon, who had never been present in the country, but had been born in Pakistan where his mother had been held against her wishes. The mother maintained Haroon was British or had his habitual residence in the UK. The Court of Appeal allowed the father to appeal against his return on the grounds that habitual residence was a matter of fact which required physical presence in the country and didn't derive from the parents' habitual residence.

Habitual Residence

In A v A (Children: Habitual Residence) [2013] UKSC 60; [2014] AC 1, the Supreme Court unanimously allowed the mother's appeal, holding that Haroon's British nationality gave it **Inherent Jurisdiction** to make an order and remitted the case back to the High Court. Lady Justice Hale concluded,

> [54] (i) All are agreed that habitual residence is a question of fact and not a legal concept such as domicile. There is no legal rule akin to that whereby a child automatically takes the domicile of his parents.
>
> (iii) The test adopted by the European Court is "the place which reflects some degree of integration by the child in a social and family environment" in the country concerned. This depends upon numerous factors, including the reasons for the family's stay in the country in question.
>
> [55] It is one thing to say that a person can remain habitually resident in a country from which he is temporarily absent. It is another thing to say that a person can acquire a habitual residence without ever setting foot in a country. It is one thing to say that a child is integrated in the family environment of his primary carer and siblings. It is another thing to say that he is also integrated into the social environment of a country where he has never been.

The Court cited two European cases, *Proceedings brought by A* and Mercredi v Chaffe [2012] Fam 22, which, more than the English courts, "focussed on the situation of the child, with the purposes and intentions of the parents being merely one of the relevant factors". To be habitually resident, the child required some integration, but not full integration; it was "possible" for a child to have no habitual residence, but only in "exceptional" circumstances.

The current position is established by Re B (A Child) [2016] UKSC 4. The parties had lived in a same-sex relationship but without civil partnership or marriage; the child, B, had been conceived through IUI. On 3rd February 2014, the biological mother, a British national of Pakistani ethnicity with sole parental responsibility, lawfully took B to live in Pakistan. Unaware, the non-biological mother had applied for shared residence; her application depended on the child being habitually resident in England at the time. She had no recourse to the Pakistani courts which did not recognise same-sex relationships, so she applied that B be made a ward of the English court.

In July 2014, Mrs Justice Hogg dismissed both applications, ruling that the child had lost her habitual residence on removal to Pakistan and the Court thus had no jurisdiction, and in August the Court of Appeal dismissed the appeal.

On 3rd February 2016, however, the Supreme Court ruled with a majority of three to two that B's habitual residence had still been in England. Hogg's ruling meant an application intended to protect her relationship with one of her parents had been dismissed "without any appraisal of B's welfare; without any knowledge of her current situation; without any collection of her wishes and feelings; and in circumstances in which no such applications can be entertained in any other court".

Wilson LJ concluded that it was "highly unlikely, albeit conceivable, that a child will be in the limbo in which the courts below have placed B". He imagined a see-saw: as the child put down roots in the new jurisdiction so her roots in the old came up. Habitual residence was "overarchingly a question of fact" influenced by the depth of the child's roots in the old jurisdiction, the degree to which the parent had planned the move and whether any members of the child's family remained in the old jurisdiction or moved with him. Hogg J had "fallen into error" through allowing Lord Brandon's observation in Re J to guide her.

Wilson weighed up the factors both enabling and preventing her disengagement from her English environment, concluding that at the time of application she was still habitually resident in England. It was not in her interest to be without a habitual residence, and she had not yet acquired it in Pakistan. Traditional English law had relied on a parent's intention, but this was not consonant with international law which required a degree of integration by the child into her new environment. Recital 12 of BIIR required the Court to take the path which best served the child's interests,

> [56] ...it makes no sense to regard a person's intention... at the moment when the aeroplane leaves the ground as precipitating, at that moment, a loss of habitual residence. At all events, and more importantly, I remain clear that such is not the modern law.

Lady Justice Hale and Lord Justice Toulson agreed; the Lords Justice Sumption and Clarke dissented.

Hadkinson Order

A rare and draconian case-management order of last resort which prohibits a party from making further applications in a case until an existing order has been complied with. The justification is that the party himself is impeding the course of justice. Named after Hadkinson v Hadkinson [1952] P 285 CA. Also known as an "unless" order.

Hague Convention

One of several international agreements, in particular the 1980 Convention on the Civil Aspects of International Child Abduction, which was originally brought into UK law by the Child Abduction and Custody Act 1985, the 1993 Convention on Inter-Country Adoption and the 1996 Convention on Jurisdiction, Applicable Law, Recognition, Enforcement and Cooperation in respect of Parental Responsibility and Measures for the Protection of Children which provides for the co-ordination of legal systems and for international judicial and administrative cooperation and which came into force in November 2012.

The Hague Conventions apply in a wider number of countries than **Brussels II Revised** (BIIR). Where there is overlap BIIR takes precedence. The Hague Convention (Article 12) demands that—

> Where a child has been wrongfully removed or retained... and, at the date of the commencement of the proceedings before the judicial or administrative authority of the Contracting State where the child is, a period of less than one year has elapsed from the date of the wrongful remove or retention, the authority concerned shall order the return of child forthwith.

> The judicial or administrative authority, even where the proceedings have been commenced after the expiration of the period of one year... shall also order the return of the child, unless it is demonstrated that the child is now settled in its new environment.

All applications to return under the 1980 Hague Convention must be made to the High Court and not to the single Family Court.

TLMP v AWP [2012] CSOH 121 is a case from the Scots jurisdiction which raises some important Hague principles. The petitioner sought return of a child under Article 12. The defendant father argued that the mother had agreed to the child's removal. The Court found the child had been wrongfully retained and ordered return but suggested the Californian court should inquire as soon as possible into whether the child's long-term interests were best served by residence with his mother or father. The Court held:

1. prompt return under the Convention is in the child's best interests and thus Article 8 of the **European Convention on Human Rights** is not violated;
2. where there is dispute over consent, the burden of proof is on the abducting parent on the balance of probability; where there is no proof either way, the Court cannot conclude that arrangements were agreed;

3. the child could not be shown to be **Settled** in his new environment because it was not known how he functioned emotionally without his mother; and

4. the defendant failed to establish the child would be at risk or would otherwise be placed in an intolerable situation were he to be returned.

When proceedings commence within a year of wrongful removal, the child must be returned.

(Article 12) The child's welfare remains paramount, and the Hague principle cannot be applied automatically or mechanically. Article 13 states that return is not required where it would "expose the child to physical or psychological harm or otherwise place the child in an intolerable situation".

When a year has elapsed, the child must be returned unless it can be demonstrated that he is "settled in his new environment".

Abduction cases thus depend on how the courts interpret the phrase "settled in his new environment". The defendant must be able to show that the present situation "imports stability when looking into the future", and has developed an attachment to the new country – whether through marriage, family, employment, etc. The term "new environment" encompasses place, home, school, people, friends, activities and opportunities but not, per se, the relationship with the defendant parent; see Re N (Minors) (Abduction) [1991] 1FLR 413 per Bracewell J at 417H-41HB.

Where a period greater than a year has elapsed before an application for return is made, the Court must consider the reason for this delay, particularly where the defendant parent has concealed the whereabouts of the child from the other. In such cases, the onus on the defendant to demonstrate that the child is settled is greatly increased; the Court must look critically at claims which are built on concealment and deceit, particularly where the defendant is a fugitive from justice in their home country.

In Re R (Child Abduction: Acquiescence) [1995] 1 FLR 716, Balcombe J ruled that in normal circumstances it is generally in a child's best interests promptly to be returned and that only in exceptional cases should a court exercise its discretion not to return. The Court should consider a child's views as likely to be influenced by the abductor – and by the knowledge that return could result in the abductor's arrest and imprisonment – and little weight should be given to them. This principle is overturned only by the demonstration that the child's views are clearly his own, and that determination will depend heavily on the CAFCASS report.

Thorpe approved Balcombe's observation in Zaffino v Zaffino (Abduction: Children's Views) [2005] EWCA Civ 1012, [2006] 1 FLR 410: in 2002 a French court ordered the mother residence and the father contact. The father appealed, but relocated to the UK prior to the hearing, so the appeal was dismissed. Contact continued intermittently. In 2005, father and son, both now in the UK, jointly applied for a variation of the order; the mother countered with an application for sole residence which was granted, she also applied under the Convention for the son's return.

The High Court found that the son objected to return, he was of sufficient age and maturity for his views to be taken into account; the judge did not order return, exercising his discretion under Article 13, Paragraph 2 of the Convention,

> The judicial or administrative authority may also refuse to order the return of the child if it finds that the child objects to being returned and has attained an age and degree of maturity at which it is appropriate to take account of its views.

The mother appealed. Thorpe and Wall LLJ allowed the appeal and ordered return. The trial judge had erred in exercising his discretion and had given insufficient weight to the order of the French court; the strong presumption was that children should be returned. Discretion to refuse return could only be used in exceptional cases, and although the child's opinion carried weight, the abduction was patent, it was clearly a French case, and French proceedings were on-going. The trial judge had satisfied the requirement that he be "plainly wrong".

In November 2012 the Hague Convention 1996 came into force which allows, under Article 24, the "advance recognition" in the new state of orders for contact made in the original state. Where that is not possible a **Mirror Order** should be obtained. This must include things like telephone calls, email, and contact by webcam.

Hand Down

To deliver the written version of a **Judgment** in a more complex case at a later date. Such a judgment will contain the dates of the judgment and handing down, lists of the judges, parties, counsel and solicitors and the **Neutral Citation**.

Handover

The point at which a child passes from the care of one parent to that of the other.

Handovers (the "switching hour") are particularly treacherous moments which can be traumatic for children and allow parents to continue animosity and conflict.

One way to prevent parents meeting is the "staggered" handover which is a safer alternative to parents meeting at the local garage or park. One parent turns up at the **Contact Centre** at an agreed time, drops the child off and leaves. The other parent turns up a little later to pick up the child. This ensures the parents don't meet and the child doesn't witness confrontation. In most cases this is what the courts should be ordering as the default position for contact rather than **Supervised Contact** because staggered handovers provide the same outcome: the children and non-resident parents remain in contact with each other and the parents do not have to attempt pleasantries which often result in argument. The typical cost of this service is £15 a session, which is money well spent compared with what it could cost if an argument breaks out.

Another option available to parents who wish to use external services for handovers is the "pick-up and drop-off". This is not available at every contact centre but is worth exploring as in some areas social services can offer it. For those parents who do not want to risk bumping into the ex in the contact centre car park even as part of a staggered arrangement, the service eliminates any possibility of contact. A member of staff can come to their home, or other pre-arranged location, pick up the child, and take him to the other parent's house. The cost can vary but usually there will be a fee for the case worker plus a mileage allowance for the journey to and from the parents. This is probably the safest of all services as there is no chance of disputing parents meeting.

Unhappily, once in court, parents are usually given a limited choice of services because CAFCASS officers themselves do not know what is available. The best solution is for parents to be prepared and approach all contact centres in their area and ask them for details of their services before going to court; they can then ask if they would be prepared to offer services such as staggered handovers and pick-ups and drop-offs. They might not offer those services on a regular basis, but the options can be explored so that, once in court, parents and children are not forced into the one-size-fits-all supervised contact in a contact centre.

Harassment

Claims of harassment are pervasive in family proceedings and the legislation is widely abused. Harassment is defined in Section 154 of the Criminal Justice and

Public Order Act 1994. A party is guilty of an offence if he intends to cause a person harassment, alarm or distress by —

a) using threatening, abusive or insulting words or behaviour, or disorderly behaviour, or
b) displaying any writing, sign or other visible representation which is threatening, abusive or insulting, thereby causing that or another person harassment, alarm or distress.

Harassment itself is not defined, but the law says,

The person whose course of conduct is in question ought to know that it amounts to harassment of another if a reasonable person in possession of the same information would think the course of conduct amounted to harassment of the other.

To make a successful allegation of harassment, the applicant must prove a "course of conduct" but, under the Protection from Harassment Act 1997, only two incidents are necessary. This means a respondent can still be prosecuted if only two incidents out of a longer list of allegations can be proved, even if they are months apart; see Lau v DPP [2000] 1 FLR 799. Nevertheless, to prove a "course of conduct" there must be cogent linking conduct between the events, and it is up to the prosecution to prove this. See R v Hills [2001] 1 FLR 580, in which a conviction was overturned.

An application to the courts is not necessary, and in the first instance the claimant should make a complaint to the police. They will probably issue the other party with a police information notice before taking further action; this has no legal status. A police constable may arrest without warrant if he reasonably suspects an offence is being committed. The defendant will then be liable on summary conviction to imprisonment for a term not exceeding six months, or a fine, or both.

The offence may be committed in any private or public place, but it is not harassment if both the defendant and the victim were inside the same building; it is a defence if the defendant was inside a building and didn't think what he was doing would be seen outside the building. It is a defence if the course of conduct was pursued for the purpose of preventing or detecting crime, if it was pursued under any enactment or rule of law or to comply with any condition or requirement imposed by any person under any enactment (such as a phone call to confirm arrangements made under a **Child Arrangements Order**), or if the defendant thought the pursuit of the course of conduct reasonable.

It is also harassment under Section 4 of the Act if a "reasonable person" would think the course of conduct could cause another to fear that abuse will be used against them. The defences are the same as above, or if the course of conduct was reasonable for the protection of the defendant or another or for the protection of his or another's property. Again, a course of conduct is defined by only two incidents.

A person arrested for harassment should demand to see the duty solicitor at the police station and not agree during the interview on any account that his behaviour could have been construed as harassment.

He should state he believes his behaviour was reasonable and cannot imagine how it could have been interpreted otherwise. If he agrees, as he will be pressured to do, then in effect he becomes the "reasonable person" required to condemn himself.

It is common to offer a reduced sentence if the defendant pleads guilty, but this should be resisted. Admitting guilt will ensure the harassment charge continues to affect future applications.

Similarly, no one innocent of committing the offence for which he is being cautioned should accept a caution; it is an admission of guilt which can be used later in a Child Arrangements dispute. The police may offer a deal to accept the caution, but it should be rejected.

It is also an offence under the Malicious Communications Act 1988 to send a message by letter, email or text, etc., which is indecent or grossly offensive, threatening or known to be false, if the intent is that it should cause distress or anxiety. It is not an offence if the message was intended to reinforce a demand the defendant had reasonable grounds for making, or if he believes the message was a proper means to reinforce the demand.

Harm

Section 31(9) of the Children Act 1989 defines "harm" as:

ill-treatment or the impairment of health or development;

"ill-treatment" includes sexual abuse and non-physical forms of ill-treatment; following amendment to Section 120 of the Adoption and Children Act 2002, this now includes "impairment suffered from seeing or hearing the ill-treatment of another";

"health" means physical or mental health; and

"development" means physical, intellectual, emotional, social or behavioural development.

Some degree of harm is inevitable in most cases involving children; in Re A & B (Children) [2013] EWHC 2305, Mr Justice Cobb admitted,

> *[6]* There is no way forward from here which does not involve the continuation of harm to the children, the risk of future harm, and/or inevitable loss to the children. The issue for me has tragically become one of balancing the risks of harm.

Section 31(2) entitles the state to intervene only where "harm" exceeds a **Threshold** and becomes "significant",

> A court may only make a care order or supervision order if it is satisfied—
>
> a) that the child concerned is suffering, or is likely to suffer, significant harm; and
> b) that the harm, or likelihood of harm, is attributable to—
>
>   i.   the care given to the child, or likely to be given to him if the order were not made, not being what it would be reasonable to expect a parent to give to him; or
>   ii. the child's being beyond parental control.

This introduces the concepts of **Significant Harm** and **Future Harm**, discussed below; see also **Care**.

Harm; Future

Section 31(2) of the **Children Act 1989** allows a court to order care or supervision where "the child concerned is suffering, *or is likely to suffer*, **Significant Harm**".

> A court may only make a care order or supervision order if it is satisfied—
>
> c) that the child concerned is suffering, or is likely to suffer, significant harm; and
> d) that the harm, or likelihood of harm, is attributable to—
>
>   iii. the care given to the child, or likely to be given to him if the order were not made, not being what it would be reasonable to expect a parent to give to him; or
>   iv. the child's being beyond parental control.

This enables intervention when no harm has befallen the child, but where it is considered "likely" that at some unspecified future date it may.

It is apparent that the **Balance of Probability** standard, which applies to actual **Harm**, cannot be applied to harm which has yet to happen. In Re H [1996] AC 563, Lord Nicholls sought to introduce a third standard of proof,

> [69] ...a real possibility, a possibility that cannot sensibly be ignored having regard to the nature and gravity of the feared harm in the particular case.

Baroness Hale conclusively rejected this approach in Re B (Children) [2008] UKHL 35; see **Burden of Proof**. Re J (Children) (Care Proceedings: Threshold Criteria) [2013] UKSC 9 established that a likelihood of significant harm means no more than a real possibility it will occur, but that a conclusion to that effect must be based upon a fact or facts established on a balance of probabilities.

The **Threshold** set by s.31(2) is intended to protect the child and his family from unwarranted interference by the state. Reasonable suspicion is a sufficient basis for investigation, and even interim protective measures, but cannot constitute a sufficient basis for the long-term intervention entailed in a care order; Lord Reed said,

> [96] ...a real possibility that [the mother] harmed another child in the past is not by itself a basis upon which the court can properly be satisfied that there is a likelihood that [she] will harm the child in question in the future.

Every case where a baby is removed at birth relies on this prediction of future behaviour; if a parent has already abused her older children then such a prediction can reasonably be justified, though past harm is not the only criterion, but all too often there is no evidence, and a prediction must be challenged in court, and the litigant must insist that the Court adheres to the facts.

Consider the following tragic case. In Re W (A Child) [2009] EWCA Civ 538, a girl, A, was taken from her mother because the new husband had been a possible perpetrator of a severe head injury against his son by a previous marriage, notwithstanding the facts that the son continued to live with his parents and the father continued to have contact. Subsequent evidence cast doubt on the injury being non-accidental, but the mother's application for residence and a stay of the adoption order were refused.

The case shows how a decision based on probability – and the preference of one expert's evidence over that of another – can go on to be accepted as a certainty ("where no certainty exists") resulting in a child to whom no harm has been done losing a mother who has never been accused of wrongdoing. As the appellate judge, Lord Justice Wilson, observed of the case,

> [5] Among its most haunting features is surely the fact that A's mother, who sits before me today, has, subject to this proposed appeal, lost her child by reference to circumstances which, largely, do not relate to her.

Harm; Significant

Section 31(2) allows the state to intervene where "harm" exceeds a **Threshold** and becomes "significant",

In Humberside CC v B [1993] 1 FLR 257, Booth J suggested that "significant" meant "considerable, noteworthy or important"; the Court should identify how and in what respects the harm is significant. In Re L (Children) (Care Proceedings: Significant Harm) [2006] EWCA Civ 1282, [2007] 1 FLR 1068, Hedley J expressed his view that significant harm "must be something unusual; at least something more than the commonplace human failure or inadequacy". Significant harm can also arise from the cumulative effect of several minor harms.

Note that significant harm refers to the effect on the child and not the intention of the parent. Cases arise – for example, where a parent goes on holiday leaving the child behind – in which the harm caused is relatively minor, but the action of the parent shows such indifference to the child's welfare that there are grounds for grave concern for his future welfare.

Harvey Order

A rare order for the allocation of the former matrimonial home whereby one party remains in residence and pays rent to the other. Named after Ormrod LJ's decision in Harvey v Harvey [1982] 1 All ER 693.

Heads of Agreement

A written summary of an agreement – usually financial – reached through successful **Mediation**, which can be worked up into a court order if the Court thinks it necessary or appropriate (see **Financial Dispute Resolution**). Sometimes also called a Memorandum of Understanding.

Hearing

A court session conducted before a judge.

Hearsay

A statement not given in oral evidence in proceedings, but which is nevertheless accepted as evidence.

High Court

Together with the **Court of Appeal** and the Crown Court, one of the senior courts of England and Wales, comprising the Queen's Bench, Chancery Division and Family Division.

High Court judges have greater powers than those in the Family Court and can hear all cases including those the **Family Court** cannot hear. Often proceedings will be at the Royal Courts of Justice (RCJ) in London, but High Court proceedings may be held at District Registries around the country.

Categories of case include inherent jurisdiction cases; applications to make a child a ward of court, or to end such an order; proceedings under the Child Abduction and Custody Act 1985, and other international abduction cases; proceedings with an international element relating to or enforcement of orders, conflict or comity of laws which have exceptional immigration/asylum status issues; declarations of incompatibility under the Human Rights Act 1998; applications for Declaratory Relief; registration of foreign judgments; registration of judgments given in a different part of the UK; registration of custody orders made in a court in another part of the UK; and Parental Responsibility Orders prior to adoption abroad.

High Court Judge

These judges are above **District Judges** in the judicial hierarchy. They are known as Mr or Mrs Justice X and all are made knights or dames on appointment (though Alison Russell QC insisted on being known as Ms Justice).

High Court judges deal with leave-to-remove cases involving particular factual or legal complexity; applications for financial relief where the parties do not consent to permission being granted and to the substantive order sought; and parental orders under the Human Fertilisation and Embryology Act 2008 where the child's place of birth is outside England and Wales.

Hold

What a court "holds" is its final decision or ruling on an issue.

Holidays Abroad

Where there is a **Child Arrangements Order** in force, a parent named in the order as a person with whom the child is to live can take the child out of the English/Welsh jurisdiction for up to twenty-eight days (Children Act 1989, Section 13(1)). In the case of a **Special Guardianship Order**, the permitted period is three months.

No one else can remove the child without the written consent of all those with **Parental Responsibility** for him or leave of the Court.

Where there is *not* a Child Arrangements Order in place, the courts tend to apply the same principle, since the law does not specifically provide for that circumstance.

If a parent wants to take the child abroad for a period longer than twenty-eight days, or if the intended period of removal coincides with a time when the child is scheduled to be with the other parent, he must obtain the written consent of all those with PR or leave of the Court.

These provisions are enforceable under Section 63(3) of the Magistrates Court Act 1980; if an adult who is "connected" with the child (see **Association**) takes him abroad for a period longer than twenty-eight days in breach of them, then a criminal offence is committed under the Child Abduction Act 1984 (see **Abduction**).

Even if the father doesn't have PR, a mother is still advised to seek his consent, and he can apply both for PR and for a **Prohibited Steps Order** to prevent travel. Removal out of the country can still constitute "**Wrongful Removal**" and he can start abduction proceedings under the **Hague Convention** on International Child Abduction. Removal is likely to be wrongful if there is a PSO in force, or a CAO regulating with whom the child is to have contact and removal breaches its terms. Case law indicates that even where the other parent has no PR, they may still be deemed a *de facto* primary carer with rights of custody; see Re B (A Minor) (Abduction) [1994] 2 FLR 249 and Re O (Abduction: Custody Rights) [1997] 2 FLR 702.

An offence is not committed if the removing parent believes consent has been given, has taken all reasonable steps to communicate with the other parent or if consent is unreasonably withheld. A parent who wants to take her child abroad when it isn't certain they will agree, will need to plan ahead and make a **Specific Issues** application, giving the reason for the trip, date and method of travel and return, where the child will be staying and with whom, and providing contact landline telephone numbers and other provisions for continuing contact. This should be recorded in the order, together with declaration that the child's **Habitual Residence** remains in England/Wales.

It may be appropriate to make a notarised agreement, pay a financial bond, provide copy air tickets or make the Court an **Undertaking** to return the child on a specific date. Alternatively, the Court may require the applicant to obtain a **Mirror Order** from the foreign jurisdiction.

It is sensible to obtain an SIO even where there is agreement: it's not unknown for parents to agree to such trips and then promptly get a PSO or contact the police and allege **Abduction**. If these precautions are not taken, a parent may find herself unable to go on the planned trip.

A parent named in a CAO as a parent with whom the child is to have contact may not take the child abroad without the resident parent's consent, but it is possible to have a direction added to the order to allow the child to be taken for contact purposes, so that the resident parent's permission isn't needed each time. If there is no such direction and the resident parent objects, the parent will need to apply to the Court, demonstrating that it is in the child's best interests.

Note that some countries will not allow a lone parent with a child to enter the country unless there is written authorisation from the other; if she has a CAO, it is advisable for her to take it, though she will need the consent of the Court to disclose it.

Holistic

Signifying the global, comprehensive analysis of a child's welfare seen as a whole, having particular regard to the circumstances set out in the **Welfare Checklist**.

The word may have been first used in this context by McFarlane LJ in Re G (A Child) [2013] EWCA Civ 965 (see **Threshold**), before being picked up by Munby LJ in Re B-S (Children) [2013] EWCA Civ 1146 and used regularly thereafter in successive judgments. McFarlane glossed his use in Re F [2015] EWCA Civ 882 (see **Leave-to-Remove**),

> [48] ...my purpose in using the word "holistic" was simply to adopt a single word designed to encapsulate what seasoned Family Lawyers would call "the old-fashioned welfare balancing exercise", in which each and every relevant factor relating to a child's welfare is weighed, one against the other, to determine which of a range of options best meets the requirement to afford paramount consideration to the welfare of the child. The overall balancing exercise is "holistic" in that it requires the court to look at the factors relating to a child's welfare as a whole; as opposed to a "linear" approach which only considers individual components in isolation.

Home Rights

The right of a party under Part IV of the Family Law Act 1996 to remain in a property during separation or divorce when it is owned by the other spouse or partner. A party can apply to register their home rights as a charge on the property with the Land Registry, so it cannot be sold or mortgaged without their knowledge, but not if the property is jointly owned with a third party.

Human Rights Act 1998

The legislation which enshrined the **European Convention on Human Rights** into English law. The articles most relevant to family law are:

Article 6: the Right to a Fair Trial,

1. In the determination of his civil rights and obligations or of any criminal charge against him, everyone is entitled to a fair and public hearing within a reasonable time by an independent and impartial tribunal established by law. Judgment shall be pronounced publicly by the press and public may be excluded from all or part of the trial in the interest of morals, public order or national security in a democratic society, where the interests of juveniles or the protection of the private life of the parties so require, or the extent strictly necessary in the opinion of the court in special circumstances where publicity would prejudice the interests of justice.
2. Everyone charged with a criminal offence shall be presumed innocent until proved guilty according to law.

President of the Family Division, James Munby, explained in Re L (Care: Assessment: Fair Trial) [2002] EWHC 1379 that what Article 6 effectively confers is an absolute right of access to a court for the resolution of disputes; see Golder v United Kingdom (1979-80) 1 EHRR 524. *Fairness* obliges all servants of the state, including social workers, to treat parents fairly and guarantees parents the right to be involved at any stage in decisions about their children and to see and comment on the evidence presented against them. This places a heavy burden upon local authorities of full **Disclosure**, and meetings with experts must be open to the parents or their representatives and properly recorded so that they acquire evidential status; see Mantovanelli v France (1997) 24 EHRR 370.

Article 8: the Right to Respect for Private and Family Life,

1. Everyone has the right to respect for his private and family life, his home and his correspondence.
2. There shall be no interference by a public authority with the exercise of this right except such as is in accordance with the law and is necessary in a democratic society in the interests of national security, public safety or the economic well-being of the country, for the prevention of

> disorder or crime, for the protection of health or morals, or for the
> protection of the rights and freedoms of others.

Despite the absence of explicit procedure, these provisions protect fairness both in the trial process and in the decision-making process at all stages of child protection; a *fair* trial is an adversarial trial in which there is **Equality of Arms**.

The word "necessary" ensures that a child cannot simply be moved into an environment that better meets his interests (see Melo v Portugal, application no. 72850/14, paragraph 89).

Article 12: the Right to Marry and Found a Family,

> Men and women of marriageable age have the right to marry and to found
> a family, according to the national laws governing the exercise of this right.

Article 13: the Right to an Effective Remedy.

> Everyone whose rights and freedoms as set forth in this Convention are
> violated shall have an effective remedy before a national authority
> notwithstanding that the violation has been committed by persons acting
> in an official capacity.

Article 14: the Prohibition of Discrimination (note that this Article applies only if a person's rights under another Convention Article are breached),

> The enjoyment of the rights and freedoms set forth in this Convention shall
> be secured without discrimination on any ground such as sex, race, colour,
> language, religion, political or other opinion, national or social origin,
> association with a national minority, property, birth or other status.

A party who relies on any right or provision in the 1998 Act must specify in his written application the right or provision which has been breached and the manner of breach. He must also specify what relief he seeks, and whether he wants the Court to declare incompatibility, in which case a Minister will be joined as a party. See Rule 29.5 of the **Family Procedure Rules 2010**.

The notorious case of P, C and S v United Kingdom (2002) 35 EHRR 31, [2002] 2 FLR 631 featured alleged breaches of these rights. P, an American, moved to the UK where she met and married C and had a daughter, S. A child by a former partner had been taken into protective custody in the US, and S was taken into care under an **Emergency Protection Order**. Wall LJ upheld the decision on appeal on the grounds that P had a personality disorder. The couple complained:

1. their human rights under Article 6(1) had been abused: they had not been involved in the decision-making process and had not been given access to representation to challenge the **Freeing Order**;
2. their rights under Article 8 had been abused: adoption was irreversible and made no provision for resuming any form of contact in the future; and
3. their rights under Article 12 had been abused.

The Court upheld the Article 6 and 8 complaints; the Article 12 complaint was not an issue separate from Article 8. Given the complexity and importance of the case, it was essential P should have had legal assistance. "The **Draconian** step" of removing a child from its mother at birth required exceptional justification which was not "supported by relevant and sufficient reasons". The case was particularly significant because Wall, who had abused the couple's right to family life and denied them a fair trial, went on to become President of the Family Division.

I

Illegitimacy

Literally, the condition of a child who cannot inherit from his father.

A child born to a married mother by another man is an 'adulterine bastard'; a child born to unmarried parents who later marry is a 'special bastard'.

The Family Law Reform Act 1987 supposedly eliminated the distinction between legitimate and illegitimate children from English and Welsh law to bring it into line with European law. This would have ended the discrimination against a child claiming financial support from his father merely because his parents were unmarried; however, a culture had already arisen in which mothers of illegitimate children preferred to claim financial support from the state rather than institute proceedings against the father. The introduction of the Child Support Act in 1991 was intended to counter this.

Prior to 1987, parental authority over an illegitimate child had been vested solely in the mother; removal of the concept of legitimacy would have given even "**Unmeritorious**" fathers parental authority, a development strongly resisted by single-mother lobby groups. Accordingly, the Law Commission had recommended that fathers of "non-marital" children should acquire parental authority only following judicial scrutiny.

The 1989 Children Act achieved a compromise, which demanded only an agreement between the mother and father to confer what was by then termed **Parental Responsibility** onto the father. PR reintroduced the distinction between legitimate and illegitimate: a child whose father did not have PR was effectively illegitimate. The judicial inquisition which would have applied to all unmarried fathers now applied only to fathers who separated from their children's mothers, regardless of whether they had been married.

From 1st December 2003, the Adoption and Children Act 2002 introduced amendments which enabled an unmarried father to acquire PR through being named on the child's birth certificate or through an order of the Court.

Section 9 of the Legitimacy Act 1976 still requires parents who marry after the birth of a child to re-register the birth within three months using Form LA1; failure to do so can theoretically merits a £2 fine.

Imerman Documents

Documents – relating, for example, to financial matters – which have been obtained illegally or fraudulently; named after Tchenguiz & Ors v Imerman (Rev 4) [2010] EWCA Civ 908.

The Court must balance one spouse's Article 6 right to a fair trial against the other's Article 8 right to privacy. Procedure is given under rule 21.3 of the **Family Procedure Rules 2010**; the correct approach was established by Mostyn in UL v BK (Freezing Orders: Safeguards: Standard Examples) [2013] UKHC 1735, and modified by Macur in Arbili v Arbili [2015] EWCA Civ 542,

> *[35]* I recognise the professional difficulties for any legal representative informed of the existence of illicitly obtained materials,... but this particular topic has been traversed at some length in *[Imerman]* sufficiently to give an adequate indication of the steps to be taken. The unlawfully obtained materials must be returned. The recipient's duty to make any relevant disclosure arising from them within the proceedings is triggered. The ability of the wrongdoer, or their principal, to challenge the sufficiency of the disclosure, is confined to evidence of their memory of the contents of the materials but is admissible.

See also Lifely; Jones v Warwick University [2003] EWCA Civ 151.

Implacable Hostility

Remorseless and irrational hatred of the other parent and opposition to sharing parenting or compliance with a court order.

Implacable hostility is unique to child arrangements disputes and only applies where no valid reasons have been given to oppose contact. Implacably hostile parents are likely to be suffering from a personality disorder: there should be psychiatric analysis and treatment available, and their children should be protected from their behaviour. Note, however, that the term is a legal one and not a medical diagnosis.

The Court must consider the reasons an order is disobeyed, why there is hostility and whether it is "implacable". The respondent can apply for relief from any sanction the Court may impose, but must supply evidence for the reasons given; under Rule 4.6 of the **Family Procedure Rules 2010**, the Court must consider all circumstances.

Re S (Contact: Grandparents) [1996] 1 FLR 158 established that it is unacceptable for a court to make no order simply because it is likely to be disobeyed; if contact is in the child's best interests, the order *must* be made; in Re J (A Minor) (Contact) [1994] 1 FLR 729, Balcombe said,

> Judges should be very reluctant to allow the implacable hostility of one parent... to deter them from making a Contact Order where they believe the child's welfare requires it. The danger of allowing the implacable hostility of the residential parent (usually the mother) to frustrate the court's decision is too obvious to require repetition on my part.

In Re P (Contact: Discretion) [1998] 2 FLR 696, Wilson J outlined three ways hostility to contact might arise and how it should be dealt with:

1. There are no rational grounds: the Court should refuse contact only where there is serious risk of emotional harm to the child.
2. The grounds are sufficient to displace the presumption in favour of contact: contact should not be ordered.
3. The arguments are rational but not decisive: in such a case the hostility itself may be of determinative importance when measured against the child's best interests.

Guidance on case management of implacable hostility cases was handed down by Mr Justice Hedley in Re E (A Child) [2011] EWHC 3521:

1. Courts must identify at an early stage those cases which will be intractable, or even difficult.
2. Parties must have the opportunity to give evidence in respect of the child's interests and not, as so often happens in fact-finding hearings, against each other.
3. Judicial continuity is of particular importance in difficult and intractable contact cases.
4. The fact that a case is intractable is not of itself sufficient reason to transfer to the High Court, for the very reason that it undermines judicial continuity.
5. If a case is transferred to the High Court, the matter should be transferred not absolutely but for directions with a view to a High

Court judge considering whether the matter should remain in the High Court; the judge considering the matter should consult with the Family Division Liaison Judge. That has the advantage of a new mind being applied to the case without necessarily divesting the judge who has had continual oversight of the case from continuing in it.

6. The child's expressed opposition to contact should be taken seriously but the judge must ask why this is the case. Is this the child's genuinely held view, or is it superficial and a protection for the child against finding herself in endless conflict with the residential parent, upon whom she is wholly dependent?

7. The Court is obliged under s.1 CA1989 to consider "the ascertainable wishes and feelings of the child concerned (considered in the light of his age and understanding)".

8. The Court must consider the child's physical, emotional and educational needs.

9. The Court must consider the likely effect on the child of any change in his circumstances: persisting with attempts at contact will be distressing to him and frustrate his desire that proceedings come to an end.

10. Persisting with contact or abandoning it may both lead to harm; the Court must consider the benefits and risks of both, ensuring that "the harm that she will suffer by the persistence with contact is proportionate to the advantage that may be achieved by it".

11. The Court finally has three options:
    a) to abandon the quest for contact entirely;
    b) to make and enforce an order for contact; or
    c) to pass the case on for further professional assistance.

Cases often fail because a parent has delayed application until the child is too old to respond well to a further order. In J-M (A Child) [2014] EWCA Civ 434, a father appealed against the refusal of his application for contact with his fourteen-year-old son. The lower courts had made no errors which would justify interference and the appeal was dismissed.

In Re A (A Child) [2015] EWCA Civ 910, the Court of Appeal declined to overturn a decision not to order contact where none had taken place for six or seven years,

> That this should be the outcome of this case is, in my view, a tragedy. It is certainly a tragedy for the Father, but, more importantly, it is a tragedy for this young man, who had a warm, easy and close relationship with his father when he was much younger before their separation took place. Some

family situations are simply not amenable to the blunt instrument of a judge sitting in a law court making an order.

While it may seem prudent to order **Transfer of Residence** early in a case, the courts often seem prepared to allow many years to pass before even considering it. Cases reach a point where an applicant who has done nothing wrong is nevertheless banned from seeing his child and from making further applications because of the relentless hostility of a personality-disordered respondent. The key to success is **Judicial Continuity**, so that a single judge can apprehend the situation more swiftly and adopt a clear and definitive approach to resolution and decide when more **Draconian** intervention should be applied. In Re C (Residence Order) [2007] EWCA Civ 866, Ward LJ rejected the mother's application to overturn the trial judge's order,

> [3] He found that [the mother's] attitude towards contact was one of implacable hostility. So the problem for HHJ Lowden was how to cope with that familiar situation. He took the course often threatened but seldom implemented. He ordered L's immediate change of residence from her mother's home to that of her father.

In Absentia

(Latin: "in the absence of") of a decision made by the Court despite the fact that one party has chosen not to attend.

In Camera

(Latin: "in a chamber" and thus also "in chambers") a hearing conducted in private to which press and public are not admitted.

In Curia

(Latin: "in a court") a hearing conducted in open court and thus the opposite of *In Camera*.

In Loco Parentis

(Latin: "in the place of a parent") relating to anyone who assumes the responsibilities of a parent.

In Utero

(Latin: "in the womb") of a **Child**: not yet born.

Infant

In legal rather than common parlance, a person who has not yet reached the age of legal majority.

Informal Notice

An application made in haste in which the applicant does not complete all the usual documentation.

Inherent Jurisdiction

The rule that a senior court has the power to try any matter which comes before it unless another court specifically has jurisdiction or its power is limited by a statute or rule.

In the Family Court this ensures that a child will always enjoy the Court's protection, even if the matter concerning him cannot proceed under the Children Act 1989. What blogging solicitor Andrew Pack has called its "magic sparkle dust" gives the Court powers that are effectively limitless, compared with the restricted powers under the Act. See Practice Direction 12D and 12.36 to 12.42 FPR 2010.

Injunction

An order obliging a party to do or prohibiting him from doing a thing.

These can serve an essential role in protecting a child or parent from abuse but can also be misused and cause impediment and delay if, for example, a party is prevented from entering his own home.

They include **Non-Molestation Orders, Occupation Orders, Domestic Violence Protection Orders, Section 91(14)** Barring Orders and **Undertakings**. An injunctive order can be made where there is only a fear or threat of violence and no violence has been proven. Injunctions constitute evidence of domestic violence under the **Domestic Violence Gateway** and support a litigant in an application for legal aid.

Before anyone can be arrested for breach of an injunction, the power of arrest must be served by handing the appropriate form to the officer in charge of the nearest police station. The orders are set out on Form FL404a for a **Non-**

Molestation Order or Form FL406 for an **Occupation Order**. After they have been served on the respondent, the **Process Server** prepares a statement of service to be served on the relevant police station. This statement will detail the date and time of service and what documents were served, and will be used as evidence the respondent knows there is an order in place. The statement is made under oath or affirmation, so it can be relied on in the civil and criminal courts.

Was the arrest valid? Has he been arrested for breach of the order or was it for something else? He will need a photocopy of the arresting officer's notebook in which the arrest was recorded. If it does not record arrest for breach of the injunction he should be released immediately.

If an injunction is to be enforceable, it must be served on the respondent personally. The applicant must provide proof that this happened, such as a statement of service from a process server. The onus is on the applicant to prove the respondent knew of the order.

If the power of arrest has not been served, the arrest is invalid, and the respondent must be released. It may be that the process server will have to be summoned to court and, if he cannot provide evidence the papers were served, the Court will have to find that they were not. In addition to the power of arrest, "a statement showing that the respondent has been served with the order or informed of its terms (whether by being present when the order was made or by telephone or otherwise)" must be delivered to the police station. The statement should record that this has been done; otherwise, the arrest is invalid, and the respondent must argue for release.

If the above fail, the respondent can either admit breach of the order and be sentenced accordingly, or the Court will have to adjourn for a full hearing which must take place within fourteen days if there are no further allegations. If this limit is exceeded, the Court's power to deal with the matter expires and the respondent should be released. If the applicant wishes to add further allegations, they must do so on Form N78; they may also do this if the respondent is released.

Inlying Expenses

(Scots) additional or unforeseen costs in relation to bringing up a child, such as school fees, music tuition, funeral costs, etc.

Inns of Court

Lincoln's Inn, Inner Temple, Middle Temple and Gray's Inn: the four professional associations to one of which a barrister must belong. Established in the middle ages, they are similar to Oxbridge colleges in layout, with dining halls, libraries, chapels, accommodation ("Chambers") and gardens.

Instruct

For a litigant or his solicitor to authorise a lawyer or **Expert Witness** to act in a case. Further instructions may be necessary during the case.

Instructing a solicitor means handing over all responsibility to him. Many things the client could have done will now be handled by the solicitor; direct communication with the other party will cease, relations break down, positions become polarised and entrenched.

Solicitors will act only on a client's instructions, though they may not make this clear, so a client can be waiting months for some action the solicitor will not take until specifically asked.

A solicitor is entitled to refuse his client's instructions and, if he is publicly funded, can refuse if he believes that following them would give the case no hope of success; he has a responsibility to spend public money effectively. Once a solicitor has agreed to take a case he is "on record" on the court file. For him then to remove himself he must either persuade his client to sign a release form or take directions from the judge. He must make an application to the Court which the client can oppose.

Under their code of conduct solicitors may only refuse to follow instruction in certain circumstances. In order to ascertain whether or not they are reasonable they will take advice from a barrister and the client will have to pay for this.

Inter Alia

(Latin: "amongst other things") used, for example, where a court may make a variety of orders.

Inter Partes

(Latin: "between parties") describing a hearing at which all parties are present.

Interdict

(Scots) a form of **Injunction**.

Under Section 14(1) of the Matrimonial Homes (Family Protection) (Scotland) Act 1981, a spouse was able to apply to the Court for a matrimonial interdict and, if circumstances warranted, for the attachment of a power of arrest under Section 15. The Act's major flaw was that the power lapsed when the parties divorced; all too often the solicitor would have to advise a client that, while the Sheriff had granted the power of arrest, it would last only a few weeks until the divorce was granted. Many clients may have wondered what on earth the point of it was. The limitation of the granting of powers of arrest to anti-molestation interdicts between spouses or cohabitants was another major disadvantage.

Section 1(2) of the Protection from Abuse (Scotland) Act 2001 improved the situation greatly. A power of arrest became available for anyone who was applying for an anti-molestation interdict. The parties did not have to be spouses or cohabitants.

The procedure is much the same as the older law: a solicitor should still apply for the attachment of the power of arrest in the same way, although it is necessary to narrate in the **Crave** that it is a power of arrest in terms of the relevant section of the Act.

A Matrimonial Interdict would not only prevent a spouse from entering the family home, but could also extend to the applicant's place of work and the children's schools, as well as a specified area around the family home. However, when applying for a Matrimonial Interdict, it is necessary to ensure she has also applied for the Exclusion Order, as the Court is prohibited from granting a Matrimonial Interdict which would prevent the named spouse from entering, or remaining in, the family home unless an Exclusion Order is sought in conjunction with the Matrimonial Interdict; Interim Exclusion Order under Section 4 of the Matrimonial Homes (Scotland) Act 1981.

This would mean that the interdicted person would have to be excluded from living in the family home. The applicant would need to demonstrate the order is necessary for them and any children to live in peace; **Domestic Abuse** is a common justification.

The Court would also, at the same time as granting an Interim Exclusion Order, grant the ancillary orders required, i.e., the order for summary ejection of the interdicted person and (non)removal of furniture and the Interdict against his entry to the house.

The Court must attach a power of arrest on application, providing the following two clauses are satisfactorily met:

1. the spouse against whom the Interdict is being granted has been heard by the Court, or has proper representation before the Court; and
2. it is necessary to attach the power of arrest to allow the applicant protection from a risk of abuse should the Interdict be breached.

In order for it to become effective, the police are notified of the existence of the Power of Arrest attached to the Interdict once the Interdict has been served. Should the two spouses live in different police areas, then both forces need to be notified.

Interim Order

An order made as a temporary measure at the commencement of proceedings, particularly in **Child Arrangement** applications.

The court process can become protracted and considerable time elapse without contact. An interim order ensures some contact between parent and child, pending a full hearing. Interim contact can be staying or visiting, or may only be indirect.

Every application should be accompanied by a submission at the **Directions Hearing** for an interim order. The applicant should advise the Court and the other side in advance that this is what he intends to do.

The criteria for ordering interim contact were established by Wall LJ in Re D (Contact: Interim Order) [1995] 1 FLR 495,

1. contact must be monitored (usually by CAFCASS);
2. the judge must have sufficient information to order contact, even if at the end of proceedings, a different order is made;
3. if the dispute is only over the amount of contact, an interim order can be made without considering any additional information.

The greatest care had to be taken in making an interim order and without hearing oral evidence, to ensure that it was in the interests of the child and that the order did not prejudice the issue. It was difficult to envisage circumstances in which an interim order for contact could properly be made where the principle of contact was genuinely in dispute and where there were substantial factual issues relating to a child which were unresolved without the court hearing oral evidence or having the advice of an expert such as a court welfare officer.

The Court is obliged to process the application and will arrange a minimum of a short hearing within a few weeks, giving the applicant opportunity to explain why his child deserves a relationship with him and why contact should continue while the Court waits for CAFCASS reports, etc. The application should focus on the best interests of the child, refer to the **No Delay Principle** and ask for a **Quantum of Contact** equivalent to the amount enjoyed before proceedings began.

If the application is opposed and the Court asked to wait until the CAFCASS or other reports are in, the applicant will need to keep pressure on the Court, asking for the earliest possible date for the hearing for interim contact and pushing it to establish a timetable of realistic targets for hearings. He must show readiness to attend court at short notice and accept a cancellation, so the matter can be resolved expeditiously.

The Court of Appeal does not welcome the appeal of interim orders; see Re J (A Minor) (Interim Custody: Appeal) [1989] 2 FLR 304.

Interlocutor

(Scots) the sheet of paper upon which the court order is written.

Intervenor

A third party who becomes involved in a case because of a specific issue.

Involvement

Under Section 11 of the Children and Families Act 2014, an additional clause was added to Section 1 of the Children Act 1989 promoting the "involvement" of both parents in their children's lives,

> A court... is to presume, unless the contrary is shown, that involvement of that parent in the life of the child concerned will further the child's welfare.

This clause cleverly incorporated the right of a child to be parented by both parents into the definition of the child's welfare and thus re-interpreted the concept to include shared parenting. This undermined the argument of those opponents of shared parenting that any presumption would contradict the **Welfare** principle. Caroline Nokes MP, a member of the Bill Committee, summarised:

> By inversing the subject of the legal right, and introducing a clause which gives this "right" not to the parent, but to the child, the Government achieves the twin objectives of enshrining shared parenting, whilst maintaining the paramountcy of the child's welfare.

To emphasise the point, the clause added the usual welfare caveats:

> a parent of the child concerned

> a) is within this paragraph if that parent can be involved in the child's life in a way that does not put the child at risk of suffering harm; and

224

b) is to be treated as being within paragraph (a) unless there is some evidence before the court in the particular proceedings to suggest that involvement of that parent in the child's life would put the child at risk of suffering harm whatever the form of the involvement.

This formula risks enabling parental exclusion when the parent himself presents no risk to the child but where his *involvement* can potentially cause harm through, for example, exacerbating conflict with the other parent.

An anti-shared parenting lobby group, the *Shared Parenting Consortium*, headed by former President of the Family Division, Elizabeth Butler-Sloss, introduced an amendment to the clause which almost certainly destroyed any effectiveness it might otherwise have had,

In subsection (2A) "involvement" means involvement of some kind, either direct or indirect, but not any particular division of a child's time.

This means "involvement" can be interpreted as indirect contact and never as an apportionment of time, Earl Howe explained,

Contact disputes are about one thing and one thing only: the amount of time that each parent believes that he or she should have with the child. That simple truth has somehow got submerged during the drafting of this Bill.

Irretrievable Breakdown

The sole ground for **Divorce** in the English and Welsh jurisdiction, and one of two grounds in Scotland: the Court must find both that the marriage has broken down and that it is irretrievable.

This principle has been criticised on two points. Firstly, it can be established only by satisfying one of the **Facts**, a divorce cannot be granted where the parties fail to do this, even where both agree the marriage is irretrievable. Secondly, even where a fact – such as adultery – is proven, the divorce may not be granted unless it is also demonstrated that the marriage as a result is irretrievable.

Adultery and "Unreasonable" **Behaviour** are the most popular motives in England and Wales (accounting for 56.5% of petitions in 2016) because it is otherwise necessary to have lived apart for more than two years. In the wiser Scots jurisdiction, the two-year wait for a no-fault separation with consent is reduced to one, while the five-year wait for separation without consent is reduced to two, and together account for 93% of divorces.

J

Join

For a court to confer party status upon an individual – such as a **Grandparent** or older sibling – who has not been a party to the case but nevertheless has a vested interest in it.

Joining a Child

If a parent is concerned that the **Best Interests of their Child** are not adequately represented, it is possible to have the child **Joined** to proceedings as a party.

A child cannot represent himself and must be represented in court either through a **Solicitor** who specialises in representing children or by a CAFCASS **Children's Guardian** who will **Instruct** a solicitor on his behalf.

Joinder can be requested at any stage in proceedings and it isn't necessary to give other parties notice. Rule 16.2 of the **Family Procedure Rules 2010** provides, "The court may make a child a party to proceedings if it considers it is in the best interests of the child to do so". Practice Direction 16A – *Representation of Children* should also be consulted.

Joinder is particularly desirable in protracted and conflicted cases which show no promise of resolution, where one parent has made allegations of abuse, and where one or both is unable or unwilling to see the case from the child's perspective. With separate representation the interests of the resident parent and of the child can be viewed as separate: the child thus becomes a player in his case and not a pawn.

A Guardian must also engage a solicitor (usually through CAFCASS Legal) and will then be responsible for instructing him or her. The Guardian will interview the parties and prepare a report. For a final hearing they will engage a barrister. In Scotland, where CAFCASS doesn't operate, a solicitor known as a *Curator ad Litem* will perform the function of the Guardian.

The Court will agree to appoint a Guardian if it is in the child's interests to do so (Rule 16.1) and if the child is considered **Competent**. This may slow the process considerably, though, and at paragraph 7.3 the Practice Direction warns against delay, so this should be an option only in an already intractable case. In some circumstances, a court will order separate representation without application, or on recommendation by CAFCASS. Once appointed, the Guardian is treated as a party to the case and must safeguard the child's interests and assist the Court as it may require.

New cases in which the child is represented are referred to in the title as "A.B. (A Child by C.D. his/her Children's Guardian)". In proceedings which the child is conducting on his own behalf through his solicitor, the case is referred to in the title as "A.B. (A Child)".

The alternative to a **Children's Guardian** is for the child to be represented by his own solicitor, independently of the parents.

Leave of the Court must be obtained, and if the Court refuses, it must give its reasons; if the child is a party and is instructing his own solicitor who considers the child has sufficient understanding to instruct, then under Rule 16.6(3) a Guardian will not be necessary. If there is already a Guardian, the child may apply for her removal.

It was formerly easy to get legal aid for children's solicitors, but this is no longer so and solicitors are advised to check on the availability of legal aid before representing a child. A guardian is normally expected to be provided by **CAFCASS**.

A child should be made party to the proceedings only in the minority of cases which involve an issue of significant difficulty. Consideration should first be given to alternatives, such as further work by CAFCASS, a referral to social services or engagement of an expert. The Court may also consider whether to transfer the case to another court. The final decision is the Court's, and at paragraph 7.2 the Practice Direction directs it to consider the following factors:

a) there has been a recommendation by CAFCASS;
b) the child's interests cannot be represented by the adult parties;
c) there is an intractable dispute; contact has entirely ceased; there is implacable hostility to contact; the child is at risk of harm;
d) the views and wishes of the child cannot adequately be met by a report to the Court;
e) an older child is opposing a proposed course of action;
f) there are unusually complex issues to be determined regarding medical issues or mental health or another matter;

g) there are international complications involving child abduction, where it may be necessary for there to be discussions with overseas authorities or a foreign court;

h) there are serious allegations of physical, sexual or other abuse beyond CAFCASS to resolve;

i) the proceedings involve more than one child and their interests conflict;

j) there is a contested issue about scientific testing.

An application for the appointment of a Children's Guardian or leave to have his own solicitor must include this evidence and be made according to Part 18 of the **Family Procedure Rules 2010**. If a solicitor instructed by a Children's Guardian considers the child is of sufficient maturity and understanding to instruct the solicitor, and the child's instructions are at odds with those from the Guardian, the solicitor must take the child's instructions and not the Guardian's (Rule 16.29(2) FPR 2010). If he receives no instructions he must act in the best interests of the child.

A precedent is Mabon v Mabon [2005] EWCA Civ 634, in which Thorpe LJ considered Article 12 of the United Nations Convention on the Rights of Children, Article 8 of the **European Convention on Human Rights** and Rule 9.2A(4) of the Family Proceedings Rules 1991 (now superseded by the 2010 Rules) and directed that three mature and articulate teenagers had a right to separate representation and to instruct their own solicitor; that their guardian might adequately represent their best interests but not their wishes: "It was simply unthinkable to exclude young men from knowledge of and participation in legal proceedings that affected them so fundamentally". The conventional "tandem model" of representation by a Guardian, who instructs a solicitor, who in turn instructs a barrister, was "paternalistic", and in conflict with the children's right to freedom of expression and participation.

In Ciccone v Ritchie (No. 1) [2016] EWHC 608, Macdonald J agreed to join the child, Rocco, against the wishes of his mother, the singer Madonna:

1. Rocco was the subject of proceedings and had the closest interest in their outcome;

2. at 15 years and 4 months he was mature, articulate and reflective and close to the upper limit of the court's jurisdiction;

3. he was the instigator of the circumstances which had led to the alleged retention and opposed return;

4. the judge had regard to paragraph 7.2(e) of the Practice Direction;

5. Rocco was already involved through an earlier attempt at mediated resolution and was present in court;

6. his clear wish and expectation were to contribute actively (not passively through the CAFCASS report), to argue his position and respond to his parents' arguments;

7. to confine him to a passive role would be detrimental;

8. to force him to wait outside in the corridor – both literally and metaphorically – would engender in him a sense of grievance and injustice;

9. if he were not joined, it would affect him adversely and he could not be expected to accept any subsequent decision of the New York court;

10. it was Rocco who would have to live with the court's decision and, if it went against his wishes, he would find it easier to live with if he had been involved;

11. the advantages to Rocco of joinder outweighed the detriments: he was not in the position of a child who had been insulated from proceedings;

12. to rely on the CAFCASS report would be inadequate – a report cannot respond proactively to evidence and submissions as they unfold; much work had already done by others in representing Rocco's views to the Court;

13. finally, joining Rocco as party would enhance the Court's understanding and provide a "moving picture" as he responded to evidence and submissions.

As a mature, articulate and reflective teenager with a strong sense of his own agency I am satisfied that Rocco needs to emerge from these proceedings, whatever their outcome, satisfied that he has participated as fully as possible in the making of the decisions that will fundamentally affect his future and with the fullest possible understanding of why those decisions have been made.

In Scotland, a child has a legal right to representation by his own solicitor.

Joint Residence

An order awarding residence to two adults – e.g. in a same-sex relationship – who live in the same house. Such orders aren't really necessary, and if the other parent is surviving and excluded, they can be provocative. Also used confusingly as a synonym for **Shared Residence**.

Judge

An officer of the court who presides over proceedings with responsibility to deal with the case justly, manage it effectively, ensure that correct procedure is followed and issue directions and orders.

Judges may do only what the law allows them to; rulings must fall within a limited range of orders and comply with the specified wording, though judges have wide **Discretion** as to how they interpret the law. Their powers are provided under legislation such as the Magistrates Courts Act 1980 and the Superior Courts Act 1981; available options are provided under the **Family Procedure Rules 2010**. These powers can be exercised on application by a litigant or on the Court's own initiative.

High court judges have an additional power – called "**Inherent Jurisdiction**" – which enables them to make orders beyond what is prescribed by Parliament.

Judgment

The spoken or written decision of a judge and the reasoning behind it.

It will usually consist of two elements, the **Ratio** and the **Obiter**. The court will indicate whether the judgment is to be read **Extempore** on the day or to be "reserved" and "**Handed Down**" at a later date. Legal spelling usually omits the *e* included in non-legal usage.

Judicatory

The system of courts of law and tribunals.

Judicial Continuity

The principle that a single **Judge** should hear a case from beginning to end.

It is an objective of the **Child Arrangements Programme** that the judge to whom a case is first allocated should manage the case through to the final hearing. Where a case is heard before **Magistrates**, at least one member of the panel, preferably the chairman, should provide continuity.

Judicial Discretion

The very wide latitude of a judge to make whatever order he thinks appropriate.

Judges are bound by the **Family Procedure Rules 2010**; should there be any doubt about whether the Court is behaving appropriately or treating the parties fairly, these rules can be referred to.

A judge need not rely on an application by one of the parties before making an order and can make an order on his own initiative (Rule 4.3). If he does, he is not obliged to allow the parties to be heard or to make representations (Rule 4.3(4)), but must advise them that they can apply to have the order **Set Aside**, **Varied** or **Stayed**.

In addition to the legislation and case law, the judgment will be influenced by the judge's own views and experience; this forms in effect a body of evidence which the parties cannot question. What professors Lynn Wardle and Laurence Nolan call "the more subtle and insipid rampage of judicial discretion" transcends case precedent and even legislation, and rose out of the doctrine of children's rights. Aristotle had warned, "the best laws should be constructed so as to leave as little as possible to the discretion of the judge", and in Hindson v Kersey [1765], Lord Camden explained, "the discretion of a Judge is the law of tyrants: it is always unknown. It is different in different men. It is casual, and depends upon constitution, temper, passion. In the best it is oftentimes caprice; in the worst it is every vice, folly, and passion to which human nature is liable". In the 1943 case of Kovacs v Szentes, the Supreme Court of Connecticut identified the challenge for litigants,

> In effect the trial judge, as a basis for *[his]* findings, made of himself a witness, and in making *[these findings]* availed himself of his personal knowledge; he became an unsworn witness to material facts without the *[parties]* having any opportunity to cross-examine, to offer countervailing evidence or to know upon what evidence the decision would be made.

Judicial Separation

A single decree in which the parties remain legally married but the obligations of the marriage cease.

The spouses no longer live together and the matrimonial property can be divided up. The same form, **D8**, and the same **Facts** on which a divorce is based are used, but it is not necessary to demonstrate **Irretrievable Breakdown**. It is suitable where irretrievable breakdown cannot be proved, where there is an objection – perhaps religious – to full divorce or, commonly, where the parties have not yet been married a year. It does not enable the parties to remarry and it is therefore almost always better to divorce rather than end up in legal limbo.

Jurat

(Latin: "he swears") the clause at the end of an **Affidavit** stating the date, place, and name of the person before whom it was sworn.

Jurisdiction

A court's geographical area of influence or its legal authority to intervene.

Where there is a question over which court has jurisdiction – Scotland or England, for example – it should be resolved expeditiously at the start of proceedings.

For a divorce petition, the petitioner must demonstrate that the court has jurisdiction; this involves demonstrating that she has had her **Domicile** in England and Wales for at least six months or been habitually resident for at least twelve (Domicile and Matrimonial Proceedings Act 1973). If the petitioner is from a Brussels II signatory country, domicile is determined under Article 3. Outside of the EU the Court will adopt a discretionary approach.

In children's proceedings, jurisdiction will normally depend on the child's **Habitual Residence**.

There are anomalies, such as Section 13 of the Children Act 1989 which refers to "the United Kingdom" but applies only in the jurisdiction of England and Wales.

Jurisprudence

The body of **Common Law** established by case precedents.

K

Kinship Care

An alternative to **Adoption** and the permanent removal of a child from his family. Under a **Child Arrangements Order** or Guardianship Order the child remains with other relatives or friends of the family.

The arrangement has become more common since Munby LJ's judgment in Re B-S; see **Threshold**. Previously, applications by family and friends were dismissed out-of-hand by local authorities, based on a brief telephone conversation. This is bad news for the industry that has grown up around adoption, but it represents a much better outcome for children and their families.

Four years after it became a statutory requirement in September 2011, one local authority in five still has no family and friends policy.

L

Law Report

An account of a case which has been worked up by a trained barrister or solicitor when the case makes a change to the law or is otherwise "reportable". It will consist of the **Transcript** but also include other elements and enhancements.

Law reports are classified using the name of the case, a brief indication of the most salient aspect which makes it a precedent or authority, the year in which it was heard, the volume of law reports in which the case is bound (referenced by an **Acronym**), and the page number on which it commences.

Lay Advisor

Someone, such as a **McKenzie Friend**, who is not legally qualified and who gives advice on behalf of an organisation in the lay advice sector.

Leave

The permission of the Court, which is required in certain circumstances such as making an application for which the applicant does not automatically qualify, taking an action which the other party opposes, or making further applications if the applicant's right to do so has been restricted under a **Section 91(14) Order**.

Section 10 of the Children Act 1989 determines who may apply for a **Section 8 Order**. Sections 10(4) and (5) determine the categories of person who may apply as of right. If an applicant cannot apply as of right he may apply with leave, and Section 10(9) sets out what factors the Court should consider in such an application; this does not represent a test: see Re A (A Child –

Application for leave to apply for a child arrangements order) [2015] EWFC 47. Section 10(8) enables the child himself to make an application and requires the Court to be satisfied the child has sufficient understanding to do so. Usually the initial judgement of the child's understanding will be made by his **Solicitor**, if he has one, but the discretion remains with the Court.

Leave to Remove
See **Relocation; External**.

Legal Aid
Funding from the taxpayer to enable a litigant to purchase legal services.

Private law litigants should understand that legal aid is no longer available for helping with costs except in very exceptional circumstances; it *is* available, however, for **Mediation** if the party meets the financial criteria. In public law it is automatically available to fight an allegation of significant harm, but not to fight the removal of a child if significant harm is proven; Munby LJ remarked,

> No doubt it is some imperfection on my part, but I confess that I struggle to understand the policy or rationale underlying this part of the scheme.

Legal aid is not normally a free service and is paid according to income: unless the litigant's income is especially low, they will have to pay monthly contributions; if they have disposable capital in excess of a certain amount they will not receive legal aid at all until their capital has fallen below the threshold.

From April 2013, the Legal Aid, Sentencing and Punishment of Offenders Act 2012 (LASPO) has ensured that legal aid is no longer normally available in family cases. The Legal Services Commission was abolished and replaced by the Legal Aid Agency, which is an Executive Agency of the Ministry of Justice.

Funding is now limited under Section 10 of the Act to "cases which are judged to have sufficient priority to justify the use of public funds". These include domestic abuse and forced marriage proceedings where the applicant can satisfy the criteria imposed by the **Domestic Violence Gateway**. Appeals to the **Court of Appeal** and **Supreme Court** still qualify, and references to the European Court of Justice, (where the area of law to which the appeal relates remains in scope). In addition, funding is available in cases where the applicant would have a right to legal aid under the Human Rights Act 1998 or European Union law.

Qualification for legal aid is determined by The Civil Legal Aid (Merits Criteria) Regulations 2013 amended by the Civil Legal Aid (Merits Criteria) (Amendment) (No 2) Regulations 2015. Legal aid is supplied on "advice" from a solicitor and is dependent on the likelihood of success, that is, its legal **Merit**. The criterion which must be satisfied in private law is that it will enable the litigant to obtain what he would regard as a significant improvement in the arrangements for his children. In public law it is that he obtains the order sought or wins the appeal. Legal aid may also be awarded if there is clear public interest with benefit to the public at large or to an identifiable group.

Litigants must also pass a "reasonable private paying individual test" which means they will get legal aid if a reasonable litigant paying his own costs would be prepared to commence proceedings and risk his own money in the same circumstances.

Unless his solicitor is confident that he qualifies, a litigant should assume that he does not and avoid the **Delay** caused by the application process.

If an application for legal aid is accepted the other party will be informed.

Legal Executive

A qualified lawyer who has trained less broadly than a solicitor and specialised earlier but who still has rights to partnership in a law firm and to judicial appointment.

Legal Services Order

A court order added to the Matrimonial Causes Act in April 2013 at Sections 22ZA and 22ZB which, in divorce or ancillary relief proceedings, enables one party to a marriage to access legal services by ordering the other to pay them a lump sum or instalments.

The Court must be satisfied that, were the order not made, the party would be otherwise unable to secure legal assistance. The order is likely to cover only a specific part of the proceedings and a second bite of the cherry is improbable. See FM v AK [2013] EWHC 4393 and Rubin v Rubin [2014] EWHC 611.

Lenocinium

(Scots) this is a Latin word literally meaning "pimping"; it is a rarely used defence under Section 1(3) of the Divorce (Scotland) Act 1976 to a divorce based on **Adultery** and is applicable if the **Pursuer** has in some manner connived in the act or has actively encouraged the defender to commit adultery, and if this encouragement was the cause of the defender committing the act (Hunter v Hunter [1883]).

Letters

Family litigation produces a large quantity of correspondence. All letters received should be filed and listed in the **Chronology** so they can be retrieved should the litigant need to refer to them. A letter from a solicitor or other party should never be destroyed, however provocative.

When letters are exhibited they should be collected together in a **Bundle** or bundles. There should be a front page attached stating the bundle consists of original letters and copies. The letters should be arranged in chronological order with the earliest at the top, clearly numbered and firmly secured.

Writing a letter is one of the most common and cheapest services a solicitor can provide. It is often effective, despite having no legal status, and a litigant will not be in breach of any law if he ignores it, though it will provoke further action which may prove impossible to ignore. Solicitors themselves will ignore a letter if they are not paid to respond. A common tactic is for a solicitor to send a letter ordering a party to leave his own home; the letter is a bluff designed to intimidate him and exploit his ignorance; the worst response is to **Move Out**, which could lose him everything, including his children.

Care should be taken with all outgoing letters; a party should temper what he says and not write anything he wouldn't want the judge to read or that can be used against him. He should be careful when referring to any point of law when writing to a solicitor and assume the recipient knows the law better than he does. Each letter should be restricted to one topic. This will oblige the solicitor to reply to each one. Letters should be kept short, accurate and to the point. A litigant must not allow himself to be bullied or intimidated and must never confess to a false **Allegation**.

Letters should be sent by recorded delivery and the receipts kept. The tracking number can be used as a reference. If no reply is received within two weeks a polite reminder should be sent, asking for a reply within seven days and reminding the recipient that Section 1(2) of the Children Act cautions against unnecessary **Delay**.

Lex Fori

(Latin: "the law of the forum") the law applicable in the particular **Jurisdiction** in which the case is heard.

Lex Loci Celebrationis

(Latin: "the law in the place of celebration") the law that applies in the jurisdiction in which a **Marriage** is celebrated.

Liability Order

A court order enabling the Child Maintenance Service to enforce payment; no longer necessary as a result of recent legislation.

Liberty to Apply

Many **Orders** will contain a clause saying something like, "There be liberty to apply as to the implementation and timing of the terms of this order".

Where an order is completely unworkable the litigant should apply for it to be **Set Aside** and make a fresh application and where it is simply wrong he should appeal it, but in other cases further intervention by the Court could make the order workable and the clause gives the litigant "liberty to apply" for appropriate orders or directions. If the order thus made amounts to a variation of the original order, it should be appealed. In *Halsbury's Laws of England*, Lord Mackay of Clashfern explained,

> The circumstances or the nature of a judgment or order often render necessary subsequent applications to the court for assistance in working out the rights declared. All orders of the court carry with them inherent liberty to apply to the court, and there is no need to reserve expressly such liberty in the case of orders which are not final. Where in the case of a final judgment the necessity for subsequent application is foreseen, it is usual to insert in the judgment words expressly reserving liberty to any party to apply to the court as he may be advised. The judgment is not thereby rendered any the less final; the only effect of the declaration is to permit persons having an interest under the judgment to apply to the court touching their interest in a summary way without again setting the case down.

Litigant-in-Person

LiP – a party to a case who attends court without representation by a lawyer, referred to in Scotland as a **Party Litigant**.

Litigants must represent themselves in court unless they qualify for **Legal Aid** or can afford a lawyer. There are arguments both for representing oneself and for being represented; unrepresented divorce cases only take three-quarters as long to resolve. Many people believe self-representation is the best option, but it isn't for everyone. Not only must the litigant become his own lawyer, understanding the law, court rules and case precedents and how they relate to his own case, but he will also be expected to stand up in court and present his case calmly and clearly in the most traumatic circumstances of his life.

If a litigant has previously been represented and intends now to represent himself, he must inform the court and his solicitor of his intent and serve notice of the change on all respondent parties through a "Notice of Change of Solicitor" on Form FP8. One copy is filed in the court office in which the application is proceeding, one to the solicitor and one to the other party or their solicitor if they are represented. Procedure is covered by Part 26 of the **Family Procedure Rules 2010**; an address to which papers may be served must be provided (Rule 26.2(2)). Until this is done this (and any fees still owing are paid) the original solicitor will be presumed still to be acting and will not release the litigant's file.

Generally, the legal profession views LiPs with distrust, although Lord Justice Munby, now **President** of the Family Division, said in a 2004 submission to the Commons Constitutional Affairs Committee that when litigants appeared in person,

> What you are getting is the facts as they see it without the assistance – and some people might put the word in inverted commas – of lawyers.

Following the cuts to legal aid, the National Audit Office reported a 30% increase in family cases in which neither party was represented; by June 2017 both parties were represented in only 19% of cases. This rise has meant that LiPs are no longer treated so leniently by the courts: they are expected to put their cases clearly and objectively, learn the relevant law; read up on their situations and keep up-to-date. Consider what Moore-Bick LJ said in R (Dinjan Hysaj) v The Home Secretary [2014] EWCA Civ 1633,

> if proceedings are not to become a free-for-all, the court must insist on litigants of all kinds following the rules. In my view, therefore, being a litigant in person with no previous experience of legal proceedings is not a good reason for failing to comply with the rules.

Neither is it the responsibility of the judge to give free legal advice, as Mr Justice Tugendhat clarified in a November 2012 defamation case,

> The court is under an obligation to do justice... But the English legal system is adversarial. The court employs no legally qualified staff to assist the judge. Not only is the court without any means to provide such assistance, the court is also obliged to be impartial. A litigant who explicitly seeks the

guidance of the court in the way that *[the litigant]* does is seeking what he may suppose to be free legal advice. But he is seeking it from a source which is unable to provide it, and it is certainly not free. The hearing before me has generated very substantial lawyer's fees, and someone has to pay them.

Litigation Friend

Someone who assists a party who lacks **Capacity**.

If a child is party but not subject to proceedings, the Court must appoint a "litigation friend" to represent him unless he has the Court's permission not to be represented or he has a solicitor and sufficient understanding to **Instruct** him. Guidance on the role of a litigation friend is provided in Practice Direction 15. Rule 21.2(1) of the Civil Procedure Rules provides that—

A protected party must have a litigation friend to conduct proceedings on his behalf.

A child's litigation friend may be a **CAFCASS** officer, the **Official Solicitor** or someone who "can fairly and competently conduct proceedings on behalf of the child", "has no interest adverse to that of the child", and "undertakes to pay any costs which the child may be ordered to pay in relation to the proceedings, subject to any right that person may have to be repaid from the assets of the child". Such a person must file a certificate of suitability with the Court and provide evidence.

Locus Standi

(Latin: "standing") the ability of an applicant to show the Court he has sufficient interest in a case to participate in it.

Lucas Direction

A direction by the judge that a lie told by a party does not of itself necessarily indicate guilt because the party may have some other reason for lying; from Regina v Lucas [1981] QB 720.

Lump Sum Order

A spousal maintenance order which orders the payment of a sum at once or in instalments in lieu of periodical monthly payments.

M

Magistrate

An officer of the court who tries simpler cases; there are two types in England and Wales:

1. Lay volunteers, also known as Justices of the Peace (JPs) who are expected to act with intelligence and integrity but who need no prior legal qualification or experience of the law; they sit as a "bench" of three with one acting as chairman, and two "wingers", assisted by a legally qualified Clerk to the Justices. Magistrates receive three days' training and are then trained "on the job"; those who deal with family matters receive additional training.
2. Stipendiary magistrates, known as **District Judges**, who sit alone.

Magistrates deal with all applications to initiate children proceedings, other than those in which there is some complexity; child maintenance proceedings; **REMO** applications; financial provision proceedings; declarations of parentage; Parental Orders under the Human Fertilisation and Embryology Act 2008; and proceedings under Council Regulation (EC) No. 44/2001 (the Judgments Regulation) and Council Regulation (EC) No. 4/2009 (the Maintenance Regulation). Magistrates should not hear any case estimated to last longer than three days.

Maintenance

Money paid by a **Spouse** for the financial support of the other or by a parent for the support of a **Child**.

Maintenance Order

An order made by the Court that one party should pay monies for the maintenance of another; they can be:

a) long-term, to maintain a spouse who cannot become financially independent after a long marriage;
b) short-term, to enable a spouse to become financially independent; or
c) nominal, where a tiny amount is paid *per annum* which can then be increased should the spouse's circumstances change – these orders are usually made where there are minor children.

Maintenance Pending Suit

A court-ordered amount of interim spousal maintenance paid until the conclusion of financial proceedings. Since April 2013, it can no longer be used to obtain funding for legal services (a "Currey" Order) for which a **Legal Services Order** must be used.

Mareva Injunction

See **Freezing Order**. Named after Mareva Compania Naviera SA v International Bulkcarriers SA [1980] 1 All ER 213.

Marriage

The legal union or contract made by two adults to live together.

The time-honoured definition provided by Lord Penzance in Hyde v Hyde and Woodmansee [1866] LR 1 P & D 130 as "the voluntary union for life of one man and one woman, to the exclusion of all others" became obsolete with the introduction of same-sex marriage on March 12th, 2014 in Scotland and March 13th in England and Wales.

Parties may marry from the age of sixteen; in England and Wales, parental consent is required up to the age of eighteen; in Scotland, it is not.

Marriage bestows legal protections which cohabitation does not, such as the right to stay in the family home while still married, financial provision on separation, the right to benefit from a spouse's pension, etc. Marriage is more enduring: the likelihood of a married couple being together for their child's sixteenth birthday is 75% compared with only 7% for a cohabiting couple.

To divorce it is necessary to have a lawfully recognised marriage, and not all are recognised in the England/Wales **Jurisdiction**. The courts strive to recognise foreign marriages and are tolerant of foreign cultures and customs which would be unacceptable in our own culture.

The courts will recognise a marriage if:

1. It is formally valid: i.e., it was performed either under the *Lex Loci Celebrationis* or under English/Welsh common law.
2. Both parties had **Capacity** to marry; i.e., they were not related to each other in a way prohibited by law. Where one has lacked capacity under their local law, but the other has not, the courts have been generous.

Parties to a marriage must be capable of giving consent – if they lack mental **Capacity** or have been forced or coerced, the marriage is **Voidable.**

A marriage in England or Wales must involve a civil ceremony whether or not it also involves a religious ceremony. Thus, a religious ceremony conducted with no attempt to comply with the Marriage Act is invalid; see Gandhi v Patel [2002] 1 FLR 602 and Akhter v Khan [2018] EWFC 54.

A marriage celebrated abroad can be proved through the production of a marriage certificate or similar document issued under the law in force in the country concerned, or a certified copy of an entry in a register of marriages kept under the law in force in that country (10.14 (1) FPR 2010). Where the document is not in English, it must be accompanied by a translation certified by a notary public or authenticated by **Affidavit** (FPR 10.14 (2)).

Marriages in exotic, foreign locations, combining wedding with honeymoon, are popular but, to be valid, must be conducted according to local law. If in doubt, parties should check with the country's embassy and not rely on their tour guide. They may need to satisfy a residence requirement or produce a **Certificate of No Impediment**. Parties who do marry abroad are advised to obtain several certified copies of the certificate as it may be difficult to obtain them later. They should also consider having the certificate translated and deposited with the General Register Office.

Martin Order

A rare order, similar to a **Mesher Order**, used to postpone the sale of the marital home to enable – usually – the wife to remain in the property, sometimes until her death, in cases where there are no children. Named after the case Martin v Martin [1978] Fam 12.

Matrimonial Causes Act 1973

The fundamental item of legislation dealing with divorce, nullity and judicial separation, and determining the transfer and settlement of property.

Matrimonial Homes (Family Protection) (Scotland) Act 1981

Legislation primarily concerned with providing rights to spouses in regard to the matrimonial home. Throughout the Act there are references to "entitled" and "non-entitled" spouses:

> The *entitled* spouse has legal title to the matrimonial property, either as owner or tenant, or is granted permission to occupy the matrimonial home from a third party.

> The *non-entitled* spouse has no legal title to the property, but under the Act is given certain rights of occupancy.

These rights automatically arise under the Act by virtue of marriage, and there is no requirement to register such rights for them to come into effect. Where both spouses have legal title to the matrimonial home, then property law rather than the 1981 Act gives both the right to occupy the home. Under s.1(1) of the Act, the non-entitled spouse has the rights—

1. if in occupation, to continue to occupy, together with any child of the family, the matrimonial home; and
2. if not in occupation, to enter into and occupy the matrimonial home.

These rights continue throughout the marriage even if the couple separate and live apart. Under s.7 of the Act as amended by Section 5 of the Family Law (Scotland) Act 2006, where—

a) there has been no cohabitation between an entitled spouse and a non-entitled spouse during a continuous period of two years; and
b) during that period the non-entitled spouse has not occupied the matrimonial home,

these statutory rights come to an end:

the non-entitled spouse shall, on the expiry of that period, cease to have occupancy rights in the matrimonial home.

A non-entitled spouse who has ceased to have occupancy rights by virtue of subsection (7) may not apply to the court for an order under section 3(1).

These statutory rights also cease once the marriage ends due to divorce, civil dissolution or the death of one of the spouses. It is important to note that, should the matrimonial home be sold to a third party, the rights of the non-entitled spouse are not defeated.

When a party moves out of the matrimonial home, it can be difficult to move back in and he can't just force his way in without risking falling foul of other laws. If a party leaves the matrimonial home for a considerable time it is no longer his home and his rights to occupy must be balanced against the other spouse's Article 8 right to privacy and family life, her home and her correspondence.

Maxim Law

A legal cult related to the **Freemen** principles. It is based on a number of maxims held to be established and universal principles of law and derived from various sources such as Bouvier's Law Dictionary of 1856, Black's Law Dictionary of 1891 and Roman law (which is why many maxims are in Latin – often inaccurately translated). Several are based on biblical sources and are therefore regarded as the word of God, and higher than "man's law".

McKenzie Friend

MF – a **Lay Advisor** permitted to provide "reasonable assistance" to a **Litigant-in-Person**.

It is a well-established practice and one may cite in support the words of Lord Tenterden CJ in Collier v Hicks [1831] 2 B & Ad 663 that,

> Any person, whether he be a professional man or not, may attend as a friend of either party, may take notes, may quietly make suggestions, and give advice.

The name derives from the divorce litigation initiated in 1970 by Levine McKenzie, a Westminster dustman, and in particular to his appeal (McKenzie v McKenzie [1970] 3 WLR 472 CA); the original McKenzie Friend was Ian Hanger, a newly-qualified Australian barrister then working a gap year in London, and subsequently a highly respected Queensland QC.

A litigant can take anyone he likes to court with him, but it is best to find someone who has acted before as an MF and has a successful track record. The purpose of allowing an LiP the assistance of an MF is to further the interests of justice by achieving a level playing field and ensuring a fair hearing. A good MF can advise on procedure and keep emotions under control and the case moving forward. Most parenting organisations will have members who work as MFs; some university law departments enable their students to act as MFs. A litigant shouldn't take anyone with an interest in the proceedings – which means family members should be avoided – and taking a new partner will be seen as provocative.

There are strict rules relating to the use of MFs and they *must* be followed. Updated guidance was issued in July 2010 by the President of the Family Division, Lord Justice Wall, in *President's Guidance: McKenzie Friends*, following implementation of the Legal Services Act 2007. Litigants intending to use an MF in court should familiarise themselves with this document. Before looking at what an MF can do, let us look first at what he *cannot* do.

It is vital to understand that an MF is NOT a legal representative in the same way a solicitor is. Section 14 of the Legal Services Act 2007 prevents an MF from performing any **"Reserved Legal Activities"** unless specifically permitted by the Court. These activities include:

1. the exercise of a **Right of Audience**;
2. the **Conduct of Litigation**.

These are the things a McKenzie Friend *can* do:

1. Provide moral support for litigants – going to court is a challenging business, and a litigant should never go alone.
2. Take notes – this is a vital function which doesn't require an experienced MF, just someone who can take rapid and accurate hand-written notes of everything said in court. The MF should note the start and end times of each session in the proceedings and, during the hearing, periodically note the time in the margin for easy reference later.
3. Help with case papers – an MF may help with the preparation of court documents but may *not* prepare them himself. In Re H (Children) [2012] EWCA Civ 1797, a father's MF gave the child's name incorrectly, from which the judge, Annabel Carr, concluded he had copied and pasted from another case, while the father maintained he had written 80% of the document himself. Carr banned the MF from further involvement, "So far as I am concerned, the documentation does cross the line, and even if it is only twenty per cent it is twenty per cent too much". Although the Court of Appeal found Carr's approach "somewhat rough and ready", it did not interfere, and the father's appeal was unsuccessful. The correct procedure if a litigant wants his

MF to prepare court documents – which is properly his own responsibility – is to apply for the MF to be allowed to Conduct Litigation.

4. Quietly give advice on any aspect of the conduct of the case. This includes points of law, issues the litigant may need to raise in court and questions the litigant may need to put to a witness.

The litigant should inform the Court in writing as soon as possible if he intends to use an MF and the MF should provide the Court with a brief CV setting out his experience and confirming he understands his role and that he has no interest in the case. The MF should be available to attend every hearing and commit to the case for its duration.

Litigants should beware MFs who have an obvious agenda and seek to run cases for their own ends; in H v Dent & Ors [2015] EWHC 2090, poor case management allowed an MF to take over a case entirely and persuade the unfortunate father – who was Bulgarian – to seek the committal of two CAFCASS officers and a solicitor, an application which was made with disregard for due process, was without merit, and an abuse of process.

In private hearings the onus is upon the litigant to show why he should have the assistance of an MF; in other hearings there is a strong presumption in favour of allowing the assistance of an MF and the onus is on the Court or the objecting party to show why he should not. If the judge refuses leave to use an MF, he must explain his reasons carefully and fully both to the LiP and to the would-be MF and allow the LiP a reasonable opportunity to argue the point. If the Court approves the use of an MF, that decision should be regarded as final.

MFs are entitled to charge for the provision of reasonable assistance and some charge £40 to £60 per hour, though this is no indication of quality or experience. An MF cannot charge for anything prohibited by the law or the Court; if the Court has given the MF leave to carry out the **Conduct of Litigation** or **Right of Audience** he can charge for both, though this provision may change. If an MF doesn't charge for his services, the LiP should at least cover his expenses, including stationery, telephone calls, travel and parking costs.

Mediation

Alternative Dispute Resolution attempted to prevent the case reaching court.

It is theoretically mandatory under Section 10 of the Children and Families Act 2014 for an applicant to attend a meeting about mediation known as a **Mediation Information and Assessment Meeting** (MIAM) before making an application to court, though there is significant evidence that the policy has failed and many litigants are bypassing this step with only 40% complying with the law. Solicitors are advising them to get their certificate signed before returning to them and progressing to court; judges are not enforcing the mediation requirement.

If the applicant contacts three mediators within fifteen miles of his home and none is able to provide an assessment session within fifteen days, the case will be allowed to progress to court. See **Child Arrangements Programme**.

A couple accepted for mediation will be offered a series of meetings with one or two trained mediators at which they can talk about arrangements for the children and finances and see whether agreement can be reached. Mediation is confidential, but if allegations of abuse are made, the mediator must contact police or social services.

Typically, there will be two to four sessions of about an hour-and-a-half each. If mediation leads to agreement, the mediator will provide a written record called the **Heads of Agreement** or **Memorandum of Understanding**. Both parties will be able to check it with their solicitor if they have one. This document is not legally binding but can be incorporated into an order if the Court thinks it appropriate.

As the Government sought to promote mediation over litigation, many solicitors re-trained; they wear only one hat at a time, however, which means that when acting as a mediator they do not give legal guidance or answer legal questions.

Legal aid is available for pre-court mediation via the Legal Aid Agency which issues certificates to mediators in the same way they do for solicitors. If the applicant does not qualify for legal aid he will have to pay upwards of £200 for the session, but this is still cheaper than asking a solicitor to negotiate a settlement. There are no costs awarded for mediation; each party must pay his own contribution.

Mediation has considerable advantages over solutions reached through protracted litigation:

1. the average cost of mediated cases involving children is a fifth that of non-mediated cases;
2. resolution achieved through mediation is a cooperative solution agreed between the parties, rather than an order imposed by a court;
3. it is therefore more likely to be successful both in the short and the long term;
4. mothers achieve better outcomes from mediation than from litigation;
5. couples who mediate are far less likely to return to court.

Mediation can enable a couple to retain a better relationship, which can be helpful for the future; but mediators can also sometimes try to cajole parties into an agreement which is not necessarily in the best interests of their child.

Once an applicant has found a mediator he should interview her before agreeing to the session; ask what she would consider a success and what her success rate is; ask whether she believes children benefit from relationships with both of their parents; ask what her views are on children who move between two homes; ask about her views on how children do in shared care situations. A good mediator will be able to talk about all of this before the mediation process begins.

To find a suitable mediator an applicant can try:

- his local Designated Family Centre
- the ADR Group;   Phone: 0117 946 7180
- the Community Legal Service (CLS);   Phone: 0845 345 4 345
- the Family Mediation Helpline;   Phone: 0845 60 26 627
- UK College of Family Mediators;   Phone: 0117 904 7223
- Family Mediators Association;   Phone: 0117 946 7180
- National Family Mediation;   Phone: 0300 4000 636

Anything discussed in mediation will not be disclosed in court; this can discourage openness and honesty and lead parents to exploit mediation as a tactical measure to qualify for court, planning their strategy in court once mediation has failed. In many cases mediation becomes a gesture, but without the commitment to make it work.

The perception is that the policy was designed to relieve pressure on the overburdened courts and ease pressure on funding: a crude attempt to mask cuts to the legal aid budget by presenting mediation as a panacea. It looked at mediation in isolation rather than in association with other techniques such as **Parenting Plans**, **Parenting Information Programmes** and **Collaborative Law**. Good lawyers were already recommending clients to use mediation and judges had the power to direct litigants to attend information sessions. It may well be that most cases suitable for mediation were already being mediated.

Mediation Information and Assessment Meeting

MIAM – a meeting an applicant is supposed to attend under Section 10 of the Children and Families Act 2014 before making his application to determine whether **Mediation** is appropriate in his particular case.

There are three points at which an applicant is expected to demonstrate his compliance with this requirement:

1. when he starts the case by submitting his C100 form;
2. at the **Gatekeeping** stage when the case is allocated to the appropriate level of judge; and

3. at the **First Hearing Dispute Resolution Appointment**.

Before making any application in relevant family proceedings, the applicant should contact an accredited mediator and provide the respondent's contact details. The mediator will then contact both parties to arrange for them to attend a MIAM to determine suitability. If parties are represented, the solicitor will contact a mediator on their behalf. The mediator can also suggest other methods of alternative dispute resolution such as collaborative law.

There are some exemptions which may apply, including:

1. agreement has already been reached;
2. the other party refuses to engage with the process;
3. the mediator determines that the case is not suitable for mediation;
4. either party has made an allegation against the other of domestic abuse which satisfies the criteria set out in the **Domestic Violence Gateway**.

Under Rule 3.10 of the **Family Procedure Rules 2010**, the Court is able to enquire whether the claim for MIAM exemption is valid; if it is not, the Court can adjourn proceedings until the parties have attended.

The Court is further required – under 1.4(2)(f) FPR 2010 – to consider at every stage of proceedings whether alternative dispute resolution may be appropriate. The Court may adjourn proceedings at any point (under Rule 3.4) to give parties an opportunity to attend a MIAM, obtain information about alternative dispute resolution or allow it to take place. The Court can make this direction on its own initiative or on application, and will tell the parties how and by when they must tell the Court whether alternative dispute resolution has been effective.

In addition to attendance at a MIAM, the parties should be encouraged to work together to produce a **Parenting Plan**. This is still an essential task even if they end up litigating. It will enable parents to understand more clearly how to continue parenting their child and it will provide a document to present to the Court when either is making a **Child Arrangements Application**.

Memorandum of Understanding

See **Heads of Agreement**.

Merit

The inherent quality of a case which justifies bringing it to court. In a children's case there will be a balancing exercise between the additional pressures and expense the case will impose on the system, and the likelihood that the case will significantly benefit the child concerned.

Mesher Order

An order preventing the sale of the matrimonial home and allowing a parent to remain in residence with the children until a triggering event ends the order. Mesher Orders are named after the case Mesher v Mesher [1980] 1 All ER 126 (actually decided in 1973).

Under Schedule 1 of the Children Act 1989, a resident parent can apply to the Court to be awarded "beneficial ownership" so that she has the right to remain living in the property while the non-resident parent's share is put on hold. This avoids transferring the property to the wife – which is unfair – or selling it – which leaves the wife with a lump sum but no home – though it is not without its own problems.

A Mesher Order typically ends when the youngest child reaches eighteen (seventeen in the eponymous case) or completes his full-time education, when the occupying party remarries or dies, or if the Court orders it. At this point the property can be sold and both parties receive their share; this provision means many fathers end up homeless with no chance of buying another property for many years. In the meantime, the home can be transferred to the occupying party with a charge-back to the other or be held in the parties' joint names on trust for sale. The first option is preferred, as decisions regarding the home need not be made by both parties, although the non-occupying party retains a share of the responsibility for maintenance and insurance proportionate to his eventual share of the proceeds.

Mesher Orders are advantageous to the occupying party if they cannot afford to move elsewhere or if it is likely the non-occupying party will choose not to contribute financially in any other way. They can, however, cause more problems than they solve when the triggering event occurs, and mothers can be left worse off than if the home had been sold and the proceeds divided up at the time of the divorce. If the father has already purchased a new home when the matrimonial home is finally sold, he will have to pay capital gains tax on the sale, so it can also be in his interest to sell on divorce. Once made, the order cannot be varied, which can lead to acrimony if circumstances change.

A father who wants to sell when his ex doesn't can either remain on the mortgage and let her pay the repayments or apply to the Court to order the sale so he can recover his share. This will cost her in legal fees, and even if she receives legal aid she will have to repay them from the proceeds of the sale. If she is using the same certificate for Children Act proceedings, she will also have to repay that funding. Better to sort things out now than accumulate debts later.

Mirror Order

An order which must be obtained from a foreign jurisdiction before the English or Welsh Court will allow a parent to remove their child to that jurisdiction for a holiday. The order will be made in identical terms to the order made in England or Wales and will confirm—

- the child's residence remains in England or Wales;
- the child will be returned at the end of the specified period; and
- the English/Welsh court retains **Jurisdiction**.

Mirror orders are not applied by many countries or applied as might be hoped. Not all countries respect them or their equivalent; India, for example, does not allow them. As a result, in many applications, the Court will seek the evidence of an expert in the law in the foreign jurisdiction. In Re AB (A Child: Temporary Leave to Remove from Jurisdiction: Expert Evidence) [2014] EWFC 2758, a mother was refused leave to take her six-year-old child on a three-week trip to India. Although the risk of abduction was low, the safeguards were insufficient.

A mirror order can cost considerably more than the planned holiday. Often, it will not be possible to obtain the order before travel or, once obtained, the parent will be able to have it varied or discharged once in the foreign jurisdiction; nor do they prevent further removal to a third jurisdiction. None of this is of comfort to the left-behind parent.

Misdirection

An error made by a judge either in relation to the law or to the facts of a case. A judge may misdirect a jury or, where there is no jury, himself.

Motion Roll Hearing

(Scots) an interim hearing.

At any time during proceedings, a litigant can request an interim measure, such as contact at a particular time, or an interdict, e.g. to prevent removal from the jurisdiction. This request is known as a "motion" and is considered at a "Motion Roll hearing". The litigant fills out a form and pays a fee. Both parties can then argue their case before the Sheriff.

A Motion Roll hearing will also be convened following a welfare report, in which, for example, a party would request the Court to allow contact in accordance with the report.

In some cases, a Motion Roll hearing will be sufficient to conclude the case, and progress to the **Proof** will not be necessary. This can mean ending up with an order for inadequate contact – or none at all – without having had the opportunity to present the evidence or examine witnesses.

Moving Out

In most circumstances the advice to a separating parent is *not* to move out of the matrimonial home. If he moves out without agreeing financial or children's matters, or there is no order in place—

1. he will be granting his spouse *de facto* custody of the children;
2. he will become liable for child and spousal support;
3. he will abandon all joint possessions and even personal possessions to his spouse;
4. he will open the way for his spouse/ex's new partner to move in to his house and become a substitute parent to his child;
5. he will give his spouse leave to petition for exclusive possession of the house in perpetuity in "the best interests of the children", thus tying up the house as an asset; and
6. he will lose his only bargaining position.

A parent who moves out makes himself a **Non-Resident Parent** with nowhere for his children to stay when they are with him; it is then uncertain a court will grant **Overnight Staying Contact**, and it won't allow him to be an equal custodial parent. If he decides to stay, an **Occupation Order** will enable the parent and children to move back into the home and oblige him to leave or be confined to part of the home, if it is large enough. If he is financially able to do so, he should try to keep the house and pay off the other parent. Until the divorce is finalised, the spouse has **Home Rights** to occupy the home, so the locks cannot be changed, though she should only enter at convenient and agreed times.

If he does decide to move out, perhaps for his own protection or that of his children, he must remember to take with him all personal documents, items of sentimental value such as photographs of the children and any items necessary for his job. If there is time, he should also take clothing, toiletries, essential cooking items, etc. It may become difficult or impossible to retrieve these later. His post will need to be redirected to his new address.

He may still find himself liable for the mortgage and for child support payments, based on a financial situation which no longer applies. He should stop paying the bills on the house unless ordered to do so by the Court: the goal is to encourage the other parent to accept a reasonable settlement and start taking responsibility. No one is liable for utilities they have not used – if the bills are in one name only, the accounts should be closed. It is reasonable to give a spouse some notice that this action is being taken, particularly if there are children in the house.

N

Name

Unilaterally changing a child's name is an issue which commonly causes great distress and protracted litigation.

A person's name is their identity; it is who they are. It provides a link to their father and forbears; it reverberates back through history. It provides information about culture, locality and occupation. For DIY genealogists, it is the key which unlocks the records. Someone whose surname has been changed is set adrift in history, without heritage, and unable to pass their name down to posterity.

A child's acknowledged name is as it appears on his birth certificate; this is regulated by the Registration of Births and Deaths Act 1953. Where the parents are married, it is the duty of either to register the birth within forty-two days. Where they are not married, they may register the birth together; if either cannot attend, they must sign a Statutory Declaration of Acknowledgement of Parentage which the other must produce to the registrar. If the father's details are not recorded they can be added later. An unmarried father must give his consent for his surname to be given to the child. Generally, it is not possible to change the name on a child's birth certificate, though there are exceptions.

There are several reasons why a mother might wish to change the name of one or more of her children; some are legitimate, some less so:

1. in her culture it is customary for a child to take his mother's name (In Re S (Change of Names: Cultural Factors) [2001] 2 FLR 1005, Wilson J allowed a Muslim mother to use Muslim names for her child but

refused to allow a formal change by deed poll from his Sikh names because they maintained the link with his father);

2. she feels she was coerced into giving the child a particular name;
3. the father was violent (or the child was conceived through rape) and use of the father's name causes her distress;
4. changing the child's name is necessary to protect him or the mother: in AB v BB and Others [2013] EWHC 227, the Court agreed the mother's security and the child's welfare justified changing the child's surname; in Re F (Contact) [2007] EWHC 2543, [2008] 1 FLR 1163, where there was a risk that the father would abduct the children, Sumner J held that a change of surname would enhance the child's welfare;
5. she has children by several fathers, and wants them all to have the same name;
6. she has reverted to her maiden name and wants her child to do so too;
7. she has re-married and thinks it is embarrassing or confusing for the child's name to differ from the rest of his family;
8. changing the child's name persuades the child or other parties that the mother's new husband or partner is really the child's father;
9. changing a child's name severs his final link with an absent or non-resident father;
10. it makes it more difficult for a father to find his child;
11. it makes it more difficult for the child to find his father.

Section 13(1)(a) of the Children Act 1989 states that, where there is a **Child Arrangements Order** in force regulating with whom the child is to live, the written consent (via letter, not fax or email) of every person with **Parental Responsibility** for the child must be obtained if the child is to be known by a new surname. A father should be expected to give his written consent, even if he does not have PR. If he withholds consent, the mother will need to make a Section 13 application for **Leave** using Form C1; there is no statutory duty on the Court to consider the **Welfare Checklist**, though in practice it will.

Where there is no CAO, legal precedent has usually applied the same rule, but decisions have not always been consistent or fully reasoned. In this circumstance, the application is made under Section 8, applying for a **Specific Issues Order** on Form C100, and the Court *is* obliged to consider the welfare checklist.

Where a father wishes to change his child's name, the degree of his commitment to and involvement with the child are significant considerations (Re W, Re A, Re B (Change of Name) [1999] 2 FLR 930).

A more insidious way of changing a child's name avoids the legal process and, thereby, the necessity of obtaining the father's consent or a court order. In such a case, the mother encourages the child to use the new name, encourages members of her family and her friends and neighbours to use the new name, and gives the new name to schools, doctors and local authority agencies.

If the father insists on the use of his child's correct name, these agencies may consider him to be acting unreasonably, or out of antipathy towards the mother. Very often a father with little or no contact with his children will not even be aware his child's name has been changed. Changing a name in this way has no legal status and should not be accepted by the courts.

Parents should seek agreement before resorting to court. An increasingly popular compromise is to use a double-barrelled name. In Re R (Surname: Using Both Parents) [2001] EWCA 1344, the Court of Appeal encouraged the parents to use both names.

If the surname of the child is legally protected by a CAO regulating with whom the child is to live, the father should initially write to the mother; if she is uncooperative, he can contact the school or doctor and remind them of the order and ask them to amend their records accordingly. If the mother does not cooperate, he'll need to apply for enforcement.

If the child's surname is not legally protected, the father will need to make a Section 8 application for a **Prohibited Steps Order**; if he is already making an application, he can avoid paying twice by putting this on his C100 form as a specific issue. He'll need to act swiftly; sometimes the courts have censured the mother but allowed the change to stand on the grounds that to change it again would cause the child further disruption.

Schools are not always familiar with the law and it can be necessary to inform them that, where a CAO is in place, it is an offence under Section 13(1) CA1989 to allow a child to be known by a new surname, unless all parties with PR have agreed.

There is a special case which applies when a child has been born and has not yet been given a name: the father can apply for a PSO to prevent the birth being registered without him and to prevent the child being given a name against his wishes. This is a very constructive use of the PSO.

Different judges have taken different approaches where there has been no Residence or Child Arrangements Order. In Re PC (Change of Surname) [1997] 2 FLR 730, Holman J considered it reasonable to apply the pre-1989 law,

> Where only one person has Parental Responsibility for a child... that person has the right and power lawfully to cause a change of surname without any other permission or consent. Where two or more people have Parental Responsibility for a child then one of those people can only lawfully cause a change of surname if all other people having Parental Responsibility consent or agree.

257

In Re T (Change of Surname) [1998] 2 FLR 620, Thorpe LJ agreed; Holman's judgment was—

> persuasively indicative... that consent of the other parent or the leave of the court... was an essential prerequisite certainly where both parents have parental responsibility.

Similar emphasis was given in Re C (A Minor) (Change of Surname) [1998]; and in Re W, Re A, Re B (Change of Name) [1999] 2 FLR 930, Butler-Sloss LJ said, without addressing the question of PR,

> In the absence of a Residence Order, the person wishing to change the surname from the registered name ought to obtain the relevant written consent or the leave of the court by making an application for a specific issue order.

In the 1999 **Court of Appeal** case of Dawson v Wearmouth, Lord Mackay extended this guidance to stop parents constantly changing and re-changing the child's name,

> The registration or change of a child's surname is a profound and not merely a formal issue... Any dispute on such an issue must be referred to the court for determination whether or not there is a Residence Order in force and whoever has or has not parental responsibility.

The mother had been married to Mr Wearmouth and had two children by him who took his surname. She divorced and subsequently had a third child, Alexander, with Mr Dawson. When Alexander was about a month old the mother and Mr Dawson separated, and she registered the boy with the surname of Wearmouth so that she and all three children should all have the same name. Mr Dawson applied to the Court for Alexander to be known by his surname.

The House of Lords refused his application. The name had already been registered and changing it would not enhance Alexander's interests. The mother, Mr Dawson and the child had not lived together as a family unit for any length of time. The mother not unnaturally argued that she and the two other children had one surname and it would do more for the unity of the family if all the children had the same surname. The Court agreed.

The flaw in this solution was that while the first two children really were the children of Wearmouth, the third was not: one of the appeal judges, Lord Jauncey, dissented from the deciding view,

> A surname given to a child at birth was not simply plucked out of the air. Where the parents were married the child would normally be given the father's surname or patronymic thereby demonstrating its relationship to him.

> The surname was thus a biological label telling the world at large that the blood of the name flowed in its veins. Alexander had not a drop of Wearmouth blood in his veins.

How the Court should decide where there is no CAO or where the father does not have PR remains moot, despite the positions taken, without argument, by Thorpe and Butler-Sloss. Judicial opinion inclines towards preserving a child's link (it may be his last) with his father. A guiding case is Re B (Change of Surname) [1996] 1 FLR 791, in which a mother applied to have the surname of her three children – aged twelve, fourteen and sixteen – changed to that of the man with whom they had been living for seven years; there was no contact with the father, and the children had been alienated. J Wilson observed,

> I do not think that to allow this change of name would be in the children's best interests. B is their father. And while... it may be true that the children will in fact insist on being called H, for me to allow this application would be to give the court's approval to a process which I do not believe is in their best interests. I think that in reality they are B and that this court should recognise that reality.

In answer to the issue of embarrassment, Wilson said,

> Miss Woolrich *[mother's Counsel]* resurrects the traditional argument that it is embarrassing for children to be known by a surname other than that of the adults in the household. But the law must not lag behind the times. In these days of such frequent divorce and remarriage, of such frequent cohabitation outside marriage, and indeed increasingly of preservation of different surnames even within marriage, there is, in my view, no opprobrium nowadays upon a child who carries a surname different from that of the adults in his home.

He also quoted Buckley J in Re T (orse H) (An Infant) [1963] Ch 238,

> it is injurious to the link between the father and the child to suggest to the child that there is some reason why it is desirable that she be known by some name other than her father's name.

The decisive principles were summarised by Butler-Sloss LJ in Re W, Re A, Re B, [1999]: where parents have been married, they share the power to register a child's name but where they have not, only the mother has that power; once the name is registered, any person who wishes to change that name must have the written consent of all those with PR or the Court's leave.

In making its decision, the Court will not give much weight to the fact that the child's name is not the same as the applicant's; where parents were married, there must be strong reasons to change the name; where they were not, the quality of the child's relationship with the father and his degree of commitment will be relevant.

Two fundamental principles emerge; the first, which presents a usually insurmountable obstacle, is that a court will allow the change of a child's name only if so doing *will enhance the child's welfare*. This must be evidenced by a CAFCASS report recommending the change; see AB v BB and Others [2013] EWHC 227. In Re W (Children) [2013] EWCA Civ 735, a decision had been made without the benefit of a welfare report and Ryder LJ granted the mother leave to appeal,

> [20] There appears to have been little or no evidence before the court relating to that important decision in the child's life. A CAFCASS officer could and perhaps should be asked to give an opinion on the subject having spoken to at least both parents, and on this ground of appeal I have much greater sympathy with the mother and I give permission for her to bring an appeal based upon that discrete issue.

See also M v F (change of surname: terminating Parental Responsibility) [2016] EWFC B59 in which a father who had sexually abused his daughter was stripped of **Parental Responsibility**.

The second principle is *whether the child's name has already been registered*. Anyone wishing to change the name will have to show why that registration was wrong or mistaken, or why the reasons for changing the name now override those for the original registration. The fact that a mother has remarried since registration and now wishes to change her child's name to match her own (or those of children born subsequently) is immaterial.

Changing a child's forename is rarer than changing a surname; though the point is seldom considered in a secular age, it is said that in English law to change the name given to a child at his baptism is unlawful since his name is given to him by God (Re Parrott, Cox v Parrott [1946] Ch 183, [1946] 1 All ER 321); a Christian name given on baptism can be changed only on confirmation, by Act of Parliament or by adding a name when a child is adopted.

Only the High Court can interfere with a parent's right to choose their child's forename (Re H (Child's Name: First Name) [2002] 1 FLR 973) and only in exceptional circumstances; Section 33 of the Children Act applies only to surnames and so the Court must use its **Inherent Jurisdiction**. In Re C (Children) [2016] EWCA Civ 374, the Court held that for a mentally ill mother to name her daughter Cyanide crossed the **Threshold** for **Significant Harm**; she was also prevented from calling her son Preacher so that, while growing up, the twins would be on an equal footing,

> *[109]* It is hard to see how (regardless of what justification may be given to her by loving carers) the girl twin could regard being named after this deadly poison as other than a complete rejection of her by her birth mother.

National Youth Advocacy Service

NYAS – a charity which can become involved in family cases in the role of **Children's Guardians** as an alternative to **CAFCASS**.

NYAS are generally viewed with suspicion by parents as they are yet another part of the system and ruthlessly commercial, but they may be able to offer a marginally better service than CAFCASS. They will also usually be able to allocate more time to a case. Particularly in difficult cases where CAFCASS are not helping the parties towards resolution, they should be considered by the Court. Consider Wall LJ's comments in A v A [2004] EWHC 142:

> *[132]* This case demonstrates what can be achieved by intelligent and purposeful social work intervention. The courts cannot expect in every case a service of the quality given to it by NYAS in this case. CAFCASS Reporting Officers in any event have a much more limited role. CAFCASS guardians, no doubt, are more tightly restrained by budgets and workloads. But there is no doubt that the excellent service provided by NYAS in this case was crucial to its successful determination.

If CAFCASS is already handling the case, NYAS can become involved only if formally appointed by the Court under Rule 16.3 **Family Procedure Rules 2010**. In Re B (Contact: Appointment of Guardian) [2009] EWCA Civ 435, proceedings had been continuing for ten years and the father had no contact. The Court invited NYAS to produce a report on re-establishing contact, but they referred him to the FPR rule. The Court rejected the father's application and the Court of Appeal dismissed his appeal.

NYAS can provide advocacy services for children and young people up to the age of twenty-five. Like CAFCASS, they do not operate in Scotland. They can be contacted on 0800 61 61 01 or emailed at help@nyas.net.

Needs, Wishes & Feelings

So that it may comply with Section 1(3)(a) and (b) of the Children Act 1989 which requires consideration of the child's "ascertainable *wishes and feelings*" and his "physical, emotional and educational *needs*", the Court may direct CAFCASS to produce a "Needs, Wishes and Feelings" report.

This is a flexible tool which can form part of the **Section 7 Welfare Report**; it can be filed as a **Children's Guardian** report, as part of a Rule 16.3 report, as part of a **Family Assistance Order report**, as a "Wishes and Feelings" statement by a child, as part of Extended Dispute Resolution, or as a source for discussion.

For this purpose, CAFCASS has prepared two sets of forms for younger and older children which the FCA will complete with the child. These are available from the CAFCASS website. There are other tools which may also be used, including computer-assisted programmes such as *In My Shoes* and *Listening to Young Children* or creative processes like drawing, clay modelling, games, music, drama, storytelling and play.

In an effort to reduce the burden on an overloaded CAFCASS, the Interim Guidance issued by the President encouraged the use of short "Wishes and Feelings" reports as a first step in resolution. The problem with this approach is that it may work in easy cases but simply postpones the point in more conflicted cases at which the issues must be confronted.

A child can be manipulated, and his legal team may be persuaded prematurely to give up the quest to restore a full relationship. A perceptive guardian should be able to see where a child's expressed wishes and feelings may lead to a result contrary to his best interests. In Re R (A Child) [2009] EWHC B38, an eleven-year-old boy had been alienated against his father; Judge Bond decided to transfer residence from the mother, and his decision was upheld in the Court of Appeal, Bond said in his judgment,

> [90] As the Guardian has recorded in her reports, R has consistently told her that he does not wish to see his father and wants contact to stop. As the Guardian had predicted in July 2008, R has become more hostile about his father. If the court were to act upon R's expressed wishes as to contact, it would cease... In considering the weight to be placed upon his view it is important to record the obvious point that R is older than at the last substantive hearing. The Guardian and Dr M have each considered the question as to whether R is able to express a view which is sufficiently balanced and considered. The advice is that in the particularly difficult circumstances of this case he is not. He has become too involved in the process to the extent that in the Guardian's view he has attempted to control the outcome... I therefore listen to and take account of R's view but it cannot be determinative of the result.

Neglect

The persistent failure to meet a child's physical or emotional needs, resulting in impairment to health or development. Neglect can occur before birth, or include the failure to protect a child from **Harm** or to provide a child with appropriate medical care. Neglect is the most common form of child abuse and the most likely reason for intervention.

Neutral Citation

A system of classifying cases introduced in 2001 which consists of the name of the case and the year and court in which it was heard.

The case name can be the name or initials of the opposing litigants (J v C) where "v" is short for the Latin *versus* – "against"; alternatively, cases are referred to using the Latin for "in the matter of" – *in re* or just *re* – and the child's initial. The court is referenced by an **Acronym**; this will often be followed by a brief indication of the most salient aspect of the case which makes it a **Precedent** or authority.

No Further Action

NFA – a formula used by the police when there is insufficient evidence to justify charging or cautioning a suspect. If further evidence comes to light, the investigation can be resumed.

No-Contact Order

The Children Act 1989 allowed an order to be made for No Contact – a relatively rare type of order which the courts preferred to avoid.

Their rarity was exploited to maintain the fiction that courts were seldom ordering a cessation of contact between children and parents, whereas it was easy to achieve the same result by means of an order for **Indirect Contact**.

The rule of thumb was that if the Court wanted to bind the non-resident parent not to seek contact, it made a **Prohibited Steps Order**; if it wanted to bind the resident parent not to allow contact, it made an Order for No Contact. It could also make both. The flexible wording of the Children and Families Act makes it possible to draft a **Child Arrangements Order** which achieves the same effect.

No-Delay Principle
(See **Delay**.)

No-Fault Divorce
The removal from **Divorce** legislation of the primordial requirement that the petitioner prove the respondent to be at fault. Divorce based on **Separation** or **Non-Cohabitation** is effectively no-fault divorce. Some campaigners advocate eliminating fault from the procedure entirely, and there is a case for making divorce an administrative process, no longer subject to judicial supervision.

Non-Accidental
An injury to a child which cannot be explained as accidental is often presumed by medical personnel to be non-accidental. This potentially reverses the burden of proof which places the onus on the doctors to show that the injury is deliberate, which is what the parents sought to argue in Re M (A Child) [2012] EWCA Civ 1580. No innocent explanation for a series of peculiar bruises had been offered and the trial judge had found that they must therefore be non-accidental. Lord Justice Ward allowed the parents' appeal and observed that,

> in finding as she did that this was a non-accidental injury, I fear the judge has not properly respected the burden which is on the local authority to demonstrate that these parents had deliberately gone about in some unknown way, with some unknown implement, to inflict these injuries on the baby.

Non-Cohabitation
(Scots) the condition of living separately for a specified period to qualify for divorce.

Where a **Pursuer** uses one year's separation as justification for divorce, the **Defender's** consent in writing is required for the application to be accepted by the Court; without consent the divorce will not be granted.

Where the pursuer seeks a divorce on the basis of two years' separation the consent of the defender is *not* required; there is however the rarely used legal defence that the divorce itself (but not the separation) would leave the defender financially destitute.

These periods must be complete before the application is made and be without a break. There is only one exception: if during the separation period the parties have lived together temporarily for not more than six months in total, in a final attempt to make the marriage or civil partnership work, they may still be eligible to apply for a divorce or dissolution under the **Simplified Procedure**. Thus, if during the separation period they have attempted reconciliation for five months, then the pursuer must wait either for at least one year and five months from the date of the original separation and obtain the consent of the defender or for at least two years and five months if consent is not given.

In 2015/16 divorce on the basis of one year's separation with consent accounted for 26% of Scots divorces while two years' separation without consent accounted for 68%.

As all matters relating to children and finances must be agreed upon prior to the Decree being granted, most couples use the intervening period to resolve these matters.

Non-Molestation Order

NMO or "Non-Mol" – an injunctive order, preventing the respondent engaging in behaviour which the applicant finds distressing.

NMOs prohibit the respondent from "molesting" the applicant or another adult or relevant child. "Molest" can be interpreted generally or can refer to specific acts. The word "molest" need not necessarily imply violence, so an order can be made, for example, on the basis of pestering rather than violence; the law offers no definition, but NMOs should not be granted on spurious grounds. Whereas **Harassment** requires a small degree of evidence, an NMO can be obtained merely on the basis that the applicant *fears* a former partner will become violent or abusive.

An NMO prohibits behaviour by the respondent which would not ordinarily be criminal. A **Penal Notice** is automatically attached so that **Breach** of the order becomes a criminal offence under the Domestic Violence, Crime and Victims Act 2004; there is a maximum custodial penalty of five years. Committal proceedings must be heard in open court. The same conduct cannot be punished both through a criminal conviction and proceedings for **Contempt of Court**.

Applications are made under Section 42 of the Family Law Act 1996 on Form FL401 and are supported by a sworn witness statement. The relevant rules of court are the **Family Procedure Rules 2010**, Part 10. There is no longer a fee to be paid.

The application is typically made *Ex Parte* or **Without Notice**, but the accompanying witness statement must set out the reasons why notice was not given. Rule 10.3 FPR 2010 demands that the application must be served on the respondent not less than two days before the date of the hearing. Allowing applications to be made *ex parte* means a parent can secure an NMO against the other without their attendance, without their knowledge and without providing them the opportunity to be heard or to present a defence (in Scotland, by contrast, *ex parte* applications are deemed inappropriate).

If the respondent's whereabouts cannot be ascertained, the Court need not serve the application and can hear it and make an order without the respondent's attendance. The Court may also transfer proceedings to another court which can make attendance less likely.

NMOs are made in closed court unless the Court directs otherwise; if the paperwork received does not contain notification of such a hearing, the respondent should return to the issuing court and get a date set.

The Court must first establish that the accused is "associated" with the applicant. If there is no **Association**, the applicant can apply instead for a restraining order under the Protection from Harassment Act 1997.

The Court will make an interim order if it thinks it is "just and convenient". "Convenient" circumstances include those where there is a risk of harm if the order is not made, where not making the order will deter the applicant, and where the respondent is evading service. The Court may also order disclosure of records from the police, social services or hospitals in order to provide confirmation.

The respondent must check the wording of the order; the rules are strict which means witness statements are often improperly made out and thus inadmissible, though this is rarely an obstacle in practice. An unrepresented respondent will find it difficult to use this defence if the applicant is represented. An offending clause can be removed under the **Slip Rule**; see Grubb v Grubb [2009] EWCA Civ 976. An interim *ex parte* order cannot be contested, but the respondent can contest having it made into a full NMO. He will need to file a sworn statement in response to the allegations made and attend the hearing.

NMOs are often made alongside **Occupation Orders** and it is important for the Court to clarify which bits are which, because it is a criminal offence to breach an NMO but not an Occupation Oder. An NMO must not be used to achieve an Occupation Order through the back door; an exclusion zone can be imposed as part of an NMO, for example, but a requirement for a party to leave his home can only be made through an Occupation Order. A party must not be put at risk of committing a criminal offence when the law does not permit that; see R v R [2014] EWFC 48, [2015] 2FLR 1005. Where there is no evidence of violence, the order should not mention violence or include any clause forbidding its use or threat. The Court's consideration in making the order must be to "secure the health, safety and well-being" of the applicant, other adult or child.

The Court can also add a "power of arrest" to the order so that if the respondent breaches it, he can be arrested, but the wording of the order must prohibit behaviour which would entitle a constable to arrest the respondent. "Power of arrest" can be added even to an order made without notice, so the

266

respondent can be arrested without being aware he has breached the order, though he can't be guilty of an offence or be convicted.

The order can endure for a specific period or terminate when the proceedings do, or another order is made; if it thinks it necessary, the Court can make the order without application. Refer to the Family Justice Council leaflet: *Protocol for Process Servers: Non-Molestation Orders* for information on the correct service of NMOs by process servers.

An NMO can be renewed via an *ex parte* hearing; the respondent must be served with a copy of the order, a copy of the application and supporting statement and a copy of the Court's reasons for renewing the order. There is no requirement to hold a subsequent *inter partes* hearing.

In Practice Guidance issued in October 2014, the President stipulated that an interim order should not normally be made for longer than fourteen days and must specify the date and time of expiry. A follow-up **Inter Partes** return hearing should be arranged to coincide with the expiry day, usually within a week, to consider all the evidence. The order must contain a statement clearly spelling out that the respondent has the right to make an application on notice to set aside or vary the order. The onus is on the applicant to persuade the Court the order should be extended beyond the date of the return hearing. One consequence of this guidance is that every application will need to be personally served twice – by the bailiff, if the applicant is in person.

In Re W (Minors) [2016] EWHC 2226, an *ex parte* order had been made with a duration of a year, clearly flouting the guidance; Mostyn J reminded practitioners of the guidance and drew their attention to an editorial in the **Red Book** encouraging judges to disregard it; this was "intemperate, disrespectful and legally wrong".

There is an argument that, since the order bans the respondent from doing what he denies doing anyway, there is no point defending, other than to avoid costs. He could therefore offer a bilateral **Undertaking** not to use violence or harassment, threaten violence, etc., in return for having no order for costs; the other party does the same which should satisfy both parties. An Undertaking can easily be made without representation, but making it will only resolve a case if the applicant accepts it.

If the order is to be appealed it must be within fourteen days, and there will then be a wait of at least three weeks for a hearing.

Non-Resident Parent

NRP – a purely financial term used to describe the parent with liability for paying child support. It replaced the unacceptably judgemental "absent parent" used in legislation in 2001, but has come to have a similar pejorative inference.

No-Order Principle

The principle in Section 1(5) of the **Children Act 1989** that, "where a court is considering whether or not to make one or more orders under this Act with respect to a child, it shall not make the order or any of the orders unless it considers that doing so would be better for the child than making no order at all".

This is a long-standing principle: Lord Justice Lindley said in 1893, "the duty of the Court is, in our judgment, to leave the child alone" (see **Welfare**). Its purpose is to establish the courts as non-interventionist and encourage parents to reach their own settlements; it was also intended to reduce the number of orders the courts were making, which had reached a very high level before 1989.

North Yorkshire Declaration

The early decision to rule out the child's biological parents as suitable carers when adoption is being considered: Named after North Yorkshire County Council v B [2008] 1 FLR 1645 and referenced in Re W (Children) [2015] EWCA Civ 403.

Notice of Proceedings

Form C6 on which the Court informs the respondent of the application or petition; see **Divorce**.

Nullity

That which does not exist or never happened – the state of a marriage rendered null by a court ruling; see **Annulment**.

O

Obiter

(Latin: short for *obiter dicta*, "things said in passing") the asides, illustrations, analogies, individual opinions and references to prior decisions within a **Judgment** which go beyond the facts of the case and are not the meat of the argument or essential to the decision.

Obtemper

Verb, to comply with (a court order). Failure to obtemper is **Contempt of Court.**

Occupation Order

An injunctive order made under the Family Law Act 1996 regulating the occupation of the family home in some way, usually in response to a relationship that has become turbulent or violent; they frequently go hand-in-hand with **Non-Molestation Orders**. An Occupation Order can (s.33(3)) —

1. enable the applicant to enter and remain in all or part of the home, and require the respondent to allow this;
2. prohibit, suspend or restrict the respondent's rights to the home;
3. prevent the respondent from living in all or a part of the home; or
4. impose an exclusion zone around the home which the respondent may not enter.

Changing the locks on a jointly-owned property without the consent of the other owner is inadvisable; they would still be entitled to gain entry, for example, by breaking a window, which could be costly. A party is better advised to write to his/her spouse, or ask her solicitor to do so, requesting that he stays away from the property and respects her privacy. If he needs to retrieve items, a mutually convenient time can be agreed. If he persists in entering the property and the resident party finds it distressing, she can investigate taking out an Occupation Order.

Applications are made using Form FL401, supported by a witness statement on Form N285 in which the reason for the application is explained and, if appropriate, the reason it is made *ex parte*. The application should include corroborative evidence such as police crime numbers, details of any contact with domestic abuse agencies, or evidence from a GP. Three copies will be required: for the applicant, the court and the respondent. If the order will entail a change in the occupier, a fourth copy will be needed for the landlord or mortgage supplier. There is no longer a fee to be paid.

The applicant must be entitled to occupy the home and must have an **Association** with the respondent (s.33(1)).

As with Non-Molestation Orders, the respondent must attend the hearing, which will be conducted in closed court unless the Court directs otherwise. He may decide not to defend, given that the relationship has broken down anyway, and will need to consider what would be achieved by defending: if he has to sell the house in any case, he should and move on. Not defending, however, can be interpreted in later proceedings as walking out on his children or an admission of whatever is alleged.

Orders are made under different sections of the Act according to the applicant's rights of occupancy and association with the respondent:

- under *Section 33*, when the applicant has a right to occupy or matrimonial homes rights in the property, there is no maximum duration;
- under *Section 35*, where the parties were married and the respondent has a right of occupation but the applicant does not and where the home was (or was intended to be) the matrimonial home; the order will prevent the respondent from evicting the applicant or allow the applicant to enter and occupy; the order cannot exceed six months, but can be extended for up to a further six;
- under *Section 36*, as under Section 35, but where the parties were not married;
- under *Section 37*, where the parties are or were married and neither has right of occupation but both are in occupation; the order regulates the respondent's occupation or excludes him but gives the applicant

no right of occupation; the order cannot exceed six months, but can be extended for up to a further six;

- under *Section 38*, as under Section 37, but where the parties were not married.

For Section 35 orders, the Court must consider the length of time since the parties ceased to live together and since the marriage was dissolved or annulled, and the existence of any pending proceedings.

For Section 36 orders, the Court must also consider the nature of the parties' relationship, the length of time during which they have lived together as husband and wife, the length of time elapsed since they ceased to live together, whether they have or have had any children together, or both have or have had **Parental Responsibility** for any children and the existence of any pending proceedings between them.

For Section 33 orders, the Court must consider under s.33(6) the housing and financial resources of *both* parties and their children and the likely impact on the health, safety and well-being of the parties and children if the order is *not* made. Under s.33(7) it must balance the risk to the child of significant harm attributable to the respondent's conduct (as defined under s.31(9) CA1989) against the risks of making the order. Precedent set by Chalmers v Johns [1999] 1 FLR 392 requires the Court to apply s.33(7) *before* s.33(6). Where the threshold is reached, the making of the order is mandatory. The criterion is the risk and not actual harm, and it need not necessarily be the child who is at risk.

G v G (Occupation Order) [2000] 3 FCR 33, in which the judge had refused to make the order, clarified that the respondent's misconduct need not be intentional: the Court must consider its impact. In Dolan v Corby [2011] EWCA Civ 1664, the Court of Appeal warned that the two sections must not be conflated and that the test demanded by s.33(7) *must* be satisfied first. There is no need to prove abuse or reprehensible behaviour, see Re L (Children) (Occupation order: absence of domestic violence) [2012] EWCA Civ 721, but if domestic abuse is not proven, the case must be *"exceptional"* if such a **Draconian** order is to be applied, and in Dolan v Corby it was.

Under the Family Law Act, a respondent can be ordered to pay rent and bills on the home from which he has been ousted and to keep it in good repair; under the Debtors Act 1869 he cannot be committed should he default.

Breach of an Occupation Order is not a criminal offence, but it *is* **Contempt of Court**, and the orders are usually made with a **Power of Arrest**. The respondent has to be brought to court within twenty-four hours of arrest or be released. A **Penal Notice** warning the recipient that he may be committed if it is proved beyond doubt he has breached the order can be attached if the Court has specifically directed it.

Occupation orders can be overturned. In B v B (Occupation Order) [1999] Fam Law 208, a father and his six-year-old daughter were evicted from their home to make way for the mother and her baby who had been living in a B&B. The local authority would not re-house the father, meaning the daughter would be forced to live in homeless accommodation or be taken into care. The Appeal Court allowed the father to return to his home while the local authority found alternative accommodation for the mother.

Official Copy

A copy of an official document supplied and marked as such by the office which issued the original.

Official Solicitor

A lawyer appointed by the Lord Chancellor under Section 90 of the Senior Court Act 1981. He is invited to act on behalf of a "protected party", defined under Rule 21.1 of the Civil Procedure Rules as "a party, or an intended party, who lacks **Capacity** to conduct the proceedings", when no other person or agency is able to do so.

The Official Solicitor will not take instruction, because the litigant is deemed to lack the capacity to **Instruct**, and will not necessarily argue for his views to be taken into account, and will act instead in his "best interests". What those are will often be determined by the other side.

It is a matter for the Official Solicitor's discretion whether he consents to act, and he cannot be compelled. Due to the relentless rise in demand, he will only get involved in cases where absolutely necessary – all other options should be explored first. If he consents to act, he may become involved in proceedings as a "**Litigation Friend**".

Opening Submissions

This is where the applicant (or his legal representative) presents his case, doing so as briefly and succinctly as possible. If it is his application, he goes first; the order in which parties should be allowed to speak is:

1. the applicant;
2. respondents with **Parental Responsibility**;
3. any other respondents;
4. the child's guardian; and
5. the child, if they are party to proceedings and there is no guardian.

If the respondent is represented and the applicant is not, the respondent's legal representative may be asked to speak first.

Opinion

(Scots) a **Judgment**.

Options Hearing

(Scots) the first hearing in divorce, financial and children's proceedings; equivalent to a **Directions Appointment** in England and Wales.

An Options Hearing is purely procedural, and the Sheriff has no power to make an order. Instead he is trying to make an informed decision as to what should be the next step in the process. The hearing is intended to give parties a chance to meet before the Sheriff in order to ascertain whether agreement can be reached without proceeding to a full **Proof Hearing** or, if this is not possible, to focus the precise disagreement between parties.

Note that hearings in Scotland are sometimes called "**Diets**".

Order

An official proclamation issued by a court. It will typically take injunctive form: directing a party to do or not do something. In family law, judges are restricted to a narrow range of orders, but within each category have wide discretion.

No party should leave court without a copy of the order. This sounds obvious, but a surprising number of litigants leave without the one thing they went to court for. To be valid it must be sealed – i.e., bear the Seal of the court.

Ordinary Procedure

(Scots) the procedure for **Divorce** in the Scots jurisdiction which must be used if there are children from the marriage under the age of sixteen (including adopted and step-children) or if the divorce is fault-based (i.e., on "Unreasonable" **Behaviour** or **Adultery**).

The **Pursuer** will write a statement detailing the irretrievable breakdown of the marriage, and on which grounds she is seeking divorce, and a statement detailing the arrangements for the children. It is important for the Court to see that the marriage has broken down irretrievably with no chance of reconciliation.

The action begins with the pursuer's solicitor drafting the summons (**Court of Session**) or initial **Writ** (**Sheriff Court**). This is a formal document sent to the Court stating all the facts. A copy is sent to the **Defender** who then has twenty-one days to seek legal advice and consider his response. When adultery is the basis for divorce, a copy is also sent to the third person involved if he or she is named in the summons or initial writ.

The Court can refer the dispute to a mediator accredited to a specified family mediation organisation at any stage in the proceedings.

Where both parties are in agreement, the action proceeds as an undefended divorce; sworn statements are usually provided by the pursuer and the solicitor submits the statements to the Court. The judge examines the case in private and the decree will be granted unless the Court requires further information.

The defender may decide to defend the action, either because he objects to the divorce itself, or because he disputes some aspect of the future arrangements for the care of any children, the proposed financial provision on divorce, or both. If, during the process, defended actions are settled by agreement, a Joint Minute of Agreement or Separation Agreement can be drawn up. If the grounds of the action are proven, the Court will grant a decree. Note that there is only one decree under Scots Law, unlike England and Wales in which there is a two-stage process.

When no agreement is reached, the pursuer needs to use the Ordinary Procedure to divorce by way of a **Writ** in which she also applies for financial relief, and the defender then has the opportunity to state his intention to make financial claims. There is then an **Options Hearing** to resolve the finances and, if there is still no agreement, the case proceeds to a **Proof Hearing** at which the Sheriff makes the financial orders and rubber-stamps the divorce. Fault-based divorces carry a heavy burden of proof should the defender choose to defend the divorce and the onus is then on the pursuer to provide that proof.

Ordinary Residence

A now out-dated concept superseded by that of **Habitual Residence**. It was described by Lord Scarman in Regina v Barnet L.B.C., *Ex parte* Shah [1983] 2 AC 309,

> I unhesitatingly subscribe to the view that "ordinarily resident" refers to a man's abode in a particular place or country which he has adopted voluntarily and for settled purposes as part of the regular order of his life for the time being, whether of short or long duration... there must be a degree of settled purpose.

Ors

Abbreviation of "others".

Orse

Abbreviation of "otherwise".

Out-of-Time

Many legal procedures must be completed within a specified time limit; for example, the response to a divorce petition. Where this limit is exceeded, the Court may proceed as if the respondent has consented. The other legal team will therefore seek to introduce delay and other obstacles to put the respondent "out-of-time".

Overriding Objective

The first rule of the **Family Procedure Rules 2010**: the requirement that the Court deals with a case "justly, having regard to any welfare issues involved". In order to achieve it, the Court as far as is practicable will,

1. deal with every case expeditiously and fairly;
2. deal with a case in ways which are proportionate to the nature, importance and complexity of the issues;
3. ensure that the parties are on an equal footing;
4. save unnecessary expense; and
5. allot to each case an appropriate share of the Court's resources, while taking account of the need to allot resources to other cases.

The parties are required to help the Court accomplish this and promote the **Welfare** principle.

P

Paralegal

One of a wide range of personnel who works in a legal environment but is not as widely qualified as a **Solicitor** or **Legal Executive**.

Parent

There is no "natural parent presumption" in family law: residence of a child is decided on consideration of its best interests, and while a parent's biological relationship with the child will be taken into account, it is not determinative.

In Re E-R (A Child) [2015] EWCA Civ 405, the trial judge had ordered a five-year-old to be moved to her estranged father on her mother's death, relying on a "broad natural parent presumption", rather than live with friends the mother had named as guardians. The Court of Appeal found there was no such presumption and none that the child should live with a testamentary guardian, whose appointment takes no effect while the other parent lives and has PR; the sole consideration was the child's welfare. In Re W (A Child) [2016] EWCA Civ 793, McFarlane LLJ clarified,

> [71] The repeated reference to a 'right' for a child to be brought up by his or her natural family, or the assumption that there is a presumption to that effect, needs to be firmly and clearly laid to rest. No such 'right' or presumption exists.

Fathers and mothers are legally recognised as parents under different conditions.

The legal *mother* is the woman who carried the child, regardless of how the embryo came to be in her womb, and regardless of her genetic relationship to it.

A man will be presumed to be the *father* if—

1. he was married to the mother at the time of birth (if he was unmarried at the time of conception the rule still applies) – this rule is known as *pater est quem nuptiae demonstrant* ("the father is he whom the marriage indicates") or *pater est* for short;
2. his name is on the birth certificate;
3. he has a **Parental Responsibility Order** by consent; or
4. there are other corroborative factors – e.g. he slept with the mother on the night of conception.

If a mother's female partner, whether or not joined by a civil partnership or marriage, is considered to be the child's other parent, no man can also be considered the child's parent, even if biologically he is the father. Such a man would therefore require **Leave** to apply for a **Section 8 Order**. Such a child would legally be fatherless.

Where two gay men care for a child, they are to be regarded as the "parents" but not as the "fathers".

A sperm donor is not regarded as the father of a child if he donates through a licensed provider. If he donates on a do-it-yourself basis, he *will* be regarded as the father and will be liable for child support; see Re M (Sperm Donor: Father) [2003] Fam Law 94. If the man dies after donation, he is not regarded as the father.

The notion of fatherhood has become fragmented and must commonly be shared between two or more men. All will have a relationship with the child, and may have a legitimate claim to contact, but cannot all be regarded as "parents" since a child can have only two – although this is contradicted, for example, by Re G (Children) [2006] UKHL 43, in which the child seems to have had three mothers.

The Human Fertilisation and Embryology Act 2008 established a third category of legal parent who is neither the father nor the mother, but the "other parent".

If the mother is in a civil partnership or marriage with another woman at the time of impregnation, the other woman is regarded as the "other parent": she has Parental Responsibility and the child is legitimate. If the other woman did not give her consent to impregnation, she is not to be regarded as the other parent.

If the mother was not in a civil partnership or marriage with another woman and no other adult is regarded under the above rules as the other parent of the child, but the mother is in an informal relationship with another woman and impregnation is carried out by a licensed provider, then the other woman is to be regarded as the other parent. If the two women are joined in a civil partnership or marriage before the birth of the child, the child is legitimate.

Parental Alienation

Conscious or unconscious behaviour by one parent which distances a child from the other; it is implicated in up to 90% of protracted cases.

The term was coined in the early 1980s by US psychiatrist Dr Richard Gardner who also proposed the term "Parental Alienation Syndrome" (PAS) to describe the condition of a child who has been poisoned or alienated through constant denigration by one parent against the other. Since Gardner's death in 2003 many other experts have acknowledged and researched the phenomenon.

Parental Alienation has become controversial. Within the fathers' movement it has become an obsession and is viewed as the driving force in every case; numerous organisations have been established solely to address the phenomenon, and even to have it made a distinct crime.

On the other side of the debate, its existence is denied entirely. This position is supported by the 2000 report into *Contact and Domestic Violence* by child psychiatrists Claire Sturge and Danya Glaser which was commissioned specifically to help resolve four cases in the Court of Appeal: Re L, Re: V, Re: M and Re: H (Contact: Domestic Violence) [2000] 2 FLR 334. The authors exceeded their remit, which was to report only on the **Domestic Abuse** alleged to have been perpetrated by the fathers in the cases, and their references to alienation are sketchy and of limited value; nevertheless, this report, in which the authors bluntly stated, "Parental Alienation Syndrome does not exist", has become influential and is regarded as providing a definitive position on alienation as well as on DV.

Psychologist Tony Hobbs warns that the review of alienation literature in the Sturge and Glaser report is "seriously flawed",

> While Sturge and Glaser have acknowledged the reality of so many of the factors involved in PAS, unlike many other practitioners around the world they have held back from identifying this constellation of factors as comprising an identifiable syndrome. This is not helpful. When an entity is identified and named, it can then begin to be effectively addressed.

The damage to relationships caused by alienation is clear and a common feature in cases. In Re W (A Child) [2008] EWCA Civ 1181, Wall LJ quoted extensively from the report by consultant child and adolescent psychiatrist, Dr Kirk Weir,

[11] Even the most neutral question became an opportunity for a torrent of vilification against the father. The interviews had an "orchestrated" feel; a sense that all knew this was an opportunity to leave me in no doubt as to their feelings. All were supporting each other and there was not a chink between them. That a child of 11 should feel it acceptable to say (without comment from his mother or siblings) that he wished his father dead says a great deal about the atmosphere which the mother has allowed to develop.... It was difficult to believe the mother was promoting contact with the father. It was clear she loathed him and regarded him as an emotional danger to her children.

Forcing contact on an alienated child against a resident parent's will is deemed to be emotionally harmful: Re D (A Minor) (Contact: Mother's Hostility) [1993] 2 FLR 1. This view should be resisted, and a court should consider the medium and long-term developmental impact on the child and not give excessive weight to a transient effect. The classic case in which a court accepted the indisputable alienation of a parent was Lady Justice Bracewell's treatment in V v V [2004] EWHC 1215 in which she transferred residence to the father,

[23] Mother is shrewd and intelligent, but twisted by an agenda of her own. She does not want to lose residence, nor does she want to go to prison for failure to comply, but she wants to eliminate contact. Therefore, she has to present herself as a parent who supports contact, but who is constrained by the need to protect the children from harm. The truth, however, is that she builds up her store of ammunition against father to use when the opportunity presents.

In the landmark case of Re W (A Child) [2014] EWCA Civ 772, the Court recognised that alienation is no less harmful to a child than physical harm. A **Fact-Finding** found that the girl had been sexually abused by her paternal grandfather, but the mother continued to make allegations that the father, too, had abused her, and prompted her to repeat these allegations; the Court had no option but to make an interim care order. Ryder LJ said,

[21] I ask the question rhetorically: given the court's findings, how could the judge leave the child with the mother? No level of sufficient support and necessary protection was described by anyone. To leave the child without protection would have been unconscionable. One has only to consider physical abuse to a child that gives rise to a similar index of harm to understand that such a position was untenable. The submission made on behalf of the mother that her care of the child had in all (other) respects been good or even better than good simply misses the point. More than that level of care was needed to protect this child from her own mother...

Parents who are implacably hostile to contact with the other will infect their children. The average age at which a severely alienated child is finally reunited with a parent is twenty-six, and they will continue to have mental health problems throughout adulthood. Alienators can be cunning, cruel and cold people, without empathy. They are skilled at drawing attention off themselves and onto the other parent. Once alienation has become successful and the child says he no longer wants to see the non-resident parent, the alienating parent will become outwardly supportive of contact, but say they must respect the child's wishes to have no contact. Attention is then thrown on to the alienated parent whose behaviour appears to be distressing the child.

Few cases, however, are "pure", and most are "hybrid" cases in which alienation is combined with other factors. Where children are not negotiating **Transitions** between their parents satisfactorily, it is easy for the contact parent to assume the resident parent is alienating the child against him and to jump to litigation. At the same time, the resident parent will assume the contact parent is a threat to the child and is possibly abusing him or her. The likelihood is that neither position is fully justified, and what is actually required is to cool the situation down and for the parents to start working cooperatively. A child in a hybrid case will normally return to the alienated parent in late teens or early twenties with few continuing issues.

Whilst alienation can be malicious and deliberate, it is far more likely that one or both parents is simply failing to understand how to facilitate the child's transitions. The child may only be starting out on the "alienation spectrum", but the anger and frustration of a rejected parent can push the child into full alienation. The alienation reaction deepens, and transitions become increasingly perilous because parents who should be working collaboratively to enable transition are too busy exchanging allegations and engaging lawyers; attitudes become increasingly entrenched and hostile and eventually the child prefers to remain with only one parent. The desperate response of the other is to make an application to court.

Parental alienation need not be overt; merely expressing anxiety each time a child visits the other parent and relief each time he returns is a form of alienation which becomes effective over time. Because it isn't officially recognised, a parent should be careful when referring to Parental Alienation "Syndrome". Simply "alienation" or other expressions such as "brainwashing", "poisoning" or "programming" are safer. **"Implacable Hostility"** can also be mentioned safely, while **"Pathogenic Care"** may be a better path to remedy.

Parental Responsibility

PR – according to the Children Act 1989, PR is "all the rights, duties, powers, responsibilities and authority which by law a parent of a child has in relation to a child and his property".

There are two types of PR: **Automatic** and **Acquired**. Mothers and married fathers have automatic PR; unmarried fathers may acquire it.

PR was the most significant new concept created by the Children Act 1989 and replaced the concept of parental rights in Section 4 of the Family Law Act 1987. There is no legal limit to the number of adults who can have PR for a child.

PR was a response to legislative changes in 1987 which removed the concept of illegitimacy and thus threatened to give fathers automatic parental authority over their illegitimate children which had previously been held only by mothers. In its *Second Report* on illegitimacy, the Law Commission recommended that fathers of non-marital children should only achieve parental authority through judicial scrutiny, to guard against "**Unmeritorious**" fathers; the 1989 Act was a compromise, whereby fathers could acquire PR either through judicial scrutiny or through agreement with the mother.

PR defines a parent's obligations towards a child; it confers no rights. In Re H-B (Contact) [2015] EWCA Civ 389, the President of the Family Division, James Munby, said,

> [72] ...parental responsibility is more, much more, than a mere lawyer's concept or a principle of law. It is a fundamentally important reflection of the realities of the human condition, of the very essence of the relationship of parent and child. Parental responsibility exists outside and anterior to the law. Parental responsibility involves duties owed by the parent not just to the court. First and foremost, and even more importantly, parental responsibility involves duties owed by each parent to the child.

In H v A (No. 1) [2015] EWFC 58, Mr Justice MacDonald observed that—

> [48] ...A parent's rights, duties, powers, responsibilities and authority... are only derived from their obligations as a parent and exist only to secure the welfare of their children. Within this context the concept of parental responsibility "emphasises that the duty to care for the child and to raise him to moral, physical and emotional health is the fundamental task of parenthood and the only jurisdiction for the authority it confers".

> [51] Where however the manner in which a parent chooses to exercise an aspect of their parental responsibility is detrimental to the welfare of the child, the court may prescribe, to whatever extent is in the child's best

interests and proportionate, the exercise by that parent of their parental responsibility.

Mr Justice Wall provided a useful pocket-guide to parental responsibility in a footnote to his judgment on A v A [2004] EWHC 142. It is important to understand this; abuse of these principles leads to endless unnecessary litigation:

1. *Decisions either parent can take independently of the other without consultation or notification:*

   a) how the child is to spend his time during contact periods;
   b) personal care for the child;
   c) activities undertaken;
   d) religious and spiritual activities;
   e) continuing to take medicine prescribed by a GP.

2. *Decisions either parent can take independently but of which they must inform the other:*

   a) medical treatment in an emergency;
   b) visits to a GP and the reasons for them;
   c) booking holidays or taking the child abroad during contact time.

3. *Decisions which must only be taken following consultation:*

   a) selecting a school and applying for admissions;
   b) contact rotas during school holidays;
   c) planned medical and dental treatment;
   d) stopping medication prescribed by a GP;
   e) attendance at school functions (so the parents may avoid meeting each other wherever possible);
   f) age at which children are allowed to watch age-restricted DVDs and video games.

Parents with PR for their child share the same responsibilities, even if one is the person with whom the child is to live and the other is not. This is a fact of which many parents, teachers, doctors and others so often seem unaware. A separated parent should take an active interest in his child's development, education and health and not leave it all to the other parent. Are all their inoculations up-to-date? Do they have any recurrent illnesses which may be cause for concern? Are they taking any prescribed drugs, and if so why? All of this involvement can later be used in court as evidence he is a fully committed parent, and not just a bystander. In Re G (A Child) [2008] EWCA 1468, Lord Justice Ward affirmed,

> A Residence Order gives the mother no added right over and above the father. That is the lesson that has not yet been fully learned in the 19 years that the Act has been on the statute book. The Residence Order does no more than its definition allows.

Parental Responsibility does not apply while the child is *In Utero* and only commences *after* a child is born; it expires once the child reaches an age at which he is able to make the decisions previously covered by PR. At the age of sixteen a child can marry with parental consent, change his name, consent to sexual intercourse, consent to medical treatment, or ride a motorcycle. At the age of eighteen he becomes a fully-fledged adult able to make his own decisions on all aspects of his life.

Although divorce doesn't affect the status of a parent's **Parental Responsibility**, he will find that schools and doctors will often act as if divorced, non-resident fathers no longer have PR. The doctor may want proof or may withhold records because he thinks the father is trying to discover his ex's address or whether she has a new partner, etc. The British Medical Association (BMA) gives this advice to its members,

> Anyone with Parental Responsibility has a statutory right to apply for access to their child's health records. If the child is capable of giving consent, access may only be given with his or her consent. It may be necessary to discuss parental access alone with children if there is a suspicion that they are under pressure to agree (for example, the young person may not wish a parent to know about a request for contraceptive advice). If a child lacks the competence to understand the nature of an application but access would be in his or her best interests, it should be granted. Parental access must not be given where it conflicts with a child's best interests and any information that a child revealed in the expectation that it would not be disclosed should not be released unless it is in the child's best interests to do so. Where parents are separated and one of them applies for access to the medical record, doctors are under no obligation to inform the other parent, although they may consider doing so if they believe it to be in the child's best interests.

The danger is that this guidance makes the doctor the arbiter of the child's best interests; determining these is not, of course, a decision a GP is professionally competent to make and, where there is a dispute, the Court must decide. In practice it may be necessary for a solicitor to write to the doctor confirming the parent has PR, and he may find that any records sent are incomplete, or have sections blanked out. All records belong to the local NHS trust. Access to medical records is governed by Section 7 of the Data Protection Act 1998.

A softly, softly approach is usually best at first and if that doesn't work a complaint to the Information Commissioner can be effective, but ultimately a non-resident parent may have to enforce his rights in the courts. Another approach is to proceed against the other parent on a **Specific Issue** application, and then subpoena the doctor to produce the medical records.

Parental Responsibility & Rights

(Scots) PRR – unlike the English and Welsh Children Act the Children Act (Scotland) 1995 makes a distinction between rights and responsibilities.

In Scotland, a parent has the *responsibility* (Section 1) to safeguard and promote the child's health, development and welfare and to provide direction and guidance in a manner appropriate to the child's stage of development. A parent who does not live with his child also has the *responsibility* to maintain personal relations and direct contact with the child on a regular basis and to act as the child's legal representative.

A parent has the *right* (Section 2) to have the child living with him or otherwise to regulate the child's residence and to control, direct or guide the child's upbringing in a manner appropriate to the stage of the child's development. A parent who does not live with his child also has the *right* to maintain personal relations and direct contact with the child on a regular basis and to act as the child's legal representative.

PRR ends when a child reaches sixteen. The responsibility to give a child guidance lasts until the age of eighteen.

Note how different this is from English and Welsh legislation under which a parent only has responsibilities. In Scots law, a non-resident parent has the right to maintain direct contact on a regular basis, and it is also his responsibility to do so. In England and Wales, a non-resident parent has no such right or responsibility, and a court cannot order him to have contact if he is unwilling; his only responsibility under the law is to provide monetary child support.

In Scotland, PRR enables a parent to "exercise that right independently of any other person with the same right, unless the right is conferred or regulated by a deed or court order which limits independent exercise"; thus, a parent may make decisions unilaterally without reference to the other.

A child's mother automatically has these responsibilities and rights under Scots law, and therefore is automatically classed as a "relevant person" with regard to court hearings involving her child.

A father only has PRR if married to the mother at the time of conception or if he marries her subsequently (Section 3(1)(b)) and without PRR cannot be considered a relevant person. If he is not married, he can also acquire these responsibilities and rights through being registered on the birth certificate as the father but only if the child was born after 4th May 2006 which is when the Family Law (Scotland) Act 2006 came into force. He can also acquire them through making a formal agreement with the mother (Section 4), and the Court can make an order either conferring these responsibilities and rights or depriving him of them (Section 11).

A father without PRR faces a lengthy and costly legal procedure to gain status as a "relevant person", even if he has a Contact Order or other (s)11 order, or a longstanding and close relationship with his child. The onus is on him to prove he has an active involvement with the child. In the case of Principal Reporter v K [2010], the Supreme Court highlighted the "burdensome procedural hurdle" which the father had to overcome, who had been afforded neither the opportunity to refute the allegations made against him, nor any right to appeal against the Court's decision. Where the unmarried father has established a family life with the child, there does not appear to be any good reason why he should not have an automatic right to participate in the decision-making process affecting his child.

Parental Responsibility Agreement

An agreement made between the parents of a child when one parent is not on the birth certificate that he or she should have **Parental Responsibility**.

The mother's signature must be witnessed by a Justice of the Peace, a Justices' Clerk, an assistant to a Justices' Clerk or an officer of the court authorised to administer oaths. The form is then sent to the Central Family Court which will rubber-stamp it.

Under the Adoption and Children Act 2002, a step-parent can acquire PR for a step-child; the agreement can only be overturned by court order. If the biological father has PR, his consent and signature will be required on the form, though his objection can be overruled if the mother applies for a PRO from the court. If the father doesn't have PR, his consent is not required, and he can't object.

This can be a sensible first step to consider for step-parents who ultimately intend to adopt, and it does not take PR away from the natural parent or subject the step-parent to examination by social services (see **Adoption of a Step-Child**).

There are three application forms: C(PRA1) is used by fathers, C(PRA2) by step-parents and C(PRA3) by a second female parent. A separate form must be completed for each child.

Parental Responsibility Order

PRO – an order made on **Application** to the Court that a father should be granted **Parental Responsibility** for the child concerned when there is no agreement with the mother.

A biological father will need to apply to the Court under Section 4 of the Children Act 1989 for a PRO, arguing why he feels his child will be disadvantaged by not having two parents with PR. He must emphasise the benefits to the child, and his willingness to exercise his responsibilities. The application is made on Form C1; he must also file Form FM1 to confirm attendance at a **MIAM**.

A man who is not the child's biological father cannot apply for a PRO, but can apply on Form C100 for a **Child Arrangements Order** in which he is named as a person with whom the child is to live, which will then automatically confer PR for the duration of the order. The order can also contain a clause stating that PR has been conferred, to make the point absolutely clear.

Most applications are granted, even to fathers who will then be denied unsupervised contact; PR gives access to the courts and further Section 8 orders, but it is no guarantee of contact with the child.

The awarding of a PRO must be in the child's "best interests"; the criteria were established by Balcombe LJ in Re H (Minors) (Local Authority: Parental Rights) [1991] Fam 151 CA, and so are known as the Re H criteria:

1. the degree of commitment which the father has shown towards the child;
2. the degree of attachment which exists between the father and the child; and
3. the father's reasons for applying for the order (this criterion allows the Court to screen for improper reasons).

In 1994 Balcombe said,

> The purpose of a Parental Responsibility Order is to give the unmarried father a *"Locus Standi"* in the child's life by conferring on him the rights which would have been automatically his by right had he been married to the mother at the time of the child's birth. The making of such an order would enable the father to contribute to the promotion of his daughter's welfare and to play the natural part of her father in her future, although it did not give the father any rights of either residence or contact.

Re H (Parental Responsibility) [1998] 1 FLR 855 established that these criteria represented a starting point and were not an exhaustive list; the child's welfare remained paramount. For example, in Re M (Handicapped Child:

Parental Responsibility) [2001] 2 FLR 342, a father who met the criteria was nonetheless denied PR because of the belief that it would have put stress on the mother and interfered with her ability to care for the child.

The Court will consider whether the father was at the birth, whether he continues contact, whether he is involved in the child's education and development, whether he contributes financially. Note that Re H shows attachment to be a two-way process.

Wall LJ provided the argument for granting PR in Re S (Parental Responsibility) [1995] 2 FLR 648,

> I have heard up and down the land, psychiatrists tell me how important it is that children grow up with a good self-esteem and how much they need to have a favourable positive image of the absent parent. It seems to me important, therefore, wherever possible, to ensure that the law confers upon a committed father that stamp of approval, lest the child grow up with some belief that he is in some way disqualified from fulfilling his role and that the reason for the disqualification is something inherent which will be inherited by the child, making her struggle to find her own identity all the more fraught.

The leading case is Re C & V [1998] 1 FLR 392, in which Ward LJ (echoing Wall) confirmed,

> It should be understood by now that a parental responsibility order is one designed not to do more than confer on the natural father the status of fatherhood which a father would have when married to the mother. There is also a sad failure fully to appreciate, when looking at the best interests of the child (which are paramount in this application, as elsewhere) that a child needs for its self-esteem to grow up, wherever it can, having a favourable positive image of an absent parent; and it is important that, wherever possible, the law should confer on a concerned father that stamp of approval because he has shown himself willing and anxious to pick up the responsibility of fatherhood and not to deny or avoid it.

Parental Responsibility; Acquired

An unmarried father does not have automatic Parental Responsibility, though there are various legal routes by which he (or a second female parent) can acquire it if—

1. the child was born after 1st December 2003 and the father's name is recorded on the birth certificate;

2. the parents both sign a **Parental Responsibility Agreement** and lodge it with the Court;
3. the Court makes a **Child Arrangements Order** in which he is named as a person with whom the child will live;
4. he is named in a Child Arrangements Order as a person with whom the child is to spend time or otherwise have contact and the Court chooses to award him PR;
5. the Court makes a **Parental Responsibility Order** in his favour; or
6. he is appointed **Guardian** of the child.

Another adult can acquire PR for a child through—

1. adopting the child;
2. making a Step-Parental Agreement with the parent (and any other person with parental responsibility) if he or she is married to, or is the civil partner of, a person with parental responsibility for the child;
3. a court order for Parental Responsibility;
4. being appointed the child's guardian – usually on the death of one parent;
5. having a Child Arrangements Order made in their favour in which they are named as a person with whom the child will live; or
6. being appointed a Special Guardian through a **Special Guardianship Order**.

When a child is in care, the local authority has PR.
Acquired PR can be taken away again by a court if it sees fit.

Parental Responsibility; Automatic

All mothers have automatic PR; a father has automatic PR only if he was married to the mother at the time of his child's birth (even if he is not on the certificate) or if he marries her after the birth.

Mothers also have the right, which fathers lack, to grant PR to a man of their choice, who may or may not be the father. A mother's civil partner will also have parental responsibility, subject to the conditions in section 42 of the Human Fertilisation and Embryology Act (HFEA) 2008.

Automatic PR can be lost only through **Adoption** or through a parental order under the Human Fertilisation and Embryology Act (HFEA) 1990.

Parental Responsibility; Delegation

A parent cannot surrender or transfer **Parental Responsibility** to another but can, under Section 2(9) of the Children Act, delegate all or some PR to someone acting on their behalf for a specific purpose, such as a medical appointment or school trip. The person to whom PR has been delegated can only do what they have been authorised to do. PR can also be delegated to a local authority, for example when a child is beyond parental control.

Parental Responsibility; Proof

There will be occasions when a father needs to prove he has **PR** for his child, perhaps to a doctor or school. He will first need to provide proof of his own identity by submitting his passport, birth certificate or photo identification, such as a driving licence. He will then need to provide a copy of one of the following documents:

1. the child's Birth Certificate – to acquire PR the father and mother must have registered the child's birth together on or after the 1st December 2003; or
2. the Marriage Certificate; or
3. a Parental or Step-Parental Responsibility Agreement; or
4. a copy of a court order giving the father parental responsibility – leave of the Court will be necessary to show this to anyone.

Parental Responsibility; Removal

A court has no jurisdiction to remove either a mother's or father's **Automatic PR** other than through adoption or surrogacy.

Acquired PR may be removed in a number of ways. Under section 4(2A) of the Children Act 1989, the Court can take away an unmarried father's PR if he has acquired it in one of the following ways:

1. he has been registered as the father on his child's birth certificate;
2. he and the child's mother have made a **Parental Responsibility Agreement**;
3. the Court has made a **Parental Responsibility Order** in his favour.

Where there is an order in place it can be discharged; the application is made on Form C1.

If a man believes he has been incorrectly named as the father, he can apply to have his PR removed by means of a Declaration of Non-Parentage under

Section 55A of the Family Law Act 1986. The court will need to confirm that he is not the father by directing a **DNA Test.**

Section 55A(1) also provides for any person with "sufficient personal interest" to apply to the Family Court or High Court for a declaration (of Parentage or Non-Parentage) as to whether or not a person named in the application is or was a parent of a child. Procedure is provided by the Family Proceedings Courts (Family Law Act 1986) Rules 2001; see Re J (A Child) [2004] EWCA Civ 184. The application is made on Form FL424 which must be obtained from the court: it isn't available on-line. The applicant must also complete and swear an affidavit. The completed application must be given to a circuit judge or higher for approval.

If a DNA test proves a man is not the biological father, he will lose PR. He cannot apply for a Parental Responsibility Order, and if the mother is trying to marginalise him his only option is a **Child Arrangements Order** naming him as a person with whom the child is to live which will automatically confer PR. He can still be awarded an order giving him contact but will not have PR for the child. This arrangement is not made clear in the Children Act, but derives from the legal definition of fatherhood, which relies initially on genetic paternity (see **Parent**).

If a mother wishes to have a father stripped of PR, she should make an application for a **Specific Issues Order** under Section 4(2A) of the Children Act using Form C100. This is an irrevocable step, and not one to be taken lightly; successful applications are very rare.

In H v A (No. 1) [2015] EWFC 58, a mother was unsuccessful in her application to have the father's PR revoked as they had been married. MacDonald J made instead a global **Prohibited Steps Order** preventing the father from exercising any aspect of his PR before each child reached the age of 18; he also relieved the mother of her obligation to inform or consult with the father, and imposed a **Section 91(14) Order.**

In Re P (Terminating Parental Responsibility) [1995] 1 FLR 1048, Singer J terminated the parental responsibility of a father who had been gaoled for injuring his nine-week-old child; Singer said,

> I believe that there is no element of the band of responsibilities that make up parental responsibility which this father could in present or in foreseeable circumstances exercise in a way which would be beneficial for the child.

In Smallwood v UK [1999] 27 EHRR 155, a father argued in the **European Court of Human Rights** that the provisions for stripping an unmarried father of PR, which do not apply to mothers or married fathers, were discriminatory. The Court acknowledged there was discrimination but argued that courts would only make orders for parental responsibility if they were able subsequently to rescind them.

In DW (A Minor) & Anor v SG [2013] EWHC 854, a father who had been convicted of sexually abusing his two step daughters was stripped of PR for his son. He, too, argued the decision was discriminatory, but Baker J held, following *Smallwood*, that there was no rights breach. The father also contended the Court should hesitate to rescind PR following amendments introduced in 2003 to make PR available to unmarried fathers. The father appealed; he could no longer argue the law was discriminatory, so he argued that —

1. social norms had changed since Re P, the Human Rights Act 1998 and the Adoption and Children Act 2002 had been introduced and it was no longer relevant to the present case;
2. the judge had failed to consider whether the mother had proved the father was a "sexual recidivist"; and
3. the judge had failed to make an order that was proportionate or to take into account the principle that orders of this kind should not be used as a weapon.

The Appeal Court argued (Re D (A Child) [2014] EWCA Civ 315) that two cases in twenty-five years was unlikely to open the floodgates to s.4(2A) applications. On the issue of the fact-findings, Baker had read and heard all the evidence over many days and had ample opportunity to assess the credibility of the witnesses; it was Baker, not the mother, who had found the father to be a "sexual recidivist"; the effect of this was to "subtly reverse the burden of proof". Although the case differed from Re P in that the father had not directly harmed D, he had inflicted devastating emotional harm on the whole family which he continued to deny. The appeal was refused.

In M v F (change of surname: terminating Parental Responsibility) [2016] EWFC B59, a father had raped his four-year-old daughter orally, anally and vaginally and was serving a long prison sentence. Miss Recorder Henley agreed to terminate the father's PR and allow a change of surname of the two children in order to protect them and the mother following his release,

> [29] By virtue of F's conduct, which involved the most heinous of offences, I am satisfied that he has forfeited any claim that he had to holding Parental Responsibility for his children. Parental Responsibility is for parents who can exercise it in the best interests of their children. [This Father's]... actions represent a catastrophic breach of trust.

Parenting Agreement

A detailed, written proposal for the day-to-day shared parenting of a couple's children after divorce or separation. It should include every child regarded as a **Child of the Family**.

A parenting agreement is not a legal contract and cannot be enforced by a court. It is intended to help separated parents who are on relatively amicable terms stay out of court by encouraging them to make practicable arrangements for their children by themselves or with the assistance of a Family Mediator, regarding things like living arrangements, discipline, schooling and medical decisions. They are more flexible than Consent Orders and can be changed easily with minimal expense. A parenting agreement is not set in stone and should be reviewed periodically as children develop.

Parenting agreements can help parents avoid the pitfalls which commonly cause antagonism and lead to court, such as changing a child's **Name**, or encouraging a child to call a new partner "Mum" or "Dad". They should help parents maintain a civil and respectful relationship, with no arguments or harsh words conducted in front of the children. Above all, they encourage parents to recognise the vital role the other plays in the child's life and to respect that; they should discourage parents from placing unreasonable restrictions on what the children can and cannot do during their time with the other parent, and help them to trust and respect each other to make considered decisions about what activities are safe and appropriate for their children to participate in.

As part of their parenting agreement, parents can develop tools to facilitate post-separation parenting, such as shared on-line calendars and communication books. The calendar will enable parents to keep each other up-to-date with important event information, like parents' evenings, sports days, examinations, social invitations, etc. A communication notebook records the highlights of the child's emotions and behaviours during the time she is with each parent; it includes observations of the child's health, feeding and sleeping patterns, language issues, mood, what soothes her, what upsets her, her daily routine, and any other relevant information. It stays with the child and is passed between parents at each transition.

It is important that parents establish stability as soon as possible after separation or divorce and a routine for their child. Stability doesn't mean she has only one home; it means the **Transitions** between homes and between parents are arranged so that they are manageable for her. A parent needs to understand how children form attachments and how these are arranged hierarchically. The only people who can mediate these attachments between the parents following separation in a manageable way for the child are the parents themselves. These arrangements should be made in the child's **Best Interests** and be explained to her; she should be involved in decisions but never be made to feel responsible for them.

Parenting Plan

A parenting plan is written to give parents the opportunity to sit down and have a constructive discussion about how their child will be parented after separation, covering all aspects of the children's lives. Ideally it will enable parents to produce a **Parenting Agreement**.

Regardless of whether parents agree things amicably or go to court for a **Child Arrangements Order**, they will need a parenting plan. There's no point a litigant taking his case to court if he doesn't know in detail what he wants from the exercise. A draft can be presented to the judge and be drawn up into an order.

Ruth Langford has written a multi-purpose parenting plan which acts as part of a parent's initial proposals to the other parent, as a discussion tool for parents to help them decide how to co-parent after separation, as part of a C100 application, or as a step in the mediation process. The plan allows for flexibility and, unlike other plans, facilitates shared parenting. It is available from: https://oratto.co.uk/wiki/family-law-solicitor/parenting-plan-may-be-in-the-best-interests-of-your-child.

Parents' Information Programme
See **Separated Parents' Information Programme**.

Part-Heard

A case in which a hearing is adjourned until another day because time has run out.

Party Litigant

(Scots) a litigant who represents himself without a solicitor or barrister.

A litigant will find it more difficult to conduct his own litigation in Scotland than in England: the system isn't designed for self-representation. Clerks of the **Sheriff Court** and the General Department of the Court of Session can give advice on procedure. Litigants should go at quiet times in the afternoon and not in the much busier morning session. Sheriff Court procedure is published in *Ordinary Cause Rules: Second Edition* by McCulloch, Laing and

Walker (now out of print); procedure in the Court of Session is published in *Green's Annotated Rules of the Court of Session* by Nigel Morrison.

The use of lay assistants or **McKenzie Friends** is not as well established in Scots courts as it is in English and Welsh ones, largely because they are not allowed to charge for their services. They weren't accepted into the Court of Session until mid-June 2010 (forty years after being accepted into the English court), following the Lord President's Act of Sederunt.

Lay representatives may make oral submissions to the Court and can conduct litigation; in the **Court of Session** they must complete a form containing certain statements and declarations. A party litigant will have to apply to the court to use a Lay Representative via a **Motion Roll**.

From April 2013, unpaid lay representatives have been able to appear in the Sheriff Court at a specified hearing for the sole purpose of making an oral submission on behalf of the party litigant at that hearing. To request such a hearing, the request should be made orally on the date of the first hearing at which the litigant wishes the individual to make oral submissions and should be accompanied by a document signed by the person named.

The sheriff will grant the request only if he or she is of the opinion that it would assist the sheriff's consideration of the case to grant it and may also of his or her own accord or on the motion of a party to the proceedings withdraw such permission.

Scottish Sheriffs and Lords Ordinary will not tolerate displays of frustration or emotion. Litigants must remain absolutely in control and be polite and respectful. They should also be aware that in Scotland costs are much more likely to be awarded.

Passport

Anyone with **Parental Responsibility** for a child can apply for a passport for him. It is not necessary to have the consent of the other parent. A father applying for a passport for his child, however, is likely to be challenged. Applicants should check first with the Passport Office that a passport hasn't already been issued.

Ownership of the passport rests with the Home Office, not with the resident parent or the parent who paid for it. If there is likely to be a dispute over the passport, it can be lodged with a solicitor for safe-keeping, though a duplicate can be issued without a parent's knowledge or consent.

It is possible to obtain a court order that the Passport Office should release information about a passport. The application is made on Form EX660 detailing the information required. Procedural details are provided in President's Direction on Communication with the Passport Service.

Pater Est
(See **Parent**.)

Paternity Fraud

The fraudulent identification by a mother of a particular man as the father of her child when she knows that biologically he is not.

Paternity fraud can occur in two contexts. Within marriage the motive is often to hide **Adultery**: the husband will bring up the child as his own, providing a home for the mother and paying for the upkeep of her child; should the marriage end, the man, and more damagingly, the child, may discover they have been deceived. If the mother is determined, the relationship established between father and child will end, and the father will lose **Parental Responsibility**, though not the right to make a **Section 8** application.

The second context is that of child maintenance, where a mother will identify a man as the father in order fraudulently to collect maintenance from him. Sometimes celebrities are named; in some cases, the alleged children are even fictitious. The fraud can be proved by means of a **DNA Test**, but it is rare there will be any consequence to the mother.

Some men falsely identified as the father subsequently seek compensation from the mother, both for the costs incurred bringing up the child and for the emotional trauma caused. The legal route is to seek damages under the tort of "deceit". Tort law involves seeking remedies for civil wrongs incurred under obligations not covered by a contract; in the tort of deceit, the claimant must prove on the balance of probability that the intention was fraudulent (Deek v Peek [1889]). He must demonstrate —

1. that the defendant made a representation (i.e., that a particular man was the father of a particular child);
2. that the defendant intended the claimant to act on that representation in such a way that damage resulted (i.e., the claimant paid for the child's upkeep, child support or school fees, or that a bond was established between father and child);
3. that the claimant acted on the falsehood and relied on it, and would have acted differently had the falsehood not been made;
4. that the claimant has suffered loss as a result of the falsehood.

Financial loss is easy to quantify, while putting a financial value (the Court's only recourse) on emotional distress is up to the judge's discretion.

Decisions in cases such as Re A (A Child: Joint Residence/Parental Responsibility) [2008] EWCA Civ 867 show that the courts can be sympathetic towards a father who has been the victim of paternity fraud (see **Shared Residence**).

In P v B (Paternity: Damages for Deceit) [2001] 1 FLR 1041, judge Stanley Burnton ruled that a man was legally entitled to recover damages of £90,000 from the mother of a child both for pecuniary loss and for the "indignity, mental suffering/distress, humiliation" caused by the false allegation of paternity.

In A v B (Damages: Paternity) [2007] 2 FLR 1051, a stockbroker claimed £100,000 for emotional hurt, and for the cost of bringing up a child and paying school fees. Judge Sir John Blofeld awarded him £22,400 in damages for the emotional distress, but would not order compensation for the costs of raising the child; Blofeld said "Mr A fell in love with his son as he believed. He loved him, he wanted him, he treasured him".

Paternity fraud is a serious issue; for many men this will be their only chance at fatherhood. By the time the fraud is discovered it may be too late for them to have another family, and yet the consequence of finding out may be the breakdown of the family, the exclusion of the father and a lonely future.

Pathogenic Care

A model pioneered by Dr Craig Childress intended to replace the concept of **Parental Alienation**.

Pathogenic care represents a paradigm shift from the Gardnerian understanding of alienation to an attachment-based model and treats it as a mental health and not a legal issue. It uses an established diagnosis accepted by the DSM IV rather than seek acceptance of a new syndrome. It is evidenced by three simple indicators:

1. suppression of the child's attachment system;
2. traits of narcissistic personality disorder in the child; and
3. delusional beliefs: the "lynchpin symptom"; children who are the victims of genuine abuse are not delusional.

"When all three of these child symptoms are present in the child's symptom display there is no other possible explanation, other than attachment-based 'parental alienation' by a narcissistic/borderline parent." The source of the delusion is the narcissistic/borderline parent; the result is the psychological control of the child.

PAUSE

A programme which works with mothers who have had successive children removed into care and seeks through therapeutic, practical and behavioural support to break the cycle.

Penal Notice

The attachment of a "Penal Notice" to the terms of an order theoretically enables punishment to be imposed on the parent who disregards it, though this is rarely enforced. The order will carry this notice:

> If you the within named do not comply with this order you may be held to be in contempt of court and imprisoned or fined.

A penal notice cannot give the power of arrest (there is no power in the Children Act 1989 to include a power of arrest); they are often little more than an idle threat. If an order to which a penal notice is attached is broken, then the remedy is to apply for **Committal**. However, following Re K [2003] 2 FCR 336, judges consider the committal of a resident parent to prison to be contrary to the best interests of the child.

Penal notices are usually used in private law children and financial cases but can also be attached to orders for contact with a child in care; see Re P-B (Children) 2009 EWCA Civ 143.

In financial proceedings, if a party does not comply with the Court's directions, the other can ask for a penal notice to be attached; if the application has **Merit**, the Court will allow it. If the defaulting party continues not to comply, the other can then apply for committal, proving their case beyond reasonable doubt. This process is rare as most parties will comply. In the case of breach of an injunction, committal is normally overnight or at most for a week.

An applicant can apply for a penal notice on paper provided the breach is unchallengeable; e.g. failing to file documents at court. The committal must be served personally to ensure the respondent is given notice of the hearing as the Court will make an order in their absence if satisfied they have received notice.

Pension Attachment Order

Requires a spouse to pay part of his pension to the other party.

Pension Earmarking

The process for arranging that, when a pension comes to be paid, a proportion is paid to the other party.

Pension Offsetting

The act of off-setting the value of a pension against some other shared asset such as the marital home.

Pension Sharing Order

PSO – orders the pension to be divided and allows a specified portion to be transferred to the other spouse on the transfer date which may be chosen by the pension provider any time within the four-month implementation period which commences when the **Decree Absolute** is granted.

A PSO can be achieved either by way of a court order, or by a qualifying agreement, pension sharing is expensive, and in instances where the **CETV** is of a low value, it may be wise to consider off-setting the share of the pension due the spouse against another marital asset, as the costs of implementing the PSO may outweigh the actual sum to be received.

If a couple have a qualifying agreement in place regarding the sharing of the pension, a court will not make a PSO.

In Scotland, only those pension credits accrued during the length of the marriage and up to the relevant date (of separation) will be subject to a PSO – this is because any pension accrued prior to marriage, or after the date of separation is not deemed a marital asset.

Per Incuriam

(Latin: "through lack of care") usually referring to an order made without proper consideration of the appropriate legislation or **Precedents**. A judgment ruled *per incuriam* cannot be used as a precedent.

Perfected

See **Seal**.

Perjury

Under the Perjury Act 1911, the act of wilfully making a statement which the individual knows to be false, or does not believe to be true, while under oath in court. In former times it was not merely a crime against the Court but also a sin against God.

While people in the Family Court certainly lie, they are seldom on oath and little evidence given is independently verifiable. Expert witnesses and social workers will be on oath, but parties will not be and claiming perjury is usually futile.

Person with Care

PWC – originally a purely financial term intended to signify the person in receipt of child support for a child. "Person" implied a wider range of liability than "parent". It has since come to be a badge worn by parents to convey entitlement and "ownership" of a child.

Personal Support Unit

PSU – a charity offering practical and emotional support to people who represent themselves in court.

Their trained volunteers see clients without an appointment and free-of-charge. Often, they will be students from the law department of the local university. The PSU cannot give legal advice; they adapt their service to the needs of those attending court alone, helping them to deal better with their case and to gain confidence, but they are limited in what they can do, and litigants may be better off with an experienced **McKenzie Friend**.

They currently operate in a number of regional courts and in London at the Royal Courts of Justice and at Wandsworth County Court, 09:30 to 16:30, Monday to Friday. They have a website at http://thepsu.org/.

Petition

The D8 Form on which a spouse petitions for a **Divorce** in England and Wales. A more comprehensible form was introduced in August 2017, in preparation for the eventual online process.

It is advisable if spouses can agree between themselves who files for the divorce and which **Fact** they will use before they start the process.

The new form is straightforward to complete, and guidance notes are provided on the right-hand side. At Section 1 the petitioner is required to provide the marriage certificate or a registered copy; permission to provide this at a later date may be obtained from the Court, but a Notice of Application must be completed, and a fee paid.

Care should be taken in Sections 2 and 3 that the parties' names and, in Section 4, the place of marriage are entered *exactly* as they appear on the marriage or civil partnership certificate. If names have been changed subsequently, evidence must be supplied for the petitioner's change but not for the respondent's.

The petitioner confirms in Section 5 that the Court has jurisdiction to grant the divorce. Both parties must have **Habitual Residence** in the England and Wales jurisdiction or one of them must have **Domicile** in England and Wales on the date the petition is issued. There is an alternative rule for a civil partnership if it was registered in England and Wales and the Court considers it to be in the interests of justice to assume jurisdiction.

The petitioner needs to state at Section 6 which fact or facts she is relying on and at Section 7 (**Statement of Case**) provide brief details:

Adultery – dates, locations and other relevant details should be given if known. It is not advisable to name the **Co-Respondent** unless the divorce is likely to be defended; their name must then be entered in Section 8. If the **Respondent** does not admit the adultery, it will have to be proved.

Behaviour – dates, location and details should be given. The first and most recent incidents and the most serious should be documented – five or six is sufficient; the petitioner must establish a pattern of behaviour sufficient to prove **Irretrievable Breakdown** to the Court.

Desertion – dates and brief details of the circumstances should be given.

When Separation is used as the reason for the divorce, both the date of separation and the date the petitioner realised the relationship was irretrievable must be given. This makes plain both the physical separation and the *intent* to separate; see Santos v Santos [1972] Fam 247.

Section 11 is called the **Prayer**; the petitioner indicates whether she wants dissolution or **Judicial Separation**.

It is normal practice to send the respondent one or more drafts before the final petition is sent to the court. This ensures he agrees to it and will not object to details of adultery or behaviour and defend the divorce; it also gives him the opportunity to request alterations. On receipt of the draft, if he is not happy, he should write a letter to his spouse, or to her solicitor if she is represented, stating that he wants specific allegations removed and requesting that it be re-written accordingly. If she does not cooperate, he can inform her that he will submit his own petition based on *her* behaviour – this is called "**Cross-Petitioning**".

Negotiation over the petition should be concluded at the draft stage, it is too late to leave it after the petition has been lodged with the court and Form D10 (the **Acknowledgement of Service**) has been received. The respondent can agree not to defend the petition provided the allegations will not be made or be used in children's or ancillary matters, but that strategy is risky.

The usual allegations of lack of sex/support/communication are nothing to worry about and are not worth defending; anything which alleges violence or abuse, financial impropriety or anything to do with parenting or treatment of the children should be challenged.

The Court will assume allegations which are not refuted to be true. This can be devastating later when financial issues or child arrangements matters are being debated. Tacitly admitting to "unreasonable" behaviour then can be interpreted to mean a parent has been violent or abusive and will be used against him in court. He will not get the opportunity to refute these allegations later.

When the Acknowledgement of Service arrives from the court, the respondent will be asked if he intends to **Defend the Divorce**. As long as he consents to the divorce itself, the petition will proceed as uncontested.

In a petition based on the fact of **Adultery**, the respondent is asked if he admits to the adultery alleged; he has the opportunity here to admit or deny the allegation. He will also be invited to agree to **Costs** and should check whether a claim for costs has been made in the petition, if he agrees and is not contesting the divorce or allegations, this can save time and won't necessarily be too expensive. If allegations have been made which he needs to refute, this is his opportunity.

If he is forced to cross-petition, he will issue his own petition using the fact either of adultery or of "unreasonable" behaviour. He is stating that the breakdown of the marriage is not his fault, but that of the petitioner. This is a tactical step, for example to avoid paying costs, or to have particularly offensive allegations removed.

Some negotiation may ensue. If the final petition can be agreed, it will save a great deal of time, expense and trauma later. The forms can still be filed with the court if the respondent doesn't agree or sign. The petitioner will file with her nearest **Divorce Centre**:

1. the Divorce Petition, Form D8;
2. additional copies for the Respondent and Co-Respondent if appropriate – the court must serve these;
3. the original Marriage Certificate or certified copy, if this is not in English, a certified translation will be needed, note that the court will NOT accept a photocopy or scanned copy of the certificate;
4. the correct **Court Fee**.

The documents can be filed by post or taken to the court by the petitioner. About 40% of first petitions are rejected, so it is vital to get the petition right, which means having it checked by a solicitor or competent **McKenzie Friend**. Petitioners should ensure the court has jurisdiction, that all details match those on the marriage certificate, and that the correct fee is enclosed.

Petitioner

The party who petitions for a **Divorce**.

Photographs

Contrary to popular belief, no law prevents taking or using a photograph of any child provided it is not indecent or manipulated in a way to make it indecent.

The Protection of Children Act 1978 makes it an offence to take, permit to be taken, distribute, show, possess with a view to distributing or showing, publish or cause to be published any indecent photograph or pseudo-photograph of a child. There are three categories of offence, A to C, depending on the depravity of the photograph.

The Act does not define indecency which is normally left to the jury to interpret – though the Obscene Publication Act 1959 defines it as having the potential to "deprave or corrupt".

Section 160 of the Criminal Justice Act 1988 further makes it an offence merely to possess an indecent photograph or pseudo-photograph of a child. A "child" is a person under the age of sixteen; "photograph" includes the negative and digital data; "pseudo-photograph" is an image, made by computer graphics, for example, which appears to be a photograph, though this is broadly interpreted. In 2008 Robul Hoque was convicted for possessing "*Tomb Raider-*style" computer graphics depicting naked children; in 2014 he was convicted again for possessing manga-style cartoons of children and given a suspended sentence.

Deliberately taking photographs of children in a public place will draw attention and possibly arouse the interest of the police; in Scotland it could constitute a breach of the peace. Many organisations will also have policies on photographing children at organised events; even if the children are the photographer's own, he should find out what rules are in place before getting his camera out. It is always a courtesy to ask a parent's permission before photographing their child, but not legally mandatory.

Potentially, photography could be considered harassment if a person were to take photographs of someone against their will and, as with other forms of **Harassment**, only two incidents are necessary to constitute a course of action.

Publication of a child's photograph in order to shame a parent who is withholding contact could also be harassment, which includes displaying any writing, sign or other visible representation which is threatening, abusive or insulting, thereby causing that or another person harassment, alarm or distress.

The **Human Rights Act 1998** protects an individual's right to respect for his private life, and breach could also be an offence. If a parent were to take a photograph of his own child in her home using a telephoto lens from a location outside her home, that would be an invasion of her privacy; so too might be taking a photograph of her in the street, depending on circumstances. As a child does not have the legal capacity to give consent, that of a parent or guardian must be obtained in writing.

It is an offence under Section 97 of the Children Act 1989 to publish (i.e., make public) or cause to be published (i.e., send photos to a third party) any material (including a picture or representation) intended or likely to identify a child involved in proceedings under the Act or under the Adoption and Children Act 2002. No known prosecutions have followed, and it is a defence if you can prove you did not know and had no reason to suspect the published material was intended, or likely, to identify the child. There is also a potential breach of the Children and Young People's Act 1933. Breach is a criminal offence and punishable by a fine. Publication only of photographs which recognisably identify a child is prohibited, so publication of the photograph of a baby can be acceptable; see Re J (A Child), Re [2013] EWHC 2694.

Physical Abuse

The ill-treatment of a child through the deliberate infliction of physical **Harm** or the failure to protect from harm. Physical abuse can also include the fabrication of symptoms or inducing illness.

Placement Order

A court order made under Section 21 of the Adoption and Children Act 2002 which authorises a local authority to place a child for **Adoption**.

Once made, the **Care Order** which originally allowed the LA to take the child into care no longer pertains, so an application can no longer be made to have it discharged. The LA now has **Parental Responsibility** for the child in addition to the child's parents.

Leave of the Court must first be obtained to oppose the order; only the LA and the child himself (through his guardian) can apply without leave. The Court must be satisfied that there has been a change of circumstances before it will grant leave. In the case of Re P (A Child) [2007] EWCA Civ 616, Wall LJ said,

> *[32]* We... take the view that the test should not be set too high, because, as this case demonstrates, parents... should not be discouraged either from bettering themselves or from seeking to prevent the adoption of their child, by the imposition of a test which is unachievable. We therefore take the view that whether or not there has been a relevant change of circumstances must be a *matter of fact* to be decided by the good sense and sound judgement of the tribunal hearing the application.

The reasons given to the Court for leave must now meet the very high standards of "arguable case" established by Lord Justice Wilson in Re Warwickshire County Council v M [2007] EWCA Civ 1084 (both sides cited Re P in support of their positions). "**Change of Circumstances**" is not defined, so even when it has been proven that circumstances have changed, the parents will remain at the mercy of the judges' discretion. The case established that the **Welfare Checklist** does not apply, as it does in applications to revoke adoption orders, and that the Court's consideration should be whether the applicant has a "real prospect of success".

Once leave has been granted, an application must be made to the same court which made the Placement Order for its revocation using Form A52 on which are set out the reasons for the application. A **Children's Guardian** will be appointed to represent the child's interests, and she will appoint a **Solicitor**. Revocation is governed by Section 24 of the Adoption and Children Act 2002.

Even after the application to revoke the Placement Order has been made an LA can still legally place the child with adoptive parents (if it has not already done so under **Foster-to-Adopt**), it is only "good practice" if the LA decides to wait for the outcome of the application. This means that a *Status Quo* can be established which will be difficult to overturn. Once a child has been placed for adoption, pending the final Adoption Order, it will be very difficult to have the order revoked.

Pleas-in-Law

(Scots) the third part of an application, giving the legal argument in support of the application; this should be brief, and argue the main principles of the relevant legislation; e.g., that it is in the child's best interest to have contact with both parents and that an order be made rather than that no order be made.

Police Protection

Section 46(1) CA1989 allows a constable to remove a child from its parents to suitable accommodation where he "has reasonable cause to believe that a child would otherwise be likely to suffer significant harm". A second officer of at least the rank of inspector – the Designated Officer – must then take an independent oversight of the situation.

The Designated Officer must inform the LA and the child's parents or those who have PR for him. Once the child is under police protection the LA can apply to the Court for an EPO.

Because this circumvents due process, it should be used only in an emergency or risks breaching a parent's human rights; see Langley and Others v Liverpool City Council and Chief Constable of Merseyside Police [2005] EWCA Civ 1173.

Position Statement

The document in which a litigant sets out his case to the Court in both children's and financial proceedings; its purpose is to give the judge an understanding of the dispute and an indication of what the parties want the Court to do in order to resolve it.

If the judge directs the parties to prepare position statements, they form part of the "**Bundle**" and the judge should read them before the next hearing. It is not always essential to produce a position statement, but it will help the parties to do so, especially if there is more evidence than there is room for on the court forms.

An applicant's position statement will conclude with why he is requesting the Court's assistance and what order he wants made. Any court orders already in place should be listed. Courts now expect applicants to draft their own orders; the wording has to be specific to make it enforceable; the applicant should be absolutely clear about what he wants, otherwise he stands little chance of getting it.

In children's proceedings, parties should not put what they themselves want in their statements, but what is best for their child: parents have no rights under the **Children Act 1989**. The **Welfare Checklist** in Section 1 of the Act will provide guidance, and all seven points should be covered. Nothing should be put into a statement which might appear vengeful, malicious or petty; nothing should go in which cannot be proved with solid evidence.

The position statement should open with some remarks about the child: a summary of his situation, any concerns about his health and development. It should include positives about the other party's parenting skills: this will contribute to presenting the child as a real person and not just an anonymous cipher; it will demonstrate that the parent knows the child well and understands the effect proceedings are having on him and prevent the other party from rejecting the entire statement out-of-hand.

It is customary now to include a brief **Chronology**: it will summarise briefly when the parties met, when they cohabited/married, when their children were born and when and why they separated. It will detail briefly the party's relationship with the child, their level of involvement in childcare, schooling and after-school activities, how contact has worked since separation and the benefits the child has derived, giving details of the issues, allegations, recommendations and orders already made.

An applicant will explain what order is sought; a respondent will explain their opposition. If the respondent agrees in principle but disputes some details, the statement will explain this. Case precedents and academic research backing up an argument can then be listed, with the full text included as evidence in a separate bundle.

In financial proceedings, a brief background to the case will open the statement, then set out the parties' ages, income and earning capacity, financial needs, obligations and responsibilities, standard of living, any physical and mental disabilities, contributions made (or not made), conduct issues (although conduct is rarely taken into account) and pensions. Written submissions are important because they set out the final arguments; they should apply the law to the facts of the case and persuade the judge that the party's position is the correct one, using the check-list in Section 25 of the Matrimonial Causes Act 1973 as a guide.

A position statement should be short and punchy – no more than two sides of A4 or four with a chronology – and like a business presentation: clear, precise and easy for the judge to read. It must conform strictly to the format specified in Practice Direction 22A. Judges don't always read statements, so it is more likely to be read if kept brief; it is important to help the judge find the salient facts. Later in a case, if there are particular problems, it may become necessary to make further statements in which greater detail is employed.

When the respondent receives a copy of the applicant's statement, they will need to produce one of their own. The applicant should not need to do anything until the case reaches court. The applicant can respond to the respondent's statement, but there is a danger of escalating a dispute through allegation and counter-allegation, which is why it is best if statements are filed and exchanged simultaneously.

Power of Arrest

Where a power of arrest has been attached to an order under Section 47 of the Family Law Act 1996, a police constable can arrest the respondent without warrant but must – under Section 47(7) – bring him before a judge within twenty-four hours (excluding Christmas Day, Good Friday or any Sunday). An arresting officer must have reasonable grounds for arrest, and the Court must be satisfied that—

1. the conduct alleged related to a provision in the **Injunctive Order** to which a power of arrest was attached;
2. the officer had reasonable grounds from what he had seen or been told to suspect that a breach had occurred; and
3. the respondent has been brought before a judge within the required time limits.

Where a power of arrest has not been attached, a party can apply to the Court to issue a warrant, substantiated on oath and showing reasonable grounds for believing the respondent has failed to comply with the injunction (Sections 47(8) and (9)).

Under the Protection from Harassment Act 1997 there is no power to attach a power of arrest to an injunction but there is power to issue a warrant on evidence (Sections 3(3) and (5)).

In either case, where a respondent is brought before a court, the breaches alleged should be written down and given to him so that he knows exactly what the case is against him.

He does not have to go to a police station or "help with their enquiries" unless he is arrested, though it may be sensible for him to cooperate if he wants to avoid arrest; he cannot be arrested simply in order to answer questions, there must be grounds for arrest.

Most arrests will be carried out under Section 24 of the Police and Criminal Evidence Act 1984 (PACE) as amended by the Serious Organised Crime and Police Act 2005 (SOCPA). PACE provides for a number of "Codes" which were amended in 2003; search of premises is dealt with under Code B, detention under Code C, tape recording of interviews under Code E, and arrest under Code G. The police must comply with this legislation; the arresting officer must give enough information for the individual to determine whether or not his arrest is lawful. The police will require the suspect's name, address and date of birth; they may also take his photograph, fingerprints and non-intimate body samples for DNA testing.

Practice Direction

Instructions issued to judges to achieve conformity and uniformity in court practice. They can be found on the justice.gov.uk website under Procedure Rules, Family Procedure Rules, Rules and Practice Directions.

Prayer

That part of a divorce **Petition** in which the **Petitioner** states what order she wishes the Court to make. The term dates to when **Divorce** was a matter for the ecclesiastical courts.

Pre-Action Protocol

Statements of best practice about pre-action conduct which have been approved by the **President of the Family Division** and which are annexed to a **Practice Direction**. See **Child Arrangements Programme**.

Pre-Application Protocol for Mediation Information and Assessment

The ruling introduced in April 2011 requiring parties to attend a **Mediation Information and Assessment Meeting** before progressing to litigation.

Precedent

A judicial decision which establishes a legal principle binding on an equal or lower court in the same jurisdiction and which may be persuasive in other jurisdictions; see *Stare Decisis*.

A precedent has two parts, the *Ratio*, which details the precedent itself, and which is binding, and the *Obiter*, which is the remainder of the judgment.

A litigant must refer to precedents which will persuade the judge to decide the case in his favour. He must also be aware of precedents indicative of an alternative decision, so he can counter the arguments the other side will bring. A **Litigant-in-Person** must become his own lawyer and his own legal researcher, familiarising himself with the law and researching precedent.

Cases must be relevant: merely because a court has made a decision in one case does not mean it will make the same decision in another; it is inadvisable to use precedents older than 2000. The litigant must be clear about the argument he is using case law to support and reference the page or paragraph number containing the supporting evidence.

The anonymisation of family cases means successive hearings in the same case can go by different names, and it is easy to get caught out by citing a case which has been overturned in a higher court. Academic research papers can also be used in support of an argument. The judgments and research papers should be included as part of the evidence in a file separate from the main **Bundle**.

Cited cases must also qualify as precedents. The **Practice Direction** *Citation of Authorities* [2001] 1 WLR 1001 makes it unlawful to cite certain categories of case in court:

1. applications attended by one party only;
2. applications for permission to appeal;
3. decisions which merely establish that a case is arguable;
4. all County Court cases other than those which deal with an issue affecting County Court decisions which were not decided at higher level.

Pre-Marital or Pre-Nuptial Agreement

A written statement agreed by a couple before marriage, setting out the division of financial assets and other arrangements in the event of divorce.

Pre-nuptial agreements have not had the recognition in the UK which they enjoy in some other jurisdictions. Their legal standing was transformed by the case of Radmacher v Granatino [2009] EWCA Civ 649. A German wife and French husband had signed a pre-nuptial agreement under German law that neither party would claim maintenance from the other; they then divorced in the UK.

The wife said she had been adamant no man should marry her for her wealth: if he was prepared to sign away his rights, then it could only be for love. The husband disputed this: his wife had told him she would be disinherited if he didn't sign; the notary who had drawn up the contract worked for the wife's family. The High Court awarded the husband funds totalling £5.6m; the wife – whose worth was in excess of £100m – appealed.

In the Court of Appeal, Thorpe LJ allowed the wife's appeal on the grounds that in the trial court Mr Justice Baron had given insufficient weight to the pre-nuptial agreement into which the parties had freely entered; such agreements, he explained, made under the auspices of a single lawyer or notary, were alien to the English system in which it is believed that a single lawyer cannot effectively represent the interests of both parties. Such agreements, therefore, must be contrary to the best interests of one party.

The Appeal Court altered the original award so that the husband would receive the various funds allotted in his role qua father, for the support of his children and to enable contact to take place, rather than in his role qua spouse, as had been the emphasis in the original award. This was an important distinction, founded in the paramountcy principle, and will apply to future cases.

A further influential finding was that, contrary to what the High Court had found, the husband had known what he was walking into, had voluntarily refused legal advice, and had knowingly signed away his rights.   Mr Granatino's appeal was dismissed by the Supreme Court. The case cautions against making legally binding commitments when in a state of infatuation which one may come to regret when passions cool. At the very least, both parties should be legally represented.

The decision has resulted in courts placing greater weight on pre-nuptial agreements; unwise agreements freely entered into, even without legal advice, may now become the primary source of decisions in divorce settlements.

For a court to set aside such an agreement, a spouse will need to show that circumstances have changed unexpectedly, and the agreement is now unfair, or was unfair when it was made – he didn't have legal advice or was coerced into the agreement, or that maintaining the agreement will subject him or his child to hardship.

President of the Family Division

The most senior judge in the Family Division of the High Court; the Presidents have been —

1st October 1971:	Sir George Baker
28th September 1979:	Sir John Arnold
11th January 1988:	Sir Stephen Brown
1st October 1999:	Dame Elizabeth Butler-Sloss
7th April 2005:	Sir Mark Potter
13th April 2010:	Sir Nicholas Wall
11th January 2013:	Sir James Munby
28th July 2018:	Sir Andrew McFarlane

Primary Carer

The dominant parent who should make all decisions concerning the child after separation, following the doctrine first formulated in the book *Beyond the Best Interests of the Child*.

Its authors were Joseph Goldstein, Professor of Law, Science and Social Policy at Yale University Law School, Albert Solnit, Director of the Yale Child Study Centre, and Anna Freud, daughter of Sigmund and Director of the Hampstead Child Clinic.

Inspired by the "**Attachment Theory**" work done by psychoanalyst Professor John Bowlby in the 1940s and using data gathered from tiny samples of terribly deprived and impaired Jewish refugees who arrived in Britain after the war and were taken into residential care, the academics ignored entirely the

310

damaging lack of stimulation the children had received and came to believe that all interaction between parents following divorce was confrontational and potentially violent and that custody should therefore be awarded only to the "psychological" parent while the other should be eliminated; shared custody would lead to damaging conflicts of loyalty. Decisions about contact with the other parent should be made only by the custodial parent,

> Once it is determined who will be the custodial parent, it is that parent, not the court, who must decide under what conditions he or she wishes to raise the child. Thus, the non-custodial parent should have no legally enforceable right to visit the child, and the custodial parent should have the right to decide whether it is desirable for the child to have such visits.

Since, as psychologist Sanford Braver says, "there is no evidence that there is a scientifically valid way for a custody evaluator to choose the best primary parent", it scarcely matters which parent is removed. Decisions determining custody were not to be based on any factors which promoted the best interests of children or which had evidential support. Belief in the permanent removal of non-custodial parents dominated family justice at least until the 1990s and still influences many practitioners, and yet this central tenet of *Beyond the Best Interests* is not only unevidenced but, worse, promotes harmful outcomes for children by giving legal support to the destruction of one of the child's most vital relationships. With the erosion of the fault concept in divorce, the theory of sole custody provided a straightforward solution to disputes which has wrought untold damage on children.

Primary Legislation

Legislation made by the legislative branch of government – the Houses of Commons and Lords – taking the form of Acts of Parliament.

Privacy

The rules which prevent access to family hearings by members of the public, the reporting of cases and the disclosure of documents.

The **Common Law** starting position is one of open justice and any derogation from this must be justified; see, for example, Scott & Anor v Scott [1913] UKHL 2, [1913] AC 417 —

> in public trials is to be found, on the whole, the best security for the pure, impartial, and efficient administration of justice, the best means for winning for it public confidence and respect.

Publication should be prevented only if it interferes with the administration of justice; see Harman v Home Office [1983] 1 AC 280: in which Lord Scarman said,

> the evidence and argument should be publicly known, so that society may judge for itself the quality of justice administered in its name, and whether the law requires modification.

These principles have been contradicted, however, by Rule 27.10 of the Family Procedure Rules 2010 in which the starting point is a closed court, though the judge is given discretion to open his court if he chooses. Family lawyers are inclined to follow this approach, with rare exceptions, but it is arguable that the FPR Committee, in incorporating this rule, acted **Ultra Vires** and beyond the authority given them by the Courts Act 2003.

Most proceedings in the Family and High Court are conducted "in private", closed to the public. Consider, for example, Mr Justice Munby's ruling in Re Brandon Webster (A Child) *sub nom* Norfolk County Council v Nicola Webster & Ors [2006] EWHC 2733 at Paragraph 77, that this rule was designed to make privacy the "default provision" and was not to be construed as indicating a heavy presumption in favour of privacy. The judge could use his discretion to open his court, though in practice judges are rarely inclined so to direct. Once media are admitted to a case, it can no longer be regarded as being held "in private".

There are some orders which must be announced in open court, such as decrees of divorce, Committal Orders and Non-Molestation Orders. The default position in the High Court, Court of Appeal and Supreme Court is that hearings are open, though most are heard in private. Rule 27.11 determines who may be permitted into the court.

When proceedings are conducted "in secret" neither the press nor the public may attend; hearings usually heard in secret include legitimacy hearings, nullity proceedings hearing evidence of sexual capacity and hearings regarding the location of an abductor.

In Re N (A Child) [2009] EWHC 1663, Munby quoted the father's McKenzie, campaigner Michael Pelling, that the test for excluding the press must be a high one,

> [96] Mere assertion, speculation and sentiment will no longer do; there must, he says, be real evidence of serious detriment to the child's interests, a party's or witness's safety, the orderly conduct of the proceedings, or to the proper administration of justice (as the case may be) before the presumption of rule 10.28(3)(f) (*now rule 27.11(2)(f)*) can be reversed.

The then President of the Family Division, Sir Mark Potter, issued a Practice Direction 27B regarding the new rules. On the practical matter of accommodating reporters, Potter directed that court staff should find larger court rooms where possible, but that proceedings should not significantly be disrupted or delayed. On the matter of impeding or prejudicing justice, Potter directed as an example that reporters should be excluded only where a witness (other than a party) will not otherwise give evidence, or where their evidence is likely to be compromised or incomplete. Reasons of administrative inconvenience are not sufficient to justify exclusion.

The assumed reason for privacy is that it protects children from being damaged or traumatised by media exposure, despite the absence of evidence that any child has been damaged in this way. This was accepted by the Court of Appeal in Pelling v Bruce-Williams (Secretary of State for Constitutional Affairs intervening) [2004] Fam 155, which said,

> [18] We have considerable sympathy for Dr Pelling's basic premise that the rationalisation of the current practice is expressed in very general terms that certainly appear to lack evidential foundation.

In Norfolk County Council v Nicola Webster and 5 Others [2006] EWHC 2733, Munby confirmed that the belief was "in significant measure speculative".

Other reasons that have been given are that the media will express interest only in notorious cases and thus give the public a distorted view of court operations, or that openness will result in the disruption of the court system through the additional demands made on staff and facilities, and that judges will worry more about protecting themselves than about protecting children.

The *real* explanation for secrecy is quite different: it is the belief that to allow proceedings in open court would severely inhibit the parties and witnesses and thus *prejudice the interests of justice*. This was expressed by the European Court in Pelling v United Kingdom 35974/97 and Bayram v United Kingdom 36337/97, 24th April 2001,

> The Court considers that such proceedings are prime examples of cases where the exclusion of the press and public may be justified in order to protect the privacy of the child and parties and to avoid prejudicing the interests of justice. To enable the deciding judge to gain as full and accurate a picture as possible of the advantages and disadvantages of the various residence and contact options open to the child, it is essential that the parents and other witnesses feel able to express themselves candidly on highly personal issues without fear of public curiosity or comment.

There is no evidence to support this view, and the argument was refuted as long ago as 1913 when in Scott v Scott, Lord Atkinson said,

> The hearing of a case in public may be, and often is, no doubt, painfully humiliating, or deterrent both to parties and witnesses, and in many cases, especially those of a criminal nature, the details may be so indecent as to tend to injure public morals, but all this is tolerated and endured, because... in public trials is to be found... the best security for the pure, impartial, and efficient administration of justice.

Michael Pelling also extracted this confession from the Court of Appeal in Dr Michael John Pelling, Appellant v Mrs Veronica Nana Bruce-Williams, Respondent; Secretary of State for Constitutional Affairs, Interested Party [2004] EWCA Civ 845,

> *[11]* In the end the more convincing defence of the practice in our jurisdiction may be the most simple, namely that it is reflective of a long standing tradition, of general but not universal application, that has been franked by the European Court as Convention-compliant.

Permitting access to the courts by accredited media is still very far indeed from creating a truly open and accountable court system and does not apply to placement or adoption proceedings. Potter's arrangements did not affect the legislation regarding publication, which meant that journalists could attend court and hear the proceedings but could not report what they heard. Transparency continues to be a much-discussed aspect of the English and Welsh system, with strongly-held views on both sides of the argument, and a further consultation introduced by Sir James Munby closed on 31st October 2014. In the summer of 2014, a group of lawyers and other legal professionals set up the *Transparency Project* with the aim of shedding some light onto the workings of the family courts without compromising children's privacy.

There is an extraordinary – and overlooked – disparity between English and Welsh and Scots family law, to the extent that it may constitute discrimination under Article 14 of the 1998 Human Rights Act. The adversarial court hearings, which in England have until very recently been conducted *in camera*, are open in Scotland and may be reported upon – though this is rare – unless there are good reasons why they should be heard in private. This dates back to the Court of Session Act 1693 which provides that the Court should sit with "open doors".

Run-of-the-mill residence and contact cases are routinely public in access to the Court, judgment and reporting at all levels of the Court and there is thus no damage to the administration of justice. However, many other hearings, such as conciliation hearings and preliminary hearings which do not require a Sheriff to adjudicate, are heard *in camera*.

There are no separate rules analogous to the Family Procedure Rules. Subject to certain changes which occurred with the enactment of the Children (Scotland) Act 1995, there are no express provisions for private hearings and thus no analogues to County Courts Rules 1981 rule1(4) (the rule enacting the presumption that ancillary relief proceedings will be in chambers in the County Courts), Family Procedure Rules 1991 rule 2.66(2) (ditto if the case was before a Circuit Judge), rule 27.11 of the Family Procedure Rules 2010, rule 3.9(1) (Pt. IV Family Law Act 1996 proceedings in chambers), and rule 4.16(7) (Children Act proceedings in chambers). The norm is open court, with parties and children named in all "family actions", and free reporting.

The Social Work (Scotland) Act 1968 introduced the Children's Hearings and Panels, which are entirely public law and not regulated by rules in the Ordinary Cause Rules. Adoption proceedings are not included and s.57 of the Adoption Act 1978 provides that adoption proceedings are heard in private unless the Court decides otherwise.

Private Family Law

That part of family law which deals with relationships between individuals, including divorce, financial disputes, child contact and custody, parental responsibility and domestic abuse.

Privilege

A party's right in certain protected situations, such as a court hearing, to refuse to disclose or produce a document or to answer a question of some special interest recognised by law.

Pro Bono

(Latin: short for *pro bono publico*, meaning "for the public good") professional legal work undertaken voluntarily and without payment. The Pro Bono Unit of the Bar Council is a charity which helps litigants access free legal help from trained volunteers who are mostly retired lawyers or students; 47% of their work is in family law. This help is available only to litigants who cannot afford to pay for legal representation and they must be referred by an advice agency, such as the Citizens' Advice Bureaux, or by their MP or solicitor.

Proceedings

Legal action taking place in a court; family proceedings are defined by Section 75(3) of the Courts Act 2003.

Process Server

Often, a private investigator who also specialises in serving legal documents on respondents. Whereas a court **Bailiff** can only serve at the address on the application, a process server can serve a party at his home, at his place of work, or in the street, and can thus be more effective.

Prohibited Steps Order

PSO – an order made under **Section 8** of the **Children Act 1989** "that no step which could be taken by a parent in meeting his **Parental Responsibility** for a child, and which is of a kind specified in the order, shall be taken by any person without the consent of the court".

Once applied, a PSO cannot be removed by agreement between the parties and can be lifted only by the Court. It is made in the **Best Interests of a Child**, often to protect the child's welfare – for example by preventing contact with an inappropriate adult. It is an **Injunction**, but does not carry a power of arrest, though the police may assist informally.

By interfering with parental responsibility, a PSO can be seen by the Court, or be presented by the respondent, as an attempt to control the respondent and restrict his or her liberties and rights, which is likely to have an adverse effect on the **Welfare** of the child by denying the **Primary Carer** reasonable freedom of choice. For this reason, they may be difficult to obtain.

In C (A Child) & Anor v KH [2013] EWCA Civ 1412, Ryder LJ reminded the Court that a PSO is not an extension of one parent's power to restrict the other, "it is a court order which has to be based on objective evidence". PSOs must not be applied to trivial issues, and their terms must be specific. Examples might include not to change the child's surname, not to give the child inappropriate medical treatment, or not to indoctrinate the child into a particular religion.

A PSO can be used to apply leverage, for example, on a parent who is refusing to agree terms of another order, but they are only ever a temporary solution, and the CA1989 prevents a court from making a PSO in order to obtain a result which could be achieved through a **Child Arrangements Order**.

Applications are made using Form C100.

Proof Hearing

(Scots) if parties are unable to reach agreement, disputes may have to be decided after often lengthy and expensive "proof hearings" where the parties give oral evidence and are subject to cross examination in open court, and where witnesses may also be called to provide testimony, or supply a written **Affidavit**. They can be reported by the media, subject to certain restrictions aimed at protecting "public morals" and children.

Subsequent hearings may be ordered by the **Sheriff**, for example, to monitor progress between the parties who are expected to attend the hearing and provide the Sheriff with sufficient evidence to enable him to conduct the hearing.

The Court may then order a report, and there may be another **Options Hearing**. There will then be a "proof **Diet**" or "diet of proof", during which evidence is heard and witnesses cross-examined. Finally, the Sheriff will make whatever order(s) he considers necessary, issued on a sheet of paper known as the **Interlocutor**.

Property Adjustment Order

A spousal maintenance order which adjusts the share in property – usually a house – say from 50/50 to 60/40. The Court can also order the sale of a property, if necessary, at a later date once minor children have grown up.

Proportionality

A concept fundamental to the operation of family law and enshrined in CA1989 s.1(5). It derives from Article 8 of the **Human Rights Act 1998** and requires that any intervention into family life must be lawful and necessary (see **Expert Witness**) and proportionate to the **Harm** the child has suffered or is likely to suffer.

Public Access Barrister

A **Barrister** who will accept **Instruction** directly from a litigant rather than through a solicitor.

Public Family Law

That part of family law which deals with relationships between individuals and the state; in Re L (Care: Assessment: Fair Trial) [2002] EWHC 1379, Lord Justice Munby cautioned,

> *[150]* ...it must never be forgotten that, with the State's abandonment of the right to impose capital sentences, orders of the kind which judges of this Division are typically invited to make in public law proceedings are amongst the most drastic that any judge in any jurisdiction is ever empowered to make. It is a terrible thing to say to any parent — particularly, perhaps, to a mother — that he or she is to lose their child for ever.

Puisne Judge

A judge of a superior court other than its chief judge.

Punishment of Children

Section 58 of the Children Act 2004 states, "Battery of a child causing actual bodily harm to the child cannot be justified in any civil proceedings on the ground that it constituted reasonable punishment". In practice "reasonable" punishment or chastisement is permissible provided it doesn't leave a mark, and doesn't involve an implement, such as a belt or cane.

Parents can be charged under Sections 18 and 20 of the Offences against the Person Act 1861 if they wound or cause grievous bodily harm to their child, or under section 47 if they assault or occasion actual bodily harm. A parent can also be charged with cruelty to a person under sixteen under Section 1 of the Children and Young Persons Act 1933 if he "wilfully assaults, ill-treats, neglects, abandons, or exposes him, or causes or procures him to be assaulted, ill-treated, neglected, abandoned, or exposed, in a manner likely to cause him unnecessary suffering or injury to health (including injury to or loss of sight, or hearing, or limb, or organ of the body, and any mental derangement)".

The exact nature of the charge will depend on the harm caused the child; injuries which would be regarded as common assault when inflicted on an adult can be regarded as actual bodily harm when inflicted on a child. As a rough guide, actual bodily harm usually involves an injury which will require some degree of medical attention; grievous bodily harm involves an injury leading to permanent physical or psychological damage or scarring.

In Re MA (Care: Threshold) [2009] EWCA Civ 853, Lady Justice Hallett said,

> [39] Reasonable physical chastisement of children by parents is not yet unlawful in this country. Slaps and even kicks vary enormously in their seriousness. A kick sounds particularly unpleasant, yet many a parent may have nudged their child's nappied bottom with their foot in gentle play without committing an assault. Many a parent will have slapped a child on the hand to make the point that running out into a busy road is a dangerous thing to do. What M alleged therefore was not necessarily indicative of abuse. It will all depend on circumstances.

It is important to distinguish between the bruises, bumps and scratches which are a normal and essential part of the rough-and-tumble of childhood and the more severe bruises, broken bones and cigarette burns which are an indication of abuse and are often accompanied by malnutrition and neglect.

The Serious Crime Act 2015 added a crime of psychological abuse to the 1933 Act in what was dubbed "Cinderella Law", and redefined "ill-treatment" as "physical or otherwise". Established case law had been careful to exclude non-physical aspects of harm, such as a parental failure to meet moral, educational, spiritual or emotional needs; normal lapses of parenting now risk being criminalised and the examples which formerly determined whether injury reached the criminal threshold are now irrelevant; parental behaviour need no longer be cruel to be criminal. It is too soon to know how this legislation will work in practice.

Purge

A committal for contempt can be "purged" if the **Contemnor** acknowledges what he has done and sincerely apologises to the Court; the sentence will then be reduced. Consider Judge Wildblood's words to Andrew Butt in the Williams v Minnock case,

> [6] You are now marked as a man who lies and who has been to prison for a serious contempt. You may well face prosecution for your lies. As far as this family court is concerned I consider that the court has sufficiently marked its deprecation of your actions and that you should now be released. I therefore accept that you should now be released from custody, having purged your contempt.

Pursuer

(Scots) the party who initiates litigation.

Q

Quantum of Contact

The amount of time a **Non-Resident Parent** gets to spend with their child. It is controversial, as agencies such as **CAFCASS** have no guidance on what the minimum quantum should be, despite good academic indications which suggest the starting point should be around 35% of a child's time. It is also a crude measure of the relationship between parent and child.

Most court orders routinely provide insufficient time: two hours every other Saturday is not unusual, and even if a parent manages to get overnight staying contact it may only be every other Saturday night. Reasonable contact will provide the whole weekend, alternate weeks, from Friday afternoon when he picks up his child from school to Monday morning when he returns him. He will also have half of all school holidays and substantial contact at half-term; he may even get some mid-week contact.

This level of contact will enable him to meet his child's school friends – and perhaps have them to stay over – and enable him to talk to his teachers; he will need a cooperative employer, though. Anything less will make maintaining a meaningful relationship more difficult. Once he has this minimum level of contact, there is no reason why he should not progress to share parenting fully.

Queen's Counsel

QC or "silk" – a senior (and very expensive) lawyer, usually a barrister; appointment by a nine-member committee is based on merit and referred to as "taking silk" after the gown worn.

Queen's Proctor

An official representing the monarch who may intervene in **Petitions** for **Divorce** or **Nullity** and, if appropriate, prevent a **Decree** *Nisi* from becoming **Absolute**. The powers of the role are set out in Section 8 of the Matrimonial Causes Act 1973. In Rapisarda v Colladon [2014] EWFC 1406, the Queen's Proctor sought to **Set Aside** no fewer than 180 decrees *nisi* and absolute.

Questionnaire

A document produced by the respondent to a **Divorce** on receipt of Form E on which he presents any queries he may have regarding discrepancies and perceived errors.

Possible questions might concern the nature of a cohabitation, the number of nights spent together and whether the relationship is sexual, undeclared capital, such as the deposit on a rented property, copies of tax returns and P60s to prove declared income, details of tax credits, council tax or utilities, or details of mileage and fuel consumption.

If there are discrepancies, a party is strongly advised to resolve these without going to court, which will almost certainly cost more than overlooking the errors is likely to do.

Quickie Divorce

One of the myths of family law; parties should normally allow twelve months for a **Divorce** with no **Consent Order** or eighteen months with, depending on how busy the particular court is. Using a high-street provider will speed things up, and using a solicitor will be faster still, but no divorce will take less than fourteen weeks, despite the impression sometimes given by the tabloid press.

R

Ratio

(Latin: short for *rationes decidendi*, meaning "the rationale for the decision") that part of a **Judgment** which contains the judge's reasoning, and which may set a **Precedent**.

A judge must provide a straightforward explanation of the reasons for a particular decision; and a losing party must understand why he lost. In Flannery v Halifax Estate Agencies Ltd (t/a Colleys Professional Services) [2000] 1 WLR 377, Henry LJ warned,

> *[382C]* ...the judge must explain why he has reached his decision. The question is always, what is required of the judge to do so; and that will differ from case to case. Transparency should be the watchword.

The then Master of the Rolls, Lord Phillips, concluded in English v Emery Reimbold & Strick Ltd [2002] EWCA Civ 605,

> *[118]* In each of these appeals, the judgment created uncertainty as to the reasons for the decision. In each appeal that uncertainty was resolved, but only after an appeal which involved consideration of the underlying evidence and submissions. We feel that in each case the appellants should have appreciated why it was that they had not been successful, but may have been tempted by the example of *Flannery* to seek to have the decision of the trial Judge set aside. There are two lessons to be drawn from these appeals. The first is that, while it is perfectly acceptable for reasons to be set out briefly in a judgment, it is the duty of the Judge to produce a judgment that gives a clear explanation for his or her order. The second is

that an unsuccessful party should not seek to upset a judgment on the ground of inadequacy of reasons unless, despite the advantage of considering the judgment with knowledge of the evidence given and submissions made at the trial, that party is unable to understand why it is that the Judge has reached an adverse decision.

Reciprocal Enforcement of Maintenance Orders

REMO – the process by which maintenance orders issued in one jurisdiction may be registered and enforced in another.

This is a reciprocal arrangement governed by international conventions, meaning that, if a **Non-Resident Parent** emigrates, there are international agreements with other countries which will enable him to be pursued for debts, particularly if the sums owed are large. Foreign maintenance orders in favour of **Persons with Care** abroad can likewise be registered and enforced by UK courts against UK residents.

The precise nature and degree of reciprocity available between the UK and another jurisdiction depends on the convention or agreement to which the other country is a signatory. A list of the REMO countries is available on the Ministry of Justice website, together with application forms.

Under the REMO scheme there needs to be a court order for maintenance rather than just a **Child Maintenance Service** assessment. It is easier to pursue a liable parent for payment if he is still a UK tax payer, or if he is working for a UK company and is paid from a UK bank account; if he is not, it will be more difficult, particularly if he lives outside the EU.

If there is no existing maintenance order, a claimant can go to her local Magistrates' Court and apply for one as part of the REMO application. The court staff will assist with this and there is no need to involve a solicitor. She will need to complete forms C1, C10 and C10A. The procedure for reciprocal enforcement is provided by Part 34 of the Family Procedure Rules 2010.

Some child maintenance agencies, such as the Australian system, may accept direct applications from UK resident parents-with-care in respect of NRPs resident in Australia.

If the PWC emigrates with her child, the chances are that contact will be severely curtailed and the NRP will have to pay child maintenance. Once the child is **Settled** in the new home the UK courts no longer have jurisdiction and Child Arrangements Orders made here will be worthless; an NRP may need to spend considerable time in the new country, and money on lawyers, to re-establish contact.

If, however, the PWC is only on a limited visa or if it can be shown that she has sufficient remaining links to deem her habitually resident in the UK, the UK courts will retain jurisdiction. This will usually be if she has property here, or active bank accounts, etc. Some countries, such as Australia, only allow immigration if the immigrant is able to support herself financially for a certain period, or if she has a sponsor who will do so. She should not therefore be claiming benefits, but the host country will not tell the NRP if she is, so it is advisable to find out what sort of visa she has before she leaves.

If the NRP does agree to the PWC emigrating, he should do so by means of a **Consent Order**, and make sure there is a clause with regard to child maintenance. If the PWC then goes to the child maintenance agency in the new country to increase payments, she is in breach of the order and the NRP can take her back to court in the UK. She will then need to attend in person or send representation, either of which will be costly. The NRP can then offer to drop his case if she drops hers.

If the Child Maintenance Service itself has no jurisdiction, maintenance has to be dealt with through REMO. If the case comes to court, an NRP will need to argue that the additional costs of contact (flights, hotels, etc.) exceed his liability for maintenance. REMO will not overturn an existing order.

Sometimes the child maintenance assessment will be for a much higher amount than the equivalent UK assessment. Presenting the foreign agency with a UK court order will not help because the UK court has no jurisdiction. The foreign agency will demand the NRP's employment and financial details; if he doesn't comply, they will base his assessment on the average UK national wage. The dispute will need to be resolved through REMO and, if necessary, through the courts. The advantage to the NRP of using REMO is that he can plead his case in a UK court and does not need to travel to the new country. An NRP who visits the country while he is in debt to their child maintenance system should be aware that he may be arrested on entry. If the UK courts through REMO decide not to take money off him, the new country will not be able to arrest him or bar him from entry.

Recital

An item of background information placed at the top of an order which does not constitute part of the order itself; it may record why the order was made, or an agreement the parties have reached.

Recorder

A solicitor or barrister who sits part-time as a judge for three to six weeks a year with the same powers as **Circuit Judges**.

Recording

Recording court proceedings in any form is a criminal offence, and litigants must rely on official recordings and transcripts.

There are occasions, however, when parents want to record social workers or other professionals; the Transparency Project identified a number of reasons why this might be:

a) they want to remember what was said;
b) they want their own record in case a dispute arises over what was said;
c) they don't trust the professionals;
d) they have previously disagreed with a professional's account;
e) they want evidence for forthcoming proceedings;
f) they want to use the recording as part of a campaign.

Covert recordings can destroy trust, look bad in court and fail to provide useable evidence. Precedents are few but in Re L (A Child) [2015] EWFC B148, a mother was only finally believed when she presented recordings in court of the abusive and racially insensitive foster carer with whom she and her baby were living.

The Transparency Project could find no law or statutory guidance which opposes the making of recordings; professionals are required by law to respect confidentiality and the privacy of parents and their children, but this doesn't apply to parents themselves, although they must abide by the laws which apply to **Disclosure** or identifying children.

As with any **Evidence**, a court must give leave for a recording to be used in proceedings and it must be relevant; recordings should be of good quality and complete – not edited highlights. A transcript should also be provided.

Parents who want to record a meeting should discuss it with the professionals beforehand and explain why and how the recording is to be used; they can offer to provide an unedited copy. If the professionals object, they should give their reasons and act within the law.

Covert recording of children – to gather evidence, for example, of the other parent's treatment of the child – is almost certainly likely to backfire; see M v F (Covert Recording of Children)]2016] EWFC 29, in which Mr Justice Jackson said,

> It is almost always likely to be wrong for a recording device to be placed on a child for the purpose of gathering evidence in family proceedings, whether or not the child is aware of its presence.

Recovery Order

A court order made to parents, police or social services to locate a child and return him to those with **Parental Responsibility**. The application is made using Form C3. Recovery may be ordered only where a **Section 8 order** (or equivalent order made in Scotland or Northern Ireland) has been breached and where a child has been snatched from a **Primary Carer** or has not been returned; it may result in a police officer taking the child by force.

Recuse

To disqualify a judge from presiding over a case on the grounds of prejudice or personal involvement.

A litigant can ask the judge to recuse himself or, should he refuse, make an application to the **Court of Appeal** for his recusal. The test is given in F v (1) M (2) D (3) N [2007] EWHC 2543: the judge must be a fair-minded and informed observer and adopt a balanced approach. Consider also Lord Bingham in the case of Magill v Weeks [2001] UKHL 67,

> [103] The question is whether the fair-minded and informed observer, having considered the facts, would conclude that there was a real possibility that the tribunal was biased.

In the case of Re O [2005] EWCA Civ 573, the applicant appealed that Judge Timothy Milligan should be recused following the imposition of a **Section 91 order** of indefinite duration. Judges Thorpe and Wall allowed the appeal; Thorpe commented,

> [5] It is abundantly plain to me that Judge Milligan must part from this case permanently. We have had the opportunity of reading what I think may not unfairly be described as gratuitous observations by Judge Milligan to the applicant on 1 November, and I can well understand how a litigant would feel that justice would not be forthcoming for him before that judge in the light of those observations.

In Re A (Children) [2010] EWCA Civ 1490, a father applied for a **Recorder** to recuse herself because in another case she was instructed by his child's guardian. The guardian had not adopted a position of neutrality and had taken the mother's position. The recorder recused herself but refused to **Set Aside** the findings she had made. The father's appeal was allowed. Patten LJ observed,

[19] Where a judge is faced with an application that he should recuse himself on the ground of apparent bias, it is in my judgment incumbent on him to explain in sufficient detail the scale and content of the professional or other relationship which is challenged on the application. The parties are not in the position of being able to cross-examine the judge about it and he is likely to be the only source of the relevant information.

Red Book

The colloquial name for the Family Law Practice, a comprehensive collection of legislation, practice directions and guidance for practitioners of family law, published annually by legal publishers Jordans.

Relocation

The permanent removal of a child by a parent from one location to another.

Relocation may be **Internal**, that is, within the UK – though it may represent a move of several hundred miles – or **External**, to a different jurisdiction. Where the intention to relocate is opposed by the other parent, the Court will have to intervene.

One in four separated mothers will relocate within four years and relocation is associated with poorer outcomes for children; relocation beyond a one-hour drive is linked to very substantially reduced outcomes. Moving across the Scots border is popular, because Scotland operates under a different legal jurisdiction and English parents must then attend court in Scotland. Moving to Scotland does *not*, however, constitute "removal from the jurisdiction" (due to a legal anomaly), so leave of the Court is not required.

Relocation; External

3129

The permanent removal by a parent of a child out of the geographical jurisdiction of the English and Welsh Courts; also referred to as "removal from the jurisdiction".

Where a parent wishes to take a child abroad for longer than twenty-eight days and written consent from the other is not forthcoming, she must make an application to the Court for Leave to Remove (LTR) under Section 13 of the Children Act; there is no requirement to seek mediation. Contested court proceedings may take six months or more, so she should ensure she has consent or an order in her hand before making any other commitments, and not rely on the verbal agreement of a parent who may throw a spanner in the works at the last moment.

A parent who applies to the Court for leave demonstrates she respects the rule of law and will accept the Court's decision and follow appropriate procedure. This gives the other parent the opportunity to prevent removal and his single chance to maintain a relationship with his child. Some applications follow an unsuccessful **Abduction** or cases where a child has been abducted and then returned under the **Hague Convention**; in such cases, the Court will not take the abduction into account.

If the application has not been made, the other parent can pre-empt the move by making an emergency *ex parte* application for a **Prohibited Steps Order**. He should also ask the Court for the children's **Passports** to be surrendered to an independent solicitor for safe-keeping until the matter is resolved.

If the country to which she is taking the child is not a Hague Convention country, the case must be referred to the High Court.

In at least half of cases where leave is granted, **Contact** between the child and the "left behind" parent breaks down within two years; this is a step, therefore, to be taken only if the relationship between the child and the "left-behind" parent has already irrevocably broken down and the parent is no longer involved.

In 2009, two studies were conducted into LTR cases. The first, carried out for the charity *Reunite* by Dr Marilyn Freeman, revealed that for many fathers, direct contact after relocation is often only "aspirational": after the costs of litigation, relocation and setting up two homes, the reality is that neither party can afford it; some fathers are bankrupted. Contact is easily thwarted once the child is in the new country; a father who has flown halfway round the world only to be sent home again will find it difficult to persevere. Contact can be unsettling for a child who hasn't seen her father for six months and will be difficult to maintain. Long journeys place considerable strain on children who can become hostile to international contact.

The second study, by Professor Patrick Parkinson of the University of Sydney, found that 59% of relocation cases required judicial determination compared with only 13% of other family cases. Costs are high; parents lose their homes; some mothers return home within a year; some fathers move to follow the mother; contact can be difficult or impossible and children are burdened by travel. In too many cases, judges rely on wishful thinking. It is important to remember the purpose of relocation in many cases is to stop contact entirely.

Undertakings made by resident parents are notoriously unreliable: they are made to secure leave for removal, not out of any commitment to protect the relationship with the other parent.

In the past, LTR cases were heavily dominated by a small number of precedents. Crudely, if a father had not been particularly involved and was merely a contact parent, Payne v Payne applied; but if parenting had been more-or-less shared and the father had been hands-on, Re Y did; more recently K v K and Re F attempted a return to first principles by focusing on the child's welfare.

A father is best positioned if he already has a **Child Arrangements Order** naming him as a person with whom the child is to live; even if LTR is granted he can certify the order under the **Brussels II** arrangements. It is possible for the UK Court to order as a condition of LTR that further disputes are resolved in the UK. This will save time and money if the respondent doesn't have to travel abroad to a foreign court and pay for legal representation. In practice, these international agreements are unnecessary where the relocating parent is of good faith, and fairly where they are not.

Poel

The first precedent is Poel v Poel [1970] 1 WLR 1469, in which a mother applied to take her three-year-old to New Zealand. The ruling by Lords Justice Sachs and Winn dominated cases for a long time:

> When a marriage breaks up, then a situation normally arises when the child of that marriage, instead of being in the joint custody of both parents, must of necessity become one who is in the custody of a single parent. Once that position has arisen and the custody is working well, this court should not lightly interfere with such reasonable way of life as is selected by that parent to whom custody has been rightly given... The way in which the parent who properly has custody of a child may choose in a reasonable manner to order his or her way of life is one of those things which the parent who has not been given custody may well have to bear.

The ruling in Lonslow v Hennig [1986] 2 FLR 387, involving two girls aged twelve and ten, shadowed *Poel*. Lord Justice Dillon granted leave to remove because, had he not done so, the mother and her new husband would have been "very disappointed". Leave was also granted in Re C [1998] 1 FLR 848 because otherwise "the mother would have to rearrange her affairs to accommodate the situation. That would not be easy and it would be stressful to her".

Payne

The second and more notorious precedent was provided by the then President, Elizabeth Butler-Sloss, and Thorpe LJ in Payne v Payne [2001] EWCA

Civ 166. A mother had applied to move her daughter to New Zealand; the lower Court rejected her application and she appealed.

The father countered the application but employed the wrong strategy and lost. Thorpe LJ had already suggested in MH v GP (Child: Emigration) [1995] 2 FLR 106 that the Court's acquiescence to the resident parent's wishes was a "presumption" which could be overturned only by an overwhelming welfare argument. Instead, the father used the recently introduced **Human Rights Act** and, in particular, the Article 8 right to respect for family life. Thorpe countered that Article 2 of Protocol 4, though not yet ratified by the UK, protected the "right to liberty of movement and freedom to choose his residence" and that the right to family life was thus not the only right to be weighed. The case was further hampered by a CAFCASS officer who was ignorant of the law and based her limited understanding on notes made by a colleague at a seminar she herself did not attend. Thorpe dismissed the importance of continuing contact because the father omitted any supportive authorities.

Thorpe held, firstly, that the Court had no right to interfere with a mother's right to move abroad if she wished to do so: it would risk the survival of the new family or blight its potential for "fulfilment and happiness". Secondly, he ruled speculatively that the mother should be allowed to remove the child from the jurisdiction since to refuse would have a "devastating" effect on her "psychological and emotional stability",

> [26] Refusing the primary carer's reasonable proposals for the relocation of her family life is likely to impact detrimentally on the welfare of her dependent children. Therefore her application to relocate will be granted unless the court concludes that it is incompatible with the welfare of the children.

Butler-Sloss summarised the criteria which would thereafter apply in LTR cases, making it clear that the principles applied only where the question of residence was not a live issue: the Court should first consider which parent should be the resident parent, taking into account where the child will live, and any plans the parent has for relocation (Paragraph 85).

    a)   the welfare of the child is always paramount;

    b)   there is no presumption created by s.13(1)(b) in favour of the applicant parent;

    c)   the proposals for relocation must be practical and include measures for ensuring continued adequate contact;

    d)   the proposals must be scrutinised with care and the Court needs to be satisfied there is a genuine motivation for the move;

e) the Court must consider the effect upon the applicant parent of a refusal of leave;

f) the Court must consider the effect upon the child of the denial of contact with the other parent;

g) the Court must consider the arrangements for ensuring continuing contact.

In practice, these criteria achieved nothing to protect contact between the child and the "left behind" parent. According to the father's counsel, Philip Cayford QC, commenting ten years later, all contact between father and daughter ceased following the mother's move to New Zealand.

Re Y

In cases in which care was shared more equitably, the courts began to leave *Payne* behind and Mr Justice Hedley's ruling in Re Y [2004] 2 FLR 330 came to be applied. The American mother and English father lived in Wales and had an informal post-divorce arrangement of nearly equally shared parenting. The child grew up bilingual with Welsh as his preferred language. The mother applied to remove the child to the USA; the father countered with an application for shared residence. The mother's application was refused and the father's accepted. The case did not fall within the ambit of *Payne*; the child's home was equally with both parents; the child's interests were best served by allowing him to remain in Wales,

> [25] ...this case falls factually outside the ambit of well-settled authorities in this area of the law. It demonstrates, in a way few cases can, quite how, when everything has been said, done and considered the ultimate test remains the welfare of the child, which in the last analysis overbears all other considerations, however powerful and reasonable they may be.

K v K

In K v K (Children) [2011] EWCA Civ 793, a Canadian mother applied to take her two young daughters to Canada. The Polish father countered that care was shared more-or-less equally; CAFCASS recommended the mother's application be refused, but Bevington HHJ granted the application. The Court of Appeal allowed the father's appeal: Bevington had rejected the CAFCASS report without sufficient explanation; she had relied on the Butler-Sloss criteria and not on Hedley and had referred only to the mother's case. The case did not fall into the traditional taxonomy of a "primary carer" or "shared care" case; each case should be decided on its own facts and merits. Thorpe said,

[39] ...the only principle to be extracted from Payne v. Payne is the paramountcy principle. All the rest... is guidance as to factors to be weighed in search of the welfare paramountcy.

[57] Where each *[parent]* is providing a more or less equal proportion and one seeks to relocate externally then I am clear that the approach which I suggested in paragraph 40 in Payne v Payne should not be utilised.

With regard to *Payne*, Moore-Bick LJ, whose experience was not in family law, observed,

[21] ...I cannot help thinking that the controversy which now surrounds it is the result of a failure to distinguish clearly between legal principle and guidance... As I read it, the only principle of law enunciated in Payne v Payne is that the welfare of the child is paramount; all the rest is guidance.

The end of Payne

In Re TC and JC (Children: Relocation) [2013] EWHC 292, Mostyn J allowed a mother's application to relocate to Australia because the father had expressed his commitment to relocate, too, if leave were granted. Mostyn updated the Butler-Sloss criteria:

1. The welfare of the child is always paramount and outweighs all other considerations, however powerful and reasonable.
2. The guidance provided by the Court of Appeal (in *Payne*) in determining welfare paramountcy is valuable: it guides the judge on what factors he should consider, it advises him on the relative importance of those factors, and it ensures consistency in judging.
3. That guidance is not confined to primary carer cases (like *Payne*) and may be applied to other types of case.
4. The guidance suggests that the following questions be asked and answered:
   a) Is the application genuine and not motivated by a selfish desire to exclude the respondent from the child's life?
   b) Is the application realistically founded on practical proposals both well researched and investigated?
   c) What would be the impact on the applicant, either as the single parent or as a new spouse, of a refusal of a realistic proposal?
   d) Is the respondent's opposition motivated by genuine concern for the child's welfare or driven by some ulterior motive?

     e)   What would be the extent of the detriment to the respondent and his future relationship with the child were the application granted?

     f)   To what extent would that detriment be offset by extension of the child's relationships with the applicant family and homeland?

5. The principles in the guidance should not be applied rigidly and the judge must be free to decide according to the unique circumstances of each case and the child's best interests.

6. There is no legal principle or presumption in favour of an application to relocate. The hearing must not get mired in arguments about whether a case is a "*Payne*" case or a "Re Y" case.

This warning was reiterated in Re Y (Children) [2014] EWCA Civ 1287, in which Ryder LJ rejected a father's application to remove his two children to Missouri. LTR cases must be decided on the facts of the case only; the sole principle to be derived from *Payne* was that the child's welfare must be the Court's paramount consideration.

In Re F (A Child) [2012] EWCA Civ 1364, the father appealed on the basis that, as he was the primary carer, neither *Payne* nor K v K applied; Munby LJ dismissed his appeal and reiterated the position established by K v K;

> *[60]* There is another lesson to be learnt from this case. Adopting conventional terminology, this was neither a "primary carer" nor a "shared care" case. In other words, and like a number of other international relocation cases, it did not fall comfortably within the existing taxonomy. This is hardly surprising. As Moore-Bick LJ said in *K v K*, "the circumstances in which these difficult decisions have to be made vary infinitely." This is not, I emphasise, a call for an elaboration of the taxonomy. Quite the contrary. The last thing that this very difficult area of family law requires is a satellite jurisprudence generating an ever-more detailed classification of supposedly different types of relocation case. Any move in that direction is, in my judgment, to be firmly resisted. But so too advocates and judges must resist the temptation to try and force the facts of the particular case with which they are concerned within some forensic straitjacket. Asking whether a case is a "*Payne* type case", or a "*K v K* type case" or a "*Re Y* type case", when in truth it may be none of them, is simply a recipe for unnecessary and inappropriate forensic dispute or worse. It is to be avoided.

In Re F (A Child) (International Relocation Cases) [2015] EWCA Civ 882, Ryder and McFarlane LLJ continued the judicial escape from the tyranny of *Payne*. The father appealed the decision to allow the mother to remove their twelve-year-old daughter to Germany. The issue was whether the judge had been deflected by the four-point *Payne* criteria from the appropriate welfare analysis (Paragraph 44). The **Ratio** in *Payne* had been "more nuanced" and had been misinterpreted; it had never been intended that the questions in *Payne* should have been "elevated into principles or presumptions"; "it would seem odd indeed for this court to use guidance which out of the context which was intended is redolent with gender based assumptions as to the role and relationships of parents with a child" (Paragraphs 17 and 18).

Ryder reiterated that the need for a "global holistic evaluation", "Where there is more than one proposal before the court, a welfare analysis of each proposal will be necessary. That is neither a new approach nor is it an option" (Paragraph 30). Consideration of **Proportionality** demands that "a step as significant as the relocation of a child to a foreign jurisdiction where the possibility of a fundamental interference with the relationship between one parent and a child is envisaged requires that the parents' plans be scrutinised and evaluated by reference to the proportionality of the same" (Paragraph 31). "The welfare of the child is the paramount consideration. That is the only true principle" (Paragraph 43). Ryder issued a warning for the future which surely sounded the death knell for *Payne*,

> *[27]* Selective or partial legal citation from *Payne* without any wider legal analysis is likely to be regarded as an error of law. In particular, a judgment that not only focuses solely on Payne, but also compounds that error by only referring to the four point "discipline" set out by Thorpe LJ at paragraph [40] of his judgment in *Payne* is likely to be wholly wrong.

In S v V (Children – Leave to Remove) [2018] EWHC 26 Mostyn J refused a mother's application,

> *[2]* The legal test to be applied is now very straight-forward. It is the application of the principle of the paramountcy of the children's best interests, as taxonomised by the checklist in section 1(3) of the 1989 Act. That principle is not to be glossed, augmented or steered by any presumption in favour of the putative relocator. Lord Justice Thorpe's famous "discipline" in *Payne v Payne* [2001] 1 FLR 1052 is now relegated to no more than guidance, guidance which can be drawn on, or not, as the individual case demands.

Relocation; Internal

The removal of a child by a parent within the jurisdiction.

Questions have arisen over whether these cases should be approached differently from **External Relocation** cases, and whether there is a test of "exceptionality" which has weighted decisions in favour of the applicant parent; both issues were raised by Re E (Residence: Imposition of Conditions) [1997] 2 FLR 638 and have now been resolved by the 2015 case of Re C.

Following HRA1998 and the 2001 decision in *Payne* (see **Relocation; External**), three cases (Re S (A Child) (Residence Order: Condition) [2001] EWCA Civ 847, Re H (Children) (Residence Order: Condition) [2001] EWCA Civ 1338 and Re S (a child) (residence order: condition) (No 2) [2002] EWCA Civ 1795) established the paramountcy of the child's welfare and that restrictions should be placed on a resident parent's movement only where the child's welfare exceptionally demanded it. In the slightly later case of Re H (Children) (Residence order: Condition) [2001] EWCA Civ 1338, Thorpe LJ answered the question whether a move to Northern Ireland was an internal or external case, "Does it matter? In practice, probably not much".

Wall LJ clarified the Court's task in E v E (Shared Residence: Financial Relief: Yardstick of Equality) [2006] EWCA Civ 843,

> *[32]* ...The function of the court is to decide whether or not the relocation is in the best interests of the children. In that context, the judge's duty is to subject the mother's relocation proposals to rigorous scrutiny, and (assuming the mother to be acting bona fide) to balance their benefits for the children, and the effect on the mother of refusing her application, against the effect on the children of the disruption of their relationship with their father.

In Re L (A Child) (Internal Relocation: Shared Residence Order) [2009] EWCA Civ 20, in which a mother appealed a judge's decision to prevent her relocation from North London to Chew Magna in Somerset, Wall repeated the principle upon which such cases should be heard,

> *[51]* ...The correct approach, in my view, is not to distinguish the case but to look at the underlying factual substratum in welfare terms, bearing in mind the tension which may well exist between the freedom to relocate which any parent must enjoy against the welfare of the child which may militate against relocation. In my judgment, it is this balance which is critical, and the danger of distinguishing the case as a matter of law is that the court will either lose sight of, or give insufficient weight to the former consideration.

In Re F (Children) [2010] EWCA Civ 1428, the recorder refused a mother's application to relocate four children from Cleveland to the Orkneys, describing the location as one of the remotest inhabited places in the UK and the application as "truly exceptional" and not in the children's best interests. The Court of

Appeal unanimously dismissed the mother's appeal, citing Re L, and considered that the recorder had erred in allowing the appeal.

In Re S (A Child) [2012] EWCA Civ 1031, the first instance judge had ruled, contrary to the CAFCASS recommendation, that the Friday to Sunday contact the father had each week did not amount to shared residence and that his overwhelming need to control the mother precluded it; the mother was the primary carer and the judge lifted a **Prohibited Steps Order** preventing a move to Norwich.

The Appeal Court rejected the father's appeal: the judge had considered all factors affecting the child's welfare and had not merely equated her welfare with that of the mother, as the father claimed; Sir Mark Potter cited Re L, emphasising the Court's duty of "global holistic evaluation",

> [36] Plainly, the fact of such an order is an important factor in the welfare equation, but I respectfully agree with counsel that it is not, in effect, a trump card preventing relocation. In each case what the court has to do is to examine the underlying factual matrix, and to decide in all the circumstances of the case whether or not it is in the child's interest to relocate with the parent who wishes to move.

The case of Re C (Internal Relocation) [2015] EWCA 1305 rejected the gendered approach taken in *Payne* (paragraph 83) and ended the different approaches to treatment of cases involving internal and external relocation: the principles established in the external cases of K v K (Children) [2011] EWCA Civ 793 and Re F (A Child) (International Relocation Cases) [2015] EWCA Civ 882 also apply to internal relocation:

1. the Court must undertake an holistic evaluation of what is in the child's best interests;
2. the child's wishes are significant and relevant;
3. where the proposed move will impact the Article 8 rights of the parties and child(ren), the Court must consider the **Proportionality** of the move;
4. seeking to fit a case into a closed category based on past precedent is unhelpful;
5. the Court must distinguish between "principle", which is binding, and "guidance", which is not;
6. guidance from earlier cases can be helpful, but the weight accorded any particular factor will vary.

A father was unsuccessful in his appeal to prevent a move from London to Cumbria; relying on the **Obiter** comments made by Black LJ in K v K that internal and external relocation cases followed different paths and by Wilson LJ in Re F that principles established in external relocation cases should not be applied to internal relocation, he argued that the first instance judge had been wrong to utilise *Payne*.

The mother argued that the same principles apply to both categories of case, that there should be consistency between the approaches taken, that the authorities can apply equally well to both categories and that *Payne* was therefore a useful tool. As Moore-Bick had identified in K v K, the controversy surrounding *Payne* arose from a failure to distinguish between principle and guidance; only the **Ratio** in *Payne* was binding. Lady Justice Hale reaffirmed: the sole criterion was the welfare of the child,

> *[51-53]* There is no doubt that it is the welfare principle in section 1(1) of the *[Children Act 1989]* which dictates the result in internal relocation cases, just as it is now acknowledged that it does in external relocation cases... I would not interpret the cases as imposing a supplementary requirement of exceptionality in internal relocation cases.

She continued,

> *[53]* One can see from the authorities, and indeed from this case, that the courts are much pre-occupied in relocation cases, whether internal or external, with the practicalities of the child spending time with the other parent or, putting it another way, with seeing if there is a way in which the move can be made to work, thus looking after the interests not only of the child but also of both of his or her parents. Only where it cannot, and the child's welfare requires that the move is prevented, does that happen.

On the matter of proportionality, Black rejected a "cross-check" against the parents' Article 8 rights: the only criterion was the child's welfare; Vos LJ concurred:

> *[84]* ...parents who are staying behind will always be able, in some measure, to pray in aid their Article 8 rights necessitating a consideration of the proportionality of any proposed interference with those rights. That consideration should be an essential part of the balancing exercise itself and should not be undertaken separately so as to disrupt a joined up decision-making process.

In Re R (Child) [2016] EWCA Civ 1016, a father sought to take the approach established in Re C further and invited the Court to order a summary return in all "internal abduction" cases, advocating that a principle analogous to **Habitual Residence** be applied. Black LJ rejected the appeal: it was not for the Court to do Parliament's job for it; all cases were to be tried on their individual merits, always guided by the child's welfare and a detailed consideration of the checklist.

Remission
See **Court Fees**.

Reporting Restrictions

Article 6 of the **Human Rights Act 1998** demands without restriction or qualification that "Judgment shall be pronounced publicly"; the Family Court, however, has traditionally refused to publish judgments (other than anonymised ones in carefully chosen cases) and, in the Court of Appeal precedent Re P-B (Minor) (Child Cases: Hearings in Open Court) [1997] 1AER 58, [1996] 2FLR 765 CA, the Court found that the practice of hearings in chambers with secret judgments was lawful and Convention-compliant.

Publication by anyone other than the judge of the details of proceedings held in private and conducted under the Children Act 1989 or the Adoption and Children Act 2002 or which "otherwise relate wholly or mainly to the maintenance or upbringing of a minor" is prohibited by Section 12 of the Administration of Justice Act 1960.

"Publication" means making information public, which includes putting information on social media, sending a text message or purely oral communication to any third party. Courts "sitting in private" include those into which accredited press are allowed but which still exclude the general public. It is moot whether such proceedings can still be said to be "in private" and whether, therefore, Section 12 still applies. This question has yet to be resolved by case law. Section 12 prevents publication of—

1. what goes on in front of the judge sitting *in camera*;
2. documents filed in court such as position statements, witness statements, reports, and legal arguments;
3. transcripts or notes of evidence, submissions and judgments; and
4. extracts, quotations and summaries of such documents, whether anonymised or not.

Section 12 does *not* of itself prevent publication of—

1. the fact that a particular child is subject to Children Act proceedings or proceedings relating to his maintenance or upbringing (this is prevented by **Section 97** CA1989);
2. the nature of the dispute (as opposed to a summary of the evidence);
3. the identity of the parties and witnesses, and of the party on whose behalf a witness has given evidence (this also is prevented by s.97 where it can lead to identification of the child); and
4. the text of any order made.

There is no time limit to this prohibition and Section 12 remains in force indefinitely after the completion of proceedings. **Breach** is a contempt of court punishable by a fine or imprisonment for up to two years. The Court must first warn the litigant of the consequences of breach and make an injunctive order with a penal notice attached.

Section 97 of the Children Act 1989 prohibits the publication of any material intended or likely to identify a child involved in proceedings under the Act or under the Adoption and Children Act 2002 in the Family Court or High Court. It also prevents identification of the child's home address or school. It does not extend to the Court of Appeal.

The default position of the courts is that children should remain anonymous unless it can be shown to be in their interest for anonymity to be lifted. As with the rules on access, there is a get-out clause in Section 97(4): "The court or the Secretary of State may, if satisfied that the welfare of the child requires it, by order dispense with the requirements of subsection (2) to such extent as may be specified in the order".

To some extent s.97 merely confirms what was already law: s.39 of the Children and Young Persons Act 1933 forbids publication of the name, address, or pictures of a child who is the subject of proceedings, or of particulars "calculated to identify" him or her. S.62 of the Children Act 2004 relaxed the s.97 rules by amending them to cover publication only "to the public at large or any section of the public".

The important ruling in Clayton v Clayton [2007] 1FLR 11 CA was that this prohibition endures only for the duration of the proceedings, and that once the case is concluded it is no offence to identify the child. The prohibition provided by s.12 of the Access to Justice Act, however, was not overturned and remains in force, thus parties and journalists may publish that a particular child was involved in proceedings once they have concluded but not the substance of the case. The Court may also apply a further injunction in order to continue the s.97 protection if it considers it necessary. Breach of s.97 is a criminal offence and the Court does not need to warn the parties or apply a penal notice. Breach is common but, so far as we can tell, there has never been a successful prosecution.

From 3rd February 2014, the President of the Family Division, Munby LJ, introduced new guidance on reporting judgments. He listed three categories:

1. Where the judge considers publication is in the public interest he must normally give permission for publication, regardless of whether or not a request has been made; if a judgment is not to be published there must be compelling reasons not to do so. Costs will be borne by the public purse.

2. If the judgment already exists in publishable form and relates to one of the matters below, the judge must normally give permission for publication unless there are compelling reasons not to do so. Costs will be divided equally between the parties.

   a) A substantial contested fact-finding hearing at which serious allegations have been determined;

   b) the making, refusal or discharge of a final care order or supervision order under Part 4 of the Children Act, except where the order is made with consent;

   c) the making, refusal or discharge of a placement order or adoption order under the Adoption and Children Act 2002, except where the order is made with consent;

   d) the making or refusal of any declaration or order authorising a deprivation of liberty, including an order for secure accommodation;

   e) any application for an order involving the giving or withholding of serious medical treatment;

   f) any application for an order involving a restraint on publication of information relating to the proceedings.

3. In all other cases permission may be given for the judgment to be published whenever a party or accredited member of the media applies for an order permitting publication and the judge concludes that permission should be given. Costs will be borne by the party applying for publication.

Where permission is given, the judgment must be made available to any person who requests a copy on payment of a charge. Judgments must be placed on the BAILII website as soon as reasonably practicable; judgments in category 3 will be placed on BAILII at the judge's discretion.

The guidance directs that public officials and expert witnesses should be identified by name unless there are compelling reasons not to do so. Names of children and their family members should not normally be published.

Anonymisation of the judgment should customarily be undertaken by the applicant's solicitor or, where an application has been made for publication, by the solicitor of the party applying for publication. The anonymised version must then be submitted to the judge for approval.

Munby's guidance creates some grey areas: for example, a litigant might post a link to the judgment on *Facebook* without further comment, but then others start linking and identifying him as the subject of the judgment, or the press pick up the case and he is named in the comments section, etc. Though his child is not identified, she may yet be identifiable.

Although the guidance was an improvement, there was no change to the legislation, and publication remained severely restricted. There was no opportunity to examine the methodology which produced the judgment, or to determine whether due legal process has been observed. Following some very inaccurate and partisan reporting of high-profile cases, further consultation was promised in August 2017.

Res Judicata

(Latin: "a matter judged") a matter which the Court has already decided, and which cannot be judged again.

Rescind

See **Set Aside**.

Reserve (1)

A judge may "reserve" a case to himself to ensure **Judicial Continuity**, or for other reasons, meaning that no other judge may hear it.

Reserve (2)

A court "reserves" **Judgment** if it does not deliver it **Extempore** on the day and **Hands** it **Down** at a later date.

Reserved Legal Activity

One of six legal activities reserved to authorised persons such as **Solicitors, Barristers, Legal Executives** and some **Paralegals**.

Performance of these activities by a non-authorised person, such as a **McKenzie Friend**, is a criminal offence under the Legal Services Act 2007 and can attract a twelve-month maximum sentence on summary conviction or a two-year sentence on indictment. The reserved activities are:

1. the exercise of a **Right of Audience**;
2. the **Conduct of Litigation**;
3. reserved instrument activities;
4. probate activities;
5. notarial activities; and
6. the administration of oaths.

Residence

Since the introduction of the Children and Families Act in April 2014, the term "residence" has effectively been eliminated. It was introduced under the Children Act 1989 and replaced the old concept of "custody". It is still preferable and more accurate to speak of "residence" than of "custody". In Re E (minors) [1997] EWCA Civ 3084, Butler-Sloss LJ said,

> [14] A residence order is not identical with a custody order and in particular the parent with whom the child does not live retains greater rights and responsibilities by virtue of his/her continuing parental responsibility for the child than under a custody order.

Residence signified only with whom a child had his primary residence, it conferred no degree of parental status and was confined to "settling the arrangements to be made as to the person with whom a child is to live"; it gave no other powers; Lord Justice Ward observed in Re G (A Child) [2008] EWCA 1468,

> [26] A Residence Order gives the mother no added right over and above the father. That is the lesson that has not yet been fully learned in the 19 years that the Act has been on the statute book. The Residence Order does no more than its definition allows.

In practice, it is inevitable that a **Child Arrangements Order** regulating with whom a child is to live and when should confer status because the parent in whose favour one is made has considerable advantage over the other.

Residence can be "sole", which means the child habitually lives with only one parent and may or may not have "**Contact**' with the other, or "shared", which means the child is able to live more or less equally with both parents. Until a Child Arrangements Order is made, both parents theoretically have residence, so an order either confirms this, or strips a parent of residence.

If a father does not already have **Parental Responsibility**, a Child Arrangements Order making him a person with whom the child is to live will confer it for the duration of the order only. A Child Arrangements Order naming him as a person with whom the child is to have contact will not do this. In the case of an unmarried father, the Court must also make a separate **Parental Responsibility Order** (Section 12 Children Act CA1989).

Residence Order

A court order introduced in 1989 determining with which parent a child should live following separation; from April 2014, existing Residence Orders became **Child Arrangements Orders**.

Resident Parent

The parent with whom the child habitually lives; see **Person with Care**.

Residual Jurisdiction

Under Brussels II, if a party does not have his **Habitual Residence** in a member state and no member state has **Jurisdiction**, a court can assume "residual jurisdiction" if the party is **Domiciled** in that state.

So, for example, an abducted child who has not yet acquired habitual residence in a new jurisdiction would come under the residual jurisdiction of the Court; a couple who have been living in the USA and have been living in the UK for only a few months would be able to divorce under the English and Welsh Court's residual jurisdiction.

Respondent

The party to whom the order applied for by the **Petitioner** (in a divorce case) or **Applicant** (in other cases) will apply.

It is essential that the respondent in a case responds! Some parenting groups recommend that respondents to a children's application ignore an application made by the other parent and don't attend court.

This is terribly bad advice. A resident parent might think she is entitled to play the **Gatekeeper** role, but the message this sends the Court is that she has no respect for its authority and doesn't care about her child's welfare. The Court may well make an order in her absence with which she will be unwilling or unable to comply. Further applications will then be made, and the court process escalates. Far better that she attends and perhaps is able to resolve differences at an early stage.

When the applicant makes his application, the papers will be served on the respondent; this will normally be done by the Court or can be done by the applicant in person, by a "**Process Server**" or by first-class or registered post. If the applicant serves them personally, the respondent should accept them and close the door; she should not get into any argument. If she already has a solicitor, the papers should be served to them. The papers will include —

1. a copy of the **Notice of Proceedings**, Form C6, which will give details of the nature of the application and the child(ren) concerned, the court, and the time and date of the hearing. This form should be taken to the court for the hearing;
2. a copy of the application form(s), C100 and C1A where relevant;
3. copies of any other papers the court office has allowed the applicant to file;
4. a blank C10A **Statement of Means**, if the applicant has asked the Court to order the respondent to make a payment for the child;
5. an **Acknowledgement**, Form C7.

The respondent must complete Form C7, entering her name, date of birth and address and her solicitor's details if she has one. There are four options for her in response:

1. She may decide she doesn't want to oppose the application. It may be for **Parental Responsibility**, for example, or a **Child Arrangements Order** which will enable both parents to put things on a clearer, firmer basis. In this case she answers "No" to Question 5.
2. She may have received a copy of Form C1A in which the applicant expresses concerns over the child's welfare. If she wants to comment on these statements, she must answer "Yes" to the second part of Question 6.
3. If she believes the applicant presents a threat to the child's welfare, she must answer "Yes" to Question 7. She may also want to complete her own C1A. Bear in mind that allegations and counter allegations of abuse get messy, and result in proceedings which can continue for many years.
4. She can make her own counter application for a **Section 8 order**. She will answer "Yes" to Question 8.

She must then sign and date the form. The response must arrive at the court not later than fourteen days before the hearing.

Revised Family Law Programme

A scheme of case management introduced in April 2010 and designed to reduce demand for and pressure on CAFCASS and the family justice system and to expedite the progress of cases through the system. Superseded by the **Child Arrangements Programme**.

Right of Audience

The question often arises in family cases as to whether a **McKenzie Friend** can directly address the Court, make oral submissions or examine witnesses.

This right to be heard is called the "Right of Audience" and is a **Reserved Legal Activity**, meaning a McKenzie has no such right automatically. It remains up to the judge of the day to exercise his discretion. The judge will be bound by the principle that his discretion is "to be exercised only in exceptional circumstances". This was the ruling of Lord Woolf MR in D v S (Rights of Audience) [1997] 1 FLR 724, when he denied a McKenzie right of audience; he added that the right was not to be a matter of consent for the parties but was to be granted only by the judge.

In Clarkson v Gilbert [2000] 2 FLR 839, Woolf allowed a husband to represent his wife; he said,

> [17] The overriding objective is that the courts should do justice. Now that legal aid is not available as readily as it was in the past means that there are going to be situations where litigants are forced to bring proceedings in person when they will need assistance. However, if they are litigants in person they must, in my judgment, establish why they need some other person who is not qualified to appear as an advocate on their behalf. In the ordinary way it will be for them to satisfy the court that that is appropriate. If somebody's health does not, or may not, enable them to conduct proceedings themselves, and if they lack means, those are the sort of circumstances that can justify a court saying that they should have somebody who can act as an advocate on their behalf.

In May 2005, the President, Sir Mark Potter, gave the following guidance and repeated it without the case citations in April 2008 in *President's Guidance: McKenzie Friends,*

> A court may grant an unqualified person a right of audience in exceptional circumstances only and only after careful consideration (D v S (Rights of Audience) [1997] 1 FLR 724, Milne v Kennedy and Others [1999] TLR 106, Paragon Finance PLC v Noueiri (Practice Note) [2001] 1 WLR 2357). The litigant must apply at the outset of a hearing if he wishes the MF to be

granted a right of audience or the right to conduct the litigation (Clarkson v Gilbert [2000] 2 FLR 839).

In Re N (A Child) (McKenzie Friend: Rights of Audience) [2008] EWHC 2042, Munby J allowed a mother's McKenzie right of audience in a case in which the father's McKenzie had already been granted it, though in the final hearing the father was represented. Munby reviewed the authorities and current court practice, and repeated the points established in Clarkson v Gilbert that there is no automatic right of audience for McKenzies: the law allows the judge unfettered discretion, and thus such an order need not only be made in "exceptional circumstances". In each case the judge must decide whether its circumstances are "exceptional". He repeated Woolf's rule, "the overriding objective is that the courts should do justice". This judgment led Potter to revise the *President's Guidance*, adding this paragraph:

> While the court should be slow to grant any application under s.27 or s.28 of the Act from a MF, it should be prepared to do so for good reason bearing in mind the general objective set out in section 17(1) and the general principle set out in section 17(3) of the Act and all the circumstances of the case. Such circumstances are likely to vary greatly: see paragraphs 40-42 of the judgment of Munby J. in Re N (A child) (McKenzie Friend: Rights of Audience) [2008] EWHC 2042 (Fam).

Section 17(1) of the Courts and Legal Services Act 1990 established the general objective of making "provision for new or better ways of providing [legal] services and a wider choice of persons providing them, while maintaining the proper and efficient administration of justice".

Section 17(3) set out the rules which applied to professional advocates or to members of other bodies which provided legal services, and which had enforceable rules of conduct.

The Act was replaced by the Legal Services Act 2007 which dropped the endorsement of alternative legal services; under Schedule 3, 1(2)(b) a McKenzie may be granted the right of audience by the judge in relation to the proceedings. This right is not transferable to other proceedings. Without the judge's consent he will be committing a criminal offence. Sometimes, a judge will invite a McKenzie to accept a right of audience without application if it is in the interests of justice.

Ordinarily, a person exercising such rights would be properly trained, be under professional discipline (including an obligation to insure against liability for negligence) and be subject to an overriding duty to the Court. These requirements are necessary for the protection of all parties to litigation and are essential to the proper administration of justice.

If a litigant wishes his McKenzie to be granted right of audience, he must make the request in writing or orally at the start of the hearing. His McKenzie must then submit a CV showing that he understands the law and his role.

The other party will be given an opportunity to object and the judge will decide. Acceptable grounds for objection are provided in paragraph 12 of the Practice Direction, while possible justifications are given in paragraphs 20 and 21.

It is unlikely the Court will allow a McKenzie to stand in for a litigant throughout the entire hearing, and more likely he will be allowed audience only at certain points. The circumstances need not be "exceptional", but it will help a case if the litigant can demonstrate that they are by using as many of the points in paragraph 21 as apply to him. It is for the litigant to argue the case, not the McKenzie.

Granting the right either of audience or to **Conduct Litigation** does not imply that the grant of the other right has been made. If both rights are sought their grant must be applied for individually and justified separately. Having granted a right either of audience or to conduct litigation, the Court has the power to remove either. The grant of such rights in one set of proceedings cannot be relied on as a precedent supporting their grant in future proceedings.

In practice many judges are allowing McKenzies right of audience without obliging litigants to make these arguments. It eases the pressure on an overloaded system by enabling arguments to be put more clearly and efficiently and it saves valuable court time as well as keeping hostilities to a minimum. This has to be in the interests of justice.

Risk Assessment

The Children and Adoption Act 2006 added a Section 16A to the Children Act 1989 in order to provide **CAFCASS** with the additional power to carry out "risk assessments". If a CAFCASS officer suspects a child to be at risk of "**Harm**" she must carry out an assessment of that harm being suffered by the child and provide it to the Court.

A risk assessment is defined as an assessment of the risk of the child suffering the harm that is suspected. The risk of harm to the child may relate to harm directly experienced by the child himself or to harm caused by the witnessing of harm.

A brief Practice Direction was issued in September 2007 on the use of risk assessments where there was suspicion of harm; it was reissued as Practice Direction 12L in 2010; it makes three requirements:

1. A CAFCASS officer must make a risk assessment and provide it to the Court if she is given any cause to suspect that the child concerned is at risk of harm.
2. She has a duty to provide the risk assessment to the Court, irrespective of the outcome of the assessment and even if she concludes there is no risk of harm to the child. She must make clear to the Court what prompted her to carry out the assessment.
3. The fact that a risk assessment has been carried out then becomes a material fact to be placed before the Court regardless of the outcome of the assessment. Thus, even where a risk assessment concludes that the child is *not* at risk, the mere fact that it was carried out will be taken into account in any decision the Court makes.

Rose Agreement

A **Heads of Agreement** which has not yet been worked up into an order, but which is approved by the judge and is therefore binding on the parties. Named after the case Rose v Rose [2002] EWCA Civ 208.

S

Safeguarding Letter

Rather than produce the full **Section 7** welfare report, which is enormously time-consuming and can introduce delay of a year or more, under the **Child Arrangements Programme**, CAFCASS will be asked to produce for the Court what is termed a Safeguarding Letter (formerly known as a Schedule 2 letter) which must be presented before the **FHDRA**.

CAFCASS will be expected to identify any issues raised in the C1A Form relating only to "safety". All other issues will be deferred to the FHDRA so that both parties can know what issues the other has raised and thus be on an "equal footing". To achieve this the **Family Court Advisor** must,

1. carry out inquiries including interviews with the parties by telephone and checks with the local authority and the police;
2. meet with the parties individually if safety issues are raised in order to clarify them;
3. record and outline safety issues in a Safeguarding Letter for the Court within seventeen days and no less than three days before the hearing;
4. *not* initiate contact with the child.

The limitations on the information the police will disclose to CAFCASS are set by a joint agreement with the Association of Chief Police Officers (ACPO) and were clarified in G v B [2010] EWHC 2630:

1. CAFCASS may not seek information on third parties such as new partners without the express permission of the Court.

2. CAFCASS may discuss the information received with the relevant party and with the other parent, but only if there are child welfare issues. They may only include in the report police information which is relevant to the child's welfare.
3. CAFCASS may not give copies of police documentation to the parties or their legal representatives, or attach copies to the report.
4. CAFCASS may pass on police information to social services but only where there are urgent child protection issues or for the preparation of a Section 7 report.

If CAFCASS receive nothing from the police or the local authority, they will report that the parties are not known to them and that there is therefore no further need for their involvement. The intention is that this should end the use of s.7 reports where they are not needed.

Under Paragraph 3.9 of Practice Direction 12B, the Court must inform the parties of the contents of this report unless it would create a risk of harm to a party or the child. The Court must also consider whether there is need for,

1. a **Risk Assessment**; or
2. a **Finding-of-Fact** hearing to determine the actuality of any allegations made.

The reality tends to lag behind the ideal and Safeguarding Letters will not always be produced to the courts on time. Unallocated cases have been reduced, but largely through the strategy of allocating more cases to each worker, and especially to managers; this doesn't necessarily guarantee the cases will be dealt with and means these cases are not always subject to regular review and monitoring.

There has been some criticism of Safeguarding Letters because they are produced to a formula, with scripted telephone calls, restricted enquiries, and a prescriptive template. Reliance on these letters in private law cases has reduced the capacity of CAFCASS to report under Section 7, with a consequent decline in its ability properly to investigate cases.

Schedule 2 Letter

Former name for the **Safeguarding Letter.**

Schedule of Deficiencies

A list of discrepancies and missing information provided during **Ancillary Relief** proceedings.

School Absence

Under Section 7 of the Education Act 1996, a parent is legally obliged to ensure his child receives "full-time" education, either through mainstream education or otherwise. Schooling must begin from the term following the child's fifth birthday; a child may leave school at the end of the school year if he has reached the age of sixteen or will reach that age before the beginning of the next school year. A parent is guilty of an offence under s.444 if his child fails to attend school "regularly" without "reasonable justification".

Taking a child out of school during term time is disruptive both to the child's learning and to the school, and a parent must have the written permission of the head. In Wales, schools can use their discretion to allow annual absence of up to ten days.

Unauthorised absence will result in the issue of a penalty notice to both parents and they may be fined £60 each per day of absence, rising to £120 if the fine is not paid promptly. Many parents consider the fines worth paying to take advantage of cheaper holidays.

In 2015, Jon Platt took his daughter on holiday in term-time, ignoring the school's refusal and subsequent fines. The LA prosecuted, and the Magistrates' and High Courts found in his favour; the LA appealed to the Supreme Court (Isle of Wight Council v Platt [2017] UKSC 28). In addressing the meaning of "regularly", the Court rejected an interpretation of "sufficiently frequently", as had been applied in earlier cases, and decided that the appropriate interpretation was "in accordance with the rules prescribed by the school"; "full-time" meant "for the whole of the time when education is being offered to children like the child in question"; the intention of Parliament had clearly been to tighten the rules on unauthorised absence. Platt was given a twelve-month conditional discharge and £2,000 fine, scant relief to his neighbours whose taxes paid the council's estimated £250,000 legal bill.

School Reports

Although the school must treat both parents equally, it is obliged to issue only one copy of a child's educational record or school report; it can only provide information to which the child has a right of access. Provided that requirement is satisfied, the school must make the child's educational record available to a parent, free of charge, within fifteen school days of receipt of his written request. This rule does not apply to nursery schools.

The school may charge for further copies but not beyond the cost of supply, so a parent should offer to pay for them and provide the school with a dozen stamped, addressed envelopes. Even if he doesn't have contact he still has a right to this information under the Education (Pupil Information) (England) Regulations 2005.

Schools & Non-Resident Parents

The choice of school is a common source of post-separation conflict. The courts take the view that this is a decision properly to be made by the parents; where agreement is impossible, a parent will need to apply for a **Specific Issues Order**. In EG v JG [2013] EW Misc 21 (CC), the court was not in a position to decide between two very similar schools and ruled instead on which parent should have the final say, concluding that it was in the children's best interests that the mother should decide, and ending proceedings which had become disproportionately costly.

A **Non-Resident Parent** must not allow himself to become excluded from his child's education: this is another area he can find challenging.

It is more difficult if he has only weekend and holiday contact, which is why midweek contact is so important, enabling a parent to help with his child's homework, visit and see the school, and meet teachers and friends. He should go to the school, introduce himself, arrange a meeting with the head, explain his situation. He can join the Parent Teacher Association (PTA), turn up at curriculum evenings, get to know all his child's teachers and discuss progress with them, etc. Remember that in many schools, family breakdown is the norm rather than the exception and they should be geared up for this.

He should get involved in every school outing he can, for example, by providing transport (he will need to have a DBS check); he can offer to take photographs on outings and sports days, and give a spare copy or disc to the principal; turn up for every school event, whether invited or not; offer to run a stall on school fairs day, or on fundraising days; write to the school on a regular basis thanking them for all they are doing for his child; he should ensure he has a record of his **Involvement**, including photographs, so that he can present it as evidence in court.

If a parent does not know which school his child attends but knows the general area, he can write to the local education authority and request this information, stating his name, the child's name and their relationship. He should ask for the address of the school and name of the head teacher, so he can write to them and ensure his continuing involvement in his child's education and development. He should state he is making the request under the

Education (Pupil Information) (England) Regulations 2005 or Section 7 of the Data Protection Act 1998. Note that not all schools (e.g. academies) are subject to the 2005 Regulations, so it is sensible to check.

Schools are required by the Department for Education to treat both parents equally, and not discriminate against non-resident parents. This is a summary of the advice given; note that it is sent only to head teachers, so other teachers may be unaware. The guidance begins with the definition of a parent from Section 576 of the Education Act 1996, which includes married and unmarried parents and anyone who has **Parental Responsibility** (PR) for the child.

Next, the guidance provides a definition of PR and the ways in which it may be **Acquired**, and notes that not only parents may have it, but that it may also be acquired by a local authority through a **Care Order**. A local authority with PR can prevent a parent having contact with their child, even though the parent also has PR. Children may also be taken into local authority accommodation by agreement with the parents without a court order. Several people, including the LA, can thus be regarded in law as a child's parents.

The guidance goes on to discuss **Section 8** orders and specifically the restrictions **Prohibited Steps Orders** and **Specific Issues Orders** impose on the exercise of PR. If either parent needs to show a school a copy of a court order they will need the consent of the Court, otherwise they could be in **Contempt**.

Schools are *in loco parentis* for the children in their care and, though they do not have PR, in the event of an accident or the need for emergency medical treatment are enabled by Section 3(5) CA1989 to "do what is reasonable in all the circumstances of the case for the purpose of safeguarding or promoting the child's welfare", for example, taking a child to hospital to have a wound stitched. The parents must then be kept informed as soon as possible, so that they can take responsibility for any further decisions necessary.

Schools are obliged by the Children Act to make the child's **Welfare** paramount and, where a parent's action makes this difficult, the school should seek resolution with the parent, but avoid becoming drawn into any conflict.

It is a legal requirement that the school registers a child using the **Name** on the birth-certificate; if necessary a parent may have to insist on this. Schools are advised that, though a custodial mother may ask a school to change her child's name in its records, she may not legally do so without the consent of all those with PR. The school must have evidence of this consent in writing, or a court order: a letter from the mother's solicitor carries no legal authority. If the name has already been changed, then it may not be in the child's best interests for it to be changed back.

Head teachers must ensure they have the full names and addresses of all adults who have PR when the child is enrolled. They must also have details of any court orders which affect the parents' exercise of PR. These records must be kept up-to-date and made available to the child's teachers; they must be forwarded to the new school should the child change schools.

If a school hasn't been given the contact details of a parent, it must remind the parent with whom the child lives that both parents have the right to be involved in the child's education and request to be given the contact details. A school can do nothing if the parent refuses, but if the other parent contacts the school directly it must cooperate.

If both parents have PR neither can take unilateral decisions about their child's education; they must consult. If they can't agree, the Court will have to impose a decision.

A school must recognise that everyone with PR has the right to participate in decisions concerning the child's education, even if only one parent is the main point of contact with the school. They must treat everyone with PR equally unless they have been shown a court order restricting a parent's PR; this must include,

1. providing parents with information, such as copies of the governors' annual report, pupil reports and attendance records;
2. enabling parents to participate in activities, such as voting in elections for parent governors;
3. asking parents to give consent, for example to their child taking part in extra-curricular activities;
4. telling parents about meetings involving their child, such as a governors' meeting on the child's exclusion.

Generally, a school will need the consent of only one parent for a child to be involved in an outside activity, unless the activity will have "a long term and significant impact" on the child or if the non-resident parent has informed the school that he wishes to be approached for consent in all such cases. Sometimes one parent will give consent and the other withhold it; this puts the school in an awkward position, and the best advice is that the child should *not* participate in the activity. The school would not be taking sides, merely protecting itself from possible legal action should, for example, the child be injured on a trip. The resident parent could be recommended to seek a court order to clarify the situation.

Scots Law

A legal system independent of and distinct from the English and Welsh which can trace its origins back to ancient Roman law and to the *Corpus Juris Civilis*. Unlike many European legal systems, it is uncodified with sources in **Common Law** and **Statute Law**.

Between the Act of Union 1707 and the Scotland Act 1998, Scotland shared a parliament with England and other countries of the UK. Nevertheless, Scots law remained fundamentally separate from English law, albeit the Union facilitated a mutual exchange of legal influences and some harmonisation of **Substantive Law.**

Since the Treaty of Rome 1957, Scotland has formed part of the European Union and thereby shares a large range of trade laws with Europe as well as the **European Convention on Human Rights.**

The Scotland Act 1998 reinstated the Scottish Parliament; while only a devolved assembly, as opposed to a fully-fledged independent institution, the Parliament has nonetheless advanced the distinctive character of Scots law into the New Millennium.

There are two levels of family court in Scotland: the **Sheriff Court** and the **Court of Session** (the English interpretation of the Latin word *"Sederunt"* – literally: "they sat"). A party can be represented by a solicitor and receive public funding even if he is resident in England (qualification criteria are much the same as they used to be in England), and by a barrister, known as an "advocate". The Sheriff Court is cheaper, because lawyers cannot charge as much, but its jurisdiction is limited, so if a party wants an English order enforced in Scotland he is better off going to the Court of Session, though he will then need to stay in Edinburgh. Correspondingly, orders made in the Sheriff Court will not be respected in England.

Civil Procedure in the Sheriff Courts is governed by the Act of Sederunt (Sheriff Court Ordinary Cause Rules) 1993, SI 1993/1956; the scope includes nearly all private law family proceedings.

Scots Law; Applications

A party from England or Wales pursuing proceedings in Scotland can still apply for an order in an English/Welsh court, which will then be easier and simpler to enforce in Scotland if the Court agrees. Care should be taken when adopting this approach, because it can be interpreted as disrespectful to the Scots courts: the **Pursuer** should make it clear that the decision was the Court's and not his.

A "Writ" must first be issued in the **Sheriff Court** or, very rarely, a "Summons" in the **Court of Session** under the **Ordinary Procedure**; it must be worded in a particular formal way acceptable to the Court; there are no forms equivalent to the C100 to simplify the process. The Ordinary Cause rules and family procedure rules are available from the Scottish Courts website. The Summons should be kept as brief and to-the-point as possible. It will have three sections: the **Conclusions**, the **Condescendences** and the **Pleas-in-Law.**

Even if the pursuer intends to self-represent it is worth paying a solicitor to help get the wording correct. The Summons must be "signetted" (i.e., stamped with the signet or seal of the Sovereign to authorise execution) and "registered" in the Register of Summary Causes at the Sheriff Court; at the Court of Session it must be "lodged for calling". The **Defender** must then lodge a notice of intent to defend and lodge the **Defences** which is the official response to the Condescendences. In this document each point raised by the pursuer must be answered, and either admitted or defended; anything not specifically denied is assumed to be admitted.

The pursuer will then be allowed a period of time in which to alter the Summons in response to what has been claimed in the Defences, and the defender will be allowed time to alter the Defences. Each side must indicate clearly what has been changed. The Scots courts are stricter than the English and Welsh, so neither side should be able to ambush the other with new claims or evidence. It is the pursuer's responsibility to keep a record of all changes, from both sides, and to lodge it with the Court prior to the first hearing.

The Sheriff will ascertain from the parties, or their solicitors if they are represented, what matters are in dispute in relation to the child. Parties will provide the Sheriff with information relating to the issues in dispute.

Solicitors (or the **Party Litigant**) put each side's case to the Sheriff, then after discussion, if an agreement cannot be reached, the Sheriff will set out a timetable on how to proceed. The Sheriff may make interim orders, or refer both parties to a family mediator, such as *Relationships Scotland*.

Scott Schedule

A commonly used document named after the surveyor who developed it as a means of presenting allegations in litigation.

It is set out as a table in which the numbered allegations are listed in one column, the respondent's comments or refutations in another and the judge's findings in a third. The allegations and responses are recorded briefly, with references to the fuller account in the **Position Statement** and the relevant page number in the **Bundle**.

Because false allegations are liable to escalate, a Scott Schedule can be a way of fixing them so that no new ones can be introduced. Providing a response to each individual allegation, however, effectively validates it and allows it to become a part of the proceedings. The Schedule can be a ruse to add additional **Delay** with the allegations amounting to no more than the entirely normal behaviour of a loving parent tested beyond endurance and the natural ebb and flow of imperfect parenting.

If the allegations are trivial, the responses can be brief, or the respondent can simply state "Admitted" or "Denied", but needs to address the allegations to ensure that the Court will be given the information necessary to allow it to come to an informed decision.

Failure to complete the Schedule when ordered can result in the case being adjourned and possible cost penalties; not responding to the specific allegations significantly increases the likelihood that findings of fact will be made which are likely to prejudice the case.

Seal

A mark the court places on a document to indicate that the court has issued it. Once it is sealed, an order is referred to as "perfected". A court order only has effect once it has been sealed.

Sears Tooth Agreement

A deed between litigant and solicitor that assigns all or part of a capital settlement to the solicitor to cover legal fees. It must be disclosed to the court and other parties. Named after the case Sears Tooth (A Firm) v Payne Hicks Beach (A Firm) and others [1997] 2 FLR 116.

Secondary Legislation

Legislation made by the executive branch of government under powers delegated by the legislature. Whereas there may be only a few dozen primary pieces of legislation each year, there will be thousands of secondary items. In the context of family law these are mainly statutory instruments.

Secrecy

See **Privacy** and **Reporting Restrictions**.

Section 1 Principles

Section 1 of the Children Act 1989 specifies four fundamental principles which determine all cases:

1. the child's welfare is the Court's paramount consideration;
2. delay is likely to be prejudicial to the child's welfare;
3. the Court is to presume that the child's welfare will be furthered by the involvement of a parent who does not put his child at risk of suffering harm; and

4. no order shall be made unless the Court considers that doing so would be better for the child than making no order at all.

Section 7 Report

A report ordered from **CAFCASS** by the Court under Section 7 of the Children Act 1989 in order to determine the welfare issues of a case.

In most cases, the **Safeguarding** (Schedule 2) investigation by CAFCASS will be sufficient, but in a case where any question concerning the **Welfare** of the child has arisen, s.7 allows the Court to request a further report which will assist the judge in understanding the case and in making an appropriate order. If allegations have been made, the Court may want to determine the veracity of these through a **Finding-of-Fact** hearing before ordering a welfare report.

To prevent litigants becoming dependent on the Court to regulate every aspect of their children's lives, it is intended that the Section 7 reports should set out phased recommendations for the short, medium and long term to be incorporated into orders. This will enable, for example, levels of contact to increase over time to a more beneficial level. If monitoring is necessary, it will be carried out by CAFCASS under the provisions of the Children and Adoption Act 2006 or by means of a **Family Assistance Order.**

The report writer is only obliged to investigate those matters which are in issue and will only interview adults who are relevant to that investigation; this may be done in their homes or over the phone. A parent should have everything he wishes to say to CAFCASS written down in front of him when he is interviewed: it is easy to forget what one wants to say when under pressure. He should be calm, collected and cooperative and not raise his voice. Everything should be expressed in a child-centred way, focused on the child's welfare and needs, using the **Welfare Checklist** as a guide, and avoiding anything which sounds selfish, or can be interpreted as disparaging of the other parent. It can help for the parent to show photos or video of himself with his children.

In 2009, the President of the Family Division issued emergency guidance instructing courts to ensure that s.7 reports were no longer requested in general terms; instead, they had to address one or more specific questions to be recorded on the order; these are governed by Rule 12.6(c) of the Family Procedure Rules 2010. Full reports examining every factor on the welfare checklist should seldom be used and come under Rule 12.6(d). The timeframe for reports is within six weeks for a single issue and within six to twelve weeks for two or more, depending on complexity. The emergency guidance – originally intended to last only six months – ended in September 2011, though the "spirit" of the agreement was expected to continue.

CAFCASS reports are usually based around a template; most – about 97% – are delivered on time, but some are still late. Once the due date has passed parties must badger CAFCASS until the report is produced. An applicant should talk to the **Family Court Advisor** about arranging interim contact while he waits for the report; if necessary, he should make an official complaint: they are violating the "**No Delay**" rule.

A party should not accept the arranged hearing date unless he has had ample opportunity to study the report and discuss it with his legal advisors. He may need to request an alternative date for the hearing. A party employing a solicitor must make sure he or she passes the report on. It should be taken into account, but the judge always has discretion whether or not to do so. If he rejects it, he must give his reasons.

In D v E [2016] EWFC 3, Macdonald J lambasted a social worker who had produced her first Section 7 report with only ninety minutes' training:

> [47] ...neither the substantive section 7 report [n]or the addendum reports contain any welfare analysis whatsoever of the issues engaged in this case nor a welfare analysis of the competing options available for C, and... I have felt unable to attach any weight to the recommendation of the social worker.

CAFCASS reports vary enormously in scope and quality; it is vital that CAFCASS is not allowed to be the final arbiter and that an inadequate or inaccurate report is challenged. A report which does not meet the national standards should not be accepted. The report must be fact-based and not reliant on opinion or jump to unsupported conclusions; if it is not satisfactory, a **Finding-of-Fact** hearing should be held to establish the truth of allegations, etc. If a litigant rejects the findings of the welfare report, the judge usually applies the same principles in G v G (Minors: Custody Appeal) [1985] 1 WLR 647 which are applied to **Appeals**.

Many non-resident parents find that Section 7 reports are difficult to challenge in proceedings; **Cross-Examination** of a report's author is allowed by the Criminal Justice and Courts Services Act 2000, which provides at Section 16(1) "an officer of the Service may, subject to rules of court, be cross-examined in any proceedings to the same extent as any witness", the Family Procedure Rules 2010 further provide at 16.33(5), "a party may question the officer about oral or written advice tendered by that officer to the court". The judge will use the officer's report as evidence but, if the report has been rejected, he may not agree to allow the examination as it would no longer be relevant and would waste court time.

Due to the increased workload of CAFCASS, courts are instructed to summon FCAs to hearings only if it is absolutely necessary; otherwise they will be excused. A litigant will need to ensure the FCA is available and that their attendance is confirmed at the pre-hearing review, ensuring they are written to, giving the date of the hearing as the courts don't always do this. He should also request in advance that copies of the FCA's notes on interviews be made available rather than the summary.

If the judge approves the FCA's attendance, he will *Subpoena* her to attend; she will then be in contempt if she doesn't, although the judge is unlikely to take any action against her. In that event she has caused additional delay, which is contrary to the welfare of the child and a complaint should be made.

Section 8 Application

In Bakir v Downe [2014] EWHC 3318, Mr Justice Mostyn stressed,

> *[8]* ...If a litigant in person wishes to make an application to the court, then he must do so in accordance with the procedure laid down by the law of the land.

> *[9]* That procedure is in Part 18 of the Family Procedure Rules. It requires an application to be made. It requires a fee to be paid. It requires a draft order to be supplied. It requires the relief that is sought to be clearly specified.

An applicant for a **Section 8 order** must prepare a **Parenting Plan** and draft an order; he must know what he wants from the Court before the hearing. Trying to bypass the procedure, by writing directly to the court, for example, is not acceptable.

Section 10 of the Children Act 1989 specifies who may make an application to the Court for any Section 8 order as of right:

- the child's parent (including an unmarried father);
- the child's guardian or special guardian;
- a step-parent who has acquired **Parental Responsibility**; or
- someone who already has a **Child Arrangements Order** in respect of the child naming them a person with whom the child is to live.

The following may apply only for a CAO:

- a party to the marriage or civil partnership in relation to which the child is a child of the family;
- someone with whom the child has lived for at least three years;
- a relative or foster parent with whom the child has lived for at least one year;
- someone who has the consent of everyone with PR for the child;

- someone who has the consent of every person named in a CAO as a person with whom the child is to live; or
- someone who has the consent of a local authority with which the child is in care.

A person who is not yet a party but has PR for the child can ask to be **Joined** as a party under Family Procedure Rule 12.3(2).

A person who cannot apply for an order as of right may apply with **"Leave"**, and Section 10(9) sets out what factors the Court should consider in such an application. These applications include those made by the child himself and 10(8) provides that the Court must be satisfied the child has sufficient understanding to make the application. Usually the initial judgement of the child's understanding will be made by his **Solicitor**, if he has one, but **Discretion** remains with the Court.

All Section 8 applications will be determined under the principles set out in **Section 1** of the Children Act. The Court must also follow the principles of the **Overriding Objective**. The Court and parties shall consider the need to ensure that children are involved appropriately in the decision-making process according to their age and level of understanding. The Court will exercise the discretion available to it, which includes the ability to cancel or repeat a particular hearing.

If the Court considers that the application, referred to as a "**Statement of Case**", is without **Merit** and has no hope of success, or is an abuse of process, or has not been made according to the rules, it can reject it. This is called "**Striking Out**" and is enabled under Rule 4.4 of the Family Procedure Rules 2010.

Once the application has been made, **Withdrawing an Application** may only happen with **Leave** of the Court.

Section 8 Order

Section 8 orders may only apply to issues of **Parental Responsibility**, and cannot be applied to issues which concern only the adults in a case. Section 8 of the **Children Act 1989** originally made provision for four types of order: **Prohibited Steps Orders, Specific Issue Orders, Contact Orders** and **Residence Orders**. In April 2014, Contact and Residence Orders were abolished and replaced by a combined **Child Arrangements Order**.

Orders made to vary or discharge these orders also come under Section 8.

A court will not normally make a Section 8 order once a child is sixteen, other than in exceptional circumstances. In Fergus v Marcail [2017] NIFam 6, "exceptional" was interpreted loosely to protect a vulnerable child from his physically and intellectually overbearing father. Most s.8 orders lapse when the child reaches sixteen, but a Child Arrangements Order regulating *only* where and when a child will live lapses when the child reaches eighteen.

Section 9 Judge

A **Circuit Judge** authorised to sit as a **High Court Judge** and do **High Court** work under Section 9 of the Supreme Court Act 1981.

Section 11 Orders

(Scots) the equivalents to the English **Section 8 Orders** relating to the exercise of parental responsibility are made under Section 11 of the Children (Scotland) Act 1995. This act led to some necessary amendment of the Sheriff Court Ordinary Cause Rules 1993 in so far as family actions were concerned, effected by the Act of Sederunt (Family Proceedings in the Sheriff Court) 1996, SI 1996/2167.

The orders defined by Section 11 are: **Residence Orders** [s.11(2)(c)], **Contact Orders** [s.11(2)(d)], **Specific Issue Orders** [s.11(2)(e)], and under s.11(2)(f) an **Interdict** analogous to the **Prohibited Steps Order**.

Section 17 Assessment

The initial assessment undertaken by social services under Section 17 of the Children Act 1989 when parents request their involvement. It will cover three areas:

1. the developmental needs of the child;
2. the capacity of the parents or caregivers to supply that need;
3. the impact of the wider family and environment on the child and on parenting capacity.

Section 20 Agreement

If a child is abandoned or a carer becomes unable to care for him, social services are obliged to provide accommodation under Section 20 of the Children Act.

Section 20 is intended to confer a duty, but local authorities misuse it as a means of taking a child into care without going through the rigmarole and expense of an application and without scrutiny by a court or the examination of evidence. All they need do is coerce a parent into agreeing, which is easily done when the only alternative offered is an **Emergency Protection Order**. The LA can avoid the costs of accommodation by placing the child with a convenient aunt or grandmother.

After a few months, the non-resident parent is advised by the LA to make a **Section 8** application; the Court's scrutiny is automatically engaged, and the cost and responsibility are borne by the court, the family or the Legal Aid Agency. If the parent tries to take the child home again – which they have the right to do because they still theoretically have PR, the LA will apply for an Interim **Care Order**. Despite the LA's conviction that the child is at serious risk of **Harm**, it has neatly sidestepped responsibility. It is a scam: care through the backdoor, and parents should be aware.

The courts are responding; consider, for example, Re CA (A Baby) [2012] EWHC 2190, the case which first highlighted misuse, "the use of Section 20 is not unrestricted and must not be compulsion in disguise", or Re P (A Child: Use of Section 20) [2014] EWFC 775, "it goes without saying that it is totally inappropriate for a local authority to hold a child in s.20 accommodation for 2 years without a plan", or Northamptonshire County Council v AS & Ors (Rev 1) [2015] EWHC 199, "the use of the provisions of s.20 Children Act 1989 to accommodate was, in my judgment, seriously abused by the local authority in this case", or Surrey County Council v M, F & E [2012] EWHC 2400,

> To use the section 20 procedure in circumstances where there was the overt threat of a police protection order if they did not agree, reinforced by the physical presence of uniformed police officers, was wholly inappropriate. By adopting this procedure the local authority sought to circumvent the test any court would have required them to meet if they sought to secure an order.

Re N [2015] EWCA Civ 1112 established that agreement *must* be in writing: it is not enough that parents don't object. If consent is withdrawn, the LA must obtain an *immediate* court order or return the child.

From April 2016 in Wales, the wording of Section 20 was transferred to Section 76 of the Social Services and Well-being (Wales) Act 2014.

Section 34 Application

Section 34(1) of the Children Act 1989 requires local authorities to enable "reasonable" contact between a child in care and his parents.

Where contact has not started, has stopped or is insufficient, an application can be made to the Court. This ensures full investigation of the issues at an early stage rather than waiting for the **Case Conference** and keeps any break in contact to a minimum. In Re C (Children) [2011] EWCA Civ 1774, contact was ordered between a mother and her sons of two hours four times a year but was not enabled. Nine months after her final contact, the mother made an application, but the boys were hostile even to indirect contact and an order was made under s.34(4) to end it; the mother's appeal was dismissed. An earlier application could have had a very different outcome.

In Re P-B (Children) 2009 EWCA Civ 143, the judge criticised a local authority for not complying with a s.34 order for contact and controversially attached a penal notice against the Director of Children's Services.

Section 37 Report

At any point in public or private family law proceedings, if he considers it necessary to protect a child's welfare, a judge may order the local authority to undertake an investigation into the child's circumstances to determine whether or not he should be placed under supervision or taken into care.

The investigation is ordered under Section 37 of the Children Act 1989. The report must be delivered within eight weeks. As part of this investigation the local authority should consider whether it needs to offer the family "services or assistance", whether it should apply for a **Supervision** or **Care Order**, or whether it should take any other action. If it decides not to, it must give its reasons to the Court.

A judge may mention a care order because he is testing a parent's commitment, and perhaps inviting an application for a **Child Arrangements Order**. If the application is not made, his only options will be to leave the children with their other parent or to put them into care. Alternatively, a judge can make an interim Care Order to allow a child time out from their other parent so that they can recover from **Alienation** and then be re-introduced to a parent without a negative attitude to contact.

Consider Re M (Intractable Contact Dispute: Interim Care Order) [2003] EWHC 1024, in which the Court ordered a s.37 report from the local authority on the basis of which it ordered residence to be transferred to the father, a supervision order to the LA, and contact with the mother to be at the LA's discretion.

Section 47 Report

If the Court is concerned about a child's **Welfare** and considers he "is suffering, or is likely to suffer, significant harm", it can order the local authority to undertake an enquiry under Section 47 of the Children Act 1989. This is similar to the powers available under s.37, but whereas a **Section 37 Report** can only be ordered as part of other family proceedings and obliges the LA to consider whether it should apply for a care or supervision order, under s.47 the LA is required to make "such enquiries as they consider necessary to enable them to decide whether they should take any action to safeguard or promote the child's welfare". It is thus more of a preliminary report to look into the child's welfare, whereas a s.37 Report is made when it is looking as if either care or supervision will be necessary.

The s.47 enquiry will be carried out by Children and Young People's Services either alone or jointly with the police. They may take "reasonably practicable" steps to obtain access to the child. This includes contacting his school or doctor and interviewing him to ascertain his wishes and feelings to which it must then give due consideration when deciding what further action to take. Anyone they contact is required to assist them with their enquiry. They will wish to interview the parents and assess their ability to provide for the child's needs.

If the LA completes its enquiry and decides action is necessary, or if it is refused access to the child, it can then take whatever action is in its power to take, such as an application for an **Emergency Protection Order**, a **Child Assessment Order**, a **Care Order** or a **Supervision Order** unless it is satisfied that the child's welfare can satisfactorily be safeguarded without its doing so. If it decides no application for an order is required, it can review the case at a later date.

Section 91(14) Order

An order made under Section 91(14) of the **Children Act 1989**, prohibiting the party to whom it applies from making further applications, or applications of a particular kind, for the duration of the order without prior **Leave** of the Court.

Such "barring" orders do not prevent further applications entirely: they are to be understood as a filter and not as a barrier; an applicant merely needs leave to make applications which previously he could have made without. Section 91 Orders are often made by judges desperate to bring protracted proceedings to a halt, which means they may be challenged on technicalities. In properly managed cases with judicial continuity they should not be necessary: parties should consider whether further litigation is really in their child's best interests.

The leading precedent is set by Re P (Section 91(14) Guidelines) [1999] 2FLR 573 CA, in which Lady Justice Butler-Sloss extracted the following guidelines:

a) S.91(14) is to be read in conjunction with s.1(1), the **Welfare** principle, and an order should be made only where the best interests of the child demand it and where the welfare of the child would be adversely affected by any future application.

Re K (Children) [2010] EWCA Civ 1365 showed the correct application of the welfare principle: a district judge had dismissed a father's contact application and imposed a s.91(14) order for a period of a year despite there being no application from the mother. The father appealed and, although the decision was unappealable, the circuit judge allowed it on welfare grounds. The mother appealed, and the Court of Appeal dismissed her appeal: the district judge had been plainly wrong,

> [15] She had, in the Judge's words, deprived the children of "a last and final chance of growing up with a real knowledge of their father" without hearing oral evidence, contrary to authority and in what, in my judgment, represented a plain breach of the father's ECHR Article 6 rights.

b) All relevant circumstances must be taken into account in considering whether to exercise the discretion.

c) Any exercise of the s.91(14) jurisdiction is a statutory interference with a person's right to access to the Court and should be used sparingly; however, the section is compliant with Article 6 of the Human Rights Act since it merely controls access and does not bar it entirely; the purpose of a s.91 order is to curb excessive litigation, not to prevent parents' access to justice. Article 6 is also interpreted to mean that a judge must give his reasons for any decision made.

Re M (A Child) [2012] EWCA Civ 446 shows that the Court's proper role is not to exclude parents from the system but to assist them to engage: a vexed father "ranted at the system", stormed out of court and applied to withdraw his application for contact and PR. CAFCASS had been unable to provide the supervised contact order and the judge, HHJ Carr QC, unreasonably looked to the father to arrange an alternative. She then over-reacted entirely and imposed a two-year s.91 order without specification. On appeal Thorpe LJ said,

> [8] Surely this was not the time to prohibit or to inhibit the father. The proper course was to, as it were, draw him back into the proceedings and not to put a barrier on his further engagement with the system.

Thorpe set aside Carr's order and **Recused** her from the case, "her reaction exceeds the generous ambit of discretion and… it was plainly wrong". He also directed the replacement of the child's Guardian.

d) The exercise of s.91(14) requires great care and is to be considered the exception rather than the rule.

In DJ v MS [2006] EWCH 1491, Coleridge J said that the trial Court judge "went too far" in seeking to relieve pressure on the mother,

> [24] ...to impose a restriction is a statutory intrusion to the right of a party to bring proceedings before the court and to be heard in matters affecting his/her child... the power is therefore to be used with great care and sparingly, the exception and not the rule... it is generally to be seen as a weapon of last resort in cases of repeated and unreasonable applications.

e) Generally, the making of a s.91(14) order is a weapon of last resort in cases of repeated unreasonable application and its use must be proportional to the harm it seeks to prevent. "**Vexatious Litigation**" in this context is litigation brought solely to "vex" or harass an opponent; a vexed parent is not necessarily vexatious.

In Re F, a restraint order was imposed on a father because the mother's **Implacable Hostility** was "so deeply rooted, and so total, that she will never agree to contact and she will always do her best to try and make sure that it doesn't happen". The decision was overturned in the Court of Appeal (Re F (Contact: Restraint Order) [1995] 1 FLR 956) by Lords Justice Waite and Nourse who held that the father had been "neither vexatious nor oppressive in his genuine attempts to further the welfare of his daughters by maintaining contact with them",

> The starting point, always, is that every child has a right to be brought up in the knowledge of his non-custodial parent. That is a right which the courts are determined to preserve... Their right to have their welfare served by re-establishing contact with their father at the earliest possible moment requires that the fullest attention should now be given [to that], with the best possible legal and medical help available.

As a precedent, Re F established that a s.91 order may be made in response to a litigant who is "vexatious" or "oppressive" in their applications but not in response to the behaviour of the respondent.

f) There may be cases where there is no history of repeated applications, but the child's welfare makes the order necessary or another order has been made (for **Child Arrangements**) and time must be allowed for it to work.

In B v B [1997] 1 FLR 139, Lord Justice Waite said that s.91 must be read in conjunction with **s.1**(1),

> The judge must, therefore, ask him or herself in every case whether the best interests of the child require interference with the fundamental freedom of a parent to raise issues affecting the child's welfare before the court as and when such issues arise.

g) A further check is to consider whether there is a serious risk that the child or his **Primary Carer** will be subject to unacceptable strain if the order is not made.

h) The order may be made without formal application or the judge may take it upon himself to impose it, provided the Court is considering an application by one of the parties for an order under the Act.

i) The order may be with or without time limit.

In Re T (A Child: Suspension of Contact: Section 91(14) CA 1989) [2015] EWCA Civ 719, the first instance judge, Judith Hughes QC, had made an order in July 2014 suspending all contact between a father and his four-and-a-half-year-old child and forbidding any s.8 application until December 2019. The Court of Appeal found Hughes had not considered the Article 8 rights of the father or child and had failed to weigh the factors summarised by Munby LJ in Re C (Direct Contact: Suspension) EWCA Civ 521 (see **Contact**),

> [57] In the circumstances, having regard to the deficiencies in the procedure, the insufficiency of a proper explanation of the rationale for the making of the order in the best interests of the child, and the absence of explanation as to the reason for its duration, we conclude that HHJ Hughes QC's order in this respect is wrong and cannot stand.

j) The order must specify precisely what type of applications are being restrained and be no wider than necessary; the Court cannot impose a blanket ban on all applications without specifying that is the case; see Re S-B (Children) [2015] EWCA Civ 705.

368

k) Without notice *Ex Parte* orders should only be made in the most exceptional and extreme circumstances.

A s.91(14) order should usually be made only on notice but may exceptionally be made without notice or even without application. Consider Re C-J (Section 91 (14) Order) [2006] EWHC 1491, in which Coleridge J held that exceptional circumstances were required before the Court could dispense with the usual procedural step of a formal application (Para. 19). Once made, the order can be difficult to overturn.

A party representing himself should consider Re M (Section 91(14) Order) [1999] 2 FLR 553 and Re C (Prohibition of Further Applications) [2002] EWCA Civ 292, which held it to be wrong in principle, except in exceptional circumstances, to place a **Litigant-in-Person** at short notice in the position of confronting a s.91(14) order which barred him from dealing with any aspect of the case relating to his children, particularly contact. Re G [2008] EWCA Civ 1468 held that a barring order should not be sprung on an unrepresented litigant. In Re C (A Child) [2009] EWCA Civ 674, the importance of following correct procedure was emphasised where the Court is considering whether to make the order against an LiP.

Where the Re P criteria are not followed, there will be grounds for appeal.

There are circumstances in which a party may wish to apply for a Section 91 Order in respect of the other party. Such an order is often the only reasonable alternative to an application for committal, which would not be in the best interests of the child or the other parent. It will bring protracted litigation to an end and force the judge to decide with whom the child is to live without going down the route of punishing the other parent for non-compliance.

An application should be supported by a detailed **Chronology** which will show that the order is necessary because the other parent has consistently ignored and refused to comply with the Court's orders and no alternative solution is appropriate. It will remind the Court of its duty to protect the child's relationships with both parents.

A **Children's Guardian** may also make a s.91 application. In Re H (A Child) [2010] EWCA 1296, the parents had been fighting over their eleven-year-old daughter for many years. A finding-of-fact found the mother's allegations against the father to be unfounded and residence was awarded to him; the mother's application for contact was dismissed and a s.91(14) order was granted on application by the Guardian. The mother appealed on the grounds that the Guardian had no right to make the application and that the judge had misdirected himself and failed to put a time limit on the order.

The **Court of Appeal** ruled the Guardian was indeed right to apply for the order, the child was a party and any party could make such an application; the judge had not misdirected himself. Only the appeal as to the duration of the order was allowed – the judge should have given a time limit or explained why he had not.

A s.91(14) order cannot be made with conditions attached, but the judge can indicate the issues to be addressed before any future application may be successful (Re S [2007] 1 FLR 482).

Section 97 Prohibition

The prohibition in Section 97 of the Children Act 1989 preventing the identification of children in proceedings. See **Reporting Restrictions**.

Seek & Locate Order

An order requiring a named party to disclose the whereabouts of a child.

If a parent doesn't know where his child is living, he can make an "application for an order for disclosure of a child's whereabouts" under Section 33 of the Family Law Act 1986. The application is made on Form C4. The order allows the Court to order anyone who may have information regarding the whereabouts of the child to disclose that information.

The applicant should provide the names of any people or agencies (such as Social Services) to whom the order should apply and specify how the information should be disclosed. He must state why the Court does not have this information, and why he believes the person or agencies to whom the order is directed should have it. If necessary, the application will be followed by a **Recovery Order** for the return of the child made under Section 34 of the Family Law Act.

Segal Order

A form of interim order for spousal maintenance made before a Child Maintenance Service (CMS) assessment which is later reduced by the amount assessed.

Although the establishment of the Child Support Agency removed from the courts jurisdiction to make a child maintenance order, a Segal Order can be made under the Matrimonial Causes Act 1973 in order to ensure that a resident parent is not left without financial means following divorce and before the CMS has made its assessment (which can legitimately take twenty-six weeks and, in reality, take months or even years). This is outside of statute and covers a situation not envisaged by Parliament. A Segal Order is defined by Thorpe LJ in Dorney-Kingdom v Dorney-Kingdom [2000] 3 FCR 20,

> *[24]* A practice has grown up, finding its origins before District Judge Segal in the Principal Registry, to make an order for spousal maintenance under s.23(1)(a) of the Matrimonial Causes Act 1973 that incorporates some of the costs of supporting the children as part of a global order. When a Segal order is made an important ingredient is that the overall sum will reduce *pro tanto* from the date upon which the Child Support Agency brings in an assessment *[i.e., monies paid through the order reduce by whatever amount is paid through the CMS]*. The utility of the Segal order is obvious, since in many cases the determination of the ancillary relief claims will come at a time when the Child Support Agency has yet to complete its assessment of liability. It is therefore very convenient for a district judge to have a form of order which will carry the parent with primary care over that interim pending the Agency's determination.

In *Dorney-Kingdom*, the orders made both at first instance and on appeal reduced *pro tanto* from the moment of the CSA assessment, but it should be noted that, though a Segal Order will include an amount of spousal maintenance to gain legitimacy through the Matrimonial Causes Act, it cannot be used to control the global sum of maintenance because from the point of assessment the Court loses jurisdiction to make any order at all and the order cannot thereafter be enforced.

Seised

Having possession of; a court is "seised" of a case when it has sufficient evidence to pass judgement.

Separated Parents Information Programme

SPIP – an awareness programme to which a court will direct parents when a CAFCASS officer has recommended accordingly. SPIPs are run by providers such as *Relate*. Both parents are expected to attend the sessions, but not together.

They are aimed at improving parents' abilities to put aside their differences and limit the negative impact that their divorce or separation has on their children by improving communication, helping them make joint parenting decisions and see the separation through their children's eyes.

SPIPs are run over two group sessions and last a total of four hours. Parents are initially asked to watch a DVD made by young people which charts the course of a case over six months. They are then asked to discuss a prepared scenario and consider it from the viewpoints of the mother, father and children. Finally, they are asked to look at the emotional effects divorce and separation can have and at the options for moving forward.

The provider only reports the parents' attendance back to CAFCASS and does not assess their responses to the programme.

Separation

(For Scots law, see **Non-Cohabitation**) this can be used as one of the **Facts** upon which a spouse bases their divorce. There are two categories:

1. The parties have lived apart for a continuous period of at least two years immediately preceding the **Petition** and the respondent consents to the divorce.

   This is often called "**No-Fault**" **Divorce** because three of the other "facts" involve an allegation of fault. Spouses can have had periods of living together as long as they do not add up to more than six months and they have been apart for at least two years altogether. The dates given on the petition must be separated by at least two years and a day. The respondent's consent is required for a petition on this ground; without consent the petition will be rejected.

2. The parties have lived apart for a continuous period of at least five years immediately preceding the petition.

   The respondent does not need to agree to this. He or she cannot defend this petition but can ask the Court not to grant the final decree because of major financial or other type of hardship.

Mere physical separation for two years is insufficient to prove "living apart" as contained in the Divorce Reform Act 1969 and the case of Santos v Santos [1972] 2 WLR 889 showed that the petitioner must also have ceased to recognise the marriage as subsisting and has no intention of ever returning to the other spouse. Lord Justice Sachs reviewed the case law, beginning with Sir Francis Jeune's observation in Bradshaw v Bradshaw [1897] Probate 24 that "cohabitation does not necessarily imply living together physically under the same roof". This was repeated in Rex v Creamer [1919] 1 King's Bench 654,

the law has regard to what is called consortium of husband and wife, which is a kind of association only possible between husband and wife. A husband and wife are "living together" not only when they are residing together in

372

the same house, but also when they are living in different places, even if they are separated by the high seas, provided the consortium has not been determined.

In Nugent-Head v Jacob [1948] Appeal Cases 321, the Court held that an American woman resident in London and her husband who had been serving overseas for a continuing period of nearly three years were still cohabiting because there had been "no rupture of matrimonial relations". Seventy years later it is unlikely the courts will be quite so insistent on observing the letter of the law, but it is worth bearing in mind.

Separation Agreement

(Scots) couples often enter into separation agreements when they initially separate, to regulate their financial affairs and the care arrangements for their children. It is common for the couple to come to an agreement regarding the division of their assets and for payment of financial support for the spouse and children and indeed for the division of assets to take place at, or shortly after, the time they separate. Thereafter, if the parties do come to divorce, the action can proceed on an uncontested basis.

Separation Agreements (formerly known as Minutes of Agreement) must be written up by a solicitor. Such separation agreements are normally registered in the Books of Council and Session located in Edinburgh which is done simply by writing a letter to them with a copy of the signed agreement and asking for it to be registered. There is a fee payable depending on the number of pages and how many copies are required; once registered, the agreement has the same effect as a divorce court decree and can be enforced (unlike the English/Welsh version).

There is only limited scope for changing the terms of a registered agreement; for example, it is possible to vary the arrangements made for the care of the children and to vary the arrangements made for the payment of maintenance for a spouse and/or children if there is a change of circumstances. Otherwise the provisions of the agreement can only be challenged if it can be shown that they were not fair and reasonable at the time they were entered into.

Separation Date

This is typically the date one spouse leaves the matrimonial home; it is a critical date for calculating the "**Equalisation of Assets**". The status of that date may change if the one who left returns for any amount of time. A separation date may be established while the couple are still together. Often, it's the date they

373

stop sleeping together in the same room, but it may require the added proviso that they have stopped doing things together as a family.

Service

The action of bringing a document to someone's attention according to the rules of court, usually by delivering it by post or otherwise to the respondent(s).

A divorce **Petition** must be served on the **Respondent** and, where appropriate, the **Co-Respondent**; responsibility lies with the petitioner.

In children cases, applications must be served on all parties with **Parental Responsibility** and anyone caring for the child at the time proceedings commence. Responsibility for service now usually rests with the court, and not with the applicant. The court must serve on the respondent a copy of the C100 application form, together with Supplemental Information Form C1A (if relevant), the **Notice of Proceedings** on Form C6, the **Acknowledgment of Service** Form C7 and a blank Form C1A.

Papers should normally be served fourteen days before the hearing, or twenty-one days if the respondent lives outside the jurisdiction in Northern Ireland, Scotland or a **Hague Convention** country within Europe, or thirty-one days if they live in a Hague country outside Europe.

If serving the papers by post fails – if, for example, no response is made to the Court within fourteen days, the applicant can pay for a court **Bailiff** to serve the papers; he will then be able to provide a certificate of service that the papers were correctly served. The applicant must complete Form D89 and provide evidence that service has not been successful, giving the respondent's address. A bailiff can only serve documents at the address on the application/petition, within the jurisdiction and during working hours. If the bailiff cannot serve the papers at that address he can be asked to serve them at an alternative address.

For service outside the jurisdiction, a court official in that jurisdiction will have to be contacted. It is often more effective to employ a **Process Server** who is able to serve at an alternative address, or in the street if necessary, and at any hour for a similar fee. Legally represented parties will have to use a process server.

If the respondent's current address isn't known, reasonable steps must be taken to ascertain it. Otherwise the applicant must consider where else the papers may be served and request the Court to direct accordingly. If the petitioner has made every reasonable attempt to serve the **Petition** on the **Respondent** but has been unable to do so, she may apply to the Court to make an order to "**Dispense with Service**".

If the respondent is a child, the papers must be served to a parent, guardian or carer (other than the applicant). If the child is represented by a

Children's Guardian, papers must be served on them and also on the solicitor if one has been appointed.

The application is deemed to have been served when the Acknowledgement of Service is returned to the court. The applicant will have to confirm that the signature on it is indeed that of the respondent. If no Acknowledgement is filed, the court may still consider that the application has been served if there is evidence to that effect.

How the papers have been served must be entered on Form C9, the **Statement of Service**. If the respondent then fails to turn up at court, there is evidence that they were appropriately informed and given the opportunity to present their case.

Under Family Procedure Rule 12.32, the respondent is expected to file a response using the Forms C7 and C1A no later than fourteen days before the hearing, and the Court may abridge this time if it thinks it necessary. This will allow him or her only two weeks at the most to read the application, find a solicitor (if required) and prepare a response. The Court must forward this response to CAFCASS on receipt.

Full information on how to serve the papers is provided in the Practice Direction 6A – *Service within the Jurisdiction*, which also covers service to forces personnel who may be overseas. Practice Direction 6B covers service outside the jurisdiction, including Northern Ireland and Scotland.

Set Aside

To rescind, cancel, repeal or revoke a judgment or order; so, doing is referred to as "rescission". Parties may rescind a divorce petition by written mutual consent, and it is not uncommon for financial orders to be set aside, but in an extraordinary 2014 case, the Queen's Proctor sought to set aside 180 decrees *nisi* and absolute: 179 Italian couples resident in Italy had given as their address a post box in Maidenhead (and one in Epsom) in order to secure a quick – but illegal – divorce (see Rapisarda v Colladon [2014] EWFC 1406).

Settled

The law frequently refers to a child who has been removed from the jurisdiction as being "*settled* in his or her new environment". This is an important concept in terms of changing a child's **Habitual Residence**, and has two components:

1. The child must be physically integrated into the new community and environment, with a new home, new or existing relatives, attending a new school, making new friends, etc.

2. The child must be emotionally and psychologically secure and stable within the new environment.

A child is usually deemed to be "settled" after a year in the new environment; once he is "settled" it is much more difficult, if not impossible, to repatriate him.

The courts will place greater emphasis on physical integration than on emotional stability. Many of these children are far from emotionally stable, yet the courts seem not to associate that with the fact of their abduction, regarding it as normal in teenagers, for example, and entirely consistent with the concept of "settlement" under the **Hague Convention** on the Civil Aspects of International Child Abduction. Thus, Sir Mark Potter could say in Re C (A Child) [2006] EWHC 1229 of a thirteen-year-old girl who had self-harmed, abused alcohol and run away with an eighteen-year-old,

> *[54]* While it is plain that A has had a history of trouble from persistent bullying by *[sic]* and a number of emotional disturbances, neither factor goes to the question whether or not she is physically settled into the community in which she has lived for 5 years. I find that she is so settled.

In Cannon v Cannon [2004] EWCA Civ 1330, Thorpe LJ said that the Court must balance the degree of "turpitude" committed by the defendant against the extent to which the twelve-month limit has been exceeded; thus, in the eyes of the court, if the abductor has managed to conceal their whereabouts for long enough, this will outweigh any degree of turpitude. The Court must also consider the difficulty of re-introducing the other parent into his child's life at this late point. The **Court of Appeal** may often remit these cases to the Family Division (and a report by **CAFCASS**) to determine where the balance lies.

Thorpe emphasised that, although the **Hague Convention** provides "a swift and summary procedure" for the return of a child, preventing an abducting parent from gaining advantage through their wrongdoing, an order for return must not be "an automatic response". Although the courts in a child's country of origin are best placed to decide matters of custody, once sufficient time has been spent in the new country, they are no better placed than the courts there because the evidence on which such a case must be decided has now shifted.

Sexual Abuse

(Child sexual abuse may be abbreviated to CSA) forcing or enticing a child to take part in sexual activities, including prostitution. Sexual activities may be penetrative or non-penetrative or may involve encouraging children to behave in sexually inappropriate ways, or making a child look at pornographic material or watch sexual activities.

Shared Parenting

The antithesis and rejection of the sole-maternal-custody model of post-separation parenting; the principle that a child will thrive best after his parents' separation if three conditions are met:

1. the child must be able to feel truly at home in both households;
2. the child's needs must be prioritised over those of his parents; and
3. the arrangements made for the child must be flexible.

Shared parenting guarantees the continuation of the child's family life, with nurture from both parents rather than just one, and from two extended families; it reassures the child he still has two parents who love him, and that though they now live in separate houses, he has a home in each. When parents share parenting, they don't have to ask each other's permission to take their child abroad, and if they are a bit late returning him, they won't be accused of abduction.

Shared parenting ensures that the responsibility of discipline doesn't fall to one parent alone while the other is relegated to being the "fun" parent; it places both parents on an equal footing with schools, doctors and other agencies, which might otherwise only be prepared to deal with the "resident" parent; it affirms that no matter what, each parent wants to, and is able to, provide a home for their child and reassures him that in the event of one parent dying he will still be cared for.

Shared parenting encourages parents to work together and support each other – a principle affirmed in Re F (Shared Residence Order) [2003] EWCA Civ 592, [2003] 2 FLR 397 – and ensures that children and parents develop meaningful and lasting relationships, instead of the artificiality and stigma of "contact"; it convinces the parents they both have an enduring role in their child's life and counters the disgraceful lie that only one parent is "caring" while the other is "deadbeat" or "absent".

Shared Residence

The legal manifestation of **Shared Parenting**, enabled by a **Child Arrangements Order** (CAO) in which both parents are named as persons with whom the child is to live. Existing Shared Residence Orders (SROs) became CAOs in April 2014.

If the Court makes the order, it will say that the children should live with the named person – either permanently, or for the period specified in the order.

It was believed at the time the Children Act was drafted that, where shared parenting was appropriate, there would be no need for an order at all and that, where there was conflict, an order for shared residence would not be suitable; the irony was that the courts had already been moving towards shared residence: over the six years before the Act, the proportion of custody orders which were shared had doubled to 26%, though there was wide regional variation, with shared orders more common in the south and rarer in the north.

In Re H (A Minor) (Shared Residence) [1994] 1 FLR 717, Lord Justice Purchas articulated the prevailing orthodoxy that such an order "would rarely be made and would depend upon exceptional circumstances". In the same year, the President, Elizabeth Butler-Sloss, said, in A v A (A Minor) (Shared Residence Order) [1994] 1 FLR 669, that such an order should be made only if there were something unusual about the case and a positive benefit in making an order which was not a conventional one, and that it was unlikely to be made if there were unresolved issues between the parents. Yet, in Re H (Shared Residence: Parental Responsibility) [1995] 2 FLR 883, Lord Justice Ward made a "therapeutic" order to articulate to the children that they "lived with the respondent and did not just visit him"; he expressed the hope that Shared Residence Orders—

> may gradually win more grudging approval from the courts if the Judges begin to acknowledge that such orders can reflect practical arrangements made by parents and their children which work well in putting into satisfactory practice that purpose promoted by the Act which emphasises that parenting is a continuing and shared responsibility even after a separation.

Butler-Sloss back-pedalled on her A v A position following the introduction of the Human Rights Act 1998. In the seminal D v D (Shared Residence Order) [2001] 1 FLR 495, she and Lady Justice Hale produced a contrary judgment which established that an SRO could still be made where there was conflict and animosity. In highly conflicted proceedings, the lower Court judge, Ansell J, had made an order, on the father's application, for shared residence,

> [15] ...the making of a joint residence order underlying the status of the parents as equally significant in the lives of the children would be likely to diminish rather than increase that conflict.

Sadly, the mother disagreed and applied to suspend or supervise the father's contact. The application was dismissed by Connor J; again, the mother appealed. Lady Justice Hale reviewed the history of shared residence in which the courts had moved away from the earlier principle that it required "exceptional circumstances"; she concluded,

> [34] ...it seems to me that there is indeed a positive benefit to these children in those facts being recognised in the order that the court makes. There is no detriment or disrespect to either parent in that order. It simply reflects the reality of these children's lives. It was entirely appropriate for the judge to make it in this case and neither party should feel that they have won or lost as a result. I would, therefore, dismiss the appeal.

Thus, at the turn of the century, this type of order had come to be seen as a way of defining an on-going situation – the children spent 38% of their time with the father – rather than prescribing a new one: the sole-residence-plus-contact paradigm remained the rule; Hale confirmed this in Re A (Shared Residence) [2002] 1 FCR 177,

> ...the law is that parents already have shared Parental Responsibility for their children... A residence order is about where a child is to live. It is very difficult to make such an order about a child who is not only not living with one of the parents but is, for the foreseeable future, unlikely even to visit with that parent. The court's order has to be designed to reflect the real position on the ground.

Thorpe LJ showed a growing acceptance of shared residence in 2003 and a rejection of the winner-takes-all approach, referring to D v D in Re A (Children) (Shared Residence) [2003] 3 FCR 656,

> There is a need for courts of trial to recognise that there may well be cases that are better suited by a joint residence order than by residence order to one parent alone. Where there is a proximity of homes and a relatively fluid passage of the children between those two homes, the judicial convention that the welfare of the children demanded a choice between one parent or the other as a guardian of the residence order in order to promote the welfare of the children no longer runs as it used to run.

D v D was also cited by Mr Justice Wall in A v A (Shared Residence) [2004] 1 FLR 1195, another case in which there was high conflict and false allegations had been made against the father. Wall made it clear that, had the parents been capable of working together, he would have made no order. Because of the high level of conflict, however, an order was necessary, and the making of the order for shared residence confirmed the parents had equal responsibility towards their children,

> If these parents were capable of working in harmony, and there were no difficulties about the exercise of shared Parental Responsibility, I would have followed Mrs P's *[the Guardian]* advice and made no order as to residence. Section 1(5) of the Children Act 1989 requires the court to make no order unless making an order is better for the children concerned than making no order at all. Here, the parents are not, alas, capable of working in harmony. There must, accordingly, be an order. That order, in my judgment, requires the court not only to reflect the reality that the children are dividing their lives equally between their parents, but also to reflect the fact that the parents are equal in the eyes of the law, and have equal duties and responsibilities towards their children.

Wall repeated Lady Justice Hale's observation that shared residence orders do not diminish the parental role of the parent who previously had sole residence, "a residence order in Mr A's favour would not, as a matter of law, diminish Mrs A's status as a parent, or remove her equal parental responsibility for the children", Wall showed how a prescriptive SRO could be used to affirm the importance of a child's relationship with both parents and their equality in the eyes of the law even in a case involving false allegations against the father and where there was tremendous conflict. His reprimand has wide application,

> This case has been about control throughout. Mrs A. sought to control the children, with seriously adverse consequences for the family. She failed. Control is not what this family needs. What it needs is cooperation. By making a Shared Residence Order the court is making that point. These parents have joint and equal Parental Responsibility. The residence of the children is shared between them. These facts need to be recognised by an order for shared residence.

By 2003, an SRO could be used prescriptively where the parental homes were close together. In Re F (Shared Residence Order) [2003] 2 FLR 397, Thorpe LJ went further by demonstrating that shared residence could also be appropriate where the parents lived far apart, in a case where the mother moved from Hampshire to Edinburgh to thwart contact,

> The fact that the parents' homes are separated by a considerable distance does not preclude the possibility that the children's year will be divided between the two homes of the separated parents in such a way as to validate the making of a Shared Residence Order.

Mr Justice Wilson concurred,

Will an order for shared residence be valuable to *[the children]* as a setting of the court's seal upon an assessment that the home offered by each parent to them is of equal status and importance for them?

Wall LJ's judgment in Re P (Children) [2006] 1 FCR 309 demonstrated how far judicial thinking had moved since 1989: the father's appeal against the decision of the trial judge was allowed on the grounds that an order for shared residence reflected the reality of the situation and that there were no compelling reasons *not* to make it. A Shared Residence Order could at last become the default position:

Good reasons are required if a Shared Residence Order is not to be made. Such an order emphasises the fact that both parents are equal in the eyes of the law, and that they have equal duties and responsibilities as parents. The order can have the additional value of conveying the court's message that neither party is in control and that the court expects parents to cooperate with each other for the benefit of the children.

The next stage was to make the SRO an acceptable order when the adult in whose favour the order was made was not biologically the child's parent. In Re A (A Child: Joint Residence/Parental Responsibility) [2008] EWCA Civ 867, a father had obtained a **Parental Responsibility Order**; CAFCASS recommended joint residence and defined staying contact. The mother responded by questioning paternity and a DNA test duly confirmed the father was indeed not the biological father. This meant he no longer had PR and could acquire it again only through a residence order. The mother was unable to accept he should have PR or any say in his child's upbringing.

The case became protracted and proceedings persisted for more than four years. The mother planned to move away, threatening to disrupt what was by then regular contact. The father obtained a **Prohibited Steps Order** and sought shared residence on the grounds that he would otherwise be marginalised; the mother objected. The Court awarded joint residence with defined generous contact and PR, but in return allowed the mother to move. The mother was also barred from introducing the child to his biological father without the Court's consent, and both parties were barred from making further applications.

The mother appealed on two primary grounds: firstly, that in the order the Recorder had erred in principle and in law, had inappropriately linked the father's PR to the mother's relocation, had unduly favoured the "social and psychological" father over the biological mother and had thus undermined the mother as biological parent. Secondly, the Court had not sufficiently considered the child's biological parentage, perpetuating a lie and excluding the biological father (who did not wish to be involved in his child's life).

In rejecting the appeal, the President, Sir Mark Potter, emphasised that the Shared Residence Order was made, not to give the father undue rights – the mother remained the primary carer, but to affirm the father's responsibilities and to ensure he was not marginalised; it was the only legitimate means by which to confer Parental Responsibility on an individual who could not otherwise apply for it. Potter also assessed the case law and current policy on Shared Residence Orders; he made an important distinction,

> The fact is, Mr A is not H's father or parent either in common parlance or under any definition contained in the Children Act or other legislation. He is not a father by biological paternity or adoption, nor a stepfather by marriage. He is a person entitled, by reason of the role he has played and should continue to play in H's life, to an order conferring Parental Responsibility upon him. He is thus a person who, jointly with the mother, enjoys the rights, duties, powers, responsibilities and authority which by law a parent of a child has in relation to that child... but he does not thereby become the father of that child.

Potter went on to summarise the status of the Shared Residence Order,

> The making of a Shared Residence Order is no longer the unusual order which once it was... It is now recognised by the court that a Shared Residence Order may be regarded as appropriate where it provides legal confirmation of the factual reality of a child's life or where, in a case where one party has the primary care of a child, it may be psychologically beneficial to the parents in emphasising the equality of their position and responsibilities.

This seems to have contradicted Hale's opinion in Re A [2002] that "a residence order is about where a child is to live". Both cases showed that a Shared Residence Order was now the most appropriate order to make when one parent was trying to marginalise the other, regardless of conflict, regardless of geographical separation, regardless of one parent continuing to be the primary carer and regardless of whether or not the other parent was the biological parent. Biology was a factor and an important one but could not be allowed to trump the child's welfare.

In Re W (Shared Residence Order) 2009 EWCA Civ, Potter affirmed his view that shared residence was the appropriate order to make when a parent was seeking to marginalise the other,

> I should make clear, however, that, although therefore an inability of parents to work in harmony does not, by itself, amount to a reason for making a shared residence order, a possible consequence of their inability to do so, namely the deliberate and sustained marginalisation of one parent by the other, may sometimes do so.

By 2010, Mr Justice Mostyn was able to say in Re AR (A Child: Relocation) [2010] EWHC 1346,

> I am clearly of the view that a joint or shared residence order should be made. Indeed, such an order is nowadays the rule rather than the exception even where the quantum of care undertaken by each parent is decidedly unequal. There is very good reason why such orders should be normative for they avoid the psychological baggage of right, power and control that attends a sole residence order, which was the one of the reasons that we were ridden of the notions of custody and care and control by the Act of 1989.

We should also dismiss the myth that ordering the sharing of residence is appropriate only where the care of the child is shared in a certain, minimum, ratio. In Re F (Shared Residence Order) [2003] EWCA Civ 592, [2003] 2 FLR 397, Lord Justice Wilson observed that such calculations were usually of limited value; he repeated this observation in Re W (A Child) [2009] EWCA Civ 370, a case in which a child would only be spending between 22% and 24% of her nights with her father. The force of an SRO was to confirm that parents had equal status and responsibilities.

Shared parenting is not a panacea, it works least well when court-ordered against sustained resistance from one parent and best where parents put aside their differences and cooperate. Non-resident parents were forced into making the application in order to avoid the sole-residence-plus-contact arrangement which so often led to the complete breakdown of the parent/child relationship. This was the consequence of the failure of parental responsibility to confer any meaningful status; litigants and judges alike were forced to use an order which was meant only to determine where a child was to live to compensate for this deficit and regulate matters of parental authority. Residence Orders were a poor substitute for this role.

As it became a more common order, there was evidence that many fathers who obtained shared residence found themselves in much the same position in practice as a non-resident father with a Contact Order: handovers were fraught or didn't happen, and the other parent continued to play a "gate-keeping" role.

In April 2014, the steady acceptance of Shared Parenting Orders was disrupted by the introduction of the Children and Families Act and the subsumption of Residence and Contact Orders into the **Child Arrangements Order**; it is unclear what the long-term effects of this will be.

Before applying for an order to share residence a parent must consider practicalities such as whether he has suitable accommodation where his child can stay overnight, whether his work is flexible enough to allow for some overnights during the week, how far from the other parent he lives, and so on.

Examining the cases in which applications to share parenting have been successful reveals some key points:

1. shared parenting must be shown to be in the child's best interests;
2. shared parenting is more likely to be ordered where parents live close to each other;
3. shared parenting is more likely to be ordered where the parents are unable to work together in harmony and there is a need to make an order;
4. shared parenting is more likely to be ordered where there is no reason *not* to make such an order.

Sometimes a parent will need to consider changing his job or life-style if an application to share parenting is to be successful; if he doesn't have suitable accommodation where his child can stay overnight, or there has been a long period of time since he last saw the child, or he has allowed a long period to elapse before making the application, he is unlikely to be successful. It is always possible to make a further application to share parenting once **Contact** has been re-established and is working well.

An application will involve **CAFCASS**. They will be guided by the **Welfare Checklist** and will want to know if there is suitable accommodation for the child, who will care for him when the parent is at work, and whether the new partner is suitable, etc. The applicant's task is to establish evidence he can present to the judge showing he is competent to care for the child, supportive of the relationship between his child and the other parent, and willing to make every effort to make a shared arrangement work.

Sharia

"The Way" – an Islamic system of law derived from religious precepts.

Sharia councils and tribunals do not amount to courts of law and cannot overrule the justice system. Some offer mediation services, but while the agreements made may carry weight, they are not binding.

Sheriff Court

(Scots) the lower level of court in the Scots judicatory. Sheriffs are ranked somewhere between **District Judges** and **High Court Judges** in the English/Welsh system and sit alone.

There are six sheriffdoms and forty-nine Sheriff Courts in Scotland; when raising an action, a litigant must make sure he is applying to the correct court, which will be the Sheriff Court in the town nearest to where the child is **Habitually Resident** (meaning that they have lived there for forty days or longer). Most cases are raised in the Sheriff Courts; it is unusual, although not impossible, to raise an action in the **Court of Session**, it is unlikely, however, that an applicant would receive legal aid for this (unless there were exceptional circumstances or complex points of law in his case) and he should be prepared for higher costs, even if representing himself.

Signposting

That step of the **Child Arrangements Programme** which directs parents to the online services which can advise and support them.

Simplified Procedure

(Scots) a DIY procedure for procuring a divorce based on **Non-Cohabitation** when there are neither children under the age of sixteen (including adopted and step-children) nor financial disputes.

The **Pursuer** completes Form SPA for one year's separation with consent or SPB for two year's separation without, giving the reason for the divorce and supporting information. She must swear before a Notary Public or Justice of the Peace that the facts given are correct, and then send the form, marriage certificate and fee to the local **Sheriff Court** or **Court of Session**. The court will send a copy of the application to the **Defender**; if he does not consent, the **Ordinary Procedure** must be used.

The court considers the application and, if all is in order, grants a decree of divorce within about eight weeks.

Sine Die

(Latin: "without a day") where a case is adjourned indefinitely without a date set to continue the hearing.

Skeleton Argument

A device used to provide an outline structure enabling the presentation of a case in court.

The Skeleton Argument or Case Theory must be no more than a page long and will go into the applicant's **Bundle** on Form N163 so that the judge can refer to it. It keeps things simple, succinct and relevant, and keeps the applicant focused.

The Skeleton Argument must be supported by evidence. It will consist of a series of numbered points backed by referenced documents. The appropriate way to do this is with the applicant's initials in square brackets at the end of the paragraph in which the reference is made together with the document number, for example, [AB1], [AB2], etc. The documents will be numbered AB1, AB2.

1. It begins by introducing the applicant and any witnesses he intends to call.
2. The "road map" is established: how the case will be presented and conducted.
3. The story leading to court and major significant events are summarised. Much of this work will already have been done for the **Chronology**. The story should be interesting and compelling, but not too long or creative.
4. The **Evidence** is presented; this is the facts upon which the judge will make his decision. The **Welfare Checklist** should be used as a guide and to provide structure. This is also where any research evidence and case **Precedents** are presented. The evidence must be relevant and presented accurately. The applicant should anticipate what the other side will say; if he were the other side's lawyer, what would his strategy be?
5. Finally, the Skeleton Argument will describe the desired outcome of the application and what order it is hoped the Court will make. For an order under **Section 8** of the Children Act, the applicant will tell the judge how he sees the relationship with his child working; again, this is work he will already have done when preparing his **Parenting Plan**.

Skype

A free system of online video calling, often and increasingly incorporated into Contact and Child Arrangements Orders following its first use in the US in 2002.

Skype parents say they feel like just another TV programme in their children's lives and can sense the relationship ebbing away with each session.

In Re W (Children) [2011] EWCA Civ 345, Wall LJ controversially overturned a decision by Judge Tyzack banning a mother from relocating her two children to Australia, saying that the father could remain in contact by Skype and that **Relocation** was in the children's best interest, despite the fact that the father lived in a mobile home with limited internet access.

In Re R (A Child: Relocation) [2015] EWHC 456, however, Mr Justice Wood rejected a mother's application to relocate a two-year-old to Hong Kong; he did not trust that the mother, once out of the jurisdiction, would adhere to the contact regime,

> [61] ...the disadvantages of Skype – as any user will know – are all too often the lack of clarity of image, the sound delay even if short and, as Miss Mills colourfully notes in her closing submissions, "You can't hug Skype".

> [65] The mother's proposals to relocate (even if her proposals for visits, telephone calls and Skype calls are carried out) in practice do not begin to make up for these losses.

Slip Rule

The rule which allows clerical mistakes and accidental omissions in judgments and orders to be corrected by the judge.

A party may also apply without notice for a correction to be made. For proceedings governed by the Family Procedure Rules the slip rule is County Court Rules (CCR) Order 15 Rule 5 or Rules of the Supreme Court (RSC) Order 20 Rule 11 and is enabled by Rule 29.16(1). In civil proceedings the rule is Civil Proceedings Rules 1998 (CPR) Rule 40.12.

A judge should not alter the substance of the judgment after he has delivered it in court, for example, by adding new reasons for his decision. He can correct manifest accidental slips and clerical errors and can add clarification. He can remove "linguistic infelicities" provided that doing so does not alter the substance. The rest follows from the principle that, once the judge is *Functus Officio*, he cannot have another go at trying the case.

Unfortunately, the Court of Appeal encourages judges in some situations to add to their reasons if there is an appeal. The judgment itself often reveals considerable working up by the judge since the hearing, including explication and case law, none of which is necessarily contained in the order itself. Some consider this unlawful and that the danger is too great that judges will simply devise new reasons to justify themselves and thereby hinder appeal. Since **Appeals** must be based on the contention that the judge misinterpreted the law (or ignored key arguments), the judgment – together with extracts from the proceedings – is essential.

Solicitor

A lawyer who practices litigation but not advocacy (the conducting of proceedings), for which he will engage a **Barrister**.

When a parent finds himself forced to litigate through the courts his first decision must be whether to be represented in court by a solicitor, or to represent himself, possibly with the assistance of a **McKenzie Friend**. There are a number of common misconceptions about solicitors which prevent litigants using them as effectively as they might:

1. A solicitor or barrister is an officer of the Court and as such his first duty is to the Court and not to his client.
2. A solicitor will often advise a client not to act precipitately or provocatively, but to be placatory, to sit it out and see what develops, when the best advice in some circumstances is to be proactive and make an application. Many cases run into trouble because a parent has delayed taking action.
3. Solicitors are expensive, between £200 and £500 per hour; a year in the Family Court can easily cost between £10,000 and £20,000.
4. Solicitors do not provide free advice; the half-hour free consultation some give is to enable them to weigh up a potential client and explain their services.

A practical compromise is for the client to represent himself in court and fill out the forms himself, using the solicitor to check them and provide particular legal advice, instructing him very carefully and precisely. When solicitors provide these specific services, it is known as **Unbundling**.

There are some circumstances, especially in high value or financially complex divorce cases, or when social services are threatening to take a child away, or where a parent has been accused of causing non-accidental harm to a child, in which appointing an experienced solicitor is a sensible, even essential, option. The client can also spend the odd hour with a solicitor if his case has met a particular obstacle with which his McKenzie is unfamiliar. There is no reason why the client, the McKenzie and the solicitor should not all get around the table to discuss strategy. This will keep down costs and can be more productive.

Solicitors' Bills

A litigant who employs a solicitor will soon find himself presented with a very big bill. The largest single category of complaints received by the Legal Ombudsman concerns the failure of family lawyers to give their clients an accurate estimate of what their services will cost. Many litigants receive bills significantly in excess of what they expect.

Litigants should always get an estimate of costs before engaging a solicitor and demand a breakdown of the bill, with time logs and every expense itemised. There is a strict time limit of one month within which the bill can be queried. The Legal Complaints Service will check the bill and their service is free, but applies only to bills which do not include court proceedings, in that case it will be necessary to apply to the court to have the bill checked, and they will charge.

A solicitor cannot begin proceedings against a litigant who refuses to pay his bill until he has informed him about these services. It is better to pay the bill before having it checked for possible remuneration or the solicitor can charge interest at a rate of 8%. At the very least, the solicitor is entitled to half his fees, all of the VAT, and all the cost of any sums he has paid out on the litigant's behalf.

Poor service is another matter; most disputes are resolved through conciliation. Failure to win a case is not sufficient grounds to withhold payment, provided the solicitor has conducted himself as he is obliged to. If the solicitor is believed to be guilty of misconduct, there is a further process.

Solicitors; Complaints

The Access to Justice Act 1999 places upon solicitors "a duty to the court to act with independence in the interests of justice", and a duty to comply with the rules of conduct of the Law Society; "those duties shall over-ride any obligation which the (solicitor) may have, if it is inconsistent with them". Any solicitor who misleads a court would be committing an offence.

A solicitor is employed by his client, even if payment is from public funding. Many of the problems litigants believe are caused by their solicitor are often systemic, but if a solicitor isn't doing his job or seems out of his depth the litigant should sack him and engage another or represent himself as a **Litigant-in-Person**.

Resolution (the family lawyers' association) sets out a code of practice which solicitors are expected to observe, but their approach is that the "guidelines" for family law practitioners are "aspirational" and not mandatory, and little can be done when solicitors breach their standards.

In the first instance, a litigant who wishes to complain about a solicitor acting in breach of the code while proceedings are on-going should send a letter headed "complaint" and address it to the complaints partner at the practice with details of the complaint and the request for a response by return. The letter should be kept short and explain that the solicitor has failed to follow instructions, answer communications or provide an adequate service. The letter should be dealt with within fourteen days. If the solicitor is a sole practitioner, then he acts as his own complaints partner.

If the complaints process has been exhausted, a litigant can approach the Legal Ombudsman, providing evidence of correspondence. Typical reasons to complain are failure to follow instructions, causing unreasonable delay, giving inaccurate or incomplete information, failure to keep a client informed or to reply to phone calls and letters or failure to give a client accurate details of costs.

If all proceedings, including those relating to costs, are completely at an end and the client does not intend to sue the solicitor for negligence, a complaint about a member of *Resolution* can be sent to The Legal Director, *Resolution*, PO Box 2108, Warwick, CV35 8YN, giving full details of the complaint and enclosing copies of any documents to be considered.

The Legal Director will acknowledge the complaint and send a copy to the solicitor concerned within seven days of receipt. The Legal Director will then contact the solicitor to discuss the complaint and to ask if they can offer an explanation and/or apology in relation to the matter. If the complaint is about a solicitor who acted for another person involved in the dispute, then the solicitor's response may be limited by client confidentiality: i.e., the solicitor's professional duty to the person for whom they acted that they will not disclose confidential information.

The Legal Director will then refer back to the complainant with any explanation and/or apology. They are obliged to refer back within twenty-eight days of receipt of the complaint. The complainant should then notify the Legal Director within twenty-eight days whether he accepts the resolution offered. If he does, the solicitor will be notified, and no further action will be taken.

Taking further action is a long process which can last more than seven months. At the end of it the solicitor will merely have been inconvenienced, and a solicitor who is not a member can still practice. It is his own colleagues who must decide the case, so there is little independent about the process.

A litigant who has suffered financial loss because, for example, his ex's solicitor fails to communicate with him when instructed – perhaps to tell him that a session of contact has been cancelled – will be better off issuing a Small Claim in the County Court for compensation of any travel costs, etc. The fee will vary according to the amount claimed; it is cheaper to claim online using the *Money Claim On-Line* service. A letter should be written to the solicitors first explaining the intended action, and settlement may be possible without going to court.

Complaints about barristers are made to the Bar Standards Board; complaints about Legal Executives to ILEX Professional Standards (IPS).

Special Contribution

See **Ancillary Relief**.

Special Guardianship Order

SGO – Section 14A CA1989, amended by Section 115(1) of the Adoption and Children Act 2002, allows one or more adults to be appointed a child's "special guardian" if the child is unable to live with his birth parents.

An SGO is more secure than a **Child Arrangements Order** because the guardian needs leave of the Court to discharge it but, unlike adoption, it does not terminate the legal relationship with the birth parents. Special guardianship confers PR on the adult in whose favour the order is made and allows him to remove the child from the UK for up to three months without consent of others with PR or leave of the Court. On making the order, the Court may also give leave for the child to be known by a new surname. SGOs lack the safeguards associated with adoption or fostering and are often made hand-in-hand with a **Supervision Order**.

Specific Issues Order

SIO – an order made under **Section 8** of the **Children Act 1989** "giving directions for the purpose of determining a specific question which has arisen, or which may arise, in connection with any aspect of parental responsibility for a child". For example:

1. what **Name** the child should be known by;
2. which **School** the child should attend;
3. whether the child should receive **Medical Treatment**;
4. how religion should be included in the child's upbringing (including ritual **Circumcision**; See Re J [1999] 2 FLR 678 and Re J [2000] 1 FCR 307;
5. whether the person with care can take the child out of the jurisdiction.

Like a **Prohibited Steps Order**, an SIO interferes with **Parental Responsibility**, taking it away from the parents and handing it to the Court; it is not to be made where a **Child Arrangements Order** could achieve the same result. When parents are eventually able to come to an agreement, an SIO can be changed or lifted, provided that to do so is in the best interests of the child.

SIOs enable parents to battle in court over whether to have a child vaccinated or to what school to send the child, not because the argument is necessary, but because it enables the parents to continue their dispute in another form. Before a party makes the application, he should ask himself if it is really essential to put his child through this.

Applications are made using Form C100.

Split Hearing

A hearing in two parts: in the first the Court makes a **Finding-of-Fact**, and in the second a decision based upon that finding.

Split hearings cause additional delay and expense, both to the parties and to the taxpayer, and consume valuable court time and resources, often unnecessarily. Clearly, there is no benefit to the Court in conducting a finding-of-fact if the outcome is to have no bearing on the final decision.

A typical example is TB v DB: in the first hearing, the Finding-of-Fact, TB v DB [2013] EWHC 2274, the Court found that the mother's allegations of violence and abuse were not proven. In the second hearing the following day, TB v DB [2013] EWHC 2275, the Court transferred residence to the father and granted the mother contact.

In the House of Lords decision in Re B [2008] UKHL 35; [2008] 2 FLR 141, Baroness Hale confirmed that a fact-finding hearing is part of the process of trying a case and not a separate exercise and that where the case is adjourned for further hearing it remains only **Part Heard**. Guidance on split hearings was issued in May 2010 by the President, Sir Nicholas Wall, who considered they were taking place when they did not need to and taking up a disproportionate amount of court time and resources.

Wall reminded judges and magistrates that a fact-finding hearing is a working tool designed to assist them to decide the case. The key factor is to decide whether finding the allegations proven or not proven "would be relevant in deciding whether to make an order about residence or contact and, if so, in what terms". Thus, a fact-finding hearing should be ordered *only* if the Court takes the view that the case cannot properly be decided without such a hearing. Even if the Court takes that view, it does not follow that such a hearing needs to be separate from the substantive hearing.

Spousal Maintenance

Monies paid after a divorce by one spouse for the financial support of the other.

This is a divisive issue: when making maintenance orders, the Court should endeavour to end the financial dependence of one party on the other as soon as practicable. In a 2015 case, a millionaire racehorse surgeon, Ian Wright, complained it would be unfair for him to continue maintenance payments to his ex-wife, Tracey, after his retirement, given that she did not work; the Court agreed, and urged her to get a job (W v W [2015] EWCA Civ 201).

Elsewhere in Europe, ex-wives are expected to be self-sufficient and ex-husbands need only pay child support; in Scotland, for example, spousal maintenance rarely continues beyond three years. The justification for such payments in the UK is that there are insufficient funds to enable a "clean break" and a wife's income is less than her husband's: their decision to raise a family together has reduced her ability to earn a living. There may be a date established for the payments to cease, by which time she must become self-sufficient, but if there are children, orders have often been open-ended, with payments ceasing only on the wife's death, re-marriage, or if the Court orders it.

If the new couple live together but have decided not to marry, it is likely they don't wish to forgo her maintenance payments. Her ex-husband may by now be in a new relationship himself and in need of the money. Any attempt by him to vary the court order will be thwarted by his ex-wife. If there are children involved, things can turn nasty.

The balance of this argument has begun to shift in favour of ex-husbands. A 2009 **Court of Appeal** decision involved a wealthy young couple with a single daughter; the trial judge ordered their capital to be split equally and the husband to pay maintenance of £125,000 a year. He appealed (Grey v Grey [2009] EWCA Civ 1424) on the grounds that his ex-wife was cohabiting with a Mr Thompson; in court, despite ample evidence, she denied this. It was only when Mr Grey **Ambushed** her during **Cross-Examination** with his knowledge that she was pregnant that she admitted she was in a "fixed, committed relationship".

Proof of **Cohabitation** does not automatically terminate maintenance; cohabitation is not the same as remarriage. The courts will take it into consideration if a woman is found to be cohabiting, regardless of her new partner's contribution; they will exercise their discretion to determine what the husband *should* be contributing according to his ability to pay (or capacity to earn) and decide whether maintenance should still be paid. Thus, if an ex-wife cohabits, she risks having her relationship exposed in court and the loss of her maintenance.

Stare Decisis

(Latin: short for *Stare decisis et non quieta movere*, meaning; "to stand by decisions and not disturb settled matters") the principle which requires judges to abide by the precedent set in previous cases.

Statement of Case

An **Application**, or the response to it, by which a litigant sets out his case.

Statement of Means

The form on which a party records his financial situation, including capital, income and outgoings, etc. In divorce proceedings, it is completed on Form D81 and in children's proceedings, on Form C10A.

Statement of Service

Form C9 which the applicant completes and returns to the court after the application has been served on the respondent.

Statement of Truth

A brief, signed declaration at the foot of a document that the writer believes the facts contained within to be true; it need not be witnessed or counter-signed. Some **Affidavits** need only be confirmed by a Statement of Truth, such as the Divorce Petition and Forms E, E1 and E2. The forms which support an application for a **Decree *Nisi***, Forms D80A to D80E, are no longer affidavits and are now Statements of Truth.

Status Quo

Or *status quo ante*. (Latin: short for *in statu quo res erant ante bellum*, meaning "in the state in which things were before the war") the established state of affairs.

Statutory Law

The body of law which has been established by Acts of Parliament as distinct from the **Common Law**. Recent legislation (since 1988) is available from http://www.legislation.gov.uk/. The site gives the option to choose between the legislation as originally enacted and the most recent update, but very recent changes will not be listed and will be available on the website of legal publisher Jordans'.

Not all legislation comes into operation; the Children, Schools and Families Act 2010, for example, was only partially enacted. Part 2 of the Act did not come into force and was eventually repealed in 2014.

Stay

A halt on proceedings, other than those allowed under the terms of the stay. If an order is being appealed, the Court may grant a "stay of order" which delays the terms of the order being implemented.

Step Parent

If a divorced or widowed parent marries again, the new spouse becomes a step-parent, though this does not carry any legal rights or responsibilities over any children. An unmarried partner is *not* a step-parent. See **Adoption of a Step-Child**.

Strike Out (1)

The Court's refusal to take all or part of a case because it has no hope of success.

When a party makes his application, the Court may decide on its own initiative or on application by the other side to reject it. This is called "Striking Out a **Statement of Case**" and is enabled under Rule 4.4 of the Family Procedure Rules 2010.

Applications which may fail under this rule include applications which set out no facts indicating what the application is about, applications which are incoherent and make no sense, applications which contain a coherent set of facts but those facts, even if true, do not disclose any legally recognisable application against the respondent, applications which cannot be justified because they are frivolous, scurrilous or obviously ill-founded.

A respondent can apply for an order under this rule if any of the above apply and they can show that the applicant's case has no chance of success or is "without **Merit**".

The Court can make alternative orders, either that the Court retain the application form until the stay is lifted or that the stay will be lifted upon submission of further documents. Striking out part of a case may help focus attention and resources on what is important. If an order to strike out the entire case is made, the proceedings will end.

The Court can make similar rulings concerning the respondent's answer if it is deemed to fail and may order clarification or additional information.

If an application is rejected, the Court must consider whether to make a limited, extended or general civil restraint order. This is in addition to the Court's powers under **Section 91(14)** of the Children Act. The respondent may also apply for such an order. There are three types:

1. A limited civil restraint order prevents the party making further applications in the proceedings without leave of the judge; he can apply for leave to appeal.
2. An extended civil restraint order prevents the party making any application "in any matter involving or relating to or touching upon or leading to the proceedings in which the order is made" without leave of the judge.
3. A general civil restraint order prevents the party making any application in any court without leave of the judge identified in the order.

Neither 2. nor 3. can be made for a period exceeding two years.

Strike Out (2)

The order of a court to delete written material so that it may no longer be relied upon.

Sub Nomine

(Latin: "under the name of"; usually abbreviated to *sub nom*) indicating that the litigation commenced under one name and continued under another.

Subpoena

(Latin: "under penalty") a **Writ** from the Court requiring a party or witness to attend, failure to comply with which is **Contempt**.

Substantive Law

The written, **Statutory Law**, in contrast to the procedural law by which the substantive law operates.

Summons

A document served on a person involved in proceedings, either giving them notice that legal proceedings have been commenced against them or requesting their attendance at court as a witness. In an attempt to simplify legal language, the term "**Writ** of Summons" was replaced in 1999 by "Claim Form", but the old term persists.

Supervised Contact

See **Contact Centre**.

Supervision Order

Part of the care process by which a child considered to be at risk remains in his home but under the supervision of social services or a CAFCASS officer.

Supported Contact

See **Contact Centre**.

Supreme Court

This replaced the House of Lords as the UK's highest appellate court in the three jurisdictions of England and Wales, Northern Ireland and Scotland on 1st October 2009, taking over the functions formerly exercised by the twelve Lords of Appeal in Ordinary. It sits in Middlesex Guildhall in Parliament Square, Westminster.

Leave to appeal must first be granted by the Court; The applicant must provide:

- the application (available from the Court's website);
- the order appealed against and the order refusing permission to appeal, with official transcripts;
- any other orders made in the proceedings, with official transcripts;
- a **Chronology**.

Further documents will have to be submitted if a hearing is granted, both on paper and on a memory stick.

The Court's decisions are binding on all other courts and will typically be heard by five judges. It has powers to overturn **Secondary** – but not **Primary** – legislation and to make a declaration of incompatibility with the **European Convention on Human Rights**.

Suspended Transfer Order

In Re A (Suspended Residence Order) [2010] 1 FLR 1679, Sir Paul Coleridge introduced the "Suspended **Residence Order**" (sometimes called a "conditional Residence Order").

Suspended Transfer Order

This is effectively a threat made by the Court that it will **Transfer Residence** if the resident parent's behaviour does not change; they are controversial and not all judges will make them. The intention is to change the behaviour, not to carry out the threat; Coleridge described it thus,

> It works in the same way as a suspended committal order but without the irritating technicalities attached to enforcement by committal. The court attaches clear conditions which if breached lead to immediate removal of the children to the other parent. The advantage of this order, in these intractable cases, is that the outcome lies entirely in the hands of the defaulting parent (which, of course, is made clear to him or her at the time of the making of the order)... There are three conditions I would attach to this suspended Residence Order approach. Firstly, and obviously, the judge must be satisfied, at the time the suspended order is made, that the alternative home is good enough. Secondly, it must be made abundantly clear to the parent concerned that you really mean what you say, and finally there must be judicial continuity throughout. The authority must come from the judge, not the process.

Re M (Children) [2012] EWHC 1948 concerned two children who wanted a relationship with their father but whose mother was blocking contact and influencing the children against him. She removed the children from Blackpool to Devon without notification and disengaged from proceedings. The Guardian recommended a derisory four hours' contact twice a year and was removed by the judge.

Jackson J found that the children's welfare would be better promoted through residence with the father but decided on balance to give the mother a final chance by making an order for contact which, if breached in the next eight weeks, would result in immediate transfer to the father.

T

Tagging

A parent who has been through the process of securing the return of a child will be keen to ensure that their child is not abducted again. One option is relatively unknown: to have the potential abductor tagged.

The principle was first established in Re C (Abduction: Interim Directions: Accommodation by Local Authority) [2003] EWHC 3065, [2004] 1 FLR 653, which formed part of the *Cannon* case. At the time there was no specific procedure; since then a procedure has been devised by the President's office whereby tagging can be arranged through the Tagging Team of the National Office for the Management of Offenders. Orders must follow this schedule of information:

1. An order needs to be made and sealed by 3.30pm on the day before its implementation.
2. A representative will attend the premises to install the device the next day. The order must contain the following information:
   a) the full name of the person(s) to be tagged;
   b) the full address of the place of curfew;
   c) the date and time at which the tagged person agrees to be at home (or any other relevant places) for the installation of the monitoring device;
   d) a schedule of the times at which the Court expects the person to be at home (or any other relevant places) so that the service can monitor compliance;

e)   the start date of the curfew and, if known, the end date, the days on which the curfew operates and the curfew hours each day;

f)   the name and contact details of the relevant officer to whom the service should report if there is any breach of the above schedule or if the person appears to have removed the tag.

Also refer to the case of Re A (Family Proceedings: Electronic Tagging) [2009] EWHC 710, which utilised this schedule. A sample order was appended to the judgment. A mother had twice abducted a child. The child was now in the father's care and the mother sought an order for contact; the father feared she would again abduct the child and it was eventually agreed between them that she should be tagged.

Taking a Case Out of the List

The removal of a hearing from that day's schedule. If for any reason the parties decide not to go ahead with a hearing – perhaps because they have reached agreement – they must inform the court as soon as possible by telephone and back this up by a letter signed, where possible, by all parties. Some background to the case and details of the order sought should be given, and an explanation of why the case is to be removed from the list.

Tandem Model

In which a child is represented in court both by a **Solicitor** and by a **Guardian**.

Tariff

The level of **Contact** ordered by the Court.

Taxing Master

A judge who decides on which costs in a case have reasonably been incurred.

Templates

The Ministry of Justice provides a series of **Child Arrangements Programme** templates for use by litigants on which to set out draft orders to be presented to the Court:

- *CAP01* – the template for a directions order made at the gatekeeping/allocation hearing.
- *CAP02* – the full template for an order for directions made at the **First Hearing Dispute Resolution Appointment**.
- *CAP02Lite* – the cut-down template for an order for directions made at the FHDRA.
- *CAP03* – the template for a **Child Arrangements Order** made at a **Dispute Resolutions Appointment**.
- *CAP04* – the template for a Final Order.

Therapeutic Jurisprudence

A model of jurisprudence in which a judge's traditional role of upholding justice and the rule of law is discarded and the court process is used to secure the best therapeutic outcome for the client: to carry out social policy rather than act as independent arbiter.

Therapeutic jurisprudence has been applied to juvenile and drug courts in the US, to domestic violence courts in the UK, and to the family court worldwide. It is spreading to the criminal courts in cases of alleged child abuse or sexual assault.

As a result, traditional legal safeguards are gravely eroded or eliminated, such as the separation of powers between the judiciary and the executive, judicial independence and objectivity, the right to be presumed innocent until proven beyond reasonable doubt to be guilty, the right to due process, the right to be tried in public, the right to confront one's accusers, the right to **Equality of Arms**, the right to consult an expert of one's choice, and even the right to communicate in confidence with one's own lawyers.

Threshold

The point at which the neglect or ill-treatment of a child necessitates the intervention of the state.

The threshold is passed when the child is suffering, or likely to suffer, **Significant Harm** and the harm, or likelihood of harm, is attributable to the care given to the child by the parents not being what it would be reasonable to expect from them: Section 31(2) **Children Act 1989**.

Before a local authority can intervene in a family, it must prove, on the balance of probabilities, the facts on which it relies, must demonstrate that these facts amount to the child suffering, or being likely to suffer, significant harm, and that the harm is the consequence of a failure of parental care, and must show that the proposed course of action is the only one possible. Failure to do this risks unacceptable social engineering: the Court has no mandate to improve on nature or secure that every child has a happy and fulfilled life; its single task is to be satisfied that the threshold has been crossed.

The starting presumption must be Lord Templeman's words in Re K D [1988] AC 806,

> The best person to bring up a child is the natural parent. It matters not whether the parent is wise or foolish, rich or poor, educated or illiterate, provided the child's moral and physical health are not endangered.

Hedley J famously elaborated on this in Re L (Children) (Care Proceedings: Significant Harm) [2006] EWCA Civ 1282, in which he dismissed the LA's application for a **Care Order** on the basis that the parents' deficiencies had "subtle and ambiguous consequences" for the children but could not amount to significant harm,

> ...Society must be willing to tolerate very diverse standards of parenting, including the eccentric, the barely adequate and the inconsistent. Children will inevitably have both very different experiences of parenting and very unequal consequences flowing from it. It means that some children will experience disadvantage and harm, while others flourish in atmospheres of loving security and emotional stability. These are the consequences of our fallible humanity and it is not the provenance of the State to spare children all the consequences of defective parenting... One never ceases to be surprised at the extent of complication and difficulty that human beings manage to introduce into family life.

In Re C and B (Care Order: Future Harm) [2001] 1 FLR 611, Lady Justice Hale defined the fundamental justification for interference in family life,

> [34] Intervention in the family may be appropriate, but the aim should be to reunite the family when the circumstances enable that, and the effort should be devoted towards that end. Cutting off all contact and the relationship between the child or children and their family is only justified by the overriding necessity of the interests of the child.

If the parents dispute a matter of concern, then it is in issue and the onus is on the LA to adduce proper evidence and prove their allegation. It is not enough merely for the LA to contend the parents do not accept the allegation made or give it sufficient standing. If the Court is to find the threshold has been crossed, it must evaluate the evidence presented and make a finding-of-fact. In Re P (A Child) [2013] EWCA Civ 963, Lady Justice Black emphasised,

[115] ...Allegations which are denied are not facts. If the local authority need to rely upon them as part of their case, they will have to produce the evidence to establish them.

The first test is to determine whether the child's carers cannot be removed from the pool of potential perpetrators; the **Court of Appeal** had to decide on this issue in Re B and W [1999] 2 FLR 833, in which a baby had suffered serious shaking injury at the hands either of her parents or of her child-minder. The LA made applications to take both the parent's baby and the child-minder's ten-month-old child into care.

At the full care hearing, the first instance judge could not find whether the injury had occurred while the baby was in the care of her parents or of the child-minder. He dismissed the LA's applications on the grounds that the threshold criteria had not been met, instead making a Section 40 order placing both children in care pending the LA's appeal.

The LA duly appealed, and the Court allowed the appeal relating to the baby but dismissed that relating to the child-minder's child. The threshold criteria had been reached in respect of the baby and the harm suffered was attributable to the lack of care; the word "attributable" did not require the Court to find that a specified individual was responsible for the harm caused, care was often shared by a number of adults. Risk had been proved and the child should not be left at risk because it couldn't be determined which adult had failed in their duty of care.

In the case of the child-minder's child there was no actual harm, so the decisive criterion was the risk of future harm; because it could not be proved that the child-minder had caused the baby's injuries, it could not be established that her child was certainly at risk of harm in the future.

The parents' appeal against the care order (Lancashire County Council v B [2000] 1 FLR 583) was dismissed; the Court ruled that the phrase, "the care given to the child", could refer to the care given by any of the care givers where care was shared: the parents could not be removed from the pool of potential perpetrators. This is now called a "Lancashire finding" after this case.

The first S in the **CAFCASS** acronym obliges social services to provide parents with the support necessary to enable them to provide care for their children at home. Section 22C of the Children Act specifies that a local authority should first attempt to ensure that a child stays with his parents, then with a person who has **Parental Responsibility** for him, or with a person who has a **Child Arrangements Order** naming him as a person with whom the child is to live; next, with a relative or friend and, finally, with another person who is also a local authority foster parent. If none of these is possible, they must find him accommodation in a children's home.

Through Section 22(4), social services are also obliged, so far as is reasonably practicable, to ascertain the wishes and feelings regarding the matter to be decided of the child, his parents, any person who is not his parent but who has parental responsibility for him, and any other person whose wishes and feelings the authority considers to be relevant.

Guidance on the principles and parameters of assessing the needs of individual children and organisational responsibilities for the safeguarding of children are to be found in *Working Together to Safeguard Children*, published by the Department for Education in 2013:

1. Assessment must be carried out early in a case so that alternatives can be tried before engaging the child protection system. It must be undertaken by a lead professional who should provide support to the child and his family, act as their representative and co-ordinate the delivery of support services.
2. Everything communicated to the family must be clear, consistent and confirmed in writing.
3. Where the lead professional believes this early support cannot resolve concerns, the case must be referred to the children's department of the LA and a social worker will then take over. The LA must acknowledge receipt of the referral and confirm what action will be taken within one working day; the full assessment must be completed within forty-five working days from the point of referral.

It is at this point that good intentions break down; the Children Act has been blamed for ending the system's reliance on forensic evidence and replacing it with an erratic decision-making process enabled by nebulous concepts such as "**Future Harm**". The quality of these decisions deteriorated following the 2007 case of "Baby P". Everyone in the system now conforms to these decisions because they fear censure if they resist and there is thus little check on the process. There is no evaluation of any harm social work itself might cause and no evidence collected on outcomes, beneficial or otherwise. The impulse is to remove children from risk, with little thought of what will happen to them once in care.

For many years, parents have complained that LAs intervene before the threshold is crossed and that parents are losing their children without justification. One case was judged by James Orrell in a mere fifteen minutes; three children were taken into care on the flimsy grounds that a bruise on the ear of one could have been caused non-accidentally. In the Appeal Court, Thorpe LJ exclaimed,

> I am completely aghast at this case. There is nothing more serious than a removal hearing, because the parents are so prejudiced in proceedings thereafter. Once you have lost a child, it is very difficult to get a child back... There is a point where a judge's brisk conduct of business in his search for protection of a child is just not acceptable. This does not seem to me like acceptable process or natural justice.

In July 2013, the Court of Appeal began to grapple with this issue in a series of rulings. Subsequent judgments have refined the approach which local authorities and judges must take. The LA's evidence must include all the realistically possible options for the child with an analysis of the options for and against each option, and an assessment of the benefits and risk of harm involved in each. There must be evidence for the lack of any viable alternative option for the child other than adoption. Too often this is missing; in a case which has received much attention, Re B-S (Children) [2013] EWCA Civ 1146, the President, Lord Justice Munby, declared,

> [30] We have real concerns, shared by other judges, about the recurrent inadequacy of the analysis and reasoning put forward in support of the case for adoption, both in the materials put before the court by local authorities and guardians and also in too many judgments. This is nothing new. But it is time to call a halt.

The LA must next prove the link between the facts (if proved) and its claim that the threshold has been crossed; it must explain why the facts justify a conclusion that the child is suffering, or is at risk of suffering, significant harm. Both local authorities and the lower courts have based past decisions on flimsy evidence and an absence of analysis. In Re V (Children) [2013] EWCA Civ 913, Lady Justice Black said,

> [88] ...Very careful consideration has to be given to whether these children's welfare required that the parents' consent to adoption be dispensed with and whether adoption is necessary. I have searched without success in the papers for any written analysis by local authority witnesses or the guardian of the arguments for and against adoption and long term fostering.

Before they make an application for care or adoption the LA must show they have fully considered *all* other possible options for the child. In Re S, K v The London Borough of Brent [2013] EWCA Civ 926, Ryder LJ lamented the frequent absence of justification,

[24] ...The reasoning was in the form of a conclusion that needed to be supported by evidence relating to the facts of the case and a social worker's expert analysis of the benefits and detriments of the placement options available. Fairness dictates that whatever the local authority's final position, their evidence should address the negatives and the positives relating to each of the options available.

In Re G (A Child) [2013] EWCA Civ 965, McFarlane LJ expressed the crux of the issue,

[49] In most child care cases a choice will fall to be made between two or more options. The judicial exercise should not be a linear process whereby each option, other than the most draconian, is looked at in isolation and then rejected because of internal deficits that may be identified, with the result that, at the end of the line, the only option left standing is the most draconian and that is therefore chosen without any particular consideration of whether there are internal deficits within that option.

[50] The linear approach, in my view, is not apt where the judicial task is to undertake a global, holistic evaluation of each of the options available for the child's future upbringing before deciding which of those options best meets the duty to afford paramount consideration to the child's welfare.

[54] ...What is required is a balancing exercise in which each option is evaluated to the degree of detail necessary to analyse and weigh its own internal positives and negatives and each option is then compared, side by side, against the competing option or options.

The final requirement is that no other option than the one proposed by the LA will do; the European Court had warned in *YC v United Kingdom* [2012] 55 EHRR 967,

[134] Family ties may only be severed in very exceptional circumstances and... everything must be done to preserve personal relations and, where appropriate, to "rebuild" the family. It is not enough to show that a child could be placed in a more beneficial environment for his upbringing.

In the influential Re B (A child) [2013] UKSC 33 in June 2013, Lady Justice Hale introduced the now common phrase "where nothing else will do",

[198] ...the test for severing the relationship between parent and child is very strict: only in exceptional circumstances and where motivated by overriding requirements pertaining to the child's welfare, in short, where

nothing else will do. In many cases, and particularly where the feared harm has not yet materialised and may never do so, it will be necessary to explore and attempt alternative solutions.

Lady Justice Black cited Hale in Re P (A Child) [2013] EWCA Civ 963,

[102] ...Re B is a forceful reminder that such orders are "very extreme", only made when "necessary" for the protection of the child's interests, which means "when nothing else will do", "when all else fails". The court "must never lose sight of the fact that *[the child's]* interests include being brought up by her natural family, ideally her parents, or at least one of them" and adoption "should only be contemplated as a last resort".

Finally, in September, the President, Munby LJ, gave his thoughts in Re B-S (Children) [2013] EWCA Civ 1146,

[22] The language used in Re B is striking. Different words and phrases are used, but the message is clear. Orders contemplating non-consensual adoption – care orders with a plan for adoption, placement orders and adoption orders – are "a very extreme thing, a last resort", only to be made where "nothing else will do", where "no other course *[is]* possible in *[the child's]* interests", they are "the most extreme option", a "last resort – when all else fails", to be made "only in exceptional circumstances and where motivated by overriding requirements pertaining to the child's welfare, in short, where nothing else will do".

Social workers reacted angrily, and Munby was criticised for his remarks which seemed to be at odds with the Government's pro-adoption agenda. He responded in April 2014 that it is Parliament and not the Government which makes the law and judges who must interpret it. In Re R (A Child) [2014] EWCA Civ 1625, he clarified that he had not changed the law and that adoption still sometimes remained the only sensible option. The evangelical adoption "tzar", Martin Narey, accused LAs of misinterpreting the judgments and issued an alarmist "myth-busting" guide, written by Janet Bazely QC, which ignored the fact that some children who would formerly have been adopted by strangers were now benefiting from **Kinship Care**. It is true that the law did not change, but the understanding of it did, and practice improved accordingly. The Government nevertheless felt its agenda was being thwarted and emptily threatened judges with a fundamental and rapid change to the law which would ensure 'courts and councils always pursue adoption when it is in a child's interests'.

In Re A (A Child) [2015] EWFC 11, Munby had to repeat yet again the logical process a court must follow:

1. Establish the facts upon evidence and not suspicion or speculation; if the parents refute an allegation, it is not a question of them not admitting or acknowledging it: the matter is in issue and the LA must prove it; Munby presented A (A Child) Re (Rev 1) [2015] EWFC 11 as "almost a textbook example of how not to embark upon and pursue a care case". Yet again, he was forced to explain the difference between evidence and an assertion and that, if parents disagree with an LA's assertion, it then becomes a fact in issue which it is the LA's obligation to prove on the evidence,

    [11] Failure to understand these principles and to analyse the case accordingly can lead, as here, to the unwelcome realisation that a seemingly impressive case is, in truth, a tottering edifice built on inadequate foundations.

2. The LA must demonstrate a link between the facts and the conclusion that the child has suffered or is likely to suffer harm;
3. Finally, the LA must resist natural temptation; Munby quoted Judge Jack in North East Lincolnshire Council v G & L [2014] EWCC B77,

    [16] ...the courts are not in the business of social engineering. The courts are not in the business of providing children with perfect homes.

In Re J (A Child) [2015] EWCA Civ 222, McFarlane LJ reiterated the *single* criterion for removing a child,

[56(vi)] It is vital that local authorities, and, even more importantly, judges, bear in mind that nearly all parents will be imperfect in some way or other. The State will not take away the children of "those who commit crimes, abuse alcohol or drugs or suffer from physical or mental illness or disability, or who espouse antisocial, political or religious beliefs" simply because those facts are established. It must be demonstrated by the local authority, in the first place, that by reason of one or more of those facts, the child has suffered or is at risk of suffering significant harm.

In Re W (A Child) [2016] EWCA Civ 793, he cautioned,

[68] The phrase "nothing else will do" is not some sort of hyperlink providing a direct route to the outcome of a case so as to bypass the need

408

to undertake a full, comprehensive welfare evaluation of all of the relevant pros and cons.

Time Limits

The court computes time limits in terms of "clear days"; the day on which the period begins and the day on which an event occurs ending the period are not included. If the period is seven days or shorter, only business days count.

Timetable

The **Child Arrangements Programme** imposes a strict timetable on cases:

- *Day 1*: the court office receives the application and checks that it has been completed correctly, particularly Section 14 regarding attendance at a **MIAM.**
- *Day 2*: the application is considered by the **Gatekeeping** team and allocated to a judge. If no MIAM has taken place the judge may direct that the parties attend one.
- The papers should be returned to the applicant sealed within two working days of issue; copies will also be served on the respondent and passed to **CAFCASS.**
- *Day 17*: CAFCASS must have completed the safeguarding checks and provided the Court with the **Safeguarding Letter.**
- *Week 5* (or 6 at the latest): the case is listed for the **FHDRA.**

There is no time limit in private law comparable to the twenty-six-week limit in public law cases, but cases are expected to be processed expeditiously with due attention paid to the welfare and development of the child, and to landmarks in the child's life.

In new cases, CAFCASS must "have regard" to the timetable drawn up for each child which will be determined by the Court answering the notional question, "By when should the question relating to this child be answered?" The answer to that question and the timetable must be recorded on the order, together with any changes to the timetable which become necessary.

While the Court awaits reports and the outcome of further hearings, it may make an **Interim Order** if it considers that to be in the child's best interests. Interim orders also help minimise the effects of delay and prevent the cessation of contact becoming the *Status Quo.*

Section 7 Reports should recommend the phasing in of Child Arrangements where possible, with contact increasing incrementally, and review hearings should be avoided.

Tipstaff

(Plural: tipstaves) the enforcement officer (who once carried a metal-tipped staff) of the **High Court** with power of arrest and duties including delivering prisoners to court and receiving abducted children. He has two assistants but can also call on any constable or bailiff in the jurisdiction to assist him.

Tomlin Order

A form of consent order designed to stay further action, but which is enforceable by either party if the other defaults; the terms may remain confidential in an attached schedule. Named after Mr Justice Tomlin from the case of Dashwood v Dashwood [1927] WN 276.

Transcript

The official verbatim text version of a **Judgment** produced by a court stenographer and classified by means of its **Neutral Citation**.

A transcript of a judgment can be ordered by completing Form EX107 at the Court Office which will send the tapes to a nominated official transcriber. The transcriber has to be paid but the transcript will be provided in electronic form by email or on disc if requested. It can then easily be transformed into a *Word* Document by a suitable OCR programme such as Office Lens.

If a litigant wants a transcript but doesn't intend to appeal, he can make an application under the County Court Act 1984.

Before transcripts are released to litigants, judges often re-write them on the pretext of checking that their judgments do not contain grammatical or spelling errors, which they are allowed to do under the **Slip Rule**. Correcting grammar can potentially change the semantics of a whole sentence.

Transfer of Proceedings

Proceedings may only be transferred following an order by a **High Court Judge**, **Court of Appeal** judge or the **President of the Family Division**. Most cases that need to be heard by a High Court Judge will still be heard in the **Family Court**.

Transfer of cases is regulated by Rule 29.17 of the Family Procedure Rules 2010 and by Sections 38 and 39 of the Matrimonial and Family Proceedings Act 1984.

The High Court has the power to transfer proceedings either down to the Family Court (s.38 MFPA 1984) or up from the Family Court to itself (s.39 MFPA 1984). A Designated Family Centre (DFC) can transfer proceedings to another DFC. This is a Part 18 application. Transfer does not affect any right to appeal or to enforce an order.

Proceedings will be transferred to the High Court if they are exceptionally grave, important or complex, in particular because of complicated or conflicting evidence about the risks involved to the child's physical or moral well-being or about other matters relating to the welfare of the child; because of the number of parties; because of a conflict with the law of another jurisdiction; because of some novel and difficult point of law; or because of some question of general public interest.

The Court must consider whether it would be appropriate for those proceedings to be heard together with other family proceedings which are pending in another court and whether transfer is likely significantly to accelerate the determination of the proceedings, where no other method of doing so, including transfer to another Magistrates' Court, is appropriate, and delay would seriously prejudice the interests of the child who is the subject of the proceedings.

Transfer of Residence

A **Child Arrangements Order** which reverses the roles of the **Resident** and **Non-Resident** parents.

If committal is considered too **Draconian**, the only logical response of a court to a parent who has consistently shown their inability to support contact between their child and his other parent and refused to **Obtemper** every order the Court has made is to transfer **Residence** to the non-resident parent who is better able to provide for the child's emotional needs. In V v V [2004] EWHC 1215, Mrs Justice Bracewell lamented the—

> [2] ...intractable contact disputes which drag on for years with little or anything to show for the outcome except numerous court hearings, misery for the parents, who become more entrenched in their positions, wasted court resources, and above all serious emotional damage to the children... Frequently... it is the mother caring for the children who is against making contact work.

411

Bracewell outlined the difficulties for the Court in what has become a defining narrative,

> [10] Currently, there are only four options available to the court and each is unsatisfactory: one, send the parent who refuses or frustrates contact to prison, or make a suspended order of imprisonment. This option may well not achieve the object of reinstating contact...
>
> Two, impose a fine on the parent. This option is rarely possible because it is not consistent with welfare of a child to deprive a parent on a limited budget.
>
> Three, transfer residence. This option is not necessarily available to the court, because the other parent may not have the facilities or capacity to care for the child full-time, and may not even know the child...
>
> Four, give up. Make either an order for indirect contact or no order at all... This is the option which gives rise to the public blaming the judges for refusing to deal with recalcitrant parents. This option results in a perception... that family courts are failing in private law cases and that family judges are anti-father.

Bracewell chose to transfer residence; as she noted, this option may not be ideal, but the hope is that whereas the first parent has been implacably opposed to contact the second will allow it, and the child will have satisfactory relations with both parents restored. Transfer of residence is nevertheless preferable to **Committal** or simply giving up.

A number of conditions must be met if an application for a Child Arrangements Order to transfer residence is to be successful:

1. the resident parent must have demonstrated **Implacable Hostility** to contact;
2. every possible effort has been made to make contact work and all have failed;
3. the non-resident parent is at risk of becoming marginalised and the child is at risk of developing psychological problems;
4. the resident parent is incapable of any insight into her behaviour and cannot see the harm it is doing the child; and
5. the non-resident parent is able to supply all the child's needs and will actively promote contact between the child and the other parent.

412

The high level of evidence required means that transfer occurs late in a case, if at all, when the best interests of the child require that it should happen at the earliest opportunity.

Re A (Residence Order) [2007] EWCA Civ 899 shows the degree of evidence and history needed if an application is to be successful. The mother of an eight-year-old was hostile towards contact and interfered with and frustrated the father's sessions over a long period. Eventually, the father issued an application for transfer in preference to an application for committal.

A psychological assessment of the mother suggested she was suffering from a personality disorder and that the dispute would eventually lead to psychological problems for the child; she was incapable of reforming her behaviour, into which she had no insight. The independent social worker indicated the assessment had led him to conclude the child should live with the father, and that, notwithstanding the child's excellent relationship with the mother, the mother was incapable of parenting the child sufficiently well and, in relation to contact, her behaviour was appalling; the father was a good father who could provide for the child's needs. The judge concluded that it would be in the child's best long-term interests to live with the father.

The mother appealed but the Court dismissed her appeal, noting that expert evidence from two sources had made strong recommendations that the child's residence be changed. Evidence of the mother's good parenting had been taken into account; it was not enough for her to complain it had not been given sufficient weight. Although the child wanted to live with the mother, his long-term interests outweighed the short-term problems he would face in making the move. The judge had presided over the case for more than two years and had had a good opportunity to engage in the problems surrounding contact and there was no ground upon which the decision could be interfered with.

In Re C (Residence Order) [2007] EWCA Civ 866, the Court of Appeal considered the case of a five-year-old who had lived all her life with a mother who had refused contact for over three-and-a-half years, resulting in the father becoming a "virtual stranger". Following, *inter alia*, V v V [2004] and Re A [2007] All ER (D) 156 (Jun), the judge made an order for the transfer of residence.

The mother's appeal was dismissed and the matter remitted back to the Court for ancillary orders relating to contact, therapy for the child and family assistance. The Court of Appeal stressed the importance of courts acting robustly in cases of failing and/or failed contact. Lord Justice Ward concluded,

> [26] As to the option to make no order, that was the option of abdication and all too frequently judges are driven to that conclusion and that is why week after week fathers come to this court protesting that the court is powerless to enforce its orders, quite unable to control the intractable, implacably hostile mother, even though the long-term damage to the child

413

is perfectly obvious. Time after time this court has to mollify the angry father, endeavouring to explain that the judge has a broad discretion and that his decision cannot be challenged unless plainly wrong. This time the boot is on the other foot, and if a different conclusion has been reached in this case then let it be shouted out from the roof-tops.

An order by the Court of Appeal to transfer residence often corrects a catastrophic succession of errors made by the lower courts. In Re A (A Child) [2013] EWCA Civ 1104, there had been no fewer than *eighty-two* court orders over twelve years; seven judges had been involved and more than ten CAFCASS officers. The father was described by the Court as **Unimpeachable** while the mother had been diagnosed with emotionally unstable personality disorder, paranoid personality traits and depression and had abused alcohol and illicit drugs. She had failed to attend the final hearing.

In October 2012, the trial judge, Alan Goldsack, nevertheless ordered residence with the mother, twice yearly indirect contact and a s.91(14) order preventing further applications until the fourteen-year-old girl, M, was sixteen – by which time, of course, no further orders could be made. The father had already spent more than £100,000 and was representing himself; he appealed on two grounds:

1. the judge was wrong in the exercise of his discretion to make an order for no direct contact;
2. where the Court itself admits that there has been a systemic failure in the provision of family justice to the case before it, the outcome should be a full re-hearing, properly undertaken before a new judge.

Lord Justice McFarlane accepted that the father was unimpeachable, that the mother was implacably opposed to contact and that contact between M and her father had been positive, though M was now stating she no longer wanted contact. It was the view of the CAFCASS Guardian and of Dr Hall, a Chartered Clinical Psychologist, that the child's wishes and feelings should not be overridden. Dr Kirkland Weir, on the other hand, believed the mother hid her opposition to contact behind the child's stated wishes and feelings, and recommended shared residence or, if that failed, transfer to the father.

What was unusual was that the father sought to use the entire twelve-year history of litigation as evidence that the system had failed to protect M's welfare and her and her father's Article 8 rights to family life.

McFarlane agreed there had been unjustified violation of M's and her father's rights, but this did not automatically justify a retrial or setting aside the judge's decision; nevertheless "with a heavy heart" he conceded that this was

414

necessary, and he transferred the case to the High Court. Lord Justice Aitkens agreed that M's—

> *[82]* ...childhood has been irredeemably marred by years of litigation. As a result of the system's failure, she has suffered the lack of a proper relationship with her father during her childhood years. Yet he, throughout, has acted irreproachably.

Months later, however, the press reported that the case had become mired in further delays and there had been no progress; the relationship between the "father with NO rights" and his daughter was "slipping away".

Transfer of residence is a balancing exercise: the courts tread cautiously and will transfer residence only if the risk of doing so is outweighed by the risk of not doing so: long-term emotional harm must exceed short-term distress. The **Threshold** proving the child has suffered emotional and physical harm must be crossed; see Hampshire County Council v Mother & Ors [2014] EWFC B126, where the Court transferred residence to the father from a delusional mother who had made a number of false allegations of sexual abuse.

In TB v DB [2013] EWHC 2275, the Court ordered transfer to the father and contact for the mother following a **Finding-of-Fact** (see split hearing) in which the Court found the mother's allegations against the father and his brother were "false and untrue". Although this would be disruptive and necessitate a change of school, Michael Keehan QC followed the Children's Guardian's recommendation and made an order in the child's best interests",

> *[10]* I simply do not believe that there is any set of orders that the court could make that this mother would not seek to circumvent. The extent and the lengths she went to, to pursue these false allegations was, in my judgment, quite extraordinary.

> *[11]* Whilst I accept that the discharging of the shared residence order and the making of a sole residence order in favour of the father carries some risks to the child, I am completely satisfied that those risks are completely outweighed by the risks to D if the current arrangements are maintained.

Transfer need not only be to the other parent; in Re H (Children) [2014] EWCA Civ 733, the Court of Appeal refused to allow an appeal of Lady Justice Parker's decision to transfer residence of two boys to their father and one to the paternal grandmother ("true as steel, stout as oak"), with weekly contact with the mother to be supervised by the local authority. She had said,

[74] I regard parental manipulation of children, of which I distressingly see an enormous amount, as exceptionally harmful. It distorts the relationship of the child not only with the parent but with the outside world. Children who are suborned into flouting court orders are given extremely damaging messages about the extent to which authority can be disregarded and given the impression that compliance with adult expectations is optional... Parents who obstruct a relationship with the other parent are inflicting untold damage on their children and it is, in my view, about time that professionals truly understood this.

Transfer ends existing child support arrangements; in Re: C (A Child) Schedule 1 Children Act Variation in August 2018, judge Booth discharged a Canadian father's obligation to pay £5,500 per month when residence transferred to him, but left in place an obligation to purchase a house for when the child was staying with his mother in England, though he reduced the specified value from £700,000 to £200,000.

Transitions

Children in separated families are obliged to move regularly from parent to parent and from home to home; they must also move from home to school and from home to grandparents and to other members of their extended family.

When transitions occur less often, or less flexibly, or when the adults begin to be agitated by transitions, or are irritable with the child, it becomes more troubling for the child to move from one to the other. A child may exhibit distress after contact, but it isn't always easy to tell if this is because the contact has been distressing, because returning to the resident parent is distressing, because the resident parent is showing distress as a result of the contact, or because the child is playing one parent off against the other. It is not uncommon for a child to pick up on a resident parent's reluctance to allow contact and to protect her by expressing his own unwillingness to spend time with the other. Children can find transitions between parents difficult and it is important for parents to be sensitive to their needs; it is quite wrong for either parent to place responsibility for enabling contact onto the child.

Sometimes the resident parent is the one who does all the boring stuff: deals with the school, ensures the homework is done, takes the child to the dentist, handles discipline; while the infrequently-seen contact parent does the fun things. The child may say he wants to go and live with the contact parent, but this can be the result of unrealistic expectations. On the other hand, children who have only limited contact with one parent and who have possibly been alienated against him are bound to favour the resident parent in any assessment of their wishes and feelings.

These situations have to be approached carefully and sympathetically; trying to force a child to agree to contact is self-defeating: children swiftly become unwilling to transition. A child whose transitions are not supported will align himself with the resident parent to the exclusion of the other, will begin other behaviours such as bed-wetting, and be disinclined to go to school and unhappy when he gets there. He will become distressed if his parent leaves the house or leaves him with a baby-sitter.

This leads to a downward spiral: a child who realises that transitions distress his resident parent will become less willing to make them; the parent who realises the transitions distress the child will tell him he needn't make them. All this makes the child's distress worse.

Each parent then blames the other: the resident parent is blocking contact and **Alienating** the child; the non-resident parent must be harming the child. The child's relationships crumble and break apart entirely; he sees his non-resident parent in a **Contact Centre** and then not at all, and for the rest of his life blames himself and, as he grows older, turns his back on the parent he blames for the loss of his relationships.

It is the responsibility of the child's parents to ensure transitions happen freely and calmly, with a minimum of stress to the child. When transitions occur regularly, but are kept flexible, when the adults on each side are relaxed and supportive, then the child is enabled to transition easily.

Trial

Can refer to the **Final Hearing** both in children's and in **Ancillary Relief** proceedings.

Turnbull Direction

A judge's caveat that an eye-witness's identification of an individual may not always be reliable and will depend on a number of variables; from R v Turnbull [1977] QB 224.

U

Ultra Vires

(Latin: "beyond the powers") a decision made beyond the jurisdiction of the Court and which can therefore be appealed and **Set Aside**.

Unbundling

A way of providing legal services in which the traditional full service offered by solicitors and barristers from instruction to conclusion is broken down into its component parts or "discrete acts of legal assistance".

This "unbundling" or "*à la carte* service" enables a **Litigant-in-Person** to seek legal advice only where he specifically needs it while retaining a **McKenzie Friend** if he wishes: he continues to represent himself. It is important that both litigant and solicitor are absolutely clear about what services the solicitor is being engaged for, and where his involvement ends. Note that, when providing an unbundled service, the solicitor has no wider duty of care to the client; see Minkin v Lesley Landsberg [2015] EWCA Civ 1152.

Undertaking

A solemn written promise made to the Court that a party will do or not do a specified act. It is *not* an admission that he has ever done the act. Undertakings are made on Form N117.

The Court may accept an Undertaking from a party rather than impose a **Non-Molestation Order**, provided that the applicant accepts it; the Court must be satisfied he does not need the threat of a criminal prosecution to persuade him to behave. Lord Justice Munby made clear in Q v Q (Contact: Undertakings) [2016] EWFC 5,

> The fact is, the law is, that an undertaking is enforceable in just the same way as an injunction. It is equally binding on the person to whom it attaches. And the court should not lend any credence to any suggestion to the contrary.

For a conviction, the applicant must apply to the same court and prove beyond reasonable doubt the Undertaking has been breached. Although the respondent signs the document in court, it must still be served on him to be valid, and the Court has no discretion to dispense with **Service**. This could form the basis of a possible defence, if he claimed he did not fully understand the nature of the undertaking made and had not been served; he is more likely to get away with this defence if he is representing himself. See Hussain v Hussain [1986] 2 FLR 271, which led to this little-used rule.

The advantage of an Undertaking is that it is something a Litigant-in-Person can easily do. The drawback is that it may nevertheless be used as an admission of guilt – not that he won't *ever* do something but that he won't do it *again*. The applicant must agree to the Undertaking; if she doesn't, she can ask the Court to make the Non-Molestation Order; this is more likely if she is legally aided and has a solicitor.

Under the Legal Aid, Sentencing and Punishment of Offenders Act 2012 (LASPO), legal aid is available only for cases involving proven domestic abuse and an Undertaking forms part of the evidence required under the **Domestic Violence Gateway**. Thus, accepting an undertaking, even if the respondent has never done what he undertakes not to do, may be regarded as evidence that the applicant is a victim of domestic abuse and qualify her to receive legal aid to which the respondent will not be eligible. It will also identify the case as one in which domestic abuse is a factor.

Unfind

Verb invented by Lord Justice Thorpe in Re L-B (Children) [2012] EWCA Civ 984 describing a judge reversing her original finding in a case.

Unilateral Divorce

A decision to end a marriage made by one spouse only and without reference to the other. The term was coined by Maggie Gallagher in her 1996 book *The Abolition of Marriage*,

The most significant practical legal change created by "no-fault" divorce in grounds was that it licensed unilateral divorce: for the first time, one spouse could successfully petition for divorce over the objections of his or her spouse, without alleging any grounds.

Unimpeachable

Another word particularly favoured by judges and a throwback to the days when divorce was a remedy available to an injured and legally innocent party. The integrity of a party who is "unimpeachable" cannot be doubted or questioned; this tends to elevate him to an entirely unrealistic infallibility, while simultaneously blackening the other party's character beyond redemption.

Universal Declaration of Human Rights

The *Universal Declaration of Human Rights* was commissioned in 1946 and adopted by the United Nations General Assembly in 1948; the following Articles may be relevant to family law:

- Article 7 guarantees equality before the law and the right to equal legal protection without discrimination;
- Article 10 protects the right to a fair and public hearing by an independent and impartial tribunal in the determination of any criminal charge;
- Article 11 demands that anyone criminally charged is presumed innocent until proven guilty and that historic offences are tried according to the laws pertaining at the time of perpetration;
- Article 12 protects from arbitrary interference a person's privacy, family, home and correspondence;
- Article 16 allows men and women to marry and found a family; marriage must be entered into only with free and full consent; it concludes, "The family is the natural and fundamental group unit of society and is entitled to protection by society and the State".

Unless Order

See **Hadkinson Order**.

Unmeritorious

Without **Merit**; especially of unmarried fathers, to justify the denial of automatic **Parental Responsibility**; an unmarried father is presumed to be unmeritorious unless either the mother or the Court agrees he is not. Also used of an application deemed to be without prospect of success or **Vexatious**.

Unpaid Work Requirement

An enforcement order of between forty and three hundred hours of unpaid work which must be of benefit to the community; formerly called Community Service.

.

V

Variation

An adjustment to an existing order made by the Court.

Varying a Child Arrangements Order

If a **Child Arrangements Order** is made with which a parent disagrees and feels unable to comply, she can appeal. If circumstances change and she wants to alter the order, she can apply for a **Variation**.

If she simply disobeys, she will be in breach and the other parent may apply for enforcement. She must show the Court what has changed, why it means she cannot obey the order and why it must be changed. Until there is a new order in place, the original stands. She will need to show that the change is "material" and that altering what the Court has already ordered will be in the child's best interests.

A parent can also apply for a variation if the other is failing to comply with the order so that it better reflects the reality on the ground.

Once **Contact** is up and running it is important to increase it periodically to the point where it reaches a reasonable level. Under the **Child Arrangements Programme**, these increments should be written into the original order, which means parents don't have to return to court repeatedly and it is cheaper and easier for everyone; alternatively, a parent can apply to the Court for a variation of the original order.

If contact has been working well and there is no incremental increase built into the order, the **Non-Resident Parent** should return to court with an application for a more realistic level of contact, or even for an order giving him

Shared Residence. It is worthwhile indulging in some horse-trading: being prepared to lose a Sunday if it means getting some mid-week contact, for example. The more a parent asks for, within reason, the more the courts are likely to award. He should tell the judge how pleased he is that he was granted the order and how well it fits with the best interests of his children. The application is likely to trigger an investigation by CAFCASS and a **Risk Assessment**.

He can ask for a variation to be allowed to pick his child up from school and drop him off at the resident parent's home; this will benefit her. It may be advisable to arrange a meeting with the head to explain how the order is to work.

The application is made on Form C2 if the original order is less than twelve months old, or C100 if it is older.

Varying a Maintenance Order

The usual justification for varying any order is a **Change** in the **Circumstances** of one of the parties. If a party loses his job, suffers financial hardship, etc., it may be appropriate for him to apply to the Court to vary the order up or down, to change the duration of the order, to discharge arrears, capitalise payments or suspend the order temporarily.

To vary a maintenance order there must be an order already in place, the payee must not have remarried, and the Court must have regard to all the circumstances of the case including any changes to the factors which the Court considered when making the original order.

The Court has wide discretion to decide whether to allow a variation and its first consideration must be the welfare of any children under eighteen. The Court must consider the factors involved in making the original order and look at what factors have since changed. The Court may also consider that there should now be a clean break, perhaps through payment of a lump sum, provided this doesn't cause the recipient "undue hardship".

Capitalisation of maintenance is enabled by Section 31(7B) of the Matrimonial Causes Act 1973; this is a tempting option for a woman who is proposing to remarry and would thereafter lose the right to regular payments, or whose ex is applying for a reduction or termination of maintenance. It can also be a sensible option for a man approaching retirement and will ensure no future applications from his former wife. Of course, if a man knows his ex is about to remarry, he should resist a Section 31 application. An application for variation may help to achieve a clean break but may also rake up old resentments and hostility; the case will go to court if the parties cannot agree.

Once the application has been made, the applicant will have to wait fourteen weeks or so for a **Directions Hearing**. The Court will determine what further information is required and whether it needs a valuation on the assets. It will set out a timetable for future hearings. At the second hearing, the Court will encourage the parties to settle and if that fails, the case will go to a **Final Hearing**, which could well be eighteen months after the initial application. In the meantime, the payer must continue paying maintenance as per the original order.

Applying for a variation will be chancy and costs will be high and possibly disproportionately so compared with any variation achieved. Parties are advised to negotiate.

In the past, maintenance orders increased over time according to the retail prices index, but this is no longer considered best practice. Recent case law indicates a tendency away from placing the onus on the payee to argue why the maintenance period should be extended to placing it on the payer to argue why it should not. In North v North [2007] EWCA Civ 760, the Court limited a wife's claim to increase maintenance because she had made no attempt to become financially independent through gainful employment and had frittered away her settlement on an extravagant lifestyle and unwise business ventures. She was nevertheless awarded an increase on the grounds that she was not to blame for the failure of the businesses in which she had invested.

Once the Court has made a **Consent Order** neither party should return to court to make further financial claims on the other. It is therefore difficult to vary a lump sum order, but the amount ordered in a Consent Order can be varied if circumstances change, and the income, resources and obligations of both parties will be taken into account as specified by Section 25 of the Matrimonial Causes Act 1973. Parties should always consider mediation before returning to court.

Vexatious Litigant

One who brings litigation without **Merit** merely to vex or harass the respondent rather than to resolve the case. In children's proceedings, an application for a **Section 91(14) Order** is the usual response.

Visiting Contact

Contact in which the child is able to visit the **Non-Resident Parent** during the day but does not stay **Overnight**.

Voice of the Child

The degree to which the "**Wishes and Feelings**" of the child are represented to the Court and influence its decision.

Article 12 of the United Nations Convention on the Rights of Children provides,

1. Parties shall assure to the child who is capable of forming his or her own views the right to express those views freely in all matters affecting the child, the views of the child being given due weight in accordance with the age and maturity of the child.
2. For this purpose, the child shall in particular be provided the opportunity to be heard in any judicial and administrative proceedings affecting the child, either directly, or through a representative or an appropriate body, in a manner consistent with the procedural rules of national law.

Children are rarely heard directly in court, and their views are usually presented through the medium of a **CAFCASS** officer. The **Children Act 1989** demands at Section 1(3)(a) that the Court considers "the ascertainable wishes and feelings of the child concerned (considered in the light of his age and understanding)" and to "his physical, emotional and educational needs".

This process does not allow the child to participate in proceedings, and it can be difficult to ascertain what the child's views really are, and they can be heavily influenced by parents and other adults with conflicting and competing interests. Even if they are truly the child's own, they may well not be in his long-term interest (a child may express a wish not to go to school, clean his teeth, or eat healthy food).

It can be challenging to get an independent view of what a child really wants, what his best interests are, and where the balance lies. One option is for the Court to enlist a **Children's Guardian**, another is for the child, especially an older child, to be **Joined** to proceedings.

The test is simply the best interests test and the starting point on "wishes and feelings" is that the older a child is the greater their significance. In Re S (Minors) (Access; Religious Upbringing) [1992] 2 FLR 313, Butler-Sloss LJ said of children who were thirteen and eleven,

Nobody should dictate to children of this age, because one is dealing with their emotions, their lives and they are not packages to be moved around. They are people entitled to be treated with respect.

It is clear, however, from cases such as RS v SS [2013] EWHC B33 or Re S [2010] EWHC 192, that even the wishes and feelings of a fourteen-year-old can be overridden if the Court considers that to do so is in the child's interest.

> [2] Section 1(3)(a) of the Children Act 1989 did not permit the court to pay no regard to the clearly and consistently expressed wishes and feelings of a child, but such wishes and feelings were to be assessed in the light of his age and understanding, in particular the impact of alienation upon the reliability of the child's wishes and feelings, and some modest signs that his expressed views might not in fact reflect his true feelings were matters to be taken into account when assessing the weight to be attached to his expressed wishes and feelings.

The minimum age is at which a child can make his or her "ascertainable feelings" known in court is often placed between ten and fourteen (the age of criminal responsibility is ten in England and Wales and eight in Scotland). CAFCASS, who are criticised for not giving children's views sufficient weight, often quote an age of eleven or twelve, based on psychological research by Jean Piaget (1896-1980) who held that a child becomes able to make "moral" decisions at that age.

In practice, age *per se* is not the measure, but the child's **Competence** (or **"Gillick Competence"**). In the family law realm, whether a child can "understand fully the nature of what is proposed" will depend not only on his intellectual development but also on the quality of the information given to him, which may well be poor, and beyond even the adults in the case to understand. The definition enables the Court to override the child's wishes if it thinks it necessary.

Children are not usually expected to have direct input into the decision of the Court; in Re M (Family Proceedings: Affidavits) [1995] 2 FLR 100, a twelve-year-old girl expressed the wish to live with her father; the Court refused, relying on the welfare officer's "instinct" that she should live with her mother. The father appealed, producing as evidence an affidavit signed by his daughter. In the Court of Appeal Butler-Sloss LJ rejected his application,

> It is not fair on children that they should be dragged into the arena, that they should be asked specifically to choose between two parents, both of whom they love, and they ought not to be involved in the disputes of their parents.

Legally, children become able to make their own decisions only between the ages of sixteen and eighteen, and it is arguably quite wrong for the courts to expect them to make irreversible decisions about their own welfare before then;

imposing such a high burden of responsibility onto children places enormous pressure on them which is liable to cause severe and long-lasting psychological damage while it absolves adults of responsibility. It isn't only irresponsible parents who escape their obligations in this way; CAFCASS is particularly keen to place more responsibility onto children.

The *Family Justice Young People's Board*, which is hosted by CAFCASS, is concerned by the lack of attention given to the views of children and young people and has produced a charter for including them in family justice decisions. Its main points are that children and young people should—

1. be at the centre of all proceedings, with their needs, wishes and feelings fully considered;
2. be kept safe;
3. be respected and treated as individuals;
4. be informed of their rights;
5. be able to meet and communicate freely with their social worker or CAFCASS officer and the judge, if of sufficient understanding;
6. be informed about the court proceedings and kept up-to-date in a clear and age-appropriate manner;
7. have the opportunity to give feedback through email, text, telephone or writing;
8. be involved in developing family justice.

There are some circumstances in which it will be appropriate for the judge to meet the child, though currently it is rare, as a judge is regarded as having no relevant expertise. The purpose of such a meeting is not evidence-gathering, which is the job of CAFCASS, but to explain proceedings to the child and reassure him that his voice is heard. The Family Justice Council issued *Guidelines for Judges Meeting Children* in 2010; in July 2014 and again in February 2015, the Government pledged that children would be able to see a judge from the age of ten, though there has been no movement on this policy since.

The Scots courts will, under Section 11(7) of the Children Act (Scotland) 1995, and so far is it is practical, give the child the opportunity to express his views and thoughts, should he wish to, and give due consideration and regard to the views expressed, taking into account the child's age and maturity.

Under Section 2(4A) of the Age of Legal Capacity (Scotland) Act 1991 a child "shall have the legal capacity to instruct a solicitor, in connection with any civil matter, where that person has a general understanding of what it means to do so".

Usually, a child of twelve years or older will be considered to have sufficient maturity, but it is possible for a younger child to present his views to the Court. Any action or decision is to be intimated to the child directly. The child's views must be recorded in writing. Rules 33.19 & 33.20 of the 1993 Rules were substituted by SI 1996/2167.

The Court remains bound by the welfare principle, i.e., that consideration of the child's welfare must be paramount at the heart of any judgment, and by the no-order principle.

If a child wishes to express his views, he should indicate that he wishes to do so using Form F9. The Sheriff must then order such steps to be taken as he considers appropriate to ascertain the views of that child. The Sheriff should not grant any order unless the child has been given the opportunity to be heard, and due weight has been given to the views expressed.

A child's views may be sought and represented in a number of different ways: the Sheriff may interview the child in chambers privately, without parents or a third party being present, or the child may be invited to attend the hearing, or a bar reporter may be appointed to obtain the child's views.

Where the child expresses a view on a matter affecting him, either personally to the Sheriff, or to a person appointed by the Sheriff, or provided in writing, the Sheriff, or the person appointed by him, must record the child's views in writing and direct that such views, and any written views, given by a child shall—

1. be sealed in an envelope marked "Views of the child - confidential";
2. be kept in the court process without being recorded in the inventory of process;
3. be available to a Sheriff only;
4. not be opened by any person other than a Sheriff; and
5. not form a borrowable part of the process (i.e., it will not determine the court's opinion).

There is no presumption that the Sheriff will keep the child's recorded views to himself, but clearly these rules do permit the taking of confidential evidence from the child even to the extent of keeping it confidential from the parties and their representatives.

Children who are party to proceedings are entitled to have their own independent legal representation throughout. Children are also entitled to apply for Legal Aid; although the usual age for understanding the proceedings is around twelve, a child of any age can apply for Legal Aid, and **Instruct** their own solicitor, providing they have a good understanding of the situation. The Scottish Legal Aid Board (SLAB) has a section on their website dedicated to children.

Void Marriage

A marriage is void if the parties were not eligible to marry in the first place.

The court will declare it "void": i.e. no marriage has taken place and any property transactions entered into on the assumption of the marriage's validity will be set aside. The statement is made on Form D80F. A void marriage *must* be ended. Under s.11 MCA1973, a marriage may be void if—

1. the parties are within the prohibited degrees of relationship;
2. one of the parties was under the age of sixteen at the time of the marriage;
3. the parties have intermarried in disregard of certain requirements as to the formation of marriage – the marriage may have violated one of the criteria which must be fulfilled for a marriage to be valid, see Sections 25 and 49 of the Marriage Act 1949;
4. either party was already lawfully married or in a civil partnership at the time of the marriage;
5. in the case of a polygamous marriage entered into outside England and Wales, one party was at the time of the marriage domiciled in England and Wales.

The prohibited degrees of relationship are defined in Schedule 1 of the Marriage Act 1949. A relationship may be prohibited due to **Consanguinity** or **Affinity**. Exceptions and changes are given in the Marriage (Prohibited Degrees of Relationship) Act 1986.

In Akhter v Khan (Rev 2) [2018] EWFC 54, a court decided a twenty-year union celebrated only under sharia law was void rather than a non-marriage and granted a Decree of **Nullity**, as this best supported the human rights of the couple, enabling their finances to be resolved as if they had been married and not cohabiting. The court did *not*, contrary to media reports, recognise a sharia marriage.

Voidable Marriage

A marriage is voidable if one of the parties was married against their will or under false pretences and need not be ended if both parties consent to it continuing.

A voidable marriage is treated as a valid marriage for all purposes up to the decree of annulment, so the finances are treated in the same way as in divorce. The Statement is made on Form D80G. Under Section 12 of the Matrimonial Cause Act 1973, a marriage may be voidable if—

Voidable Marriage

1. there has not been **Consummation** of the marriage; i.e., the parties have not had sexual intercourse since the marriage; any sex before is irrelevant; without consummation it is impossible to commit **Adultery** and an **Annulment** is the appropriate way to end the marriage rather than divorce;
2. either party didn't consent to the marriage (see **Duress**);
3. either party was suffering from mental disorder at the time of the marriage;
4. the respondent was suffering from communicable venereal disease at the time of the marriage;
5. the respondent was pregnant by a third party at the time of the marriage;
6. one party has, since the marriage, been issued with an interim **Gender Recognition Certificate**; or
7. the respondent's gender has become the acquired gender at the time of the marriage.

W

Wardship

See **Guardian**.

Warning Notice

Since the implementation of the Children and Adoption Act 2006 in December 2008, all **Contact Orders** and **Child Arrangements Orders** or **Variations** on existing orders have carried a "warning notice".

The notice must apply both to the **Respondent** and to the **Applicant**. Warning notices are covered under Rule 12.33 of the Family Procedure Rules 2010. An application to have a warning notice attached to an order made prior to 8th December 2008 is made on Form C78.

Breach of the order will result in a range of sanctions beginning with an **Unpaid Work Requirement**. Further breach may result in an additional Enforcement Order, an extension of the Enforcement Order to make the work requirement "more onerous", a fine or **Committal** to prison if consistent or flagrant breach is considered **Contempt of Court**.

There is no retrospective appending of warning notices to existing orders, but all existing orders become Child Arrangements Orders which carry warning notices automatically.

Three types of warning are possible,

1. A warning (in accordance with Section 13 of the Children Act) that where a Child Arrangements Order regulating with whom the child is to live is in force, no person may cause the child to be known by a new

surname or remove the child from the UK without the written consent of every person with **Parental Responsibility** for the child or leave of the Court. This does not prevent removal, for a period of less than twenty-eight days, by the person in whose favour the order was made.

2. A warning that it may be a criminal offence under the Child Abduction Act 1984 to remove the child from the United Kingdom without leave of the Court.

3. Advice that any person with Parental Responsibility for the child may obtain guidance on what can be done to prevent the issue of a passport to the child. They should write to UK Passport Agency, Globe House, 89 Eccleston Square, London, SW1V 1PN.

Wasted Costs Order

An order made by a court under the Courts and Legal Services Act 1990, s 4(1), that a litigant's costs be paid by their legal representative. The criteria were set out in Re A Barrister (wasted costs order No 1 of 1991) [1993] QB 293, [1992] 3 All ER 429,

- Has the legal representative of whom complaint is made acted improperly, unreasonably or negligently?
- If so, did such conduct cause the applicant unnecessary costs?
- If so, is it, in all the circumstances, just to order the legal representative to compensate the applicant for the whole or part of the relevant costs?

In Ridehalgh v Horsefield [1994] Ch 205, the Court of Appeal provided definitions,

- "improper" involves a significant breach of duty by reference to the code of professional conduct which, in turn, might justify suspension, striking off, fines or suspension from the legal profession;
- "unreasonable" means vexatious, designed to harass the other side rather than resolve the case;
- "negligent" denotes incompetent behaviour but not in a technical sense.

In HU v SU [2015] EWFC 18, Keehan J made an order against the mother's solicitors and reiterated these fundamental principles,

i. court orders must be obeyed;
ii. a timetable or deadline set by the Court cannot be amended by agreement between the parties; it must be sanctioned by the Court;

iii. any application to extend the time for compliance must be made *before* the time has expired.

Welfare

The over-ruling principle of the Children Act 1989 is the welfare of the child; it embodies the **"Best Interests of the Child"** principle within the law and is expressed in the Act like this,

> When a court determines any question with respect to—
>
> a) the upbringing of a child or
> b) the administration of a child's property or the application of any income arising from it
>
> the child's welfare shall be the court's paramount consideration.

This reveals the origin of welfare in the administration of property; as the Lord Chancellor, Lord Eldon**Error! Bookmark not defined.**, said in 1827,

> This court has not the means of acting, except where it has property to act upon.

Note that if the proceedings relate to the child but *not* to his upbringing or the administration of his property or income, then his welfare is *not* the Court's paramount consideration, though it may be material. Examples of such a case would be where the Court is considering whether to **Commit** a parent to prison (see A v N (Committal: Refusal of Contact) [1997] 1 FLR 533), making a **Finding-of-Fact** or when deciding whether or not to grant **Leave** to an adult to apply for a s.8 order. The principle also does not apply if a statute expressly states it should not.

S.1(3) CA1989 provides a guide to what a court should take into account when considering a child's welfare in the form of the **Welfare Checklist**, but it doesn't define "welfare" itself, nor the crucial concept of "paramountcy".

The child's welfare was first enshrined in statute and given preferential status by Section 5 of the Guardianship of Infants Act 1886 which enabled the Court to make an order for custody "having regard to the welfare of the infant" and to the conduct and wishes of his parents; this gave mothers rights equal to those of fathers. Sections 1 and 2 of the Custody of Children Act 1891 enabled the Court to interfere with these parental rights in the interests of the child's welfare.

In McGrath [1893] 1 Ch 143, Lindley LJ extended the concept of a child's welfare from the merely material and financial to the moral and religious,

> The duty of the court is, in our judgment, to leave the child alone, unless he is satisfied that it is for the welfare of the child that some other course shall be taken. The dominant matter for the consideration of the court is the welfare of the child. But the welfare of a child is not to be measured by money only, nor by physical comfort only. The word welfare must be taken in its widest sense. The moral and religious welfare of the child must be considered as well as its physical well-being. Nor can the ties of affection be disregarded... The court has to consider, therefore, the whole of the circumstances of the case, the position of the parent, the position of the child, the age of the child, the religion of the child so far as it can be said to have any religion, and the happiness of the child.

Thus, the welfare of the child had come to be as important a consideration as the rights of the parents. Section 1 of the Guardianship of Infants Act 1925 provided,

> Where in any proceedings before any court... the custody or upbringing of an infant, or the administration of any property belonging to or held on trust for an infant, or the application of the income thereof, is in question, the court, in deciding that question, shall regard the welfare of the infant as the first and paramount consideration, and shall not take into consideration whether from any other point of view the claim of the father, or any right at common law possessed by the father, in respect of such custody, upbringing, administration or application is superior to that of the mother, or the claim of the mother is superior to that of the father.

Lord Guest interpreted this in J v C [1970] AC 668,

> even prior to the 1925 Act the paramount consideration in regard to the custody of infants was the infant's welfare. The father's wishes were to be considered but only as one of the factors as bearing on the child's welfare. The father had no "right" as such to the care and control of his infant children.

Lord McDermott noted that welfare "was being regarded increasingly as a general criterion which was not limited to custody disputes between parents". He continued that the words of the 1925 Act "must mean more than that the child's welfare is to be treated as the top item in a list of items relevant to the matter in question". He continued,

> I think [the words of the 1925 Act] connote a process whereby, when all the relevant facts, relationships, claims and wishes of parents, risks, choices and other circumstances are taken into account and weighed, the course to be followed will be that which is most in the interests of the child's welfare as that term has now to be understood.

Thus, the welfare of the child is the Court's sole consideration in relation to which all other factors are weighed and are relevant only in so far as they serve it. The wishes even of **Unimpeachable** parents become immaterial. Barrister Susan Maidment called the 1925 Act "a political device to actually deny women equality of parental rights": while the progressive diminution of paternal authority was accepted as inevitable, the lawmakers sought to ensure that this authority would not fall into the hands of mothers.

In deciding J v C, the Court ignored a precedent – Carroll (An Infant) [1931] 1 KB 317, 356 – that the wishes of a child's parents should be decisive unless they had neglected their duties and ruled that a ten-year-old should stay with his Protestant foster parents in England rather than return to his natural Catholic parents in Spain. This set a new and alarming precedent: ensuring the removal of a child from unimpeachable parents who had done nothing wrong merely because an outsider could better promote its welfare. The "child's best interests" now meant that the biological bond, the behaviour of either parent, the wishes of either parent, or their ability to care for their children counted for nothing if another adult could offer the child a better home. The child of poor but adequate parents could be taken and reallocated to more affluent adoptive parents, and the welfare principle ensured it would be "in the child's best interests".

J v C unravelled the careful compromise of the 1925 Act which had ensured that the child's welfare should be the paramount consideration, but not the only one. Section 31 of the Children Act 1989 later restricted this power by requiring the Court to find "that the child concerned is suffering, or likely to suffer, **Significant Harm**".

Welfare Checklist

Section 1(3) of the Children Act 1989 and (more extensively) Section 1(4) of the Adoption and Children Act 2002 (ACA2002) set out the matters to be considered when a court determines any question relating to a child's upbringing or property.

a)   *The ascertainable wishes and feelings of the child concerned (considered in the light of his age and understanding)*

435

The Court must consider the child's wishes and feelings if he is mature enough to express them; this is achieved through a **Needs, Wishes and Feelings** report. CAFCASS will record and interpret what the child expresses and how he behaves, seeking input from other practitioners if necessary. This maturity and understanding are referred to as **Competence**.

In Re H (Children) [2014] EWCA Civ 733, Lady Justice Parker made it clear that "ascertainable" does not mean the same as "expressed" – that is, a CAFCASS FCA must *ascertain* what the real wishes and feelings of the child are and not merely rely on what he *says*.

b)   *His physical, emotional and educational needs*

Physical needs cover things like appropriate accommodation, food, clothing and medical requirements. The courts will also consider how a parent's work routine affects his ability to care for his child, how close to the school he lives, what transport he will use. The parent should also consider things like child minders and after-school clubs.

Emotional needs are less clear-cut, but the Court will consider the effect on the child of any continuing conflict or exposure to arguments. Can handovers be conducted civilly? Will he be separated from a sibling or a relative he is close to?

Parents should be able to agree their child's education together, otherwise the Court will have to make the decisions for them. What impact will a change of school have? Will the child be able to maintain contact with old friends?

If necessary, CAFCASS will elicit information from the child's school, his doctor, health visitor and other professionals who are involved with him.

c)   *The likely effect on him* (the ACA2002 adds *"throughout his life"*) *of any change in his circumstances*

The Court will consider any change in residence and separation from one or other parent, especially a move abroad, and changes in schooling, etc.

d)   *His age, sex, background and any characteristics of his which the Court considers relevant*

The Court is looking here particularly at issues surrounding "diversity" and how they are being addressed and met by each parent.

This includes any disability he has, his heritage, culture and religion (so far as he can be said to have any).

The older a child is, the less willing the Court will be to make an order; ordering a teenager to have contact with a parent against his will can be counter-productive if the child thinks his views are being ignored.

The effects of separation on a child will be reduced if he can continue with familiar activities; older children will require more flexibility than younger ones. Whether children are still breast-feeding will also influence how a court decides. Boys and girls have different needs and require each parent to a different extent at different times of their lives.

e) *Any harm which he has suffered or is at risk of suffering*

The Court will have to consider any allegations of abuse made by one parent against the other. They will also want to know if the child has witnessed domestic abuse. They will seek input from schools, social services, and agencies like the NSPCC, and consider in particular whether any action has been taken to protect the child.

The Court will also consider the effects on the child of continuing conflict; many professionals in the family justice system believe the greatest harm is caused a child by witnessing conflict between his parents. Conflict will be less where parenting is shared.

f) *How capable each of his parents, and any other person in relation to whom the Court considers the question to be relevant, is of meeting his needs*

CAFCASS should assess the parents and any other relevant adult, bearing in mind what has been said about them by the other parties, and their attitude to the child's wishes and feelings. In reality these assessments can be very perfunctory.

Parents often make allegations that the other is unable properly to care for their children. No one is born a parent, and we all have to learn; a parent who is denied that opportunity will be less capable. If his child has special educational or medical needs it is important he knows how to provide these, and there is no shame in his asking for help from the appropriate quarter.

g) *The range of powers available to the Court under this Act in the proceedings in question*

The Court has wide powers to make a variety of orders, though its first duty is to make **No Order** unless absolutely necessary.

Welfare Officer

A **CAFCASS** officer who has been asked to produce a **Welfare Report**.

Welfare Report

See **Section 7 Report**.

Welfare; Scotland

Scots law combines the **Welfare** Principle of English/Welsh law, which makes the child's welfare the Court's paramount consideration, with the **No-Order Principle** into Section 11(7) of the Children Act (Scotland) 1995 which replaced s.3(2) of the Law Reform (Parent and Child) Act 1986.

Section 11(7) requires that when considering whether or not to make an order regarding parental responsibilities, parental rights, guardianship, administration of a child's property, and Section 11 orders for residence and contact, etc., the Court —

> shall regard the welfare of the child concerned as its paramount consideration and shall not make any such order unless it considers that it would be better for the child that the order be made than that none shall be made at all.

The Act also requires the Court to give the child the opportunity to express his views and to take his views into consideration, while taking account of his age and maturity.

The Court would also consider those involved in the application, normally the mother and father. While the mother has a *de-facto* relationship with the child, the onus is on the father to prove his reasoning for either applying for or defending the application, so his motive will be a consideration. The courts will consider if those involved are able, or will be able, to co-operate with sufficient willingness.

The courts may also consider the arrangements for the non-resident parent to see his child. If the resident parent doesn't agree with the contact arrangements, the Court may make a Contact Order.

Other factors are: the domestic living arrangements of the child currently in place, the person/parent best able to meet the daily needs of the child/children, the working arrangements of the person applying for the order, and whose arrangements are most conducive to the primary needs and care of the child. In the case of a very young child, the Court will presume that the child is better left in the care of the mother – however each case is considered on its own merits.

There is no Scottish equivalent of CAFCASS, so welfare reports are prepared by lawyers known as *Curators ad Litem*. A litigant who is not receiving Legal Aid will have to pay £5,000 or more, depending on the reporter's costs – e.g., how far he has to travel to interview witnesses, etc. There is no right to challenge the report or cross-examine its author.

Wishes & Feelings

See **Needs, Wishes and Feelings**, **Voice of the Child** and **Welfare Checklist**.

Withdrawing an Application

A litigant who decides he can no longer pursue an application which concerns the welfare or upbringing of a child may only withdraw it with **Leave** of the Court, even where withdrawal is unopposed.

The Court is obliged to manage the case and consider the terms of withdrawal and any further steps that may be necessary. It would not serve the ends of justice, however, to compel a party to pursue a case from which he wished to withdraw; see Ciccone v Ritchie (No. 2) [2016] EWHC 616.

Rule 29.4 of the Family Procedure Rules 2010 requires the applicant to produce a written request, setting out his reasons. He can make the application orally in court if the other parties to the case are present.

In Re D [2004] EWHC 727, Mr Justice Munby had described the father as "consistent and sincere in his wish for contact",

> a balanced, fairly well-integrated man who could acknowledge both his own deficits as well as reflect on his past behaviour and consider errors, misjudgements and misdemeanours. His view of others was equally balanced; he had no difficulty in adopting another's perspective and could easily acknowledge alternative viewpoints and alternative hypotheses.

The mother, however, had been allowed consistently to obstruct contact. The case had been plagued by delay: a penal notice was added, a year later a suspended sentence was imposed, and after another year the mother was committed. All her allegations proved groundless. Finally, the father applied in despair to withdraw his application, prompting Munby to make this criticism of the system,

[4] Those who are critical of our family justice system may well see this case as exemplifying everything that is wrong with the system. I can understand such a view. The melancholy truth is that this case illustrates all too uncomfortably the failings of the system. There is much wrong with our system and the time has come for us to recognise that fact and to face up to it honestly.

In April 2007, a father had applied to withdraw an application made the previous January for contact with his son with whom he had a "warm, easy and close relationship". The CAFCASS officer "in express terms, advised against the application being withdrawn" but the father pressed ahead, and the Court acquiesced. The mother was "at the severe end of the spectrum in terms of depression and anxiety" and "attracted a diagnosis of PTSD"; she had—

[14] ...started using emotional blackmail and went further to say that I had touched my son's private parts. I felt that matters were getting out of control and I became concerned that she may be on the verge of having a nervous breakdown. Also the judge had said that [B] had to undergo a psychological assessment. At that moment I decided to withdraw my case to give [the Mother] space and time to relax and forget about the stress and pressure of the court proceedings.

It was "the most ill-advised decision that he has made in his life". Three years later, in November 2010, he made another application for contact, but due to further delays, it was another four years before it came to court. By this time, the mother's mental state had deteriorated, and the boy had been severely alienated against his father. The application was rejected, and an order made for very limited **Indirect Contact**; the father's appeal failed (Re A (A Child) (Contact Order: Child's Contact with Father Where Contact Detrimental to Mother's Mental Health) [2015] EWCA Civ 910).

Without Notice

Also referred to as an "application not on notice", an application made without giving the other side notice or the opportunity to oppose.

The hearing is thus held *Ex Parte* and the Court hears only one side of the case and makes a decision without requiring all parties to be present and without notice to the respondent. In 2014, the President, Sir James Munby said,

There are only two justifications for a without notice order. One is that it is so urgent that there simply isn't time to notify the other side. Now that in the modern world of modern technology will be a pretty rare case. You can usually give somebody half an hour's notice.

The other context is where there is a real reason why you cannot safely give notice to the other side because they may do something irreparable in the gap between giving them notice and the hearing.

Such applications may only be made exceptionally where —

1. for the applicant to give notice to the respondent would enable the respondent to take measures which would defeat the purpose of the application;
2. it is necessary to conceal the application from the respondent (such as emergency medical treatment the respondent would be likely to disrupt);
3. there has literally been no time to give notice of the application to prevent a specific action (such as taking a child abroad);
4. giving the respondent notice would expose the child to unnecessary physical or emotional risk.

Without notice applications are usually made in crisis situations in which the child is at risk, when the applicant needs a **Prohibited Steps Order**, a **Specific Issues Order**, **Non-Molestation Order** or an **Emergency Protection Order** very quickly – for example, to prevent removal of the child from the jurisdiction, or when an order has been breached. The order will be made only for a short period and will invariably be followed by a hearing on notice to review the application.

Where a litigant needs to make an urgent application without notice there is no requirement to attend a **MIAM** and the application will bypass the normal allocation process.

In practice, when the applicant submits his C100 he must give the other side or their legal representative the opportunity to appear; otherwise, he must seek an **Abridged Notice** for them to return to court in forty-eight hours. He then has to use a **Process Server** to serve the documents on the respondent or their legal representative so that he has evidence of service if they don't turn up

If he does not provide his full application at the same time, he must do so within forty-eight hours. If he makes an application without notice, he must pay his fee and will then have to wait until a judge becomes available. Of course, any decision made will be contested later, and he must be prepared.

Getting an *ex parte* hearing entails going to the court and waiting to see the duty judge, which can mean hanging about all day. If the judge won't allow an *ex parte* application he may allow an urgent – i.e., within forty-eight hours – **Inter Partes Hearing** where both parties are present.

For further guidance, see Re J (Children) (*Ex parte* orders) [1997] 1FLR 606 and Re S (A Child) (Family Division: without notice orders) [2000] 1FLR 308.

Without Prejudice

Protective wording on an offer of settlement to ensure that if refused it will not be shown to the Court and prejudice proceedings. If the judge sees it, he may have to **Recuse** himself. Used in financial matters but not appropriate to children's proceedings.

Witness

A person who gives evidence by witness statement to support the argument of a party or who attends court to speak on their behalf.

Litigants should not call friends and family members to provide a general paean to their parenting skills; Wall LJ explained in Re H (Children) [2012] EWCA Civ 1797,

> The reasons for this are threefold. Irrespective of the quality of the witness, often the witness is partisan in favour of one party rather than the other. Secondly, what matters of course is the judge's assessment. And thirdly, what also matters is that the witness can rarely give direct evidence about the issues which the judge has to decide.

The judge will seek evidence on a parent's parenting skills from **CAFCASS**, not from witnesses. A witness should be used only to prove or disprove a particular fact. Witnesses need to be able to provide first-hand evidence, not "hearsay". Seeing a bruise is evidence, but assuming that a parent caused it is hearsay; actually witnessing the parent causing it is first-hand evidence. Hearsay evidence is worthless and should be rejected by the Court.

Generally, witnesses submit their evidence in written **Statements** or **Affidavits** and are required only to attend court for the final hearing. Statements must be presented in the appropriate format set out in Practice Direction 22A; they must carry a clause saying that the evidence presented is true and they must be signed. The witness must be able to attend court; a statement provided by a witness who can't or won't attend carries little weight.

If a party wants to challenge evidence provided by other witnesses, they must be called to court so that they can be cross-examined; see Family Procedure Rules 2010, Rule 24. If evidence is not challenged, the Court will accept it as true.

Only the Court can order a witness to be called and if he wishes, for example, that a doctor or psychiatrist should give evidence, or that a CAFCASS officer should be available for cross-examining, a party must therefore ask the Court to make a **Direction** accordingly and give the Court a list of witnesses. The Court may issue a Witness **Summons** (particularly if the witness refuses)

Writ

on Form N20 which can be used to "require a witness to attend court to give evidence, to produce documents to the court, or both". The form must be filed at least seven days before the hearing and served on the witness at least four days before. A fee must be paid and the witness's travel expenses and compensation for loss of time. Two copies of the form should be filed with the court. If the witness then fails to attend once they have been **Subpoenaed**, they will be in contempt.

Writ

A court's written command that someone act or refrain from acting in a particular way.

Wrongful Removal

The removal of a child from the jurisdiction without legal authority or observation of correct legal process (see **Hague Convention**).

Xydhias Agreement

A financial agreement negotiated between spouses which has not yet been drawn up into an order, but which may nevertheless prove binding.

In Xydhias v Xydhias [1998] EWCA Civ 1966, the parties reached **Heads of Agreement** after extensive negotiation and agreed that only a forty-five-minute final hearing was necessary to resolve some minor issues. The husband then withdrew all offers and demanded a fully contested final hearing. The Court made an order much on the lines of the original agreement and the husband appealed. The **Court of Appeal** dismissed the appeal: the Court had an interest in avoiding unnecessary "adversariality" and litigation.